T0230952

The Digital Gaming Handbook

The Digital Gaming Handbook

Edited by
Roberto Dillon

CRC Press
Taylor & Francis Group
Boca Raton London New York

CRC Press is an imprint of the
Taylor & Francis Group, an **informa** business

First edition published 2021
by CRC Press
6000 Broken Sound Parkway NW, Suite 300, Boca Raton, FL 33487-2742

and by CRC Press
2 Park Square, Milton Park, Abingdon, Oxon, OX14 4RN

ISBN: 978-0-367-22384-7 (hbk)
ISBN: 978-0-367-51376-4 (pbk)
ISBN: 978-0-429-27459-6 (ebk)

Typeset in Minion
by Deanta Global Publishing Services, Chennai, India

Contents

Editor, ix

Contributors, xi

Introduction, xv

PART I **Game Analysis, Player Experience, and Accessibility**

CHAPTER 1 ▪ Analyzing Games with the AGE and 6-11
Frameworks   3

ROBERTO DILLON

CHAPTER 2 ▪ Designing Player Interdependence to
Enhance Players' Social Experience in
Multiplayer Games   19

KATHARINA EMMERICH

CHAPTER 3 ▪ Game Accessibility: Getting Started   37

THOMAS WESTIN, IAN HAMILTON AND BARRIE ELLIS

PART II **Gamification and Serious Games**

CHAPTER 4 ▪ Gamification for Good: Addressing Dark
Patterns in Gamified UX Design   53

OLE GOETHE

CHAPTER 5 ▪ The Social Media Game? How Gamification
Shapes Our Social Media Engagement   63

DAYANA HRISTOVA, SUZANA JOVICIC, BARBARA GOEBL AND
THOMAS SLUNECKO

CHAPTER 6 ■ Games for Health   95

ANDRÉS ADOLFO NAVARRO-NEWBALL

PART III   **Game Design, Level Design, and Storytelling**

CHAPTER 7 ■ Free to Play Mobile Game Design
Fundamentals   117

SIMON ROZNER

CHAPTER 8 ■ Evergreen Game Design Principles   127

ROBERTO DILLON

CHAPTER 9 ■ Architectural Spaces and Level Design in
Modern Games   141

CHRISTOPHER W. TOTTEN

CHAPTER 10 ■ Encouraging and Rewarding Repeat Play
of Storygames   163

ALEX MITCHELL

PART IV   **Game Development and Technology**

CHAPTER 11 ■ How We Make Mobile Work: An Indie
Perspective   185

JAMES BARNARD

CHAPTER 12 ■ The Development and UI Design of
an Interactive Game Map   199

TOMASZ ZAWADZKI, KORNELIUSZ WARSZAWSKI, SLAWOMIR KREZEL
AND SLAWOMIR NIKIEL

CHAPTER 13 ■ Challenges in Designing and Implementing
a Vector-Based 2D Animation System   245

JIE JIANG, HOCK SOON SEAH, HONG ZE LIEW, AND QUAN CHEN

CHAPTER 14 ■ Best Practices for Pixel Art   275

CINDY LEE

CHAPTER 15 ▪ Making Sound Decisions in Game Audio   287

GWEN GUO

CHAPTER 16 ▪ Making It Real   303

ANDRE PONG AND JUSTIN NG

CHAPTER 17 ▪ Player Locomotion in Virtual Reality Games   313

ANDREY KREKHOV AND KATHARINA EMMERICH

CHAPTER 18 ▪ Working Everywhere and Nowhere.
A Practical Guide to the Virtual Office   331

ALLAN SIMONSEN

PART V **Game History, Society, and Culture**

CHAPTER 19 ▪ A Short Summary of Mobile Games' History   341

SIMON ROZNER

CHAPTER 20 ▪ Retrogaming as a Form of Digital
Preservation: A Cultural and Technological
Approach   359

MARCO ACCORDI RICKARDS, MICAELA ROMANINI AND
GUGLIELMO DE GREGORI

CHAPTER 21 ▪ Diversity in Games: How and Why?   383

ALAYNA COLE

INDEX, 389

Editor

Dr. Roberto Dillon is the author of five books published by AKPeters, CRC Press, and Springer. He is active both as an indie developer and as an academic in the field of game design and development. His games have been selected for such events as Sense of Wonder Night in Tokyo and FILE Games in Rio de Janeiro, besides reaching top positions on Apple's App Store across several countries and categories.

He is currently the Academic Head of the School of Science and Technology at James Cook University Singapore where, as an Associate Professor, he lectures game design and project management classes. In 2013, he founded the JCU Museum of Video and Computer Games, the first museum of its kind in Southeast Asia.

Contributors

Marco Accordi Rickards
Director
VIGAMUS
Link Campus University
Rome, Italy

James Barnard
Springloaded Software
Singapore

Alayna Cole
Defiant Development/Queerly
  Represent Me
Brisbane, Australia

Guglielmo De Gregori
VIGAMUS Foundation
Rome, Italy

Katharina Emmerich
Department of Computer
  Science and Applied Cognitive
  Science
University of Duisburg-Essen
Duisburg, Germany

Barrie Ellis
OneSwitch
Essex, UK

Barbara Goebl
Faculty of Computer Science
University of Vienna
Vienna, Austria

Ole Goethe
Westerdals Department of Film
  and Media
Kristiania University College
Oslo, Norway

Gwen Guo
Imba Interactive
Singapore

Ian Hamilton
Independent
Bristol, UK

Dayana Hristova
Department of Philosophy
University of Vienna
Vienna, Austira

Jiang Jie
School of Computer Science and
  Engineering
Nanyang Technological University
Singapore

Suzana Jovicic
Department for Social and
    Cultural Anthropology
University of Vienna
Vienna, Austria

Slawomir Krezel
Department of Computer
    Engineering
University of Zielona Gora
Zielona Góra, Poland

Andrey Krekhov
Department of Computer
    Science and Applied Cognitive
    Science
University of Duisburg-Essen
Duisburg, Germany

Cindy Lee
Springloaded Software
Singapore

Alex Mitchell
Department of Communications
    and New Media
National University of Singapore
Singapore

Andrés Adolfo Navarro-Newball
Department of Electronics and
    Computer Sciences
The Pontifical Xavierian University
Cali, Colombia

Slawomir Nikiel
Institute of Control and
    Computation Engineering
University of Zielona Gora
Zielona Góra, Poland

Justin Ng
Gattai Games
Singapore

Andre Pong
Gattai Games
Singapore

Chen Quan
Department of Computer
    Engineering
Nanyang Technological
    University
Singapore

Simon Rozner
Rovio
Espoo, Finland

Micaela Romanini
VIGAMUS
Link Campus University
Rome, Italy

Allan Simonsen
Boomzap Entertainment
Singapore

Thomas Slunecko
Faculty of Psychology
University of Vienna
Vienna, Austria

Seah Hock Soon
School of Computer Engineering
Nanyang Technological University
Singapore

Christopher Totten
Modeling, Animation, and Game
  Creation (MAGC) Program
Kent State University
Kent, OH

Korneliusz Warszawski
Faculty of Electrical Engineering,
  Computer Science, and
  Telecommunications
University of Zielona Gora
Zielona Góra, Poland

Thomas Westin
Department of Computer and
  Systems Sciences
Stockholm University
Stockholm, Sweden

Tomasz Zawadzki
Social Sciences Institute
Maynooth University
Kildare, Ireland

Liew Hong Ze
Multi-plAtform Game Innovation
  Centre (MAGIC)
Nanyang Technological University
Singapore

Introduction

DIGITAL GAMES HAD AN extraordinary evolution during their short history, especially if we look at the last couple of decades—long gone are the days where computer games were a simple form of entertainment. Now games are a very pervasive medium, able to influence almost every facet of our culture and society by pushing both technology and creativity to new heights.

This anthology aims at showcasing a snapshot of the current "state of the art," including many different perspectives and areas as discussed by leading academics and successful developers from all over the world. Some chapters will be more theoretical in nature while others will be quite practical. Most importantly, though, each author has drawn from their own personal experiences and expertise, making this volume a unique mix that surely has something interesting to offer every reader.

Overall, the volume is divided into five main sections:

- Game Analysis, Player Experience, and Accessibility

- Gamification and Serious Games

- Game Design, Level Design, and Storytelling

- Game Development and Technology

- Game History, Society, and Culture

In the first section, "Game Analysis, Player Experience, and Accessibility," we start with a practical introduction to the AGE and 6-11 Frameworks, with detailed examples on how to apply these game analysis tools in practice to analyze, discuss, and critique different types of games. Katharina Emmerich from Universitat Duisburg-Essen then analyzes the concept of player-interdependence in depth, explaining how fostering communication and increasing players' sense of social presence can have beneficial effects on the overall playing experience within the context of multiplayer co-op games. This first section is then closed by Thomas Westin (Stockholm University), Ian Hamilton (independent), and Barrie Ellis (OneSwitch. co.uk) who present thoughtful guidelines for designing more accessible games in "Game Accessibility: Getting Started."

The second section, "Gamification and Serious Games," opens up with Ole Goethe (Kristiania University) with "Gamification for Good: Addressing Dark Patterns in Gamified UX Design" where the Norwegian professor exposes deceiving UX practices to manipulate user behavior and calls for gamification designers to be responsible for their actions. Scholars from the University of Vienna, Dayana Hristova, Suzana Jovicic, Barbara Goebl, and Thomas Slunecko, follows by explaining how gamification changed different social media platforms such as Snapchat, Instagram, and Facebook in "The Social Media Game? How Gamification Shapes Our Social Media Engagement." The section is wrapped up by Andres Adolfo Navarro-Newball from the Potificia Universitad Javeriana Cali, presenting the state of the art in games for health.

The third part centers on "Game Design, Level Design, and Storytelling" and is kickstarted by Rovio's Battle Studio lead game designer Simon Rozner discussing the nuts and bolts of mobile games in "Free to Play Mobile Game Design Fundamentals." How to find inspiration thanks to some well-thought-out examples from old concepts is the topic of the following chapter, "Evergreen Game Design Principles." Level design then gets the center stage thanks to Christopher Totten (Kent State University) and his chapter "Architectural Spaces and Level Design in Modern Games." Storytelling wraps up the section with Alex Mitchell from the National University of Singapore who explains how to increase replayability in story-based games in "Encouraging and Rewarding Repeat Play of Storygames."

Part Four, "Game Development and Technology," is the most articulated in the whole volume with eight chapters. The section is opened by Springloaded's founder James Barnard discussing his experiences in moving and adapting from a AAA environment to indie development in "How We Make Mobile Work: An Indie Perspective." Then Tomasz Zawadzki (Maynooth University), Slawomir Nikiel, Slawomir Krezel, and Korneliusz Warszawski (University of Zielona Gora) guide us step by step in developing a game map from start to finish in "The Development and UI Design of an Interactive Game Map." Professor Seah Hock Soon leads a team from Nanyang Technological University including Jiang Jie, Liew Hong Ze, and Chen Quan in explaining the "Challenges in Designing and Implementing a Vector Based 2D Animation System" while Springloaded lead artist Cindy Lee shows us how pixel art can still be relevant and a beautiful artistic choice for modern games in "Best Practices in Pixel Art." After discussing graphics, we come to audio with Imba Interactive's co-founder Gwen Guo showcasing her approach for "Making Sound Decisions in Game Audio." Virtual reality (VR) is next, with the multiple-awards winning team from Gattai Games, Andre Pong, and Justing Ng, explaining their approach in "Making it Real," as well as Andrey Krekhov and Katharina Emmerich (Universitat Duisburg-Essen) who discuss in detail one of the most critical aspects for an effective VR immersive experience, i.e. "Player Locomotion in Virtual Reality Games." Allan Simonsen from Boomzap Entertainment wraps up the section with "Working Everywhere and Nowhere. A Practical Guide to the Virtual Office," outlining how his studio managed to establish itself as one of the main indie players across Southeast Asia by working remotely.

Last but not least, the *Handbook* ends by touching on other very relevant areas of modern games culture, outlining why history and its preservation is so important for today's developers and also stressing the importance of diversity for growing a healthy and successful industry. In Part Five, "Game History, Society, and Culture," we once again meet Simon Rozner in "A Short Summary of Mobile Games' History," who is followed by Italian scholars Marco Accordi Rickards, Micaela Romanini (Tor Vergata University, Rome), and Guglielmo De Gregori (VIGAMUS Foundation) discussing "Retrogaming as a Form of Digital Preservation: A Cultural and Technological Approach." Alayna Cole (Defiant Development/ Queerly Represent Me) then closes the volume with her powerful message about diversity: "Diversity in Games: How and Why?"

The game industry is a wonderfully diverse and exciting world that is constantly evolving in new, unexpected directions. While we cannot know where it is going next, our journey is surely going to be a worthwhile one. I hope this *Handbook* offers its readers a unique perspective on the present trends and how these are effectively rooted into a past that was as exciting for the pioneers that preceded us. Maybe, all this will help inspiring us in taking the next step towards the future.

Roberto Dillon
Singapore, January 2020

I

Game Analysis, Player Experience, and Accessibility

CHAPTER 1

Analyzing Games with the AGE and 6-11 Frameworks

Roberto Dillon

CONTENTS

1.1	Introduction	3
1.2	The AGE Framework	4
1.3	The 6-11 Framework	4
1.4	How to Analyze Games	8
	1.4.1 Game Analysis: *Frogger* (Konami, 1981, Arcade)	8
	1.4.2 Game Analysis: *Loading Human* (Untold Games, 2016, PC/PSVR)	11
	1.4.2.1 Color Appreciation	13
	1.4.2.2 Self-Identification	13
	1.4.2.3 Curiosity	15
	1.4.2.4 Gameplay: Storytelling and Puzzle Solving	15
	1.4.2.5 Actions: Movement and Object manipulation	16
1.5	Conclusions	17
	References	17

1.1 INTRODUCTION

Among the different models conceptualized to help game designers analyzing the inner workings of games, the AGE (Actions, Gameplay, Experience) and 6-11 Frameworks (Dillon, 2010) have been adopted by both industry and academia thanks to their simplicity and ability to synthesize in an easy to understand diagram* how players' engagement can develop around a specific set of emotions and instinctive behaviors thanks to actual gameplay features. See, for example, Marins et al. (2011), Kerlow et al. (2012) and Göbel (2016).

1.2 THE AGE FRAMEWORK

Inspired by the original MDA model (Mechanics, Dynamics, Aesthetics) proposed in Hunicke et al. (2004), the AGE framework was gradually formalized following the original work in Dillon (2010) and ultimately finalized in Dillon (2016). Like the original MDA, it breaks down a game into three different conceptual layers. At the most basic level we have the **Actions**, which represent the atomic actions a player can perform in a game. These are usually described in terms of verbs like moving, jumping, kicking a ball, punching, shooting, taking cover, shifting tiles, etc. By combining the possible actions according to the game rules, we move to the next layer, i.e. the **Gameplay**. This can also be described either in term of more general verbs or higher-level concepts like fighting, race to an end, avoidance, territorial acquisition and so on. Through the gameplay, players aim at overcoming some form of challenge or achieving a certain goal as requested by the game and, in doing so, the typical sequence of failures, successes and rewards will manage to engage them emotionally in what the model describes as the third, highest level: the **Experience**, i.e. the emotional experience that engages players during the game.

It is important to understand how the concepts outlined in the model do not work in isolation but are inherently related to each other: players apply the predefined rules to give a purpose to the available actions, producing the resulting gameplay. This then is used to overcome the specific challenges the game is all about and these provide players with a reason to immerse themselves in the gaming world and get emotionally engaged in what they are doing, as summarized in Figure 1.1.

1.3 THE 6-11 FRAMEWORK

Analyzing Actions and Gameplay should be relatively straightforward, but the Experience involves emotions and can be, henceforth, subjective. How shall we describe it then? And, even more importantly, how to actually connect it to the actual gameplay that is happening on the screen? The

---

* The diagrams summarizing the analysis are often referred to as "on the way to fun" diagrams, as first presented in Dillon (2010)

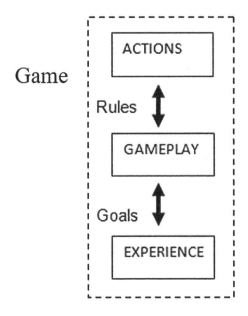

FIGURE 1.1 A game seen under the schematic representation of the AGE model: players perform a specific action that, in accordance with the game's own rules, allows for the emergence of one or more types of gameplay. Through gameplay, players aim at overcoming a series of challenges or reaching a goal and, in doing so, they can get emotionally engaged and immersed in the virtual world.

original MDA tried to solve this problem by means of the "8 Kinds of Fun" taxonomy while the AGE framework here adopts another model, the 6-11 framework.

The idea behind the latter is that games can be so engaging at a subconscious level because, in general, they successfully rely on a subset of a few basic emotions and instinctive behaviors, which are well known in psychology and deeply rooted in all of us. In particular, the six emotions originally included in the model, involving both positive and negative emotions, are:

1. **Fear:** one of the most common emotions in games nowadays. Think of survival horror games or dungeon explorations in RPGs for plenty of examples.

2. **Anger:** a powerful emotion that is often used as a motivational factor to play again or to advance the story to correct any wrongs that some evil character has committed.

3. **Pride:** rewarding players and making them feel good for their achievements and successes is an extremely important motivational factor. Players need to feel good about what they just did and aim at even higher successes.

4. **Joy/Happiness:** arguably, one of the most relevant emotions for having a fun gaming experience.

5. **Sadness:** despite being an emotion that doesn't seem to match with the concept of "fun," this negative emotion has always played an important role in games and designers have always been attracted by it as a way to reach new artistic heights and touch more complex and mature themes.

6. **Excitement:** most games worth playing should achieve this and it should happen naturally as a consequence of successfully triggering other emotions and/or instincts.

Moving to the instinctive behaviors, the framework discusses games in terms of the 11 following behaviors:

1. **Survival (fight or flight):** the most fundamental and primordial of all instincts, triggered when faced with a life threat. According to the situation, we will have to decide whether we should face the threat and fight for our life or try to avoid it by finding a possible way to escape. Relying on this instinct is very common among many modern videogames, especially first-person shooters (FPS) and survival horror games.

2. **Self-identification:** people tend to admire successful individuals or smart fictional characters and naturally start to imagine of being like their models. This is common of all entertainment, especially those based on storytelling, and it is even more relevant in games where, thanks to their interactive nature, players actually have a chance of wearing the hero's shoes.

3. **Collecting:** a very strong instinct that motivates players to look for and form patters of objects by completing sets with a common theme. It also relates to our hunting instinct. While always present in many games since the early days of the medium, it has been extremely prominent in the last few years via the infamous "loot boxes," pushing players to desperately look for rare items.

4. **Protection/Care/Nurture:** arguably the "best" instinct of all: the one that pushes every parent to love their children and every person to feel the impulse for caring and helping those in need despite the possible dangers, including countless princesses in distress and kidnapped girlfriends.

5. **Aggressiveness:** the other side of the coin, usually leading to violence when coupled with *greed* or *anger*. It is exploited in countless of games, too, especially in FPS and fighting games.

6. **Greed:** this is another typical human behavior that is responsible for the addictive qualities of many games: hoarding resources, virtual money and so on is a common habit and motivational factor across many games.

7. **Revenge:** another powerful instinct that can act as a motivational force and is often used in games to advance the storyline or justify why we need to annihilate an alien or an enemy.

8. **Competition:** the need for measuring our skills against those of others is one of most important instinct in relation to gaming, whether the competition happens within the game itself or outside the game, by means of leaderboards. Without it, many games would lose much of their appeal.

9. **Communication:** the need for expressing ideas, thoughts or just gossip, was one of the most influential for human evolution. It can be used to great effect in games too, while seeking information by talking to a non-playing character (NPC) or while sharing experiences with other players in chatrooms and forums.

10. **Exploration/Curiosity:** all human discoveries, whether of a scientific or geographical nature, have been made thanks to these instincts that always pushed us towards the unknown. Many adventure games rely on curiosity alone to engage players and push them to progress.

11. **Color Appreciation:** scenes and environments full of vibrant colors naturally attract us, whether it is an abstract or a photorealistic setting. This is often important to capture players' attention and interest from the get-go. Note this is about the artistic use of colors and the palette used to make graphics attractive regardless of the technical specs, screen resolution or even the actual number of colors used.

1.4 HOW TO ANALYZE GAMES

The AGE framework may be seen then as a canvas where we can use any of these elements to discuss how games successfully engage players emotionally and how emotions and instincts are then the driving forces that make players act in the game.

For example, we can imagine a horror game scaring the player with a sudden encounter with a monster in a dark room. This will likely trigger the player's survival instinct, pushing him to find a way to answer the threat, for example. by escaping and avoiding the danger, which is made possible by the actions the game offers, like the ability of running or hiding somewhere. All these pieces of information can be assembled together in diagram form where Experience ultimately leads the player to "fun" and is linked to the Actions via the Gameplay as exemplified in Figure 1.2.

With the basics now discussed, let us try to use the framework step by step, starting with a very simple game at first and then progressing to a more articulated example to analyze in detail a modern game.

1.4.1 Game Analysis: *Frogger* (Konami, 1981, Arcade)

In *Frogger* (Figure 1.3), players control a small frog that, starting from the bottom of the screen, needs to find a safe haven by navigating a trafficked highway and a river.

Our analysis can proceed either in a top-down approach, from the Experience down to the Actions, or the other way round, in a bottom-up style. Let's start with the latter by identifying the Actions first and then go up to towards the Experience.

So, what are the "Actions" in *Frogger*? Let's start by playing the game and ask ourselves *"What can I do?"* If there is any doubt here, the best way

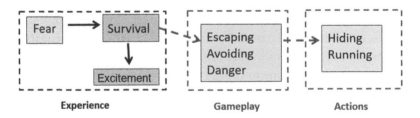

FIGURE 1.2 An example of a simple "On the Way to Fun" diagram outlining the Experience, Gameplay and Actions for a generic horror game: the survival instinct is what motivates the player to escape (Gameplay) by using the available abilities at his disposal (Actions). Fear and Survival also lead to Excitement, delivering a "fun" experience overall.

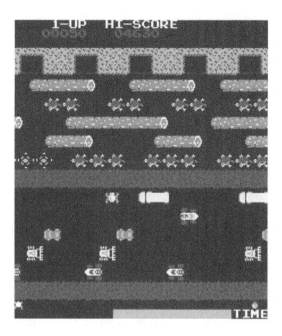

FIGURE 1.3 *Frogger* (© 1981 Konami): was it an engaging and fun game? Why?

to proceed is to check the game controls as the actions, by definition, are necessarily tied to them.

In *Frogger*, this analysis is extremely simple as we only have a joystick that allows us to move left, right, to advance and to retreat.

With the Actions clearly identified, we can now proceed to the next stage and analyze the gameplay. For doing so, we should ask ourselves something like *"What are the game rules allowing us to use the Actions for?"* Or, more simply, *"What are we actually doing in the game?"*

In the case of *Frogger*, we are trying to avoid the speeding cars and then jumping on the floating logs to reach a safe haven at the top of the screen. In game design terms, we can say the gameplay is about "avoidance" of different hazards together with a "race to an end" component. By describing the gameplay in these terms, we have also identified the goal and we are then ready to discuss the emotional Experience. For this, we have now to ask ourselves *"How does the gameplay make me feel?"*

This is the most subjective part of the analysis and can obviously be quite tricky, but we can rely on the 6-11 framework to guide us in the process.

Most likely, we would point out that, while playing the game, we were **excited** by the fast action of moving across the highway and river and then

happy for successfully reaching the end. Notice that we have already identified the two main emotions that make *Frogger* fun and enjoyable but why were we happy? Because we felt **proud** for our success!

Indeed, **pride** plays an important role here and, in fact, it usually resolves into Joy and Happiness. Our experience is gradually taking shape.

Now, what is it we are actually proud of? Surviving the perils we had to face across the road and river! So, **survival** is the main instinct at play here and it actually drives us towards the goal of the game. In the process, we may also realize that, by looking at the cars approaching from all directions, we might have felt a bit scared and that we have unconsciously taken the role of the frog, i.e. we identified with it.

The whole analysis can then be summarized into an "on the way to fun" diagram like the one shown in Figure 1.4.

Anyway, as stated earlier, analyzing the Experience can be quite subjective so some players may see things a bit differently.

For example, they may have not thought they were taking the role of the frog in the first place but, on the other hand, they simply thought their role was to "help" the unlucky frog to safely reach the pond. In this case, **Identification**, **Fear** and **Survival** wouldn't play any role in their emotional experience. Instead, they would be substituted by **Protection**. In this case, the frog is not an avatar, but it simply acts as a character the player has to save and rescue.

Under this assumption, the resulting "on the way to fun" diagram would be modified like Figure 1.5.

What if instead we decide to analyze the game following a top-down approach?

FIGURE 1.4 "On the way to fun" diagram for *Frogger*.

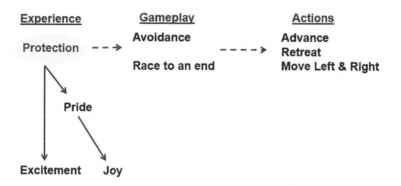

FIGURE 1.5 Alternative AGE analysis for *Frogger*: we are not the frog, we are just there to help it.

Again, we start our analysis by playing the game but this time we try to figure out the Experience first by asking ourselves *"How is the game trying to motivate me? How do I feel while playing?"* This should lead us to question our relationship with the playable character: is it an avatar (*"I'm playing as this little frog who has to cross the street"*), which will lead us to the Identification-Fear-Survival route, or just a character we have to protect (*"I have to help this poor little thing!"*), leading us to the version with Protection at its core. Once the emotional analysis is in place, we can proceed downwards with the questions we saw earlier for identifying the Gameplay and then how this originates thanks to the available Actions.

Anyway, regardless of our starting point, either the Actions or the Experience, we should arrive to the same result at the end of our analysis.

1.4.2 Game Analysis: *Loading Human* (Untold Games, 2016, PC/PSVR)

Naturally, not all games are as straightforward as *Frogger*, though. How can this approach to game analysis help us gaining valuable insights on a modern and much more complex title? As an example, let us try to discuss a recent VR-based PC and PS4 game, *Loading Human*, developed by Untold Games and released in 2016. This was an ambitious project and a launch title on the PSVR platform. Nonetheless, despite the hard work that was put in the project by its developers, the game was met with mixed reviews (Metacritic, 2016). Can an analysis based on the AGE framework help in identifying the game's strong as well as weak points?*

---

* Be aware the following analysis will necessarily include a few spoilers.

By proceeding with a top-down approach, i.e. by playing the game and trying to outline how it aims at engaging players emotionally first, we can easily understand how the design wanted to immerse players in a rich emotional experience. First and foremost, by making the player become the leading character, Prometheus, the Experience clearly began with the **Self-Identification** instinct. This should be achieved naturally thanks to the VR perspective and by offering a visually stimulating environment (**Color Appreciation** to help drawing players into the gaming world). These, then, set the stage for making the player curious enough to proceed in unfolding the mysterious story.

Indeed, **Curiosity** should be the "leitmotif" to keep players engaged and motivated throughout the game, also thanks to our **Protection** instincts. For the latter, the starting point is the desire to save our dying father and then help/protect our romantic interest Alice, engaging the player with different emotions as the game advances the well written storyline.

Ultimately, the emotional experience can be outlined in Figure 1.6.

Like all good old adventure games since the days of *Maniac Mansion* on 8-bit home computers, all these emotional hooks to engage players should be achievable by a **gameplay** revolving around storytelling and the solution of environmental puzzles which are, in turn, advanced by the simple **actions** of navigating the different locales to find and manipulate various objects.

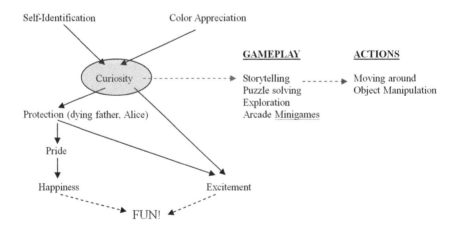

FIGURE 1.6 Thanks to the "On the way to fun" diagram, we can easily visualize how *Loading Human* aims at providing a rich emotional Experience, with *curiosity* being the central component to keep players engaged into specific forms of Gameplay. These are obtained via straightforward in-game Actions involving movement and object manipulation.

If everything fits in place as planned, the game should then be able to provide a fulfilling emotional experience, ultimately leading to excitement for solving the various puzzles and advancing the storyline while also making players proud and happy for achieving their goals, delivering a fun and memorable overall experience.

Unfortunately, not all reviewers appreciated the final result so let's try to use the earlier diagram as a starting point to discuss the game piece by piece and figure out where the game eventually fell short of expectations.

1.4.2.1 Color Appreciation

Let's quickly discuss the game's environment and aesthetics first. Textures, shaders, models, sound design and so on are above average for an early PSVR game and certain environmental details are actually very effective in making the virtual world feel believable and real. For example, early in the game the player has an opportunity to stand on the deck of his base, staring at the beautiful desolated landscape while a menacing thunderstorm is approaching. If the player stays there long enough, he can witness lighting strikes in the distance, with thunder realistically arriving only a few seconds later. This is a beautiful little detail that can effectively increase the feeling of being immersed into a believable virtual world.

1.4.2.2 Self-Identification

Virtual reality should make this fundamental aspect of games played in a first-person perspective very straightforward and easy to accomplish. The onboarding process/tutorial here works well and players have a chance to know more about the world the game takes place in by checking out newspaper articles and TV news, which are easily available and scattered all around. All of these are great ways to enhance the feeling of immersion. Despite this, in *Loading Human*, achieving an effective identification with the player's character can be quite challenging from a psychological perspective due to a questionable choice in designing the character of Prometheus himself.

This is a very important point that can be illustrated by referencing Half Life (Valve, 2009) and its sequels, which are FPS classics. These games made the self-identification aspect between the player and Gordon Freeman, the playable character, one of their most significant and acclaimed features, effectively breaking the fourth wall between the game and the player. In those games the player is Freeman, who is just an empty shell to be filled.

In game design terms, Freeman is an "avatar" not an "actor," which is typical of third-person games.* To fully achieve this, Freeman never speaks directly in the game: he has no voice because his voice is the player's own actions.

The hidden problem in *Loading Human* is that Prometheus is still essentially designed as an actor and not as an avatar: he just keeps talking by his own will and has his own independent voice throughout the game. This may cause a disconnection between players and Prometheus that can ultimately break the subconscious feeling of being the main character because the player loses control whenever he says or thinks something we don't necessarily expect.

The reason why Prometheus talks so much are easy to understand (e.g. advancing the storyline, items description, hints and so on) so this was a natural design choice but it would have probably been more effective to design some of those interactions in a different way. Specifically, throughout the game the player is assisted by an AI companion named Lucy. This NPC could have played an even bigger role and several of those tasks could have been delegated to her instead, short item descriptions could also be shown on the objects themselves while looking at them. It should also be noted that dialogue was very linear throughout the game with no branching. This can also be perceived as very limiting since players will feel like they have no control whatsoever as there are no decisions to take in what Prometheus says.

Indeed, advancing dialogue thanks to simple multiple choices would have helped greatly for achieving the self-identification aspect of the game, for feeling in control of the avatar and *being* Prometheus. Note that it may not really matter whether the game has a truly branching storyline or is still based on a linear narrative, with the final outcome being essentially the same regardless of the player's own dialogue choices: as pioneer game designer Mel Croucher of *Deus Ex Machina* fame (Automata, 1985) once said, it is all "*bunkum*," i.e. smoke and mirrors, so giving players an illusion of control may have been enough here to effectively increase immersion.

In *Loading Human*, unfortunately, we can say that the self-identification aspect of being the hero of the story was not fulfilled while this should have been a pillar of the emotional experience as outlined by the AGE analysis. The lesson to learn here is that, in first-person games and even more so in VR experiences, it is extremely important for the player to

---

* Think of Geralt of Rivia in the *Witcher* series (CD Project Red, 2007–15) for a typical actor.

feel fully in control of their avatar. This also means players should get the impression they are doing all the talking or are, at the very least, responsible for it and what is being said follows their own choices. The avatar should never talk by himself otherwise it becomes much closer to being an actor, making a true first-person immersion and self-identification much more challenging, if at all possible.

1.4.2.3 Curiosity

Curiosity is generally the main driving force behind adventure games and *Loading Human* is no exception. As discussed, the rich environment and overall game aesthetics do a proper job in making the player interested in the virtual world and, consequently, willing to unfold the upcoming plot. This is what pushes the player forward and links the emotional experience to the actual gameplay, as shown in Figure 1.6.

1.4.2.4 Gameplay: Storytelling and Puzzle Solving

Generally speaking, gameplay in adventure games tends to be based on puzzles. These works in symbiosis with the abovementioned "curiosity" instinct to reinforce each other, i.e. curiosity motivates players to solve puzzles and each puzzle should advance the story providing new hooks to keep players engaged, hence willing to find out what happens next.

Loading Human has an interesting and mature storyline which is advanced thanks to several environmental puzzles involving objects manipulation. Unfortunately, these fall mostly in the "ordinary use" of objects and don't require much lateral thinking, a must-have ingredient in adventure games to engage players effectively and offer a rewarding and memorable experience. For example, going to a specific location for making tea would be an effective tutorial puzzle to teach players movement and objects handling, even though there is nothing exciting or original about it, but it is just too mundane if placed well into the adventure, as it happens in the game.

Besides puzzles, a notable feature of the gameplay here is the presence of arcade style minigames as well as wireframe sequences where players are tasked to reconstruct some aspect of a scene by linking different elements together. Overall, these can help in providing a change of pace and take a short break from the main story but one such episode in particular was actually detrimental to the emotional experience: a section of the game involves the player trying to rescue his romantic interest Alice from a fire. While in the middle of the action the scene is suddenly interrupted with no warning and the player is asked to complete a wireframe sequence to identify the fire source. There is no timer involved (hence no urgency to find a solution while the damsel in distress was supposed to be in a life-threatening situation) and the abrupt change in gameplay here can actually break all the excitement that could have been achieved for rushing in and saving Alice. Breaking the rescue scene was also a missed opportunity for enhancing the protection instinct and rewarding players for their bravery. On the other hand, tracking back the causes of the fire may have been an interesting exercise once the danger was over and before getting back to the main storyline to relax a bit and take a breath.

In the end, the gameplay in *Loading Human* showcases a good story but a closer look at how the story actually unfolds, thanks to its puzzles, shows how the latter are too simple to effectively engage players. The lack of puzzles involving interesting solutions based on lateral thinking makes progress less rewarding and, most importantly, may fail in keeping players' curiosity alive. Since curiosity is supposed to be a central component of the experience, this can be a major problem. Unfortunately, action sequences are also not exciting enough to effectively provide a change in pace and can even be detrimental to some important emotional components. Ultimately, a closer look at the gameplay trying to relate it to the intended emotional experience shows how the former is not able to effectively support the latter.

1.4.2.5 Actions: Movement and Object manipulation

All the gameplay elements discussed are implemented thanks to specific actions, here essentially revolving around movement and manipulation of objects.

The latter worked very well but movement had issues that were often pointed out by reviewers as playing often induced motion sickness. This was, and still is, a common problem in VR and developers keep trying new approaches. In this specific case, the game offered too much freedom of movement to players: for example, it was possible to turn around while moving or looking down for items on the floor while walking and then bumping into objects and furniture, abruptly stopping Prometheus. If playing while sitting down, these kind of interactions could trigger discomfort and motion sickness. In a game that involves a significant amount of movement across different rooms to accomplish the required gameplay, this can obviously become a serious issue.

1.5 CONCLUSIONS

Based on clear definitions and a limited, but flexible, palette of building blocks, the AGE and 6-11 frameworks can be useful tools in both game analysis and design: by framing the most important elements of a game into an easy to understand diagram form, they can help in conceptualizing a coherent system and check that all different elements fit together properly and support each other effectively. In relatively simple games, like many mobile and casual titles, the analysis process can be very straightforward and self-explanatory, while in more complex games, it can still outline the most important components and point in the right direction for further discussion.

REFERENCES

Dillon, R. (2010). *On the Way to Fun: An Emotion-Based Approach to Successful Game Design*. Boca Raton, FL: A K Peters.

Dillon, R. (2016). Towards the definition of a framework and grammar for game analysis and design. In M. J. P. Wolf (Ed.), *Video Games and Gaming Culture (Critical Concepts in Media and Cultural Studies)*, pp. 188–193. Routledge.

Göbel, S. (2016). Serious games application examples. In R. Dörner, S. Göbel, W. Effelsberg, & J. Wiemeyer (Eds.), *Serious Games*. Cham, Switzerland: Springer.

Hunicke, R., LeBlanc, M., & Zubek, R. (2004) *MDA: A Formal Approach to Game Design and Game Research*. Available at http://www.cs.northwestern.edu/~hunicke/MDA.pdf. Last accessed: April 11, 2020.

Kerlow, I., Khadafi, M., Zhuang, H., Zhuang, H., Azlin, A., & Suhaimi, A. (2012). Earth girl: A multi-cultural game about natural disaster prevention and resilience. In A. Nijholt, T. Romão, & D. Reidsma (Eds.), *Advances in Computer Entertainment. ACE 2012. Lecture Notes in Computer Science, vol 7624*. Berlin, Heidelberg: Springer, pp.521–524.

Marins, D. R., de O. D. Justo, M., Xexeo, G. B., de A. M. Chaves, B., & D'Ipolitto, C. (2011). SmartRabbit: A mobile exergame using geolocation. *Brazilian Symposium on Games and Digital Entertainment (SBGAMES)*, pp. 232–240.

Metacritic. (2016) *Loading Human: Chapter 1*. Available at https://www.metacritic.com/game/playstation-4/loading-human-chapter-1.

CHAPTER 2

Designing Player Interdependence to Enhance Players' Social Experience in Multiplayer Games

Katharina Emmerich

CONTENTS

2.1	The Social Player Experience	19
2.2	Player Interdependence	21
2.3	Approaches to Design for Player Interdependence	22
	2.3.1 Complementarity and Coupled Interactions	22
	2.3.2 Level Design	25
	2.3.3 Interface Design	27
2.4	Challenges Regarding Player Interdependence	29
2.5	Conclusion	31
References		32

2.1 THE SOCIAL PLAYER EXPERIENCE

The appeal of multiplayer games lies in the rich opportunities for social interaction that they offer. People play such games to spend time with friends and family, as well as to establish new relationships (ESA—Entertainment Software Association, 2018; Kaye & Bryce, 2012). Players appreciate the social interaction and the feeling of being socially connected.

Many current games feature multiplayer modes or are completely focused on social play to enable social experiences. The additional social layer is a strong motivation for players and an important aspect of the overall experience of playing (de Kort & Ijsselsteijn, 2008; Stenros, Paavilainen, & Mayra, 2011). Apart from the commercial success of multiplayer games, research confirms the positive impact of the presence of co-players: studies indicate that players experience higher positive affect and enjoyment when they play a game with other players compared with playing the same game alone (Gajadhar, Kort, & Ijsselsteijn, 2008; Lee, Wyeth, Johnson, & Hall, 2015; Mandryk, Inkpen, & Calvert, 2006; Peng & Crouse, 2013; Tamborini, Bowman, Eden, Grizzard, & Organ, 2010; Weibel, Wissmath, Habegger, Steiner, & Groner, 2008).

According to different theories, the positive experience in multiplayer games results from the satisfaction of social needs (Kaye & Bryce, 2012; Tamborini et al., 2010) and socio-psychological effects such as emotional contagion, which can intensify the experience (de Kort & Ijsselsteijn, 2008; Isbister, 2010; Kaye & Bryce, 2012; Stenros et al., 2011). One well-established theory of motivation, which is often referred to in digital games research, is the self-determination theory (Ryan, Rigby, & Przybylski, 2006). This theory states that a person's intrinsic motivation is determined by basic psychological needs. Based on the self-determination theory, game enjoyment can be defined as the satisfaction of the needs for autonomy, competence, and relatedness (Tamborini et al., 2010). More precisely, Ryan et al. (2006) define five aspects that influence the motivation to play: (1) perceived autonomy; (2) perceived competence; (3) perceived relatedness; (4) perceived presence; and (5) intuitive controls. The third aspect, perceived relatedness, describes the feeling of being connected with others, and is particularly relevant for multiplayer games. Results of a large online survey by Vella, Johnson, and Hides (2015) indicate that players perceive higher autonomy for solitary play sessions, whereas relatedness is mostly associated with social play.

Another concept that accounts for the social experience in digital games is social presence. In general, social presence describes the "sense of being with another" (Biocca, Harms, & Burgoon, 2003, p. 456). It is associated with the awareness that another social entity—such as a co-player or an in-game character—is part of the gaming situation (de Kort & Ijsselsteijn, 2008). Social presence can be used to describe the social richness and quality of a play setting and the extent to which the experience of players is influenced by it (de Kort & Ijsselsteijn, 2008; de Kort,

Ijsselsteijn, & Poels, 2007; Hudson & Cairns, 2014a, 2014b). High social presence is related to a sense of deep psychological and behavioral involvement with the other players (Hudson & Cairns, 2014b) and supposed to contribute to a positive player experience.

Considering the aspects mentioned above, we can conclude that a high perceived social presence and a high feeling of relatedness is beneficial for players' enjoyment and, consequently, the success of a multiplayer game. Hence, game designers may strive for fostering the social aspects of the player experience. One way to do that is to create interdependence between players.

2.2 PLAYER INTERDEPENDENCE

In this chapter, we define player interdependence as the degree to which players are influenced by and dependent on another player's actions to reach the games goal. Usually, there is at least some degree of interdependence between players in multiplayer games due to the general goal structure, which defines the main interaction pattern between players (Adams, 2010). Basically, players either have opposed goals, resulting in competition, or they work together towards a shared goal, fostering cooperation (with hybrid forms such as team competition being common, as well) (Adams, 2010; Fullerton, Swain, Hoffman, & Isbister, 2008; Waddell & Peng, 2014). Hence, the behavior and the performance of co-players always influence a player's own actions. In games with cooperative elements, the experience of interdependence is particularly important and more complex than in straight competitive games, because players must coordinate their actions, build common strategies, and help each other.

A high player interdependence fosters players' interaction and group forming (Ducheneaut & Moore, 2004). Moreover, it can contribute to the emergence of group flow: players engaging in the same activity experience a comparable level of flow (Kaye & Bryce, 2012). The concept of flow was coined by Csikszentmihalyi (2009) and describes a desirable mental state of total engagement that can be achieved if an activity is challenging and at the same time intrinsically motivating. Based on focus groups, Kaye and Bryce (2012) identified several factors that can support group flow, one of which is interdependence.

Interdependence is also related to the experience of social presence. In common questionnaires that assess social presence, such as the Social Presence in Gaming Questionnaire (SPGQ) (de Kort et al., 2007), the Competitive and Cooperative Presence in Gaming questionnaire (CCPIG)

(Hudson & Cairns, 2014a, 2014b), and the Networked Minds Questionnaire (NMQ) (Harms & Biocca, 2004), the interdependence between players is taken into account on certain subscales. For instance, the third subscale of the SPGQ, *behavioral engagement*, refers to the experience that one's actions are dependent on the actions of the co-player(s). The NMQ contains the subscale *perceived behavioral interdependence* and the CCPIG includes similar items regarding the behavioral interdependence of players in the subscales *team involvement* and *attention*. Hence, researchers consider interdependence as an important aspect contributing to perceived social presence and a positive social experience.

In the following, we will discuss different ways to design for interdependence to increase players' social interaction in multiplayer games.

2.3 APPROACHES TO DESIGN FOR PLAYER INTERDEPENDENCE

There are several ways to increase the interdependence between players by design. We categorize different approaches into three main groups: complementarity, level design, and interface design.

2.3.1 Complementarity and Coupled Interactions

As stated above, a certain degree of player interdependence is created by the general goal structure of a game. Besides, the level of interdependence is further shaped by the roles and abilities that are assigned to each player by the game. In general, player roles and abilities can either be symmetric or asymmetric (Fullerton et al., 2008; Harris, Hancock, & Scott, 2016; Schell, 2010). In many classic games (e.g., chess), all players have the same roles and abilities, providing a symmetric game design. In this case, all players have the same opportunities and can perform the same actions, inducing no direct interdependence. In contrast, asymmetric games assign different player roles, so that each player has unique characteristics and capabilities, which complement each other. This kind of complementarity is a commonly used pattern in cooperative games (Rocha, Mascarenhas, & Prada, 2008). By providing complementary roles, games can create high interdependence between players. For instance, in most roleplaying games there are healers who can restore health but cause little damage, whereas warriors are strong damage dealers but cannot restore health by themselves. Hence, players must work together to be able to defeat the enemies.

Depping and Mandryk (2017) evaluated the difference between high and low interdependence in a custom two-player game using either complementary player roles with different abilities or the same role for both players. The results of the study indicate that high interdependence induced by complementary abilities of players leads to higher experienced relatedness and increased game enjoyment compared with the game version with low interdependence. The authors conclude that this form of interdependence can foster team building among player groups and a positive player experience.

Apart from the enhancement of interdependence between players, complementary roles and abilities can make the game more interesting and enjoyable for all players, as they avoid one player taking the lead and making decision for the entire team (Zagal, Rick, & Hsi, 2006). Decision-making processes and the coordination of actions become more important. Moreover, with different roles, a game also supports different playing styles, thereby satisfying several player preferences.

A design pattern that is closely related to complementary player roles is the creation of synergies between abilities (Rocha et al., 2008). This means that one player can have a direct effect on the abilities of another player. For instance, one player might increase an enemy's vulnerability to another player's attacks. To create such synergies, players do not necessarily have to have complementary roles, but both patterns are often combined to enhance interdependence. Reuter, Wendel, Göbel, and Steinmetz (2014) discuss game design patterns for collaboration in digital games and summarize them in three categories: general, gates, and support. All patterns in the support category describe player properties or abilities that provide benefits for co-players, for instance, by preventing or removing negative effects or by restoring capabilities.

On a more general level, Beznosyk, Quax, Lamotte, and Coninx (2012) differentiate between closely coupled and loosely coupled collaboration of players: a close coupling between players means that their actions and decisions directly influence each other, whereas loosely coupled players are more independent. Based on this concept of coupling, the authors investigated the influence of interdependence on players' experience in casual games. The results of their study indicate that players prefer games that include closely coupled interactions, that is to say a high interdependence. The participants reported higher perceived excitement, engagement, replayability, and challenge in the closely coupled condition. This finding is supported by the work of Harris et al. (2016), who compared players' ratings of different degrees of asymmetry and interdependence in a custom collaborative game. Participants in their study reported that they preferred being dependent on each other, because they did not like the feeling of being useless in the case of low interdependence: players want each players' actions to be significant and necessary to succeed as a team, rather than being self-sufficient. In two subsequent studies, Harris and Hancock (2019) further investigated players' experiences regarding varying degrees of asymmetry and interdependence. In line with previous results, both asymmetry and high interdependence were preferred by participants and led to higher ratings of social presence, connectedness, immersion, and behavioral engagement, confirming the potential of designed interdependence.

At the same time, high interdependence in terms of complementary player roles and closely coupled interactions increases the complexity of game balancing. It is important that each combination of roles and abilities is fair and offers interesting choices and experiences for all players. If one role is perceived as superior or inferior, this lack of proper balancing may result in demotivation and frustration. Besides, the requirement to coordinate actions can increase the level of challenge and may cause frustration if players fail to coordinate themselves properly (Beznosyk et al., 2012; Harris et al., 2016).

Apart from complementary roles and abilities, interdependence can also be created by means of game resources in several ways (Björk & Holopainen, 2005). Players can be forced to interact with each other, if required resources, such as certain items, are unequally distributed. For instance, one player may have access to a locked chest, whereas the other player possesses the key. If players need the content of the chest to proceed, they must work together to open it. Moreover, Seif El-Nasr et al. (2010) define "limited resources" as a cooperative game design pattern that can encourage players to get in contact and share or exchange resources. By generally shortening the supplies, players are more likely to trade and think about the best ways to use them. Finally, if players have access to a shared pool of resources, this also increases interdependence. In such a case, a player must consider the needs of the co-players and coordinate the usage of shared resources.

Information can be considered as a special kind of resource, which can have a significant influence on players' communication and interaction (Björk & Holopainen, 2005). An asymmetric distribution of information among players leads to an imbalance of knowledge. In competitive games, players can try to obtain an advantage and preempt the others by gathering important exclusive information. For instance, if the goal of the game is to find a treasure chest first, the player who finds a treasure map has an advantage and might try to keep this information as a secret or even start bluffing and disseminating misinformation. In contrast, in collaborative games, asymmetric information can foster players' communication, because they must create a common knowledge base needed for coordinating their actions. The process of sharing information while adhering to certain rules can even be the core challenge of a collaborative game.

The distribution of information can be combined with different player roles and perspectives. For instance, one player can take the role of a navigator, having access to maps and world information, while another player can walk through the world and interact with objects. In such a case, both players have complementary roles, perspectives, and information, resulting in high interdependence.

2.3.2 Level Design

Another way to increase players' interdependence is to create specific level structures that force players to interact with each other or to coordinate their actions. There are two main level design approaches in this context: first, using shared objects and obstacles that players must use or overcome together (Seif El-Nasr et al., 2010) and, second, introducing distinct areas for each player (Reuter et al., 2014).

Cooperation-oriented obstacles can be created by designing shared puzzles (Seif El-Nasr et al., 2010). Such puzzles include tasks that can best be solved if players work together. The interdependence between players is highest if it is not possible to overcome the obstacle alone. A classic example is a cooperative switch puzzle: a door can only be opened if two distant levers are pulled at the same time. This way, a single player cannot proceed alone. Instead, two players must synchronize their actions and are, thus, dependent on each other. Similarly, interdependence can be induced by having players interact with the same object simultaneously (Seif El-Nasr et al., 2010). A box blocking the way can be too heavy for one single player, whereas a group of players is able to push it away. Reuter et al. (2014) call this design pattern *concurrency*.

A less obvious type of shared obstacle that induces cooperation is a sharply increased difficulty in certain game areas so that a single player cannot (or only hardly) pass them. This approach is common in massively multiplayer online games: whereas players can explore large parts of the game world alone, other parts (e.g., dungeons or raids) require the formation of player groups due to a high number of strong enemies

(Ducheneaut & Moore, 2004). This way, players are strongly encouraged to cooperate without the inclusion of specific cooperative game mechanics or obstacles.

It is also possible to increase players' interdependence by separating levels into distinct player areas with limited access and unique possibilities of actions. Though being separated, such a setting can lead to high interdependence if all players must perform certain actions on their path to make the game proceed for the entire group. For instance, one player may activate a mechanism that opens a door on another player's path. Due to the distinct areas that players "control" on their own, players may experience high autonomy in addition to the feeling of relatedness to the others. However, it should be considered that such a level design can result in unfavorable waiting times for players who are quicker than their co-players. Hence, during the design process downtimes should be evaluated and balanced carefully.

Such a separation of player areas can either be continuous—for instance, if players have different roles and related perspectives on the game world during the entire game—or temporary. In this context, Reuter et al. (2014) introduce the concept of *gates*: they define points in the game where players must split up (separation gate) or reunite (gathering gate) before they can continue. Using these patterns enables the design of temporary distinct player areas inside a level to increase interdependence while at the same time emphasizing that each player's individual contribution is significant to proceed.

In an empirical study, Emmerich and Masuch (2017) investigated the impact of high and low player interdependence on the player experience. They created two versions of a custom two-player platformer game and varied the degree of interdependence by using separated player areas. In the first version, each player had to overcome obstacles and was able to manipulate certain objects, such as moving platforms, in their own area to do so (low interdependence). In the other version, players could not control their own area but only the objects in the other player's area, so that they must help each other (high interdependence). A comparison of both game versions shows that players communicated differently and had different social experiences. In the high interdependence group, there were less utterances of frustration and more communication regarding the coordination of common strategies. Perceived social presence was also significantly higher. The results indicate that player interdependence induced by the level design can change the way players communicate and pay attention to each other.

2.3.3 Interface Design

Finally, player interdependence can also be induced by specific interface configurations. This concerns both the input and the output side; hence both will be discussed in this section. Regarding the output interface, it can make a huge difference in terms of player interdependence whether players share a single screen or have their own screens. If players have their own displays, they can have different views on the game world and see information the other players have not, for instance, regarding their characters' stats. This way, players are rather independent with respect to the interface. However, individual screens can support interdependence-inducing game design patterns such as asymmetric information distribution. A shared screen, in contrast, discloses all information to all players, so that they can retrace each other's perspectives and actions. Seif El-Nasr et al. (2010) differentiate three camera settings: split screen, one character in focus, and all characters in focus. Whereas split-screen settings simulate several displays and thereby provide independence and autonomy regarding players' navigation, a shared camera setting demands players to agree upon the direction of movement.

Apart from classic display settings with either one shared screen for a co-located group of players or individual screens for each players, modern games and systems offer innovative design spaces with new interface opportunities. One example is the use of virtual reality headsets. Such head-mounted displays provide a high level of sensory immersion, but also separate the players from each other (Liszio & Masuch, 2016). Hence, their representation inside the game world must be considered carefully, so that they are still aware of their social presence. Another innovative approach is *second screen gaming*, which refers to the idea of adding additional devices to the gaming scenario to display game content (Emmerich, Liszio, & Masuch, 2014). Equipping players with additional displays can offer a range of design possibilities, which can support the establishment of interdependence between the players. For instance, a mix of private and public displays facilitate the asymmetric distribution of information. Moreover, different devices can be linked to distinct player roles and perspectives.

The design of the input interface—the controls of a game—can also have significant impact on players' interdependence. In common multiplayer settings, each player has their own input device, for instance, a gamepad or mouse and keyboard as well as their own game character. To increase players' interdependence, their inputs can be coupled closely by giving them shared control. Shared control can be understood as a special control mode that gives players collective control over game characters, either by giving all players control over all existing game characters or by enabling players to control one single character simultaneously (Seif El-Nasr et al., 2010; Sykownik, Emmerich, & Masuch, 2017). This can lead to seemingly chaotic gameplay but can also induce a lot of fun due to the special challenge of coordinating inputs.

As there are manifold possibilities to implement shared control, Sykownik et al. (2017) introduce a classification of different types of shared control. The authors consider two main dimensions: the locus of manipulation and the timing. Locus of manipulation is a term that refers to the in-game position of a player's manipulation of the game world. This can, for instance, be an avatar, a cursor, or a game object (such as a block in *Tetris*). Players can either control a mutual locus of manipulation (e.g., a shared game character) or several distinct ones (e.g., different game characters or different body parts of the same character). Regarding the aspect of timing, Loparev, Lasecki, Murray, and Bigham (2014) differentiate between simultaneous control and control alternation. The traditional passing of a gamepad in co-located couch settings can also be regarded as a form of alternating control: players switch between phases of active game control and passively watching other players.

Any type of shared control increases players' interdependence compared with traditional control patterns, as the input of one player effects the other players. This effect is probably strongest for simultaneous control over a shared locus of manipulation, because the input of each player is directly combined, and any conflict becomes directly apparent. The differences between shared control modes and traditional control modes in terms of player experience and communication have been evaluated in studies. Emmerich and Masuch (2017) compared two different versions of a custom testbed game, in which players control several blocks and must navigate them to predefined target positions by solving puzzles. In one version, players have control over distinct blocks in the level. They can switch between their blocks anytime, but one player cannot control the blocks of the co-player and vice versa. In the second version, all players can take control over all existing blocks. This means they have shared control over distinct characters. The results of the study show that players perceived less autonomy and competence in the shared control condition, whereas perceived social presence was very high in both game versions. At first glance, the results speak against a positive impact of shared control on the player experience. However, the study tested only one specific implementation of shared control. Hence, game designers who consider implementing shared control as an interesting feature should carefully account for players' needs for autonomy and competence (Emmerich & Masuch, 2017).

In another study, Sykownik et al. (2017) compared different implementations of shared control in a custom game with a single avatar that was controlled by four players. All tested shared control modes elicited high levels of fun and provided entertaining experiences. This positive effect can be mainly attributed to the high interdependence between players, as players' cooperation was the core game mechanic of the game. Perceived autonomy and competence were also satisfactorily high. An evaluation of the perceived social presence of the players indicates that the forced collaboration between them can foster team cohesion between co-players and thereby enhancing their relationship. In sum, the results of the study underline the potential of shared control for developing innovative, highly social experiences. At first glance, the results of both studies reported above seem to partly contradict each other. It has to be noted that the games used in both studies differed regarding the locus of manipulation: in the study by Emmerich and Masuch (2017) players had control over four distinct characters, whereas the second study focused on the use of a single mutual avatar. The latter type of shared control might be more favorable in terms of players' need satisfaction.

2.4 CHALLENGES REGARDING PLAYER INTERDEPENDENCE

In the previous sections, we have learned about the potential of player interdependence in terms of the enhancement of the social player experience and discussed different ways how the interdependence between players can be fostered by design. Though the results of related studies indicate that a high player interdependence, particularly in collaborative games, can increase players' perceived social presence and enjoyment, there are also challenges that game designers have to consider before relying on related design patterns.

As stated above, the balancing of the interdependence between players is important, particularly if asymmetry and complementary player roles are used (Harris & Hancock, 2019). Though distinct roles can serve diverse playing styles and preferences (for instance, some players like to take the lead, whereas other players like to be supportive), it must be prevented that some roles are perceived as generally less favorable than others. If players perceive their specific role or task in a game as less significant than those of other players, they may get frustrated because they feel that they cannot contribute to the team's success. Similarly, an unbalanced level of difficulty of different player roles can lead to the perception of unfairness. Both too high and too low challenges impede a positive experience. Finally, a high interdependence can lead to situations in which one player has to wait until the other player has performed a certain action or overcome a challenge. Such waiting times must be kept as short as possible. If they are unavoidable, game designers should consider integrating features that prevent boredom while waiting. For instance, if waiting players can observe the other players and provide feedback or help, they are still passively involved in the gameplay.

Apart from a positive effect on perceived social presence, a high level of interdependence between players can also have negative side effects on players' experience during play. High interdependence may interfere with feelings of autonomy, which is an important need to be satisfied during play according to the self-determination theory (Emmerich & Masuch, 2017; Sykownik et al., 2017). Interdependent players are forced to cooperate, which limits their freedom to explore the game world on their own and to try out their own ideas. Moreover, players are not in full control over their success or failure in the game if their destiny is coupled with other players. If players do not trust their co-players or perceive them as incompetent, they will get frustrated. Consequently, game designers should consider players' need for autonomy and integrate game features that promote it. Harris and Hancock (2019) point out that in this context the "rhythm of interdependence" is also important. Based on the feedback of participants in their study, the authors report that players would opt for varying degrees of interdependence in a full-fledged game. This can be achieved by alternating game scenes that require close collaboration with scenes that focus on players' individual contributions. This way, the challenges are more diverse, and players can experience both individual success and high sociability.

Another important aspect regarding the implementation of player interdependence is player communication, because there is a higher need for discussing strategies. If players are forced to coordinate their actions due to high interdependence, then they should have the opportunity to communicate properly. Hence, game designers must consider which communication channels are necessary to promote players' interaction. Results of a study by Gajadhar, de Kort, and Ijsselsteijn (2009) indicate that in online play settings, verbal communication with co-players can significantly enhance the social player experience and players' enjoyment. Moreover, the participants reported less perceived challenge and frustration if they were able to talk to each other during play, showing that audio cues facilitate coordination. Apart from verbal communication, game designers can consider integrating additional communication channels such as visual cues (e.g., video chat) and in-game communication mechanics. So-called cooperative communication mechanics (CCMs) enable players to share information or to direct attention to a specific part of the game world by using in-game features. A simple example is a ping system: players can create a visual and/or audio cues in the game world in order to highlight points of interest for another player. Vaddi, Toups, Dolgov, Wehbe, and Nacke (2016) studied CCMs and compared them with voice communication using the cooperative mode of the game *Portal 2* (Valve, 2011). The authors found that players preferred direct verbal communication and that their performance was better if they were able to discuss strategies and puzzle solutions. However, players also appreciated the availability of CCMs and used them a lot to further specify what they were planning. Hence, in-game mechanics are valuable as they can enhance players' communication and should be considered by game designers.

2.5 CONCLUSION

In this chapter, we have discussed the potentials and challenges of the design of player interdependence in digital games. A high interdependence between players fosters communication and interaction and, thus, is a means of increasing players' social experience in terms of social presence, connectedness, and enjoyment. However, a close coupling between players also entails several challenges. As pointed out, game designers should consider issues of balancing, self-determination, and communication mechanics, which are particularly important in the context of interdependence design.

There are diverse possibilities to constitute player interdependence, which we have clustered in three main categories: complementarity, level design, and interface design. Different player roles and abilities, specific level structures, joint puzzles, player screens, and shared control are exemplary game design patterns, which add to the connection between players. Using such game patterns to create player interdependence can contribute to a game's appeal, if the challenges and issues mentioned above are carefully considered during the design process.

REFERENCES

Adams, E. (2010). *Fundamentals of Game Design* (2nd ed.). *Voices that Matter.* San Francisco, CA: New Riders.

Beznosyk, A., Quax, P., Lamotte, W., & Coninx, K. (2012). The effect of closely-coupled interaction on player experience in casual games. In M. Herrlich, R. Malaka, & M. Masuch (Eds.), *LNCS Sublibrary. SL 3, Information Systems and Application, Incl. Internet/Web and HCI: Vol. 7522, Entertainment Computing-- ICEC 2012: 11th International Conference, ICEC 2012, Bremen, Germany, September 26-29, 2012. Proceedings,* pp. 243–255. Berlin/New York, NY: Springer.

Biocca, F., Harms, C., & Burgoon, J. K. (2003). Toward a more robust theory and measure of social presence: Review and suggested criteria. *Presence: Teleoperators and Virtual Environments,* 12(5), 456–480. doi: 10.1162/105474603322761270

Björk, S., & Holopainen, J. (2005). *Patterns in Game Design. Game Development Series.* Boston, MA: Charles River Media.

Csikszentmihalyi, M. (2009). *Flow: The Psychology of Optimal Experience* ([Nachdr.]). *Harper Perennial Modern Classics.* New York, NY: Harper & Row.

De Kort, Y. A. W., & Ijsselsteijn, W. A. (2008). People, places, and play: Player experience in a socio-spatial context. *Computers in Entertainment,* 6(2), 1–11. doi: 10.1145/1371216.1371221

De Kort, Y. A. W., Ijsselsteijn, W. A., & Poels, K. (2007). Digital games as social presence technology: Development of the social presence in gaming questionnaire (SPGQ). In L. Moreno (Ed.), *Proceedings of the 10th Annual International Workshop on Presence,* pp. 195–203. Barcelona: Starlab.

Depping, A. E., & Mandryk, R. L. (2017). Cooperation and interdependence: How multiplayer games increase social closeness. In B. Schouten, P. Markopoulos, Z. Toups, P. Cairns, & T. Bekker (Eds.), *Proceedings of the Annual Symposium on Computer-Human Interaction in Play - CHI PLAY '17,* pp. 449–461. New York, NY: ACM Press. doi: 10.1145/3116595.3116639

Ducheneaut, N., & Moore, R. J. (2004). The social side of gaming: A study of interaction patterns in a massively multiplayer online game. In J. Herbsleb & G. Olson (Eds.), *Proceedings of the 2004 ACM Conference on Computer Supported Cooperative Work - CSCW '04.* pp.360–369. New York, NY: ACM Press. doi: 10.1145/1031607.1031667

Emmerich, K., Liszio, S., & Masuch, M. (2014). Defining second screen gaming: Exploration of new design patterns. In Y. Chisik, C. Geiger, & S. Hasegawa (Eds.), *Proceedings of the 11th Conference on Advances in Computer Entertainment Technology - ACE '14* pp.1–8. New York, NY: ACM Press. doi: 10.1145/2663806.2663855

Emmerich, K., & Masuch, M. (2017). The impact of game patterns on player experience and social interaction in co-located multiplayer games. In B. Schouten, P. Markopoulos, Z. Toups, P. Cairns, & T. Bekker (Eds.), *Proceedings of the Annual Symposium on Computer-Human Interaction in Play - CHI PLAY '17,* pp. 411–422. New York, NY: ACM Press. doi: 10.1145/3116595.3116606

ESA – Entertainment Software Association. (2018). *2018 Essential Facts About the Computer and Video Game Industry.*

Fullerton, T., Swain, C., Hoffman, S., & Isbister, K. (2008). *Game Design Workshop: A Playcentric Approach to Creating Innovative Games* (2nd ed.). Amsterdam/London: Morgan Kaufmann.

Gajadhar, B., de Kort, Y. A. W., & Ijsselsteijn, W. A. (2009). See no rival, hear no rival: The role of social cues in digital game settings. In F. J. Verbeek, D. Lenior, & M. Steen (Eds.), *Proceedings of the 13th CHI Nederland Conference, June 11, 2009, Leiden*, pp. 25–32. CHI-NL.

Gajadhar, B. J., de Kort, Y. A. W., & Ijsselsteijn, W. A. (2008). Shared fun is doubled fun: Player enjoyment as a function of social setting. In P. Markopoulos, B. de Ruyter, W. IJsselsteijn, & D. Rowland (Eds.), *Fun and Games: Second International Conference Proceedings*, pp. 106–117. Berlin, Heidelberg: Springer Berlin Heidelberg.

Harms, C., & Biocca, F. (2004). Internal consistency and reliability of the networked minds social presence measure. In M. Alcañiz Raya & B. Rey Solaz (Eds.), *Proceedings of the Seventh Annual International Workshop on Presence 2004.* Editorial de la UPV.

Harris, J., & Hancock, M. (2019). To asymmetry and beyond! In S. Brewster, G. Fitzpatrick, A. Cox, & V. Kostakos (Eds.), *Proceedings of the 2019 CHI Conference on Human Factors in Computing Systems - CHI '19*, pp. 1–12. New York, NY: ACM Press. doi: 10.1145/3290605.3300239

Harris, J., Hancock, M., & Scott, S. D. (2016). Leveraging asymmetries in multiplayer games: Investigating design elements of interdependent play. In A. Cox, Z. O. Toups, R. L. Mandryk, P. Cairns, V. vanden Abeele, & D. Johnson (Eds.), *Proceedings of the Annual Symposium on Computer-Human Interaction in Play - CHI PLAY '16*, pp. 350–361. New York, NY: ACM Press. doi: 10.1145/2967934.2968113

Hudson, M., & Cairns, P. (2014a). Interrogating social presence in games with experiential vignettes. *Entertainment Computing*, 5(2), 101–114. doi: 10.1016/j.entcom.2014.01.001

Hudson, M., & Cairns, P. (2014b). Measuring social presence in team-based digital games. In G. Riva, J. Waterworth, & D. Murray (Eds.), *Interacting with Presence: HCI and the Sense of Presence in Computer-Mediated Environments*, pp. 83–101. Warsaw, Poland: De Gryter Open. doi: 10.2478/9783110409697.6

Isbister, K. (2010). Enabling social play: A framework for design and evaluation. In R. Bernhaupt (Ed.), *Evaluating User Experience in Games: Concepts and Methods*, pp. 11–22. London: Springer London.

Kaye, L. K., & Bryce, J. (2012). Putting the "Fun Factor" into gaming: The influence of social contexts on experiences of playing videogames. *International Journal of Internet Science*, 7(1), 23–36.

Lee, C., Wyeth, P., Johnson, D., & Hall, J. (2015). Flow during individual and co-operative gameplay. In A. L. Cox, P. Cairns, R. Bernhaupt, & L. Nacke (Eds.), *Proceedings of the Annual Symposium on Computer-Human Interaction in Play - CHI PLAY '15*, pp. 103–107. New York, NY: ACM Press. doi: 10.1145/2793107.2793142

Liszio, S., & Masuch, M. (2016). Designing shared virtual reality gaming experiences in local multi-platform games. In G. Wallner, S. Kriglstein, H. Hlavacs, R. Malaka, A. Lugmayr, & H.-S. Yang (Eds.), *Entertainment Computing - ICEC 2016*, pp. 235–240. Cham: Springer International Publishing.

Loparev, A., Lasecki, W. S., Murray, K. I., & Bigham, J. P. (2014). Introducing shared character control to existing video games. In M. Mateas, T. Barnes, & I. Bogost (Eds.), *Proceedings of the 9th International Conference on the Foundations of Digital Games, FDG 2014, Liberty of the Seas, Caribbean, April 3-7, 2014*. Society for the Advancement of the Science of Digital Games.

Mandryk, R. L., Inkpen, K. M., & Calvert, T. W. (2006). Using psychophysiological techniques to measure user experience with entertainment technologies. *Behaviour and Information Technology*, 25(2), 141–158. doi: 10.1080/01449290500331156

Peng, W., & Crouse, J. (2013). Playing in parallel: The effects of multiplayer modes in active video game on motivation and physical exertion. *Cyberpsychology, Behavior and Social Networking*, 16(6), 423–427. doi: 10.1089/cyber.2012.0384

Reuter, C., Wendel, V., Göbel, S., & Steinmetz, R. (2014). Game design patterns for collaborative player interactions. In *DiGRA '14 - Proceedings of the 2014 DiGRA International Conference*.

Rocha, J. B., Mascarenhas, S., & Prada, R. (2008). Game mechanics for cooperative games. In *Zon Digital Games 2008*, pp. 72–80. Porto, Portugal: Centro de Estudos de Comunicação e Sociedade, Universidade do Minho.

Ryan, R. M., Rigby, C. S., & Przybylski, A. (2006). The motivational pull of video games: A self-determination theory approach. *Motivation and Emotion*, 30(4), 344–360. doi: 10.1007/s11031-006-9051-8

Schell, J. (2010). *The art of game design: A book of lenses* (Reprinted.). Amsterdam: Elsevier/Morgan Kaufmann.

Seif El-Nasr, M., Aghabeigi, B., Milam, D., Erfani, M., Lameman, B., Maygoli, H., & Mah, S. (2010). Understanding and evaluating cooperative games. In E. Mynatt, D. Schoner, G. Fitzpatrick, S. Hudson, K. Edwards, & T. Rodden (Eds.), *Proceedings of the 28th International Conference on Human Factors in Computing Systems - CHI '10*, pp. 253–262. New York, NY: ACM Press. doi: 10.1145/1753326.1753363

Stenros, J., Paavilainen, J., & Mayra, F. (2011). Social interaction in games. *International Journal of Arts and Technology*, 4(3), 342. doi: 10.1504/IJART.2011.041486

Sykownik, P., Emmerich, K., & Masuch, M. (2017). Exploring patterns of shared control in digital multiplayer games. In A. D. Cheok, M. Inami, & T. Romão (Eds.), *Advances in Computer Entertainment Technology 14th International Conference, ACE 2017*, pp. 847–867. Cham: Springer International Publishing.

Tamborini, R., Bowman, N. D., Eden, A., Grizzard, M., & Organ, A. (2010). Defining media enjoyment as the satisfaction of intrinsic needs. *Journal of Communication*, 60(4), 758–777. doi: 10.1111/j.1460-2466.2010.01513.x

Vaddi, D., Toups, Z., Dolgov, I., Wehbe, R., & Nacke, L. (2016). Investigating the impact of cooperative communication mechanics on player performance in portal 2. In *Proceedings of Graphics Interface 2016, Victoria, British Columbia, Canada*, 1–3 June 2016, pp. 41–48. doi: 10.20380/GI2016.06

Vella, K., Johnson, D., & Hides, L. (2015). Playing alone, playing with others: Differences in player experience and indicators of wellbeing. In A. L. Cox, P. Cairns, R. Bernhaupt, & L. Nacke (Eds.), *Proceedings of the Annual Symposium on Computer-Human Interaction in Play - CHI PLAY '15*, pp. 3–12. New York, NY: ACM Press. doi: 10.1145/2793107.2793118

Waddell, J. C., & Peng, W. (2014). Does it matter with whom you slay?: The effects of competition, cooperation and relationship type among video game players. *Computers in Human Behavior*, 38, 331–338. doi: 10.1016/j.chb.2014.06.017

Weibel, D., Wissmath, B., Habegger, S., Steiner, Y., & Groner, R. (2008). Playing online games against computer- vs. human-controlled opponents: Effects on presence, flow, and enjoyment. *Computers in Human Behavior*, 24(5), 2274–2291. doi: 10.1016/j.chb.2007.11.002

Zagal, J. P., Rick, J., & Hsi, I. (2006). Collaborative games: Lessons learned from board games. *Simulation and Gaming*, 37(1), 24–40. doi: 10.1177/1046878105282279

CHAPTER 3

Game Accessibility

Getting Started

Thomas Westin, Ian Hamilton and Barrie Ellis

CONTENTS

3.1   Introduction   37
   3.1.1   Brief History of Game Accessibility and Guidelines   38
   3.1.2   Game Accessibility Guidelines   42
   3.1.3   Applying Game Accessibility Guidelines   42
3.2   Example   43
   3.2.1   Barriers   43
   3.2.2   Working With Guidelines   44
   3.2.3   Summary   48
3.3   Concluding Remarks   49
References   50

3.1 INTRODUCTION

Disability occurs through mismatched interactions, between a person's abilities and the requirements of their environment. This can be particularly vexing when barriers present difficulty performing day-to-day tasks. This is known as the social model of disability. The social model was developed in the 1970s by disabled people to replace the medical model of disability, which views disability as a personal attribute.

Barriers do not only cause difficulty through interaction with permanent physical conditions; they can also be temporary (e.g. a broken arm, a headache), situational (e.g. playing in bright sunlight, while holding a baby or a beer), or have simple differences. Barriers in games are put there by designers and developers, often unknowingly and often unnecessarily. Accessibility is the process of avoiding or removing these barriers.

There are two main approaches to accessibility in general: inclusive design is a pragmatic approach that considers what is possible in practice based on available resources and other limitations, as opposed to universal design (Benyon, 2019). An important way in which games differ significantly from other industries is that some barriers are desirable and necessary to give the game its rules and challenge, and without rules and challenge, the experience would not be a game. Which barriers are necessary is specific to each individual game. This makes game accessibility an optimisation process, identifying and avoiding or removing as many unnecessary barriers as possible while maintaining an enjoyable experience.

By being aware of design alternatives and knowing how to apply them, designers can make choices for inclusive game design and accessibility early on in the design process. This is essential. Retrofitting can be much more expensive and difficult, reducing both the scope of what can be considered and the effectiveness of solutions. This chapter aims to help game designers get started. However, this chapter would not be possible to write without the work of many people over many years, so we will begin with a historical perspective. After this, an introduction to current guidelines is presented followed by guidance of how to work with them.

3.1.1 Brief History of Game Accessibility and Guidelines

Esther played against Tom, but the two of them were so clumsy, and the speed of the ball so relatively fast, that they had no chance of stopping it, or of scoring points against each other except by chance.

(Horwood, W., 1987. *Skallagrigg.* London, UK: Viking.)

This passage, taken from the novel *Skallagrigg* (Horwood, 1987), imagines a game of *Pong* between two disabled characters. Esther with cerebral palsy and Tom with Down syndrome. Both were fascinated by 'television games', but swiftly frustrated by the barriers. This experience mirrors the on-going struggle of disabled gamers wherever gaming technology offers few concessions to access needs. Happily, people (like you?) have long sought to find and share ways to remove barriers to enjoyable play.

In the 1970s, blind computer operators played text games such as *Lunar Lander* with touch-typed input and an Optacon hand-held scanner for reading (Wikipedia, 2020). This device converted computer printouts to a jostling array of raised pins possible to read with a finger. From the 1980s onwards, blind gamers would more commonly use home micros and external speech synthesisers to play the likes of BBC Micro *Football Manager*. Some mainstream games became blind accessible unintentionally through sound alone by players such as Jordan Verner, completing N64 *Zelda Ocarina of Time* using in-game sound and spoken help guides. Equally impressive was blind gamer Brice Mellen defeating Ed Boon at his own game, *Mortal Kombat*.

Throughout this period to current times, a small sub-sector of both hobbyist and professional audiogames have arisen: games written for (and often by) blind people designed to be played through audio alone. Some of these games aimed to be a rich experience for sighted and unsighted alike to bring players together, such as the Taito supported 'Space Invaders for Blind' in 2003.

The advent of iOS in the late 2000s brought with it a significant boost in accidentally blind-accessible games due to native apps' compatibility by default with system level text to speech, as seen in *Hanging with Friends* (Frum, 2011). At time of writing the industry is going through another fundamental shift. Software engines have always posed barriers via the incompatibility of their output with text to speech software. However, both Unity and Unreal have announced their work to solve this. Mass market games from *Minecraft* to *The Division 2* are implementing voiced menus, driven in large part by CVAA legislation. (FCC, n.d.). Over and above this, AAA games such as *Madden* and *Killer Instinct* have put significant effort into blind-accessible gameplay.

Deaf people rarely found themselves completely shut out of video games in the early days. Arcade games such as Williams' 1980 classic *Defender* disadvantaged players if they were unable to hear panicked sounds of human abduction, but few games were unplayable. That changed in the 1990s with CD-ROMs and full motion video. Games with spoken dialogue without subtitles often became impossible to follow. Games such as *Zork: The Grand Inquisitor* put this right with a subtitles option. Subtitling reached a tipping point in 2008, when the first *Assassin's Creed* game launched with none at all, to some public uproar. As a result, subtitling in-game dialogue became a publisher level requirement for all Ubisoft games, which in turn was an important step in pushing adoption across the wider industry. Despite this, there is still much room for improvement in their structure, comprehensiveness and presentation. Games also took a greater interest in conveying sound effects and mood music, critical for building atmosphere and giving people a fuller experience. To this day, games rarely have captions or visual equivalents for important non-speech audio, locking deaf or hard of hearing players out from a fuller experience. One notable early exception is Valve's captioning for sound effects and important musical cues in *Half Life 2* and *Portal*.

Physically and learning-disabled players have often benefited from standard features, such as remapping and difficulty options. The 1972 Odyssey Magnavox featured a speed control for all ball games to slow play to a crawl, hugely beneficial for motor, sight and cognitive accessibility. Atari, at their peak, used what was almost a standard connection method for joysticks, leading to a massive range of controllers shared across many systems. Atari also included a 'Special Feature' option in some of their most successful VCS console games such as *Missile Command* making play far easier. This accessibility feature was promoted on their boxes allowing people to know about it prior to purchase. Upfront communication of accessibility functionality is something still rare to find today. But although these mass market considerations are also beneficial for accessibility, often people need more, particularly with the increasing motor and cognitive demands that games and standard controllers have presented over the years.

Where more was needed, people have often turned to customising and scratch building controllers and software or asking for accessibility updates. Ken Yankelevitz (Figures 3.1 and 3.2), Brilliant Computing,

FIGURE 3.1 Two children playing *Bowling* using a fingertip controller (left player) and mouth control (right player). (Photo via Lynn Given [née Yankelevitz]. With permission.)

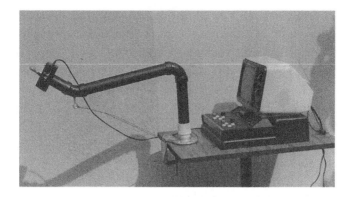

FIGURE 3.2 Ken Yankelevitz custom Atari VCS mouth control in 1982 (left). (Photo via Lynn Given [née Yankelevitz]. With permission.)

OneSwitch.org.uk, Evil Controllers and many others have long served physically disabled gamers with custom controllers. Some large gaming companies such as Nintendo, Namco and most recently Microsoft with the Xbox Adaptive Controller have also delved into this world.

Historically, players have often had to resort to many methods of 'cheating' and hacking to open up access to otherwise unplayable games, including those lacking meaningful difficulty adjustments. This has steadily become far more difficult to do with walled garden gaming platforms and a fear of on-line 'cheating'. Game accessibility has long been a game of catch up. Updating a game, however, has never been easier, thanks to the shift from physical media to digital distribution. Building accessibility in from the outset is much easier too, due to the rapid growth of information and knowledge sharing. Much of this improvement of knowledge is thanks to the web. Accessible gaming groups and people such as Audyssey, Without Wheels, the IGDA's Game Accessibility Special Interest Group, Funka, BBC, OneSwitch, UA-Games, Eelke Folmer, AbleGamers and SpecialEffect were some of the early pioneers in building and sharing game accessibility expertise and information (OneSwitch, 2009). Something the web also helped facilitate was the refinement and spread of more structured game accessibility design help (OneSwitch, 2019).

There has also been progress at system level. The inclusion of accessibility software tools in computer operating systems became more common in the late 1980s and 1990s. Pushed by the Trace Center, Wisconsin on the back of disability rights in education campaigning, the likes of IBM, Apple and Microsoft saw the benefits of including text to speech, magnifiers, on-screen keyboards, sticky keys and so on. More people could use their machines. Slowly, in the late 2010s, these types of features would surface in the likes of the PlayStation 4, Xbox One and Nintendo Switch. All of these things and more, driven by tireless advocacy on many fronts, have led to the current state of affairs in the gaming world. A time when it is not unrealistic to expect reasonable accommodations being made for humans of a very wide range of abilities.

3.1.2 Game Accessibility Guidelines

This chapter aims to get designers started with a freely available web resource of Game Accessibility Guidelines (GAG). The GAG is a living document with advice, examples of accessibility in games and quotes from disabled people. The production of GAG was a group effort by a core team consisting of developers, specialists and academics and validated through a broad pool of developers and gamers. The resource has been continuously updated since the release in 2012, based on developer input, gamer input, advances in technology and new examples of good practices.

The guidelines are divided into three main categories: Basic, Intermediate and Advanced, and sub-divided into Motor, Cognitive, Vision, Hearing, Speech and General. The Basic guidelines are design alternatives that are easy to apply for most game mechanics. The Intermediate guidelines remove barriers for many people but may take some more resources to implement and may not be applicable for all game mechanics. The Advanced guidelines may be complex to apply and are most relevant for specific niche groups of people. To learn more, please see the GAG website.*

3.1.3 Applying Game Accessibility Guidelines

To get started with the basics we'll use a simple racing game as an example. A complete analysis of how individual features could be implemented is beyond the scope of this chapter; instead, we will focus on the process involved.

The process will be as follows: 1) familiarisation with the guidelines; 2) evaluate and plan for guidelines relevant for the game mechanics; 3) prioritise and schedule guidelines earlier that you estimate have the largest

---

* http://gameaccessibilityguidelines.com

production impact if considered later in the design process; 4) implement and test with disabled people; and 5) inform users about the game accessibility features.

3.2 EXAMPLE

3.2.1 Barriers

For the purposes of this discussion, let's consider a basic racing game, with a simple main menu consisting of the following items: New game, Load saved game, Options (containing screen resolution and volume), Exit. Even the relatively simple set of information and interaction in that initial menu can present barriers. For example:

1. Information presented solely through visuals.

2. Presentation of text, including how it is affected by the background it appears over.

3. Inconsistency and complexity of language, including clarity of outcomes.

4. Complexity of menu structure and interaction.

5. Interface elements are hard to select, due to size, motion or having to hold a button down for a period of time, or inaccessible using the standard gameplay controls.

Once past the menus, the game itself may also present barriers. For example:

1. Information presented solely through visuals, perhaps also with low contrast.

2. Difficulty distinguishing the car from the track and other cars (colour, shape etc).

3. Complexity of controls make them hard to learn and use.

4. Requiring both interactions and decision making at very fast speeds.

5. Information about laps, position, speed etc hard to see or understand.

6. The player has difficulty restarting the game.

So even within the scope of a simple menu structure and mechanic there is clearly significant opportunity for increasing the base of players who are able to have an enjoyable experience.

3.2.2 Working With Guidelines

The first step, before working on the game, is to already have some familiarity with best practice guidelines. Next, again before any work starts, consider which are relevant to your game; which elements of your design might present barriers relating to player motor, vision, hearing, speech and cognitive abilities. Reviewing the guidelines again will help with this. The site offers a downloadable Excel checklist format.*

Remember though that guidelines are only a generalised framework; you are the creative problem solver and guidelines are a tool, a source of information to help drive that problem solving, not standards or hard constraints. You may identify barriers specific to your game that are not covered by guidelines or want to figure out alternative solutions; when doing this the key principles to consider are: 1) communicate information in more than one way; and 2) allow flexibility in how players experience your game. Most accessibility barriers can be resolved using these two high level principles.

Ideally you should also involve disabled people to identify barriers they may face with your specific game; this can even take place in the form of formative user research before any work is done, based on previous/competitor products. As with user research in general, a caveat is that the information is specific to the individuals you test with, but if used together with guidelines, your own assessment and where necessary expert advice, the different methods of identifying barriers complement each other well. The more information you have, the more robust your solutions will be.

Next, whittle down the list according to which items are relevant to the concepts you have in mind and which are possible given the constraints of the technology and budget and timescales you are working with. Also think about which barriers are necessary and unnecessary – which barriers are an essential part of what makes the game enjoyable, and which get between players and the kind of emotional experience you want them to have. For example, 'Do not make precise timing essential to gameplay' might not be a reasonable thing to aim for in a racing game. For this game you may end up with something like the following:

---

* http://gameaccessibilityguidelines.com/excel-checklist-download/

- Basic guidelines:

  o Ensure that all areas of the user interface can be accessed using the same input method as the gameplay.

  o Allow the game to be started without the need to navigate through multiple levels of menus.

  o Use an easily readable default font size.

  o Use simple clear language.

  o Use simple clear text formatting.

  o Provide high contrast between text/UI and background.

  o Ensure that all settings are saved/remembered.

  o Allow controls to be remapped/reconfigured.

  o Include tutorials.

  o Avoid flickering images and repetitive patterns.

  o Ensure no essential information is conveyed by colour alone.

  o Ensure no essential information is conveyed by sounds alone.

  o Offer a wide choice of difficulty levels.

  o Provide separate volume controls or mutes for effects, speech and background/music.

- Intermediate guidelines:

  o Support more than one input device.

  o Make interactive elements that require accuracy (e.g. cursor/touch-controlled menu options) stationary.

  o Ensure that all key actions can be carried out by digital controls (pad/keys/presses), with more complex input (e.g. analogue, speech, gesture) not required and included only as supplementary/alternative input methods.

  o Avoid/provide alternatives to requiring buttons to be held down.

o Allow the game to be started without the need to navigate through multiple levels of menus.

o Provide gameplay thumbnails with game saves.

o Provide separate volume controls or mutes for effects, speech and background/music.

o Ensure screen reader support.

o Provide an option to adjust contrast.

o Allow the font size to be adjusted.

o Include assist modes such as auto-aim and assisted steering.

o Provide a manual save feature.

o Provide an autosave feature.

o Include an option to adjust the game speed.

Note: 'Advanced' is not covered here as they are usually niche complex considerations.

The next step is to prioritise and schedule. The guidelines already suggest some priorities, the basic/intermediate/advanced categorisation is based on a balance of how many people benefit; how much of an impact it makes on the experience of people who benefit the most; and typical difficulty/effort of implementation. So, in general aim to meet the basic items first, although prioritisation will also be affected by your own production issues and technologies, publishers/platform/legal requirements and so on.

There will be items that just aren't achievable, considerations that aren't possible due to mechanics, budget, technology or even just internal politics, particularly if it's only the first or second game that you're considering accessibility on. **Do not let this discourage you**. View accessibility as an optimisation process rather than a bar to hit/miss; every single thing you're able to do simply makes your game more enjoyable for more people.

Although what you aim for will likely change quite a bit as development progresses, having a list upfront means you're in a position to identify which items need to be considered before any design or development work starts. So, spend some time considering dependencies and scheduling, which items can be addressed through a design decision versus feature development. Which items need to be considered before any wireframing or design, which items in place for prototyping and so on. Also consider who in your team will be working on each item, assigning specific individuals/disciplines owners where applicable (and ideally a single person with overarching responsibility too). A proven strategy can be to produce separate small lists for specific teams or individuals of only considerations that are relevant to them, and get their buy-in on this general approach (with recognition that it will likely evolve) before their work starts. Having this to refer back to can be extremely valuable, particularly in more fraught later stages of development.

Also look at which considerations you can treat as success criteria of a feature, rather than distinct backlog items in their own right. For example, you may have an item on your backlog for addressing text size. Instead, have 'adequate text size?' as a requirement that must be met for any UI backlog item before it can be moved across into the 'done' pile. This is hard to do when you're starting out, but as your company gains more experience with accessibility you should be able to identify opportunities. This should all give you a clear picture of where in the backlog and scheduling items need to sit. There may be items that seem like a given, so not worth considering. For instance, keeping interactive elements stationary, or avoiding the need to hold down buttons. Even if an item seems like a given, it's still worth keeping an eye on. Issues can easily creep in later in production as the game evolves.

So, you have a plan of what to consider and when to consider. Next comes implementation. Keep your original plan handy, refer back to it regularly (at key milestones at a minimum) and adapt as necessary. Guidelines give you a good initial framework to base your solutions on, but they are often purposely high level to allow flexibility in your solution to fit the unique barriers and constraints and opportunities presented by your game. The best solutions come from empowered designers and developers rather than generalised specifications, and there is also great opportunity for innovation and moving the industry forwards. So, if you feel like there is a different approach that would suit your game well, take the guideline as a description of the problem space and go ahead and push the boundaries. Often the solutions you will find are ones that make the game better for all players, but it is critically important not to rely on assumptions. Always remember that you have tools to ensure your approach works the way you intend, to gain more information to feed into your problem solving – user research, expert review, wide scale player feedback like betas and social media and forum requests.

Even when designing precisely according to an existing specification or an example from an existing game, still validate. If your budget doesn't stretch to formal user research, you can make use of cheaper methods like posting a mock-up or prototype on social media and asking for feedback. If you're asking for people to give up significant amounts of their time to help make your game better you should be compensating them for their time, but if it's just a case of some quick feedback through an email or tweet many people are very happy to help you out for free. Whichever method you're using, do all that you can to make people feel like their feedback is welcome and wanted. There are lots of people who feel reluctant to speak up, having been discouraged through past experiences with both developers and fellow gamers, so any efforts you can make here are important.

Once you are getting closer to launch and have a more solid picture of what kind of considerations will be in the game, think about how this will be communicated to players. You cannot take it for granted that players will know about what you have considered or know to look through menus to find options. You can let people know in-game through tutorials, loading screen hints, start-up menus etc, and also let people know publicly through social media, blog posts, feature lists on digital storefronts and press kits, and through features being present in demo builds at conventions. Aim to let people know at least some information before the game launches, so they can get in on pre-released and pre-launch hype as much as everyone else, safe in the knowledge that they will indeed be able to play.

3.2.3 Summary

- Consider accessibility from an early a stage as possible, ideally before any design or development work starts.

- Think about all the barriers your game may present for people with varied motor/cognitive/hearing/vision/speech ability, which of those barriers are essential for making your game enjoyable and which get between players and the kind of emotional experience you want them to have.

- Think about communicating information in more than one way and giving players flexibility in how they experience your game.

- When planning, prioritising and implementing do not be discouraged by not being able to achieve everything you want to – every consideration no matter how small makes a positive difference to your game.

- Treat guidelines as a tool and source of information, combine with other methods where possible and feel free to go beyond them.

- Assign owners, ensure different teams/disciplines know which considerations they are responsible for.

- Think about accessibility as a success criterion for existing backlog items.

- Involve disabled people both as a way of identifying barriers and validating solutions.

- Keep referring back to and adapting your plan throughout development.

- Give players the information they need to make informed purchase decisions.

3.3 CONCLUDING REMARKS

Hopefully, you now a have a good idea of how you can work with the Game Accessibility Guidelines for your next or even on-going game project. Remember, it is always better to try and do something than nothing, and if you don't make it right the first time, just continue and you will make it better the next time. Think of it this way: even though game accessibility has been around since the 1970s, it was not until recent years that it was considered industry wide, so you are in good company when taking your first steps. We are all in this journey together, all of our efforts will help each other. Everything you do no matter how small doesn't just benefit your own game, it helps push the industry in general to a better place.

If you want to learn more about game accessibility, see related resources at the IGDA Game Accessibility SIG* (GA-SIG) website.† You are also welcome to join the GA-SIG, simply by signing up to the mailing list or social media channels on the website. That way you will get in touch with many experts who are active in this field.

---

* SIG: Special interest group
† https://igda-gasig.org/

REFERENCES

Benyon, D. (2019). *Designing User Experience*. London, UK: Pearson Education Limited.

Frum, L. (2011). Voice controls let blind gamer 'hang' with friends online. *CNN Business*. Available at https://edition.cnn.com/2011/11/30/tech/gaming-gadgets/blind-social-gamer/index.html.

FCC. n.d. 21st Century Communications and Video Accessibility Act (CVAA) [Online]. Available: https://www.fcc.gov/consumers/guides/21st-century-communications-and-video-accessibility-act-cvaa [Accessed 12 May, 2020].

Horwood, W. (1987). *Skallagrigg*. London, UK: Viking.

OneSwitch. (2009). Game accessibility sites. *SwitchGaming*. Available at https://switchgaming.blogspot.com/2009/07/game-accessibility-sites.html.

OneSwitch. (2019). Game accessibility guidance 2019 update. *SwitchGaming*. Available at https://switchgaming.blogspot.com/2019/01/game-accessibility-guidance-2019-update.html.

Wikipedia. (2020). Optacon. Last modified 17 March 2020. Available at https://en.wikipedia.org/wiki/Optacon.

II

Gamification and Serious Games

CHAPTER 4

Gamification for Good

Addressing Dark Patterns in Gamified UX Design

Ole Goethe

CONTENTS

4.1	Introduction	53
4.2	Related Work	56
4.3	Gamification for Worse	56
	4.3.1 Privacy	56
	4.3.2 Dependency	57
	4.3.3 Exploitation	58
4.4	Open Questions on Gamification	59
4.5	Conclusion	60
References		60

4.1 INTRODUCTION

We spend much of our time in finding the trustworthiness in our day-to-day lives while doing tasks. We continually assess trustworthiness in both the people that we meet as well as in the products and services that we choose to interact with. In assessing that trustworthiness, researchers have found that the following three components come into play most of the time (Albrechtslund, 2007):

- **Integrity:** to do the task with the best intentions by heart

- **Competence:** to handle the task and the associated challenges

- **Capability:** to deliver timely outcomes and the expected level of finish

These three fundamentals are applied to both people and products having the same results. Since these fundamentals form the decisions users are making on a day-to-day basis, they can be considered when applying gamification design to generate experiences that our users recognize as trustworthy enough to interact with. Producing this trustworthiness implies that users will feel confident when it comes to sharing their data with businesses and it allows them to use that data to create more value for them (Kahneman, 2011).

At heart, the experiences must retort sustainably to the user needs. Those requirements may not always be recognized or articulated openly by the users themselves—it is, after all, the task and responsibility of the user experience practitioners to expose and innovate for the unspoken needs—but the design must also be aligned with an essentially wholesome, positive outcome (Pawlowski, 2017).

However, the dark patterns, on the other hand, are not errors. They're prudently made with a solid understanding of the human psychology, and they usually don't consider the user's interest. Dark patterns have been part of our lives for decades without most people knowing; be it about a weight loss medicine that is sold with the slogan of "reduce 10 kg in a week," or some credit card statements claiming a 0% balance transfer but don't clarify that this percentage will rise way higher unless the consumer chooses to have a long-term agreement. It is of no surprise that dark patterns have made their way into gamification contexts as well (Leavitt & Shneiderman, 2006).

As known, gamification is the use of visuals and design components from games in non-gaming contexts to enhance user engagement and motivate users to change their behavior. Hence, user engagement and motivation are the key outcomes of gameful system design (O'Brien & Toms, 2008). In our context, user engagement is an active relationship between a consumer and a product or service, with engagement measured with metrics of recency, frequency, duration, virality and ratings. Metrics from these categories can be used to form an "E-score" (i.e. engagement score), which is a single number defining the level of user engagement (Zichermann & Cunningham, 2011). Engagement also has a strong relationship with user experience, since it reinforces affective meaning, interaction, feedback and user control, which culminates in a positive user experience. However, gamification faces a big challenge since it is very difficult to maintain long-term relationships with users; i.e. "keeping engagement levels high" is hard but is achievable through positive reinforcements and actions towards mastery (Deterding, 2011).

With this in mind, the darkness could quickly make its place since the User eXperience (UX) design choices are being chosen to be intentionally deceptive (Bardzell & Bardzell, 2013). To urge the user to give up somewhat more than they realize. Or to agree to things they perhaps wouldn't if they honestly understood the decisions they were being urged to make. To put it simply, dark pattern design is dishonesty and deceitfulness by design.

The technique, as it is online today, frequently feeds off and gains the fact that content-overloaded customers skim-read stuff they're provided with, particularly if it looks dull and they're in the middle of trying to do something else—such as sign up to their desired service, complete their purchase, reach to something they want to look at or know what their friends have sent them (Fogg, 2009).

Manipulative timing is a vital component of dark pattern design (Benford et al., 2015). For example, when you see a notice, you can control how you respond to it. Or if you even notice it. Pauses usually pile on the cognitive overload—while the deceptive design uses them to make it more difficult for a web user to be completely in control of their abilities during an important moment of decision.

In terms of visuals, brightly colored "agree and continue" buttons are a recurring feature of this flavor of dark pattern design. These eye-catching signposts appear near universally across consent flows—to encourage users not to read or contemplate a service's terms and conditions, and therefore not to understand what they're agreeing to.

This often works because humans are lazy in the face of boring and/or complex looking material. And because too much information easily overwhelms. Most people will take the path of least resistance. Especially if it's being reassuringly plated up for them in handy, push-button form. At the same time, dark pattern design will ensure the opt out—if there is one—will be near invisible; Greyscale text on a grey background is the usual choice (Seaborn, & Fels, 2015). Some deceptive designs even include a call to action displayed on the colorful button they do want you to press—with text that says something like "Okay, looks great!"—to further push a decision. Likewise, the less visible opt out option might use a negative suggestion to imply you're going to miss out on something or are risking bad stuff happening by clicking there (Wyie, 2014).

4.2 RELATED WORK

To better understand gamification design, we need to better grasp game design. It has been more than 30 years since the initial voices were heard concerning the lack of a critical language for examining and speaking about game design (Costikyan, 1994). Scholars and design practitioners have since replied to that call by suggesting ways of understanding games, categorizing them, criticizing them and more. Hunicke et al. (2004) proposed a framework for understanding games and reducing the gap "between game design and the development, game criticism, and practical game research," while Zagal et al. (2005) developed an ontology for telling, examining and reviewing games, by defining a ladder of concepts abstracted from the analysis of numerous specific games.

In 2010, Bergström et al. proposed using the game design patterns to ratify and codify knowledge for game aesthetics. This idea was widened by Björk and Holopainen (2005), who developed a group of almost 300 gameplay patterns. These patterns vary from the original structure in building by replacing the problem solution pairs with the cause and consequences groups that label possibilities for the instantiation of a pattern and the possible consequences that pattern might have in a game design.

A negative experience may encompass not only the game-like experience; it can include something one experiences after the gamified experience due to its design. Even so, this definition quickly runs into problems: it ignores the will and desires of the user (Eşanu, 2019).

The users' prospects and understanding of the experience are maybe more important than if the experience was positive or negative. If we consider the interaction with a system as a contract, where a system offers one thing, but then provides another that the user was not aware of, such a contract would be problematic. and would be considered by society as unethical or illegal, even if the intentions and outcomes were well-meaning (Deterding, 2011).

4.3 GAMIFICATION FOR WORSE

4.3.1 Privacy

Gamification designers commonly use their knowledge of cognitive psychology and usability to design the best experience for you as possible. However, they sometimes also apply their understanding of psychological biases to create UX that herd and misdirect you to take a path or decision you didn't mean to intend for. Instead of designing with the users' best interests at heart, they design for their business' goals, whether that is more sales, more data or more subscribed users (Fogg, 2009). These dark patterns are ethically problematic since they nudge you towards particular choices and actions that may be against your own interest. They take your agency away without you knowing. For instance, in most of the cookie consent banner used by companies, we see that they highlighted the text "Trust and transparency is important to us" in bold letters and hyperlinked a few keywords with blue font. Users who do not read the block of text carefully will miss that "by continuing to use the site, including closing or clicking off the banner, you consent to the use of advertising and analytics technologies" (Jeffrey & Shaowen, 2015).

Note as well the usage of visuals in the consent form, which is meant to trigger users to click the most prominent button in order to continue quickly onto the site compared with the sparse "Learn More" option, which also is passively worded. The imbalance of visual representation between the options is a dark pattern meant to dissuade you from noticing the Learn More button. Once you click the Learn More button, you will often find that your privacy settings are set to the least privacy-friendly settings.

Another example of using formatting as a dark pattern is the invisible unsubscribe option. Companies bury the option in a jumble of text at the bottom of the page or format it to make it look like it's not a link.

The importance of visual design and communication is paramount in any interface's effectivity and functionality. Through formatting text fonts, buttons and color blocks, gamification designers can trigger the desirable action from the user, directly or through learned associations. For some businesses, more clicks mean more money, so the right visual cues are key (Harry, Marc, Jeremy, & James, 2015).

Gamification designers by using visual cues could easily gain access to an excess of user data without informing, empowering and enabling the people they served as customers to make choices. In fact, data sharing activities were deliberately "designed away." With time, these kinds of activities established a power imbalance. The companies who controlled the data had (and still have) the power (Zichermann & Cunningham, 2011).

4.3.2 Dependency

With regards to apps usage, there is a lifecycle of each app that must be noted. At the end of the lifecycle, there may be no more need for the app; however, creating user dependency through dark patterns in the UX design of the app, a user may still be compelled to use the app even after he/she no longer is in need to use the app (Dicheva, Agre, & Angelova, 2015). For instance, if you are on track after following a strict gym routine for months, after adopting the gym mode or fitness related app, is the app still needed to continue the same routine or lifestyle? Here is when the context matters and to manipulate the context, to keep the app under constant usage, dark patterns in gamified UX design of the app are applied.

However, context can dynamically change user experience and increase app engagement by reminding users when they are able to make a smart health decision and by using "gym mode" to get the app ready for a user's workout as they are entering the gym (Adkins, 2016).

4.3.3 Exploitation

Gamification design can exploit the lack of user understanding and especially play with their psyche. There is an increasing interest in applying the insights and results from psychology and behavioral economics from games. How can we make a line between using this knowledge to deliver more interesting, engaging and satisfying the gamified experiences (good) and misusing player's cognitive biases and probably irrational behavior to make more money? (Achterbosch, Pierce, & Simmons, 2007).

The psychologist Madigan's analysis (2012) of the *Sims* game identifies several "psychological shenanigans" that have been leveraged to encourage people to spend more time and money on the game. The implication is that the player is being manipulated towards spending money they would not have otherwise.

The case for pop-ups is similar. It's a common situation in case of pop-ups with confirmations. You read, and you don't know whether to press OK or CANCEL—both seem to fit. Problems also occur with ambiguous checkboxes during payments and subscriptions (Madigan, 2012).

Another approach is the roach motel business model. A user wants to say goodbye, but it is not easy to do so. This happens, for instance, after you signed up to an app, but then getting out of it is hard to figure out. You are suddenly not given an easy way to cancel the automatic renewal (Montola, 2010).

For instance, some companies are using the above trick to convert their leads to paying customers. They make it so easy to sign up for an account, make the fine prints unnoticeable. Everything is aligned to the laws. The worst part is—they make it difficult for their users to terminate the subscription. Some companies also sell their products in a bundle without offering the separate purchase option. Their customers are forced to buy the extra items or services because they are part of the deal (Agnieszka, 2019).

4.4 OPEN QUESTIONS ON GAMIFICATION

The dark patterns in UX gamified design are based on how the users behave and then exploiting the user behavior. Now you have read some of the examples of dark pattern design, apart from not repeating the above design, what else can you do to ensure that your design is ethical? The answer is simple—ask yourself why you design the product or feature in that way, how you collect data and why do you need the user data and so on. If your true answer is something like giving your users a more meaningful user experience—you are a designer with great ethic. What makes a designer good is not about how much money a designer brings to a business, it's about how much a designer cares about the users. Thus, we pose the following questions:

- What is the motive of using dark patterns in gamified UX design besides user engagement and dependency?

- If the user engagement is achieved, what are the adverse effects dark patterns in gamified UX design may bring to the users?

- Is it possible to obtain user engagement and behavioral change without using dark patterns in gamified UX design?

- Even if users are aware of the deceptive UX patterns in a gamified design, why don't they tend to avoid it?

- How can designers create gamified UX design that both provides access to marginalized users and brings them opportunities to engage?

- How do the demographic factors like language, age, gender, income, lifestyle and so on affect the engagement level in a gamified UX design and how do designers apply dark patterns to each group?

- While creating strategies for your gamification design, what protective tools are put in place to provide user engagement without compromising on regulatory compliances and design ethics?

4.5 CONCLUSION

Dark gamified design patterns use all of the powers of visual design with the flair of a magician's misdirection, and the language of a shady sideshow barker. These patterns are in direct opposition to concepts we celebrate in design, such as empathy, human-centered and inclusive. Dark patterns rob users of their agency (Davis, 2009). If users feel cheated by dark patterns, why do these patterns persist? Dark patterns emphasize short-term gains and offenders include some of the world's biggest brands. A successful project is one that covers both aspects of increasing engagement through pleasurable activity and satisfying the bigger picture—the original purpose for the design (Hunicke, LeBlanc & Zubek, 2004). Overall, gamification is a game-logic design "weaved" carefully into a system to encourage behavioral change, not to manipulate user behavior. Good design—and a great company—is all about giving meaningfulness to our fellow humans. In fact, it's not really limited to a company—it's society as a whole. At the end of the day, you should evaluate what you really want from your customers. Do you just want them to use your service or do you want more? A good brand is liked. A great brand is loved and respected. You'll probably never reach that point if you use dark patterns.

REFERENCES

Achterbosch, L., Pierce, R., & Simmons, G. (2007). Massively multiplayer online role-playing games: The past, present, and future. *Computers in Entertainment*, 5, 4.

Adkins, S. (2016). *The 2016–2021 Global Game-Based Learning Market*. Serious Play Conference.

Albrechtslund, A. (2007). Ethics and technology design. *Ethics and Information Technology*, 9, 63–72.

Bardzell, J., & Bardzell, S. (2013). What is "critical" about critical design? *CHI 2013*, 3297–3306.

Bardzell, J., & Bardzell, S. (2015). *Humanistic HCI*. Vol. 8. Morgan Claypool Publishers, Williston, VT, pp. 1–185.

Benford, S., Greenhalgh, C., Anderson, B., Jacobs, R., Golembewski, M., Jirotka, M., ... & Farr, J. R. (2015). The ethical implications of HCI's turn to the cultural. *ACM Transactions on Computer-Human Interaction*, 22, 1–37.

Bergström, K., Björk, S., & Lundgren, S. (2010). *Exploring Aesthetical Gameplay Design Patterns: Camaraderie in Four Games*. Proceedings of the 14th International Academic MindTrek Conference: Envisioning Future Media Environments, Tampere, Finland.

Björk, S., & Holopainen, J. (2005). *Patterns in Game Design*. Hingham, MA: Charles River Media Inc.

Bogost, I. (2007). *Persuasive Games.* Cambridge, MA: The MIT Press.

Bowman, N. (2014). *The Ethics of UX Research.* Retrieved from https://www.uxbooth.com/articles/ethics-ux-research/.

Brignull, H. (2011). *Dark Patterns: Deception vs. Honesty in UI Design. Published in Interaction Design, Usability.* Retrieved from https://www.90percentofeverything.com/about/.

Brignull, H., Miquel, M., Rosenberg, J. & Offer, J. (2015). Dark Patterns - User Interfaces Designed to Trick People. http://darkpatterns.org

Cieplińska, A. (2019). *5 Common UX Dark Patterns — Interfaces Designed to Trick You!* Medium.com. Retrieved from https://medium.com/beautiful-code-smart-design-by-10clouds/5-common-ux-dark-patterns-interfaces-designed-to-trick-you-61fdede9718c.

Daniel, B., & Erik, N. (1999). Toward an ethics of persuasive technology. *Communications of the ACM,* 42, 5, 51–58.

Davis, J. (2009). *Design Methods for Ethical Persuasive Computing.* Proceedings of the 4th International Conference on Persuasive Technology - Persuasive'09. New York, NY: ACM Press.

Deterding, S. (2011). Situated motivational affordances of game elements: A conceptual model. *CHI2011,* 3–6.

Dicheva, D., & Dichev, C. (2015). Agre, G. and Angelova, G., "gamification in education: A systematic mapping study." *Journal of Educational Technology and Society,* 18, 75–88.

Eşanu, E. (2019). *Gamification: Motivation Model: The Broken Way of Carrot and Stick.* Retrieved from Uxplanet.org.

Fogg, B. J. (2009). *A Behavior Model for Persuasive Design.* Proceedings of the 4th International Conference on Persuasive Technology. ACM.

Harris, L. (2007). *Diplomacy. In Hobby Games: The 100 Best.* J. Lowder (Ed.). Renton, WA: Green Ronin Publishing.

Haynes, T. (2018). *Dopamine, Smartphones & You: A Battle for Your Time.* Retrieved from http://sitn.hms.harvard.edu/flash/2018/dopamine-smartphones-battle-time/.

Hullett, K., & Whitehead, J. (2010). *Design Patterns in FPS Levels.* Proceedings of Foundations of Digital Games Conference, June 19–21, Monterey, CA.

Hunicke, R., LeBlanc, M., & Zubek, R. (2004). *MDA: A Formal Approach to Game Design and Game Research.* Proceedings of the Challenges in Game AI Workshop, 19th National Conference on Artificial Intelligence (AAAI '04, San Jose, CA), AAAI Press, San Jose, CA.

Huotari K., & Hamari, J. (2012). *Defining Gamification - A Service Marketing Perspective.* Proceedings of the 16th International Academic MindTrek Conference, Tampere, Finland, October 3–5.

Kahneman, D. (2011). *Thinking, Fast and Slow.* New York, NY: Farrar, Straus & Giroux.

Leavitt, M. O., & Shneiderman, B. (2006). *Research-Based Web Design & Usability Guidelines. US Department of Health and Human Services Usability User Experience Basics.* Retrieved from http://www.usability.gov/what-and-why/user-experience.html.

Madigan, J. (2012). *Seven Psychological Sins of SimCity Social*. Retrieved from www.psychologyofgames.com/2012/07/sevenpsychological-sins-of-simcity-social.

Montola, M. (2010). *The Positive Negative Experience in Extreme Role-Playing*. Proceedings of Nordic DiGRA 2012, Stockholm, Sweden, DiGRA.

Nathan, K. (2018). *How to Avoid UX Dark Patterns (When Asking People for Their Data)*. Medium.com. Retrieved from https://medium.com/greater-than-experience-design/how-to-avoid-ux-dark-patterns-when-asking-people-for-their-data-c8ea01565312.

O'Brien, H. L., & Toms, E. G. (2008). What is user engagement? A conceptual framework for defining user engagement with technology. *Journal of the Association for Information Science and Technology*, 59(6), 938–955.

Pawlowski, M. (2017). *Principles for Gamification in User Experience*. Retrieved from https://www.mobileuserexperience.com/principles-for-gamification-in-user-experience/4656/.

Schell, J. (2008). *The Art of Game Design: A Book of Lenses*. Burlington, MA: Morgan Kaufmann.

Seaborn, K., & Fels, D. I. (2015). Gamification in theory and action: A survey. *International Journal of Human-Computer Studies*, 74, 14–31.

Wyie, J. (2014). *Fitness Gamification: Concepts, Characteristics, and Applications*. Elon University, Elon, NC.

Zagal, J. P., Björk, S., & Lewis, C. (2013). *Dark Patterns in the Design of Games*. Chania, Crete, Greece: Foundations of Digital Games.

Zagal, J. P., Mateas, M., Fernandez-Vara, C., Hochhalter, B., & Lichti, N. (2005). Towards an ontological language for game analysis. In S. de Castell & J. Jenson (Eds.), *Changing Views: Worlds in Play, Selected Papers of DIGRA 2005*, Vancouver, Canada, pp. 3–14.

Zichermann, G., & Cunningham, C. (2011). Gamification by design: Implementing game mechanics in web and mobile apps. In *Gamification by Design: Implementing Game Mechanics in Web and Mobile Apps*, p. 208. O'Reilly Media, Inc.

CHAPTER 5

The Social Media Game?

How Gamification Shapes Our Social Media Engagement

Dayana Hristova, Suzana Jovicic,

Barbara Goebl and Thomas Slunecko

CONTENTS

5.1	A Double-Edged Game	64
5.2	Gamifying Social Media	65
	5.2.1 Interrelation between Gamification and Social Media	66
	5.2.2 Persuasive Design Application	67
5.3	Analytic Approach	68
	5.3.1 Selected Platforms	68
	5.3.2 Selected Gamification Elements	69
5.4	Gamification Elements in Snapchat, Instagram and Facebook	70
	5.4.1 Points	73
	5.4.2 Leaderboards	75
	5.4.3 Badges and Achievements	76
	5.4.4 Levels	77
	5.4.5 Stories and Theme	78
	5.4.6 Clear Goals	79
	5.4.7 Feedback	80
	5.4.8 Rewards	81
	5.4.9 Progress	82
	5.4.10 Challenge	83

5.5 Discussion   84
    5.5.1 Gamification Elements Discussion   84
    5.5.2 Snapchat, Instagram and Facebook Discussion   86
    5.5.3 Is Social Media Turning Into a "Social Media Game"?   86
5.6 Ethics   87
    5.6.1 Social Comparison   88
    5.6.2 Intransparent Psychological Models   88
    5.6.3 Surveillance   89
    5.6.4 Morally Obliged to Have Fun?   90
5.7 Outlook   90
References   91

5.1 A DOUBLE-EDGED GAME

Game elements and principles are steadily spreading to a multiverse of non-game domains (Deterding, Sicart, Nacke, O'Hara & Dixon, 2011). Gamification has been endorsed as a booster of user engagement (Deterding, Dixon, Khaled & Nacke, 2011; Hamari, Koivisto & Sarsa, 2014) and has become a trend in the business world (Bogost, 2014), popular discourse (Selinger, Sadowski & Seager, 2015) and scientific literature* (Hamari et al., 2014). Though its efficiency is highly dependent on the context and the users† addressed (Hamari et al., 2014), it is celebrated for its potential to evoke motivation and joyful involvement. Parallel to its rise to a global trend, gamification has also been criticized as a consulting gimmick and a tool for the exploitation of employees, customers and users (Bogost, 2013, 2014). Critics of gamification regard it as an attention economy‡ tool that is used to seduce people into "willing self-surveillance" (Whitson, 2014), generating data (Lampe, 2014), devoting attention and time for the profit of businesses (Bogost, 2014).

On a psychological level, gamification evokes further concerns due to its reliance on principles similar to the addictive design of gambling. Gamification's focus on flow (Csikszentmihalyi, 1997) as the main virtue of uninterrupted online involvement resembles the *machine zone*

---

* Google scholar search for "gamification" returns over 46,000 results as of August 2019.
† By "users" we mean active prosumers (Toffler & Alvin, 1980) that appropriate, shape and re-invent online tools. We consciously chose the term "users" since it is commonly used in tech and online discourse.
‡ The term "attention economy" refers to an approach in which human attention is understood as a limited resource that serves as a "new currency of business" (Davenport & Beck, 2001).

that Natascha Schuell (Schuell, 2014) reveals as the core of slot machines' psychological mechanisms. *Machine zone* refers to a design strategy that "uses obfuscation in user interface to entice non-reflexive and prolonged engagement with a digital device" (Gekker, 2016). This principle is best exemplified by the statement of one of Schuell's informants: "I don't want to win, I want to continue" (Schuell, 2014). Similarly, gamification is not per se about winning but about perpetuating the flow of joyful involvement. This very flow is what designers of online environments aim at. In particular, designers of social media attempt to harness the power of computer games to involve and entertain people. If the dominant narrative of the time is "fun is good" (Selinger et al., 2015), app designers can hardly ignore it.

This chapter acknowledges the complexity of gamification beyond a mere hopeful utopia of motivation on the one hand, or a dystopic weapon of control on the other. In our opinion, gameful applications hold a great potential to enhance users' experience, in particular with regard to involvement and fun. Nevertheless, we also acknowledge that gamification can turn into *exploitationware* (Bogost, 2013) for the purposes of manipulation and surveillance. Hence, we encourage transparent applications that comply with ethical guidelines. These principles are also a part of our interdisciplinary research on gamification and social media use among adolescents, specifically with regard to privacy and the transparency of applied psychological models (Goebl et al., 018; Goebl et al., 2019; Jovicic, Goebl & Hristova, 2019). As part of our empirical research, we co-designed a serious game together with adolescents revealing issues of gamification and social media use. We subscribe to Waltz and Deterding's mediating position that recognizes gamification's problematic aspects but also its relevance (Walz & Deterding, 2015) in the ludic century (Zimmermann, 2014). With the coming-of-age of the *digital natives* (Prensky, 2001) in industrialized societies, gamification cannot simply be ignored as it starts to shape the new standards for mediated communication and work. Therefore, it is necessary that its issues are addressed in a more nuanced manner* and beyond a "good-evil" simplification.

5.2 GAMIFYING SOCIAL MEDIA

Being aware of this ambiguous potential is crucial since gameful approaches have become influential in various fields such as education (Davis & Singh,

---

* For an overview of critical approaches to gamification, see Oravec (2015).

2015; de Freitas et al., 2017), environmental issues (Froehlich, 2014; Dumit, 2017), rehabilitation (Mihelj et al., 2012) and, more notably, social media (Lampe, 2014). Social networking sites (SNS)* and their gamified features have become an integral part of the daily life of billions of people worldwide. Social media shapes the new standard for online social interaction through gamified elements (e.g. points, leaderboards and badges). Upon closer examination, the symbiosis between social media and gamification is not fortuitous. According to Lampe, "both genres of interaction combine social and technical architectures to shape and enable user practice" (Lampe, 2014). Indeed, the success of social media and gamification seems to heavily rely on channeling and altering social practices through new technological affordances.†

5.2.1 Interrelation between Gamification and Social Media

Hamari and Koivisto describe gamification as "a manifold socio-technological phenomenon with claimed potential to provide a multitude of benefits such as enjoyment as well as social benefits through communities and social interaction" (Hamari & Koivisto, 2015). Online community building is undoubtedly at the heart of SNS' mission, yet the alleged social benefit has an equally powerful dark side, for instance, in the context of social comparison (Panger, 2014) enabled by quantification (Whitson, 2014). For example, *Likes* in various forms do not merely boost users' confidence (Burrow & Rainone, 2017) but also provide a leeway for competition often resulting in power struggles and envy (Weinstein, 2017; Panger, 2014). *Likes* and followership become powerful tools for negotiating hierarchies and social status. Community building and social comparison are closely intertwined aspects of social interaction, especially in the context of gamified social media that quantifies social bonds and appreciation. The interplay of such aspects contributes to the ambiguous effects of SNS on users' well-being (Weinstein, 2018).

Considering the pivotal relevance of social motivations for the functioning of gamification, it is not surprising that it resonates so profoundly with social media. Previous research indicates that social motivations are, indeed, strong predictors of whether gamification is perceived positively

---

* In this chapter, social media is used as an umbrella term including social networking sites (SNS) and instant messaging (IM) services that also include additional social features (e.g. WhatsApp, Snapchat).
† The term affordance (Gibson, 1966) originates from ecological psychology and refers to the action opportunities that the environment (may it be offline or online) offers to an agent.

or negatively (Hamari & Koivisto, 2013). Hamari and colleagues argue that gamification should, hence, "be imbued with mechanisms that afford for social interaction in order to enhance social influence and the perception of reciprocal benefits" (Hamari & Koivisto, 2013).

Gamification has become an integral part of designing SNS to such an extent that it would be difficult to imagine social media without it. Indeed, one could hardly picture platforms like Facebook without gamified tokens such as Likes and Views, that by quantifying social relations, enabling social comparison and high scoring* among other relational practices. Lampe argues that this incorporation of gamification in social media is not a coincidence since early social media designers were familiar with games' principles and readily applied them to the emerging SNS domain (Lampe, Ellison & Steinfield, 2006). Designers were aware of the power of gameful experiences and could successfully implement structural gamification (e.g. badges, leaderboards) and content gamification (e.g. making content more story-like) (Kapp, 2012) in the social media services they were working on. SNS platforms have been since relying on quantification and gamification tools that help them retain users' attention for as long as possible.

5.2.2 Persuasive Design Application

As mentioned above, gamification's main objective to maximize users' involvement in an activity overlaps with one of the main concerns of social media: encouraging users to engage more actively with its platforms, to generate content and to interact with others (Lampe, 2014). Hence, technical affordances are created in order to incite desirable behaviors that signify active use.

The wish to spark such behaviors is where social media gets intertwined with persuasion. There is a salient parallel between social media and games with regard to persuasive techniques. *Microsuasion* describes persuasive elements that are applied in an otherwise non-persuasive context and are not to be confused with macrosuasion products (e.g. preventive serious games for health) that are created for the sole purpose of behavior change. According to Fogg, "video games are exceptionally rich in microsuasion elements. The overall goal of most games is to provide entertainment, not to persuade. But during the entertainment experience, players are bombarded

---

* *High score* refers to the practice of comparing one's points to one's own previous score. In SNS, for example, a user can compare the likes she got on her last post to her previous posts and try to maximize the likes she would get the next time.

with microsuasion elements, sometimes continuously, designed to persuade them to keep playing" (Fogg, 2003). In a similar vein, social networks' primary purpose is not to persuade but to facilitate communication and community building online. However, SNS apply gamification elements to persuade users to spend more time with their platforms (Lampe, 2014) and, hence, to produce more data and meta-data. De facto, gamified elements serve as a microsuasion and a productivity tool (Whitson, 2014) for SNS nudging its users to generate more content. This is also in line with Bogost's term *persuasive games* (Bogost, 2013) that he proposed as an alternative to the, in his opinion misleading, term "gamification." Due to gamification's potential behavioral, social and motivational impact on users, it is crucial to scrutinize gamified elements used by social media platforms in the light of motivational psychology and persuasive design. In the following section, we will present an overview and analysis of gamification elements used by three major social media platforms—Snapchat, Facebook (including the Messenger app) and Instagram as of August 2019.

5.3 ANALYTIC APPROACH

5.3.1 Selected Platforms

Snapchat, Instagram and Facebook were selected due to their strong impact on shaping the face of social media today.

- Facebook is the largest SNS with the highest number of active users worldwide: 2.41 billion monthly active users as of June 2019 (Zephoria, 2019). It is also the oldest of the three platforms: founded in 2004. It is safe to say that Facebook heavily shaped users' understanding of social media platforms. It also popularized *Likes**—points awarded by other users as a sign of their appreciation for a piece of content.

- Instagram is a photo-sharing platform that has gained high popularity, especially among young people. In 2012, the platform was bought by Facebook, Inc. In the last few years, the platform progressively gained more attention also due to its successful implementation of online marketing strategies. For example, influencer marketing became a hype over the last few year due to its potential to reach and appeal to a vast number of users on Instagram (De Veirman et al., 2017). In this business model, influencers—people who have accumulated a large

---

* The capitalized element names refer to the gamification element type (e.g. Points), the names written in italics are the specific element names introduced by the platforms (e.g. *Likes*) and the normal font names – items from the element category.

followership in Instagram—are often approached by businesses with offers to advertise their products on the platform.

- Snapchat is the platform that popularized highly disruptive new rules and elements to the social media format in recent years. It capitalizes on ephemeral content that disappears upon being viewed and it also offers a variety of creativity tools (augmented reality filters, video and picture editors etc.). The platform has also shifted away from classical gamification elements that are based on the accumulation of items (e.g. *Likes*) and has brought forward elements that thrive in its ephemeral environment: *Snap Streaks* and *Stories*. Whereas *Stories* disappear after 24 hours along with their views metrics, *Snap Streaks* allow users to get points for their pictures exchange even when the sent content is long gone from their chats. In other words, this relational score—the *Snap Streak*—quantifies the number of days in a row that content (even after its disappearance) has been exchanged.

5.3.2 Selected Gamification Elements

To the present date, a universal gamification elements classification has not yet been agreed upon in scientific literature since "it is unclear which affordances are unique to games as well as which psychological outcomes can be strictly considered to stem from games" (Hamari et al., 2014). As Sailer and colleagues point out, game elements classification attempts "should help to grasp how diverse game elements could possibly look like, but they should be understood as non-exhaustive lists" (Sailer, Hense, & Klevers, 2014). Whereas multifaceted accounts of possible gamification elements (Marczewski, 2015; Robinson & Bel- lotti, 2013) are available, we adopted a more concise framework for our analysis: Hamari, Koivisto and Sarsa's categorization of ten motivational gamification affordances (Hamari et al., 2014). This categorization was selected since it is based on elements that are most commonly applied in existing gamification applications rather than on theoretical approaches to what elements could be conceived of. The selected ten types of elements (Hamari et al., 2014) are also commonly present in the body of literature on gamification elements:

- **Points** (Hamari et al., 2014; Marczewski, 2015; Sailer et al., 2014; Werbach & Hunter, 2012)
- **Leaderboards** (Hamari et al., 2014; Marczewski, 2015; Sailer et al., 2014; Werbach & Hunter, 2012)

- **Badges and Achievements** (Hamari et al., 2014; Marczewski, 2015; Robinson & Bellotti, 2013; Sailer et al., 2014; Werbach & Hunter, 2012)

- **Levels** (Hamari et al., 2014; Kapp, 2012; Marczewski, 2015)

- **Story and Theme** (Hamari et al., 2014; Marczewski, 2015; Robinson & Bellotti, 2013)

- **Clear Goals** (Hamari et al., 2014; Kapp, 2012; Marczewski, 2015)

- **Feedback** (Hamari et al., 2014; Kapp, 2012; Marczewski, 2015)

- **Rewards** (Hamari et al., 2014; Kapp, 2012; Marczewski, 2015)

- **Progress** (Hamari et al., 2014; Marczewski, 2015; Sailer et al., 2014)

- **Challenge** (Hamari et al., 2014; Marczewski, 2015; Robinson & Bellotti, 2013)

This chapter does not offer an exhaustive account of all gamified mechanisms used by Facebook, Instagram and Snapchat but rather an analysis of their most prominent features. Table 5.1 consists of feature lists provided by official SNS resources (e.g. user support and blog entries), by systematic investigation of apps and by lists provided by the platforms or by external analysts. Some gamification features applied on the platforms fulfill multiple functions and will, therefore, be presented in several gamification categories that apply to them. Furthermore, we focus on the gamified affordances intended by designers rather than on those playfully invented and spread by the prosumers in practice*. Challenges that have not been introduced by the platforms' developers have been excluded from this analysis.

5.4 GAMIFICATION ELEMENTS IN SNAPCHAT, INSTAGRAM AND FACEBOOK

This section introduces an overview of gamification elements used in Snapchat, Instagram and Facebook, as well as the motivational mechanisms that underpin their intended influence. The work of Sailer, Hense, Mandl and Klevers (Sailer et al., 2014), as well as of Zhang (Zhang, 2008), will be used to analyze the motivational appeal of these gamification elements. For each type of gamified elements, we will first outline its applications in the three platforms and then analyze its motivational pull with regard to different theories. According to Sailer and colleagues, there are six main perspectives in motivation research (Sailer et al., 2014): *the trait perspective, the behaviourist learning perspective, the cognitive perspective,*

---

* One example is the ice bucket challenge that went viral on various social media platforms in 2014.

TABLE 5.1   Gamification Elements in Snapchat, Instagram and Facebook as of August 2019

Elements	Snapchat	Instagram	Facebook
Points	Views (Stories) Snap Streaks Snapchat Score	Views (Stories, Videos) Reactions (Stories) Posts Followers Following	Views (Videos, Stories) Reactions (Posts, Stories) Shares Friends Followers
Leaderboards	–	–	–
Badges and Achievements	100 Streaks Charms	–	Friendversaries Fundraising Top Fan Badge
Levels	–	–	–
Story or Theme	Stories Stickers Lenses Thematic Snaps My Year in Snaps	Stories Posts Memories	Stories Posts Memories Fundraising Emotions and Actions Friends' Birthdays
Clear Goals	"Snapchat is for friends. Find them in your contacts" "Enable Location to explore Snap Map" "Try with a friend" (lense)	Recommended or Recent Stories: "Watch all"	"Say hi to … with a wave" "Say hi to your new FB friend" "What's on your mind?" "Add a short bio/links" Birthdays: "help your friend celebrate"

(Continued)

TABLE 5.1 (CONTINUED)   Gamification Elements in Snapchat, Instagram and Facebook as of August 2019

Elements	Snapchat	Instagram	Facebook
Feedback	Views (Stories) Chat Notifications Hourglass	Views (Stories, Videos) Chat Notifications "You are all caught up"	Views (Stories, Videos) Chat Notifications Fundraising Bar Voting Bar
Rewards	Icons for: • 100 Streaks • Friend Emojis Videos for: • My Year in Snaps • Pull-To-Refresh Lenses for: • Birthdays	Icon for: • "You are all caught up"	Icon for: • Marriage Announcements Videos for: • Friendversary • Year in Review • Birthday Stories
Progress	–	"You are all caught up"	Fundraising Bar Profile Info (complete)
Challenge	Streaks Snap Games	–	"Did you know?" Instant Games

the perspective of self-determination (Ryan, Rigby & Przybylski, 2006), *the perspective of interest* (Krapp, 1993) *and the perspective of emotion* (Astleitner, 2000). Following Sailer and colleagues' example, we combine facets of those perspectives to characterize the variety of gamification elements used in social media. For each item, we will indicate the perspective with reference to which element is analyzed.

5.4.1 Points

Points are one of the most influential and widely applied gamification elements across multiple domains (Hamari et al., 2014; Sailer et al., 2014; Werbach & Hunter, 2012). All three platforms have some form of Points, i.e. numerical values that are used for quantifying activity. Facebook features few different manifestations: the number of *Reactions* (*like, love, haha, wow, sad, angry*), *Views* (of videos and stories*), *Shares, Friends* and *Followers*. Similarly, Instagram also applies many variations of Points: *Likes, Video Views, Story Views* and *Reactions*, number of *Followers, Following* and *Posts*. Most of these metrics are also visible to one's friends and followers and hence also enable social comparison. *Story Views* and *Reactions* are an exception since they can only be viewed privately by the user for the 24 hours in which the content is displayed to other users. In contrast to the two platforms, Snapchat offers a less diverse scope of Points manifestations: *Story Views, Snap Streaks* and *Snap Score*. As with Facebook and Instagram, Story Views in Snapchat are not publicly displayed. The platform supports a further gamified feature called *Snapchat Score*. This overall score accounts for the number of snaps the user has sent altogether, in addition to the points the user has gained by playing *Snap Games*. *Snapchat Score* is visible for all of the user's contacts thereby enabling social comparison among users. A further development has been the introduction of *Snap Streaks*: a numerical feature that has been highly influential among adolescents in shaping their socio-communicative culture and practices. In order to uphold a *Streak*, one needs to send and receive at least one picture or video per day with the same friend. Hence, this gamified element motivates users to actively use the platform on a daily basis and to generate content in order to maximize their Streak count. As already mentioned, the Streak score allows users to gather points despite the fact that the content of their snaps disappears. In other words,

---

* The Story feature originates from Snapchat and was subsequently adopted by Facebook and Instagram in 2016.

Snap Streaks provide a long-lasting quantification that thrives within the context of ephemeral communication.

In more general terms, "points function as immediate positive reinforcements" (Sailer et al., 2014) that are valuable as immediate feedback (*behavior learning perspective*), and hence as an enabler of flow (Csikszentmihalyi, 1997) (*perspective of interest*) experiences (Sailer et al., 2014). Points are also virtual rewards (*behaviorist learning perspective*) for actions (Sailer et al., 2014): for example, *Snap Streak* score rewards users for composing and viewing at least one snap daily. However, there is a difference between points visible only privately to the user and points that are also publicly accessible to one's network. Publicly visible points also serve social functions such as signifying social relatedness (Zhang, 2008) or enabling social comparison (Burrow & Rainone, 2017; Panger, 2014). Publicly available points of various types also enable the negotiation of social status and power relations (*trait perspective*) (Sailer et al., 2014) with individuals establishing leadership and followership (Zhang, 2008) relations. This is exemplified by the social practices unfolding around *Likes, Views, Followers* and *Streaks*. According to Burrow and Rainone "with billions of likes conferred daily, the common Facebook user may be justified in worrying less about whether anyone will like what they post and instead wonder just how many likes they will receive" (2017).

Points also have a social and psychological impact since they can foster higher self-esteem (Burrow & Rainone, 2017) and social relatedness (Zhang, 2008). For example, in the case of *Snap Streaks*, users develop their streak as a quantified friendship project based on shared daily effort. Paradoxically, points can trigger exactly the opposite processes, too: questioning self-worth and developing a dependence on the number of likes received (Burrow & Rainone, 2017). As previously mentioned, these quantified social appreciation tokens also enable competition, unfavorable social comparison and envy (Panger, 2014; Vogel, Rose, Roberts & Eckles, 2014; Weinstein, 2017) among users. Furthermore, in our empirical research among Viennese adolescents, we observed that quantification leads to users keeping a personal high score (Hristovaet al., in prep). For example, they are trying to match and excel their own like scores with each further posting. Commonly, users also develop strategies of how to maximize their score, for example, through adjusting the timing and frequency of their posts (Hristova et al., in prep.). All aforementioned experiences, be them positive or negative in valence, are powerful motivators that gamification, particularly in the field of social media, has been able to utilize.

5.4.2 Leaderboards

In contrast to other gamified online platforms,* Facebook, Instagram and Snapchat do not, to our knowledge, include Leaderboards. Until 2018, Snapchat used to feature a *Best Friends* list that propelled contacts with whom one communicated most often to a privileged section similar to the quick-dial list of mobile phones. Initially, this list was also visible to all users (SocialBuzz, 2016) and functioned as a leaderboard of social related-ness (*self-determination perspective*) (Ryan et al., 2006; Sailer et al., 2014). This motivated users with a strong affiliation motive (Sailer et al., 2014) since the *Best Friends* feature revealed who are the people with whom one communicates most frequently. Being on top of the leaderboard could also be connected to power motives (*trait perspective*) (Sailer et al., 2014) when the *Best Friend* title is viewed as a token of dominance over other competi-tors for the status. This applies especially in the case of love interests. The leaderboard of social relations, combined with the disappearance of chat messages and photos, has been reported to elicit jealousy among Snapchat users (Utz, Muscanell & Khalid, 2015; Social Buzz, 2016). In 2018, the plat-form removed this feature, however, the *Friend list* emojis are still avail-able but are no longer visible to one's entire network.

Despite the notable absence of Leaderboards as a gamification mecha-nism, prosumers often use the platforms to create leaderboards of a sort in their offline interaction. For example, in our empirical work with ado-lescents, we noticed that they often knew by heart who has the highest streak among them (Hristova et al., in prep.). This online achievement was perceived as important and also provided a ground for the negotia-tion of social status outside of the social media context. In Instagram, one could compare account or hashtag statistics and generate the list of the top Instagram accounts or hashtags. However, this is done externally by reviewers and is not an automatic feature of the app. Furthermore, the scores of top accounts are out of reach for the average users, who can pri-marily compare with peers from their own social network. To sum up, it occurs peculiar that the highly popular Leaderboards (Hamari et al., 2014; Marczewski, 2015; Sailer et al., 2014; Werbach & Hunter, 2012) have been largely absent from Facebook, Instagram and Snapchat. The reasons for this need to be further scrutinized in depth in future research.

---

* For example, StackOverflow and Dict.cc among others.

5.4.3 Badges and Achievements

Snapchat has been intensively implementing badges and achievements. Up until April 2019, the platform also had a *Trophies* feature including 52 achievements one could unlock using the app. In 2019, the feature has been removed and replaced by *Charms* (Snapchat, 2019). *Charms* enable less competition and comparison than *Trophies*. For instance, badges are automatically generated for astrological compatibility and for a shared average *Snap Score* of two users. *Charms* are also different from *Trophies* in one more significant way: whereas *Trophies* were visible to all user's contacts, *Charms* are only displayed between two contacts. Visibility can affect the motivational pull of the gamification element. For example, this badge can bring satisfaction with one's personal achievement even if seen only by the particular user. When displayed to others it can, in addition, work as a token of power and social status. Another achievement that has been displayed only to the pair of directly involved users is the 100, 200 and so on days streak milestone. However, these icons are only visible to each of the two users and they can then decide if they would like to share with others.

While Instagram does not have an explicit Achievement feature, its users generally highly regard and strive for reaching a high likes or followers score. An example are shout-for-shout campaigns where a user can invite their network for participation, for example, by the outreach: "help my friend reach 10K followers." In the last few years, Facebook has invested into signifying and celebrating achievements such as fundraising results and yearly Facebook friendship anniversaries (*Friendversaries*). In 2019, the platform also added a *Top Fan* badge that is awarded to users who have most often visited a certain Facebook fan page. The badge can also be displayed on one's own Facebook wall where all of their friends can view it.

The drive to achieve something, or to master a competence, resonates with the way Badges and Achievements are used in the three social media platforms discussed here. For example, important achievements such as reaching the 100 days streak are shown only to the two people holding the streak. They may decide to then share this achievement in their story, but it would not be automatically displayed to others. Similarly, Friendversaries on Facebook need to be approved by one of the friends before being posted to their wall, and Charms on Snapchat are only associated and displayed to the two people involved.

According to Sailer et al., Badges "fulfill the players' need for success and thereby address people with a strong power motive" especially since they also work as "virtual status symbols" (Sailer et al., 2014). Furthermore, the author argues that they also appeal to fulfill the need for achievement (*trait perspective*) (Sailer et al., 2014) that creates a feeling of competence (*self-determination perspective*) (Sailer et al., 2014; Ryan et al., 2006). In particular, one of the new Snapchat *Charms* calculates the average *Snapchat Score* of the pair of users. The score can be within the scope of five different tiers of achievement (from *newbie* to *hero*). This particular type of badge also facilitates group belonging and emphasizes membership (*trait perspective, self-determination theory*) (Sailer et al., 2014; Ryan et al., 2006).

5.4.4 Levels

Levels, in the strict sense, have not been adopted by Instagram and Facebook. Only Snapchat includes a few elements that fulfill functions somewhat similar to those of Levels. Passing the threshold of 100 days *Snap Streak* is signified as a transition of importance. This is not to say that the task difficulty is increased after achieving the 100 count: the streak maintenance procedure remains the same. However, our research participants report (Hristova et al., in prep.) feeling that their streak score is even more at stake when it grows beyond significant milestones such as 100 or 200 streaks. The same applied to the already inactive feature of *Trophies*, where the account would receive a different icon depending on their *Snap Score*. This principle is now partially outsourced to the above-mentioned average score Charm where users are assigned one of five levels of Snapchat mastery depending on their average *Snapchat Score*. Despite the tiered structure of this charm, there is no increase of task difficulty with the label upgrade. There is one more mechanism on Snapchat that resembles levels: the *Friend Emojis* that are being upgraded when two users snap with each other most frequently for (1) two weeks and then (2) two months or to signify that they have become each other's #1 best friend. Again, there is no clear increase of difficulty or leveling, however, users often apply strategic communication in order to improve their status with selected contacts (Hristova et al., in prep.).

The main motivations triggered by the outlined level-like elements in Snapchat can be subdivided in the following major categories: (1) achievement motive (*trait perspective*) (Sailer et al., 2014); (2) belonging (*trait perspective*) (Sailer et al., 2014); and (3) power motive (*trait perspective*) (Sailer et al., 2014) and leadership–followership (Zhang, 2008). The achievement motive applies to streaks and the average score Charm in particular where the "level" upgrade is triggered by a transition on a quantitative scale. The belonging and power motives are intertwined in gamification elements such as Streaks and Friends Emojis. The desire to receive a token that signifies one's relation may be provoked by the symbolic and sentimental value of the token or by the wish to display the relation to others, and hence, claim desired social status. For example, a person may desire to be their significant other's best friend on Snapchat because it would signify a positive emotional experience of closeness. However, the same wish may be dictated by the need to confirm the social relationship (and its intensity) and protect it against potential competitors (Utz et al., 2015).

5.4.5 Stories and Theme

Stories are a storytelling practice based on content disappearing after 24 hours and are an integral part of all three social media platforms. Wargo (2015) explores how Snapchat stories are used for the purpose of creative storytelling and sharing phenomenological experiences and emotions from one's embodied perspective. Apart from *Stories*, Snapchat allows users to save their pictures to *Memories*—the app gallery where snaps are stored that would otherwise disappear from users' conversation. The platform also offers thematic and sponsored *Lenses*. The users need to switch on their selfie camera and can then play with the selected augmented reality lens that adds virtual features (e.g. animal features or marketing signs) to their image in real time. The sponsored lenses are developed for the purpose of online marketing campaigns.* A further vehicle for narratives and themes is *Snapchat Stickers*. Users can manually search for stickers with resonating narrative or emotional value. However, a selection of stickers is also automatically recommended to the user based on parameters such as local time (e.g. time stamp or a moon/sun image), weekday and weather (e.g. clouds and rain images). Finally, the platform sends thematic snaps to its users for special occasions, for example, Mother's Day.

Facebook and Instagram primarily allow their users to share experiences through posts. Posts are their most fundamental broadcasting affordance and the main source of content for the two networks. However, Facebook attaches further story-sharing affordances to their posts, such as the *Emotions* and *Activity* labels. Users can label the feeling of their post, for example, *feeling wonderful* or can signify the activity that the post is related to *traveling, attending, eating, listening to* or supporting among others. Each activity and emotion has a particular emoji that is displayed

---

* An example is the success of the Taco Bell augmented reality lens in 2016.

along with the post's content. Other thematic and storytelling features in Facebook are *Friendversaries*, friends' birthdays and fundraising for a particular cause. Facebook and Instagram also have a *Memories* function that retrieves older photo content and periodically presents these reminiscences to users.

The goal of all these particular features is to encourage emotional sharing and experiencing (Zhang, 2008). While joyful stories may foster positive feelings (*perspective of emotion* [Astleitner, 2000]) they also may invoke negative emotions such as jealousy (Weinstein, 2017, 2018). They are also important from the *perspective of interest*: "gamification meets players' interests and sparks interest for the situational context" (Sailer et al., 2014). This is exemplified by Snapchat stickers or sponsored (often commercial) lenses that are supposed to entice users to devote their attention to certain themes and stories.

5.4.6 Clear Goals

In this subsection, we focus on explicit Clear Goals that the platforms provide to their users. Basic goals defined by the platforms, such as "message," "search" and "edit profile" are excluded from this analysis because they are interfaces for the most basic platform functions. Instagram generally abstains from setting many explicit goals for their users with one exception. In addition to the basic action affordances mentioned above, Instagram recommends recent stories to its users by displaying them at multiple occasions in the feed and blending in the button "watch all."

In contrast, Facebook is full of verbally formulated goals. The focus of these commands is to nudge users to communication or to content creation: birthday wishes—"help your friend celebrate their birthday"; saluting new friends—"say hi to your new Facebook friend"; posting content—"What's on your mind, …?" Whereas these goals are purely verbally formulated, actions such as waving at friends as a simple conversation starter are introduced both via an icon (a waving hand) and a corresponding verbal phrase: "Say hi to … with a wave." Similarly, Snapchat relies mostly on blends of verbal commands and symbols to set clear goals for its users. For instance, the message "enable location to explore Snap Map" is pictured on a world map and "try with a friend" is displayed next to filters and lenses (Snapchat, as of August 2019). However, Snapchat also uses purely verbally phrased calls for action as in the case of the message "Snapchat is for friends. Find them in your contacts." In design terms, involving the user with verbally phrased goals is a very common way to lend social characteristics to an online platform and to stimulate the user to act upon the digital product (Fogg, 2003). In other words, "whether asking questions, offering congratulations for completed tasks, or reminding the user to update software, dialog boxes can lead people to infer that the computing product is animate in some way" (Fogg, 2003). According to Sailer, these explicit formulations can be motivating as they set clear and achievable goals that motivate the users to complete them (Sailer et al., 2014). Furthermore, according to *perspective of interest*: "Players are likely to be motivated if gamification enhances the feeling of flow by providing a clear goal" (Sailer et al., 2014). Last but not least, when completed, the tasks may create the sense of competence and achievement (Zhang, 2008). To sum up, clear goals are important from the *cognitive perspective* and from the *perspective of interest* (Sailer et al., 2014).

5.4.7 Feedback

Feedback is a well-known psychological and interface design mechanism (Bogost, 2014), however, feedback is also deemed absolutely essential for providing gameful experiences (Hamari et al., 2014; Kapp, 2012; Marczewski, 2015). For instance, the immediacy of feedback is regarded as one of the keys to enabling flow for gamers or users (Sailer et al., 2014). In this subsection, we exclude platform-enabled feedback from users, for example, likes because users need to actively do something (click the like button) to generate them. Instead, we will focus on the feedback provided by the SNS themselves. Furthermore, we will not go into presenting Achievements and Rewards, although they can be seen as subsets of the more general category of Feedback.

The three platforms provide somewhat similar feedback, for instance, using chat notifications and the views (story or video). In the case of *Views*, all three platforms automatically give numerical feedback when content has been seen. No additional actions are required by the user apart from viewing the content. The view count of stories across all platforms is visible only to the user who posted the story. In contrast, the video views of Facebook and Instagram can be seen by all users who have access to the video. The second type of Feedback common among all platforms at hand are the chat notifications. Whereas Instagram simply informs that the chat message has been seen, Facebook (and Messenger) also displays the exact time at which the message was viewed. Snapchat's *Friends Screen* goes one step further as it utilizes more nuanced notifications to inform users whether their snap has been sent, opened or screenshoted in addition to informing about the type of message (audio/chat). Snapchat's screenshot notification has been steadily used by adolescents to protect their privacy. Our young informants mostly keep their peers accountable for screenshoting shared content (Hristova et al., in prep.). Overall, these notifications offer control to the users: to monitor the interaction of peers with their content. However, our informants disclose that these notifications can also trigger frustration, for example, when they reveal that the sent message or snap has been ignored (Hristova et al., in prep.).

Each platform also includes further Feedback elements. For instance, Facebook displays fundraising bars showing what amount of money has already been raised with respect to the preset goal. Instagram recently started notifying its users when they have viewed all the new posts from the last 48 hours. The message "you're all caught up" is displayed in the feed and aims to provide users with a sense of control and an overview of their activity on the platform. Snapchat has one further prominent feedback feature that is relevant for *Snap Streak* holders. An *Hourglass* is displayed if only four hours are left until the streak is lost. The function induces a sense of urgency and danger as it signals to users that their streak is going to perish if they and/ or their streak partner do not snap. Hourglass nudges users to continue using the platform in order to retain the reward of their gamified communication. The phenomenological experience of Instagram's "You're all caught up" and of Snapchat's Hourglass differs significantly. This indicates the variety of behavioral and emotional responses that can be prompted by feedback mechanisms. However, on a deeper level, both share common traits since they provide immediate, relevant feedback that motivates users and supports their behavioral learning process and habit formation (Sailer et al., 2014). Sailer also adds that feedback is crucial for users (*perspective of interest*) as it provides a sense of control and, hence, they "are likely to be motivated if gamification enhances the feeling of flow by providing a direct feedback" (Sailer et al., 2014).

5.4.8 Rewards

In this categorization of gamified elements, rewards and achievements go hand in hand: rewards signify particular achievements through digital tokens. For example, Snapchat features reward icons for *Friends List* emojis and *Charms*. The platform also awarded users a special icon when they reach 100 streaks and, hence, symbolically celebrates their success. Furthermore, Snapchat creates videos, for example, for the app's pull-to-refresh-feed action and for My Year in Snaps. Lastly, the platform offers a birthday lens that celebrates the user's personal occasion on the platform. To our knowledge, Instagram generates only one reward of this type: the icon presented together with the "you're all caught up" feedback. Facebook offers a wider range of reward types. The platform endows its users with icons, for example, for marriage announcements and animated videos for *Friendversaries* (including shared content, number of shared likes etc.), *Year in Review* and in 2019 has announced *Birthday Stories* that users can upload to celebrate their friend's birthday. In this case, the reward is the colorful frame that celebrates the personal occasion. Marcewski describes this game element as "fixed rewards schedule" since the rewards come on a regular yearly basis (Marczewski, 2015).

Fogg states that "one of the most powerful persuasive uses of language is to offer praise" (Fogg, 2003). According to his research, upon receiving praise, research participants "felt better about themselves, were in a better mood, felt more powerful and felt they had performed well, found the interaction engaging, were willing to work with the computer again, liked the computer more [and] thought the computer had performed better" (Fogg, 2003). Further research also confirms the efficiency of rewards in fostering user motivation based on the drive for achievement, competition, membership (*trait perspective*) and immediate feedback (*behavioral learning perspective*) (Sailer et al., 2014).

5.4.9 Progress

Few manifestations of the Progress feature are used by Facebook and Instagram. Facebook uses closed scales in their Fundraisers feature to display users' progress on the objective of gathering a predefined amount of money. The progress bar indicates how much of the set money amount has already been donated. The fundraisers and their friends can, hence, monitor the progress of the campaign. Furthermore, this visibility enables social comparison. A less obvious manifestation of the progress feature in Facebook is the appeal to users to complete and update their profile information. In a different implementation of this element, since 2018, Instagram informs its users that they have scrolled through all the new posts in their feed by displaying the "You're all caught up" message. Progress features satisfy the achievement motive that enables progress motivation (Sailer et al., 2014). Furthermore, such gamification elements aim to promote a sense of increased autonomy and control for the users (Zhang, 2008). As previously commented in the section "Feedback," SNS has opposite effects, such as loss of control, which can occur should the user fail to reach the progress report (in this case: the "You're all caught up" message). Finally, progress bars provide feedback and clear goals (*perspective of interest* and *cognitive perspective*) as well as foster mastery (*cognitive perspective*) (Sailer et al., 2014).

5.4.10 Challenge

All in all, Challenge is not that widely adopted by Instagram, but was featured to a different extent in Facebook and Snapchat. Both platforms offer challenges for individuals as well as more social challenges where at least two people can be involved (be it in a competitive or cooperative manner). Facebook incites a mild social challenge in their "Did you know?" section where users are invited to answer questions asked by their friends. Furthermore, worth mentioning are Facebook's instant games and Snapchat's Snap Games. Both Snapchat and Facebook include games on their platforms, Snapchat produced their own games, available next to the filters, while Facebook mostly hosted externally produced games such as Farmville. Both platforms currently offer various single-player and multiplayer games.

There are also differences in the way Facebook and Snapchat offer challenges to their users. Whereas Facebook features a simple "play" button to start interacting with the game, Snap Games proactively challenge users. For example, "Can you topple the tree?" is the challenge that aims at motivating Snapchat users to play a Beaver Snap Game. Furthermore, game participation in Snapchat also contributes to raising the user's *Snapchat Score*. In other words, the in-game challenges also translate into out-of-game benefits for the purposes of gamification. In a broader conceptualization of the term "Challenge," *Snap Streaks* can also be seen as an open challenge to reach a high streak number with a friend. In the past, Snapchat also featured the *Trophies* function that was entirely comprised of challenges. As already mentioned, this function was replaced by the less challenge-oriented *Charms* that aims to celebrate friendship (Snapchat, 2019).

Instagram generally abstains from platform-driven challenges. Nonetheless, users create their own challenges such as like-for-like campaigns or follower shout-outs "Let my friend ... get 10 000 followers." This is provoked by an achievement motive that thrives on success and progress-related motivation (Sailer et al., 2014). Lastly, when the challenge is accomplished, the enjoyable feeling of being competent is evoked (Sailer et al., 2014; Zhang, 2008).

5.5 DISCUSSION

Upon outlining and analyzing the main gamification affordances used by Snapchat, Instagram and Facebook as of August 2019, we move on to discussing the major findings of this analysis.

5.5.1 Gamification Elements Discussion

A general comparison between the three platforms reveals that Facebook and Snapchat both use a large variety of gamification elements. Based on the categorization of gamified elements introduced in this chapter, both Snapchat and Facebook feature eight out of ten types of gamification elements. In comparison with those two platforms, Instagram seems to apply a more limited number of gamification mechanisms covering six out of ten types of elements. Half of the gamification elements types (five out of ten) were used by all of the examined platforms: Story, Points, Feedback, Clear Goals and Rewards. The following points summarize the use and motivational mechanisms of gamification elements as discussed above.

- Facebook and Instagram use a larger variety of quantifying gamification elements such as **Points**. Instagram and Facebook mostly use Points that are publicly displayed with the exception of their story views. Snapchat, on the other hand, sets a new standard for the use of Points through their *Snap Streaks*. Streaks pioneered metrics that also work in the context of ephemeral communication. As mentioned above, this type of elements motivates by offering immediate feedback and reward for actions thereby enabling flow. They can also boon self-esteem as well as social comparison and the feeling of social relatedness.

- **Story**: All three platforms seem to share strong affinity to Story or Themes, such as stories and *Memories*, present in all of these platforms. Stories motivate by enabling emotional sharing and experience that is aimed at boosting the user's interest for the situational context beside the specific communicational goals.

- **Feedback**: All platforms feature views (of stories and/or videos) and a more or less detailed version of chat notifications. Immediate Feedback provides a sense of control and, hence, the feeling of flow.

- **Clear Goals**: Whereas Facebook and Snapchat heavily rely on verbally formulated or multimodal (verbal command and a sign) Clear Goals, Instagram barely uses them. Clear Goals are integrated into the platforms due to the sense of control, competence and achievement they evoke, which, allegedly, can also induce a feeling of flow.

- **Rewards** have been more heavily adopted by Snapchat and Facebook than by Instagram. Frequently, Rewards are videos and appealing graphic tokens visualizing and celebrating various achievements. User motivation is increased by pleasure as well as by the drive for achievement, competition and membership.

Approximately a third of the element types (three out of ten) were used by two of the platforms: Badges, Challenges and Progress. The **Badges** and **Challenges** types were both present only in Snapchat and Facebook. In the case of Badges, Snapchat and Facebook apply elements, which are displayed to the users in private and can be shared with others, if desired. The only exception is the *Snapchat Score* that is displayed in the user profile for their contacts to view. With regard to Challenges, both platforms offer individual and more social options for involvement. Badges and Challenges motivate by inciting alleged feeling of competence (upon achieving a goal) but also a sense of membership and power. **Progress** is used both by Instagram and Facebook to account for user activity on the platforms. Instagram applies it in order to inform users that they have viewed all recent posts. Facebook uses Progress elements for fundraising and profile completion statistics. Progress is yet another mechanism that motivates through inducing the sense of control and power.

A fifth of all element types (two out of ten) were not explicitly present in any of the three platforms. Surprisingly, the otherwise popular gamification elements **Levels** and **Leaderboards** have not been applied by the examined SNS. However, **Level**-like elements have been applied by Snapchat. The used elements resemble levels but do not include a progressive task difficulty increase. Their motivational pull is based on providing a sense of achievement, belonging and power. Features similar to **Leaderboards**, for example, Snapchat's *Best Friends,* have been removed from the apps, possibly due to their potential of inspiring negative social comparison and power relations.

As it became apparent from the detailed analysis section, prosumers' agency plays a significant role in understanding gamification. Some gamification elements may not be present as digital items, but their principles can still be recognized in the prosumers' practices revolving around the platform. This is exemplified by the case of leaderboards in the Gamification elements section of this chapter.

5.5.2 Snapchat, Instagram and Facebook Discussion

We will now briefly sum up the gamification tendencies of each platform. In the course of its existence, Facebook has integrated an increasing variety of gamification elements. After Snapchat successfully implemented *Stories*, Facebook and Instagram also adopted the feature in 2016. The main types of elements that the platform used are Clear Goals, Points, Story and Reward. Instagram follows Facebook's model in some regards, most notably in its application of Points and Feedback. It has also adopted memories from Facebook and the story features from Snapchat, focusing on visual storytelling. However, it also experiments with new types of features that are not yet used in other platforms, such as the "you're all caught up" feedback which notifies users that they have seen all new posts. Snapchat is a highly gamified platform that has introduced many gamification innovations: such as *Snap Score*, *Snap Streaks* and *Hourglass* nudge, *Charms* (previously *Trophies*) and *Snap Games*. It operates mainly with Rewards, Stories and Badges.

5.5.3 Is Social Media Turning Into a "Social Media Game"?

The abundance of gamification elements deployed in social media brings up a question: is social media turning into a game? The answer is less obvious than a simple "yes" or "no." First, we need to clarify that some gamification features are inherent to social media. Existing gamification applications commonly use elements such as social network, social status and social discovery (Marczewski, 2015) to gamify various tasks and services. These features are so essential for social media that they can barely be regarded as an extra layer "added" by gamification.

Social media sites are primarily online platforms "that allow people to communicate and share information" (Cambridge Dictionary, 2019). SNS offer platforms filled with interactional affordances and spaces for hosting user-generated content while trying to increase involvement and commitment (e.g. in terms of time spent). They are also best practice examples of user experience (UX) principles. SNS, similar to games, also need to integrate two opposing principles: being challenging and enabling. According to Koster, "UX design is about removing problems from the user. Game design is about giving problems to the user" (Koster, 2015). Whereas social media may add gamified challenges in order to involve its users more intensely, its primary function is to enable online social communication, or in Koster's terms, to "remove problems from the user."

In SNS, competitive elements are used but they do not define the architecture of the site in its entirety: everyone can use the platforms and those who would like to compete can do so. Hence, social media is less explicitly focused on challenges than games. The affordances for challenges on SNS are often optional and not a necessary prerequisite for the use of the platform. For example, comparing the score of features quantifying social appreciation (likes, reactions, followers) has been simply afforded by the platform and is not built as a formally regulated competition that is clearly defined by social media designers. Anyone can use Snapchat, but some users also decide to attempt keeping *Snap Streaks* for as long as possible. Both types of users enjoy the benefits of enabled online creative communication with their peers, but some also opt for the gameful challenge offered by the platform. The users who take up the challenge may also be able to profit from the social capital associated with performing well with the goal of upholding streaks. When examined in the context of social media, Koster's statement suggests a more hybrid nature of SNS (Koster, 2015). Gamification elements are both an intrinsic part of SNS and add an extra layer to them. While competition may be a core mechanic in some games, SNS carry a different culture and competitive elements are possible but not a prerequisite for participation. Hence, social media can not be categorized as a full-fledged game but rather as a widely gamified system.

5.6 ETHICS

Although multiple gamified mechanisms have been continuously applied by SNS, their ethical implications for the users remain open for discussion. We will now briefly examine some of the main ethical concerns of gamification within the context of social media.

As laid out in the previous sections, gamification can be criticized as an *exploitationware* (Bogost, 2013)—a set of tools that that are designed with the intention to harness the engagement power of games for the purposes of attention economy (Davenport & Beck, 2001) and data production. To paraphrase Whitson (Whitson, 2014), the goal of gamification is to make social media corporate dystopias (intransparent business models and privacy violations) appear as if they were *heterotopias*—rich spaces that "mirror, reflect, represent, designate, and speak about other sites, while at the same time suspending, neutralizing, inverting, contesting, and contradicting these self-same sites" (Foucault, 1986; Whitson, 2014). We now focus further on specific controversies surrounding gamification in social media: social comparison, intransparent psychological models, surveillance and the moral obligations of fun.

5.6.1 Social Comparison

Social comparison and its use for power negotiation is selected due to its relevance for multiple gamification elements, for example, Points, Leaderboards, Badges and Achievements, Progress and Rewards. As visible from our social media analysis, SNS provide multiple affordances for the social comparison game between users (Vogel et al., 2014; Panger, 2014). For example, *Likes* are not only a token of social appreciation and reciprocity, they are also often used in a gamified manner when users try to accumulate more likes on their next post than the previous one or to receive more likes than their peers. In other words, *Likes* are used in a multifaceted manner for the goal of competition against oneself or against others—which is one of the main motivational affordances according to Zhang (Zhang, 2008).

Recently, some social network sites tried to adapt their use of *Likes* due to their impact as vehicles for social comparison. Competition per se must not be seen as negative but has implications that may not be desirable, for example, focusing primarily on the number of likes than on the content of the post. Instagram stated this as the main reason to commence tests in 2019, in which they removed the like score on their platform in Canada. The tests were an attempt to reduce the sense of competition among users (Forbes, 2019). However, Hamari and Koivisto warn that removing a gamified feature that users are involved with may lead to frustration (Hamari et al., 2014). In other words, removing features, such as *Likes*, that enable social comparison may frustrate users whose social media use heavily relies on accumulating, displaying or comparing the number of likes. It is hence an open question whether removing features that afford social comparison would solve related problematic aspects of SNS.

5.6.2 Intransparent Psychological Models

The psychological models behind persuasive design are not always transparent for the users. The aforementioned gamification elements exploit some of the users' core motivation mechanisms such as their need for competence, achievement and power. Gamified mechanisms also aim at inducing positive emotions (Astleitner, 2000) and a sense of social relatedness and flow (Sailer et al., 2014). Such mechanisms are not explained to users, although prosumers may have an intuitive understanding of them. The persuasive power of elements that are based on psychological research and are designed to alter behavior (Fogg, 2003) incites spending more time with apps and producing more data behind the "digital curtain" (Zuboff, 2019), which data can then be commercially used. Effectively, users are facing teams of scientists, managers and designers that have access to big data gathered in server farms. Navigating online environments becomes a matter of protecting one's own attention from the digital tools that are designed to captivate and to "hook" (Eyal, 2014). Still, some of our informants describe feeling like social media apps are neutral but it is them, the users, who have a weak will, cannot focus and, hence, spend too much time on SNS (Hristova et al., in prep.). We argue that more transparency regarding the use of psychological models behind gamified social media apps is needed (Goebl et al., 2019; Goebl et al., 2018; Jovicic et al., 2019). Instagram provides an example of such initiatives with its alleged attempt to protect users from spending too much time on SNS through the "You're all caught up" feedback. This feedback was speculated by some analysts to be a response to the *Time Well Spent* initiative (TechCrunch, 2016). Instagram is also said to be currently developing further tools that could help users protect themselves from excessive use of the platform. However, it is important to evaluate the efficiency of applied measures in order to prevent the use of features which just seemingly enhance ethical design, but instead serve as a distraction from other attention economy practices applied by social media platforms.

5.6.3 Surveillance

What happens with data generated during gamified activities? This question has become a major concern with regard to the gamification trend. Whitson points out that gamification entices users to involve in a "willing self-surveillance" (Whitson, 2014), producing online content and data (Lampe, 2014). She also warns against the so called "functional creep": a term describing "how data collected for one purpose is then applied to new ones" (Whitson, 2014). In her words, free play provides fewer reasons for users to resist gamification. Meanwhile, their behavior is closely surveilled (Zuboff, 2019) and this surveillance is framed as fun (Albrechtslund & Dubbeld, 2005). According to Whitson's approach, gamification is a highly instrumental tool of governance. Its proponents try to justify it by arguing that "surveillance is not about discipline and control, but is geared toward providing meaningful feedback and rewards" (Whitson, 2014). However, it is important to keep in mind that with advancing data harvesting, storage and mining capacities, it progressively becomes easier for tech and social media corporations to uphold global surveillance campaigns.

5.6.4 Morally Obliged to Have Fun?

Finally, it is important to point out that there is an ongoing interplay between affordances shaped by designers and user preferences. On the one hand, designers are contracted by SNS companies to create more appealing and involving digital products that invite users to spend more time on their online platforms. On the other hand, users are motivated by various gratifications to engage with a platform and they hence desire an adequate and satisfying product. Selinger and colleagues formulate this dilemma in the following way: "If fun is so good for us, are we then obliged to let/make people have fun?" (Selinger et al., 2015). In our opinion, steps towards establishing and applying standards for ethical design worldwide should be undertaken. This also includes more transparency concerning issues such as priming through hidden persuasion techniques and their underlying psychological models (Goebl et al., 2018; Goebl et al., 2019; Hristova et al, in prep; Jovicic et al., 2019).

5.7 OUTLOOK

The abundance of gamification elements deployed in social media turns it into a highly influential, captivating medium somewhere in between a game and an open platform for social interaction. A wide variety of motivational mechanisms are addressed through gamified elements, nudging the user to experience a sense of achievement, competence and social relatedness. Appreciation and sharing, but also social comparison enabled by aptly designed user interfaces contribute to flow and active engagement. However, the issues of surveillance and lack of transparency contextualize the utopian visions of gamification within a neoliberal attention economy harnessing user involvement for profit. Through social media, gamification sets foot in the life of billions of people around the world. Therefore, its issues need to be addressed not only in scientific research but also in the business world and popular discourse. Since play needs a safe space to unfold, ethical guidelines for the use of gamification in social media should be developed. This would enable prosumers to communicate and to grow through gameful involvement.

REFERENCES

Albrechtslund, A., & Dubbeld, L. (2005). The plays and arts of surveillance: Studying surveillance as entertainment. *Surveillance and Society*, 3(2/3). 216–221.

Astleitner, H. (2000). Designing emotionally sound instruction: The feasp-approach. *Instructional Science*, 28(3), 169–198.

Bogost, I. (2013). Exploitationware. In J. M. C. Richard & R. Shultz Colby (Eds.), *Rhetoric/Composition/Play Through Video Games*, (pp. 139–147). Springer.

Bogost, I. (2014). Why gamification is bullshit. In S. Waltz & S. Deterding (Eds.), *The Gameful World*, (pp. 65–79). Cambridge, MA: MIT Press.

Burrow, A. L., & Rainone, N. (2017). How many likes did i get?: Purpose moderates links between positive social media feedback and self-esteem. *Journal of Experimental Social Psychology*, 69, 232–236.

Cambridge Dictionary. (2019). *Social Media*. Retrieved from https://dictionary.cambridge.org/de/worterbuch/englisch/social-media [accessed 23 August, 2019].

Csikszentmihalyi, M. (1997). *Finding Flow. The Psychology of Engagement with Everyday Life*. New York, NY: Basic Books.

Davenport, T. H., & Beck, J. C. (2001). *The Attention Economy: Understanding the New Currency of Business*. Brighton, MA: Harvard Business Press.

Davis, K., & Singh, S. (2015). Digital badges in afterschool learning: Documenting the perspectives and experiences of students and educators. *Computers and Education*, 88, 72–83.

de Freitas, S., Gibson, D., Alvarez, V., Irving, L., Star, K., Charleer, S., & Verbert, K. (2017). *How to Use Gamified Dashboards and Learning Analytics for Providing Immediate Student Feedback and Performance Tracking in Higher Education*. Proceedings of the 26th International Conference on World Wide Web Companion, 429–434.

De Veirman, M., Cauberghe, V., & Hudders, L. (2017). Marketing through instagram influencers: The impact of number of followers and product divergence on brand attitude. *International Journal of Advertising*, 36(5), 798–828.

Deterding, S., Dixon, D., Khaled, R., & Nacke, L. (2011). *From Game Design Elements to Gamefulness: Defining Gamification*. Proceedings of the 15th International Academic Mindtrek Conference: Envisioning Future Media Environments, 9–15.

Deterding, S., Sicart, M., Nacke, L., O'Hara, K., & Dixon, D. (2011). *Gamification: Using Game-Design Elements in Non-Gaming Contexts*. CHI'11 Extended Abstracts on Human Factors in Computing Systems, 2425–2428.

Dumit, J. (2017). Game design as STS research. *Engaging Science, Technology, and Society*, 3, 603–612.

Eyal, N. (2014). *Hooked: How to Build Habit-Forming Products*. Penguin UK.

Fogg, B. J. (2003). *Persuasive Technology: Using Computers to Change What We Think and Do*. San Francisco, CA: Morgan Kaufmann.

Forbes. (2019). *Instagram May Be Getting Rid of 'Likes' on Platform.* Retrieved from https://www.forbes.com/sites/nicolemartin1/2019/04/30/instagram-may-be-getting-rid-of-likes-on-platform/ [accessed 15 May, 2019].

Foucault, M. (1986). Other spaces+ the principles of heterotopia. *Lotus International*, 48, 9–17.

Froehlich, J. (2014). Gamifying green: Gamification and environmental sustainability. In S. Waltz & S. Deterding (Eds.), *The Gameful World*, (pp. 563–596). Cambridge, MA: MIT Press.

Gekker, A. (2016). Casual power: Understanding user interfaces through quantification. *Digital Culture and Society*, 2(1), 107–122.

Goebl, B., Hristova, D., Jovicic, S., Slunecko, T., Chevron, M.-F., & Hlavacs, H. (2018). *Towards a More Reflective Social Media Use Through Serious Games and Co-design.* Joint International Conference on Serious Games, 229–234.

Goebl, B., Hristova, D., Jovicic, S., SluneckoT., Chevron, M.-F., & Hlavacs, H. (2019). *Fostering Social Media Literacy Through a Participatory Mixed-Methods Approach: Discussion of Workshop Findings.* 2019 IEEE 7th International Conference on Serious Games and Applications for Health.

Gibson, J. J. (1966). *The Senses Considered as Perceptual Systems.* Houghton Mifflin.

Hamari, J., & Koivisto, J. (2013). *Social Motivations to Use Gamification: An Empirical Study of Gamifying Exercise.* Proceedings of the 21st European Conference on Information Systems, 105.

Hamari, J., & Koivisto, J. (2015). Why do people use gamification services? *International Journal of Information Management*, 35, 419–431.

Hamari, J., Koivisto, J., & Sarsa, H. (2014). Does gamification work? A literature review of empirical studies on gamification. *Hicss*, 14, 3025–3034.

Hristova, D., Dumit, J., Lieberoth, A., & Slunecko, T. (2020). Snapchat streaks: How adolescents metagame gamification in social media. 4th International GamiFIN Conference, GamiFIN 2020.

Hristova, D., Jovicic, S., Goebl, B, & Slunecko, T. (in prep.). Changing the social media game: The practices of Viennese adolescents surrounding snapchat gamification.

Jovicic, S., Goebl, B., & Hristova, D. (2019). Verspielte grenzen des digitalen: Relationalität und Verhandlung gamifizierter Räume in Wiener Jugendvereinen. *Mitteilungen der Anthropologischen Gesellschaft in Wien*, 149, 177–194.

Kapp, K. M. (2012). *The Gamification of Learning and Instruction.* San Francisco, CA: Wiley.

Koster, Raph. (2015). *Game Design vs UX Design.* Retrieved from https://raphkoster.com/2015/06/29/game-design-ux-design/ [accessed 15 May, 2019].

Krapp, A. (1993). Die Psychologie der Lernmotivation. Perspektiven der Forschung und Probleme ihrer pädagogischen Rezeption. *Zeitschrift für Pädagogik*, 39(2), 187–206.

Lampe, C. (2014). Gamification and social media. In S. Waltz & S. Deterding (Eds.), *The Gameful World*, (pp. 463–480). Cambridge, MA: MIT Press.

Lampe, C., Ellison, N., & Steinfield, C. (2006). *A Face(book) in the Crowd: Social Searching vs. Social Browsing.* Proceedings of the ACM Special Interest Group on Computer-Supported Cooperative Work, 167–170.

Marczewski, A. (2015). *Even Ninja Monkeys Like to Play: Gamification, Game Thinking & Motivational Design*. London: Blurb Inc.

Mihelj, M., Novak, D., Milavec, M., Ziherl, J., Olensek, A., & Munih, M. (2012). Virtual rehabilitation environment using principles of intrinsic motivation and game design. *Presence: Teleoperators and Virtual Environments*, 21(1), 1–15.

Oravec, J. A. (2015). Gamification and multigamification in the workplace: Expanding the ludic dimensions of work and challenging the work/play dichotomy. *Cyberpsychology: Journal of Psychosocial Research on Cyberspace*, 9(3). 1–13.

Panger, G. (2014). *Social Comparison in Social Media: A Look at Facebook and Twitter*. CHI'14 Extended Abstracts on Human Factors in Computing Systems, 2095–2100.

Prensky, M. (2001). Digital natives, digital immigrants part 1. *On the Horizon*, 9(5), 1–6.

Robinson, D., & Bellotti, V. (2013). *A Preliminary Taxonomy of Gamification Elements for Varying Anticipated Commitment*. Proceedings ACM CHI 2013 Workshop on Designing Gamification: Creating Gameful and Playful Experiences.

Ryan, R. M., Rigby, C. S., & Przybylski, A. (2006). The motivational pull of video games: A self-determination theory approach. *Motivation and Emotion*, 30(4), 344–360.

Sailer, M., Hense, J. M., & Klevers, M. (2014). Psychological perspectives on motivation through gamification. *Interaction Design and Architecture Journal*, 19, 28–37.

Schuell, N. D. (2014). *Addiction by Design: Machine Gambling in Las Vegas*. Princeton, NJ: Princeton University Press.

Selinger, E., Sadowski, J., & Seager, T. (2015). Gamification and morality. In *The Gameful World: Approaches, Issues, Applications*, 371–392.

Snapchat. (2019). *Snapchat Charms*. Retrieved from https://support.snapchat.com/en-US/a/trophies [accessed 22 May, 2019].

Social Buzz. (2016). *How to Remove Snapchat Best Friends*. Retrieved from https://youtube.com/watch?v=Pw-cJG-znwU [accessed 23 August, 2019].

Techcrunch. (2016). *First Look at Instagram's Self-Policing Time Well Spent Tool*. Retrieved from https://techcrunch.com/2018/06/16/time-on-instagram/?guccounter=1gucer eferrerus = aHR0cHM 6Ly93d3cuZ29vZ2xlLmNvbS88 gucer eferrercs = NEf Klv0ZEfohseF dsQAGYg [accessed 23 August, 2019].

Toffler, A., & Alvin, T. (1980). *The Third Wave* (Vol. 484). New York, NY: Bantam Books.

Utz, S., Muscanell, N., & Khalid, C. (2015). Snapchat elicits more jealousy than facebook: A comparison of snapchat and facebook use. *Cyberpsychology, Behavior, and Social Networking*, 18(3), 141–146.

Vogel, E. A., Rose, J. P., Roberts, L. R., & Eckles, K. (2014). Social comparison, social media, and self-esteem. *Psychology of Popular Media Culture*, 3(4), 206–222.

Walz, S. P., & Deterding, S. (2015). An introduction to the gameful world. In *The Gameful World: Approaches, Issues, Applications*, 1–13.

Wargo, J. M. (2015). Spatial stories with nomadic narrators: Affect, snapchat and feeling embo- diment in youth mobile composing. *Journal of Language and Literacy Education*, 11(1), 47–64.

Weinstein, E. (2017). *Influences of Social Media use on Adolescent psychosocial Well-Being:'omg'or 'nbd'?* (Doctoral dissertation). Harvard Graduate School of Education.

Weinstein, E. (2018). The social media see-saw: Positive and negative influences on adolescents' affective well-being. *New Media and Society*, 20(10), 3597–3623.

Werbach, K., & Hunter, D. (2012). *For the Win: How Game Thinking Can Revolutionize Your Business*. Wharton Digital Press.

Whitson, J. R. (2014). Foucault's Fitbit: Governance and gamification. In *The Gameful World—Approaches, Issues, Applications*.

Zephoria. (2019). *Social Media*. Retrieved from https://zephoria.com/top-15-valuable-facebook-statistics/ [accessed 23 August, 2019].

Zhang, P. (2008). Motivational affordances: Reasons for ICT design and use. *Communications of the ACM*, 51(11), 145–147.

Zimmermann, E. (2014). *Position Statement: Manifesto for a Ludic Century*. In *The Gameful World: Approaches, Issues, Applications*. Cambridge, MA: MIT Press.

Zuboff, S. (2019). *The Age of Surveillance Capitalism: The Fight for a Human Future at the New Frontier of Power*. London, UK: Profile Books.

CHAPTER 6

Games for Health

Andrés Adolfo Navarro-Newball

CONTENTS

6.1	Introduction	95
6.2	Previous Work	98
	6.2.1 Health Personnel Training	98
	6.2.2 Patient Training	100
	6.2.3 Therapy	103
	6.2.4 Health Policies	104
6.3	Designing Games for Health	105
	6.3.1 Basic Principles from the Entertainment Industry	105
	6.3.2 Towards the Automation of Games for Health Development	107
6.4	Beyond Human Health	108
6.5	Other Uses of Game Technologies in Health	108
6.6	Discussion	110
6.7	Conclusion	111
References		111

6.1 INTRODUCTION

Computer games use technology and favour learning, discovery and creativity [1]. The potential of computer games in relevant tasks has been widely demonstrated [2]. Indeed, serious computer games rely on entertainment to allow advancing training, education, health, public policies, strategy, mental calculation and decision-making, among others [1, 3]. In health, either computer games or computer games' technologies have been used for several years to support health-related tasks [4]. One example is *LapSim* (Figure 6.1):

> In 1995 in Gothenburg, Sweden, Dr. Anders Hyltander, a senior GI surgeon at Sahlgrenska University Hospital, believed that novice surgeons could be trained in critical skills and procedures long before entering the operating room. He theorised that real-time simulators could be developed to bridge the gap between classroom pedagogy and patient. Together with three young and skilled software engineers, Dr. Hyltander tested that hypothesis to great success. [5]

Nowadays, computer games and computer games technology's applications are broad. Figure 6.2 [6] shows the most common applications:

- **Health personnel training** [7]: This is related to surgery training for surgical planning, new surgeons' training, nurses training, etc. (Figure 6.2).

- **Patient training** [8]: This is related to making patients understand medical procedures or to build up healthy habits.

- **Therapy** [9]: This is related to motivating patients with temporary or chronic pathologies or diagnostics to re-gain or gain some skills.

- **Health policies understanding** [10]: This is related to strategies or experiments to promote health policies among the population.

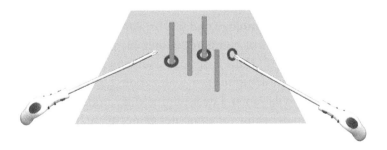

FIGURE 6.1   Basic medical task training adapted from *LapSim* [6]. This minigame requires the trainee to insert rings in the sticks using medical tools. The game is aimed at acquiring the dexterity skills required for laparoscopic surgery.

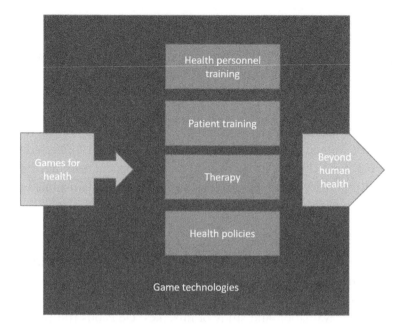

FIGURE 6.2 Summary of games for health technology. The figure shows the four main categories. In addition, it shows that games for health can go beyond human health and that the fact a solution uses games technologies does not mean that the final application is a game.

Computer games technologies used in health are also diverse and include, among others:

- **Sensors [11, 12]:** Sensors are used to gather and measure patient or trainee data.

- **Virtual reality [13]:** VR is used to simulate health environments as realistically as possible.

- **Mobile devices [14]:** Mobile devices are used to interconnect and favour mobility in health games and health systems in general.

However, the use of game technologies does not necessarily mean that the health application will be a game, as discussed later. Despite this, games seem to be a tool to enhance learning, practice and make it more enjoyable. Minigames seem to be a good way to implement games for health as they allow focusing on concrete tasks [15, 16] (Figure 6.1). We present an overview of how games can be used to favour health. Section 6.2 discusses previous works related to games for health and explain examples of each of the categories shown in Figure 6.2. Section 6.3 describes principles and methods for developing games for health. Section 6.4 discuses games for health applications beyond human beings. Section 6.5 explains the use of game technology for health in non-game environments. Section 6.6 presents a discussion and Section 6.7 is the conclusion.

6.2 PREVIOUS WORK

We present and discuss a representative example of games for health. The most common application of games for health are [17] referred to in Figure 6.2 and include health personnel training, patient training, therapy and health policies understanding. Next, we briefly explain some examples for each of these categories.

6.2.1 Health Personnel Training

Diverse surgical scenarios can be reproduced using virtual reality. They offer the advantage of repeatability of the training sessions and objective measurement of the developed skills without risk for the patient. These allow for the evaluation and study of mistakes. De Paolis [18] presents a serious game for training on suturing in laparoscopic surgery. He proposes a set of parameters to assess the level of skills developed by the trainees and focuses on the physical modelling of the virtual environment. Assessment is done by means of a thread and the two clamps controlled by two haptic interfaces. The goal of the system is to develop in the trainee important skills required in laparoscopy surgery, such as:

- Good eye-hand coordination
- The ability to manipulate the surgical instruments
- Techniques for performing the suture node

The game was developed under the following requirements:

- The behaviour and appearance of the human tissue and suture thread should be as realistic as possible within the simulation.
- The number of fiducial points on the tissue, test duration time, number of elements of the thread and the size of the tissue must be configurable.
- The trainee must receive feedback through a haptic device that simulates the force of the virtual surgical forceps.

- The skill of the trainee during the execution of the task must be measured.

Numerical indicators to measure the trainees' skill include:

- Time elapsed between the completion of the node and the first contact of the needle with the tissue (duration).
- Maximum distance between the real point of entry of the needle into the tissue and the ideal point indicated by a marker (accuracy).
- Maximum force used during the simulation in order to pierce the tissue by means of the needle (force peak).
- The sum of the forces applied to the tissue over the threshold of breakage of the tissue (tissue damage).
- Difference between the tangent and the normal to the surface at the point of the needle entry (angle of entry)
- Total distance travelled from the needle in order to complete the task (distance).

The overall score is the average of all previous specified parameters, except from distance. Figure 6.3 schematises the system (for more details see Figure 4, p. 484 in De Paolis [18]).

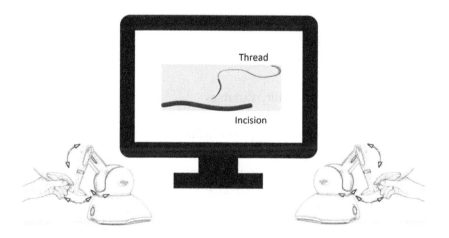

FIGURE 6.3 Serious suture game using two haptic devices. The incision and thread are shown in the interface.

Ribeiro et al. [19] describe a game to train the general public personnel in basic life support (BLS). BLS is used before patients can be given full medical care in victims of life-threatening illnesses or injuries and usually occurs in pre-hospital settings. This game was developed in collaboration with health care professionals, to train and evaluate the public in BLS (Figure 6.4). Within the game, the player chooses either to play in training mode or in evaluation mode. In training mode, the player can train the different game cases. If the player chooses the wrong procedure, a warning appears. In disastrous or emergency events, a layperson may become the first health personnel at hand, thus, some knowledge is of benefit. The training could be extended to medical personnel specialised in disaster response and nurses.

Another example of this kind of game is described in the previous section (Figure 6.2). Overall, the idea of this sort of game is to simulate real environments where medical procedures or protocols may develop as realistically as possible. These may require accurate models, tasks and triages.

6.2.2 Patient Training

Users participate and engage in an activity if they are motivated. Motivation can be achieved through video games as they offer fun experiences. Ijaz et al. [20] propose an exergame platform used to investigate motivation and physical activity and to favour activities related to wellbeing. They study player's experiences related to:

- Enjoyment
- Player's motivation
- Perceived experiences
- Physiological and vitality variables

In *Pokémon Ride*, the player explores Sydney in a DeskCycle and throws Poké balls to appearing Pokémons. The game displays information related to real-time performance and physiological information. In *Balloon Shooter*, the player rides on a DeskCycle near Sydney Hyde Park and shoots balloons. The game displays information on heart rate, time spent and calories. Figure 6.5 shows the idea. For images of *Pokémon Ride* and *Balloon Shooter* refer to Ijaz et al. [20, Figures 2 and 3, p. 3].

Herrera, Navarro and Marín [21] explain how a simulated cavity navigation environment can be used to support pre- and post-procedural

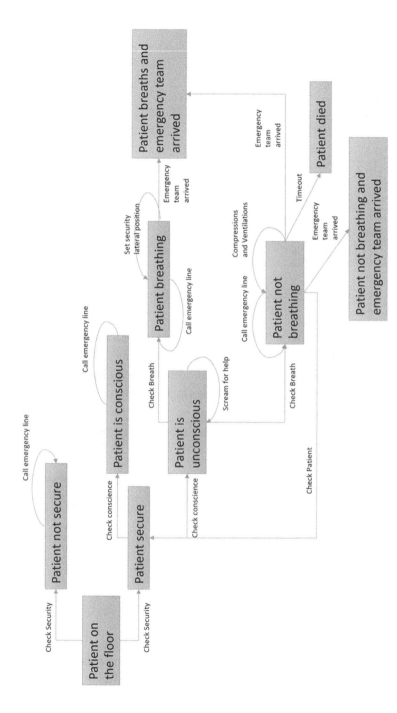

FIGURE 6.4 State machine in a VR game for BLS training. (Adapted from Ribeiro, C., Tiago, J., Monteiro, M. & Pereira, J. (2014). *SeGTE: A Serious Game to Train and Evaluate Basic Life Support.* 2014 International Conference on Computer Graphics Theory and Applications (GRAPP), Lisbon, Portugal, pp. 1–7. Images from the virtual environment can be seen in Ribeiro et al. [19], Figure 2.)

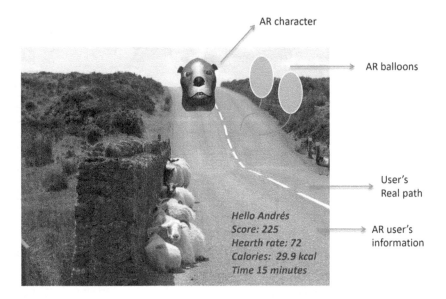

FIGURE 6.5 Games favouring wellbeing in players. AR content is superimposed on the path to motivate exercise.

education of patients by interactively showing them the pathology and the medical procedure that is going to take place. The doctor must follow the marked path while explaining the procedure to the patient. Indeed, most patients stated that they would feel confident after an explanation with the simulation environment (Figure 6.6).

Overall, the idea of these sort of games is to motivate healthy practices among people and to make them understand medical procedures better.

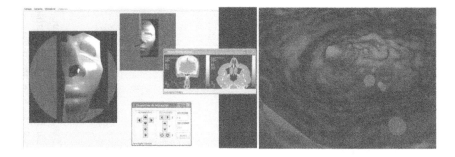

FIGURE 6.6 Interactive navigation system. Left: otolaryngology procedure. Right: inside a 3D reconstructed stomach. The dark grey spheres are mistakes in the paths. The medium grey spheres mark the suggested expert path. The light grey spheres are successful path coincidences by the user. Both systems were also used to explain the procedure to a group of patients.

6.2.3 Therapy

Therapy activities may not be easily accessible due to cost and demand. Additionally, therapy sessions may be laborious and non-motivating. Navarro-Newball et al. [22] propose a video game for therapy related to speech mechanisation in children with auditory deficiency using cochlear implants. The application workflow is as follows. It starts with an initial task list given to the patient's parents by the therapist. The task list contains a file that is uploaded by the video game and must be practiced by the child using a microphone. Then, the result is stored and received by the therapist. The process must be repeated until the patient achieves correct pronunciation. To complement the therapy activities, the game proposes a series of minigames displaying various pronunciation challenges. Minigames are implemented as challenges. A challenge is completed once a minigame is successfully repeated at least eight out of ten times. One example challenge consists of filling buckets with food for feeding a bear. If the corresponding phoneme is pronounced correctly, the corresponding bucket will be filled with food (Figure 6.7).

Henriksen et al. [23] explain a game aimed at recovering patients with upper limb amputations affected by phantom limb pain (PLP). The system was implemented using motion capture sensors and haptic feedback.

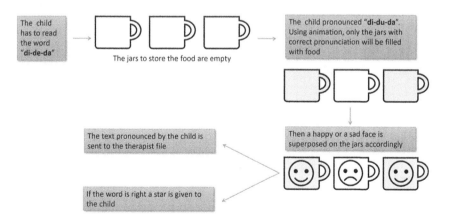

FIGURE 6.7 The system recognises incorrect pronunciation after listening to the child and gives feedback or comments visually upon it. The result is saved and handed to the therapist. (Adapted from Navarro-Newball, A. A., Loaiza, D., Oviedo, C., Castillo, A., Portilla, A., Linares, D., & Alvarez, G. (2014). Talking to Teo: Video game supported speech therapy. *Entertainment Computing*, 5(4), 401–412. doi: 10.1016/j.entcom.2014.10.005.)

It includes a bending game to grab, move, bend and release; a location discrimination game (Figure 6.8); and a frequency discrimination game where users are able to distinguish haptic frequencies. There is evidence that with these games, patients gain control of the amputated limbs.

Overall, the idea of these sort of games is to aid people with difficulties performing a physical or cognitive task gain some control and overcome their limitations. It is common that these sorts of games rely on technologies such as sensors, pattern recognition and haptics.

6.2.4 Health Policies

Public health policies should be efficiently communicated to assure democratic access to health and the quality of life of the population. Games can show rich combinations of text, audio, graphics and interaction, and may allow great flexibility for presenting health content. They can stimulate the user to act instead of passively receiving information. Indeed, gaming may be used to create many kinds of social connections. Games can be used to empower the players [17]. For example, Guana et al. [24] present a game

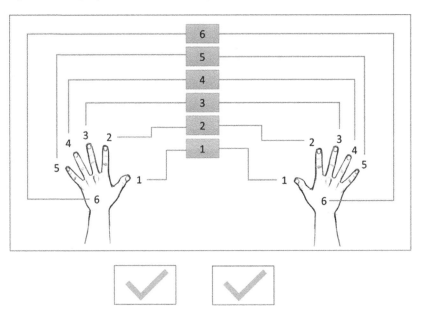

FIGURE 6.8 Location discrimination game [23]. Locations are placed symmetrically and indicated by images of hands. Participants receive tactile feedback from one of six electrodes placed on a stump. The participant has to find the electrode where the stimulation was delivered. (Redrawn by Andrés Adolfo Navarro-Newball. The original image can be found at Henriksen et al. [23], Figure 3.)

that can support education on reproductive health for governments and health organisations. UnderControl [24] is focused on teens and young adults and educates players about contraception and sexually transmitted illnesses (STIs). In this game, the player has to place a variety of contraceptives with diverse defensive capabilities that impede sperm to reach a female egg. Enemies are new STIs and the player can use different contraceptive methods depending on the level (Figure 6.9).

Overall, the idea in these types of games is to communicate health policies and education to society. The games can be focused on the portion of the population to whom the policy or campaign is oriented. It is common that these kinds of games use technologies such as highly interconnected WEB or mobile applications.

6.3 DESIGNING GAMES FOR HEALTH

In this section, we discuss some universal game design principles that can be applied for games for health design; then, we present a proposal for automatic games for health development.

6.3.1 Basic Principles from the Entertainment Industry

Both games for health and games for entertainment allow player's engagement over long periods of time. Chances are that the longer a player plays a game for health, the better the player's improvement. Ushaw et al. [25]

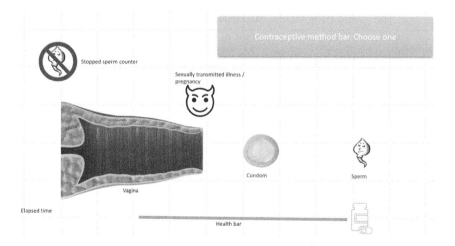

FIGURE 6.9 A variety of contraceptive methods can be used to avoid sperm contact with the female egg. (Redrawn by Andrés Adolfo Navarro-Newball. For images of UnderControl refer to Guana et al. [24], Figure 1.)

state that player engagement techniques from the entertainment industry can be transferred over to games for health. To achieve that, they propose design practices that 'bring a heightened sense of engagement and replay value to games for patients that do not distract from the main health benefit' such as [25]:

- **Platform and Input Device:** hardware platform and input device should be chosen according to the medical intentions of the game. Choices depend on the research needs and the target group of users. For example, while most people are familiar with touchscreen interaction due to the proliferation of smartphones and tablets, a traditional joypad may seem better to those unfamiliar with modern console gaming. Available systems need to be compared as each one has strengths suited to specific needs of gaming health projects.

- **Player Feedback and Player Ability**: feedback is required for retaining user's attention. It should not be punitive but encouraging, rewarding and positive. The reward should outweigh the penalty as the idea is to encourage ongoing participation with the game by providing longer term goals and feedback to the player. This can be done implementing an achievement scheme [9 as cited in 16].

- **Comfort Rewards:** implementing a comfort rewards scheme as a microlevel mechanism to provide constant positive encouragement as the game progresses. Successful completion of a task should be measured using a broad range of parameters. This means that if the player is making a reasonable effort, the game decides that the task was achieved. The player will more likely continue the more rewarding the experience is. If the latter happens, continued engagement is promoted.

- **Level Structure:** the content of each level should become more challenging as the player makes progress. Levels limit the ways players interact allowing consistent focus on the specific behaviour of interest.

- **Focused Player Action:** to encourage the player to focus on one particular action at any time is of great benefit (Figure 6.2). Focus on specific player actions is enabled from clear player feedback, comfort rewards and a level-based structure. The parameters of success can be more tolerant, making positive feedback more likely if the game is focused on assessing whether one task has been achieved. Additionally, focusing on one task favours clarity on the medical study that the game for health is enabling.

- **In-Game Help:** the option to ask for help should be available at any point and not just after failing to accomplish a task. Instructions should be available on screen and simply presented.

- **Inclusive of Family:** players enjoy involving other family members in the game. This increases dosage time as games are played communally with some element of competition.

- **Simplicity of Game Design:** accessibility increases when innovation or complication in the game design are avoided. Tasks such as matching an icon to a target, gauging the length of time to hold down a button and guiding an avatar through a series of gates can be integrated into gameplay because they are easily understood. Simple and well-known game genres may be applicable.

Although the previous principles are for games aimed at patients, these concepts could be extended to medical personnel in training. However, some parameters should allow for less tolerance as it is expected that medical personnel are less prone to mistakes than patients.

6.3.2 Towards the Automation of Games for Health Development

Best practices can be applied during the design and implementation processes. For example, Matínez et al. [26] propose a computational tool for constructing personalised minigames aimed to support language therapy in children with hearing loss. They apply the Software Product Line Engineering (SPLE) paradigm. SPLE enables the efficient management of a set of products that have common and variable elements and belong to a domain. This way, it is possible to share reusable aspects, satisfy specific needs of a market and software can be developed in a prescribed manner. This kind of paradigm enables users to configure new products. Figure 6.10 exemplifies this idea [27]. Here, the tool has three main modules. In the therapist's module, the therapist personalises and assigns the activities to be carried out by the child. In the child's portal, the child performs the activities assigned by the therapist. The minigames generator creates the game in real time. It is important to consider that 'the selection of a video game engine to develop core assets of a Software Product Line (SPL) of

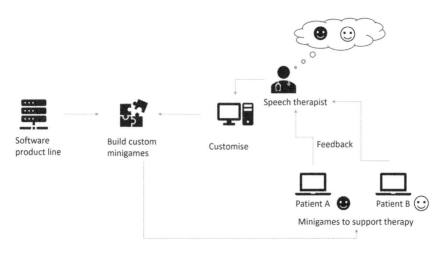

FIGURE 6.10 A health minigame generator using SPLE. (Adapted from Martinez, J., et al. (2018). *Using Software Product Lines to Support Language Rehabilitation Therapies: An Experience Report.* 2018 ICAI Workshops (ICAIW), Bogota, pp. 1–6. doi: 10.1109/ICAIW.2018.8554992; Figure 1.)

minigames could be highly influenced by the requisites of the SPL, differentiating it from the usual selection criteria applied when building complex video games' [28, p. 1].

Thus, software engineering methods and commercial principles can be extended for use in the development of serious games for health.

6.4 BEYOND HUMAN HEALTH

Xu et al. [29] describe a system to train in dog anatomy supported by virtual reality. The system was implemented using a game engine and the virtual reality toolkit (VTK). It is focused on veterinary assessment for veterinary students studying anatomy (Figure 6.11). Thus, game technologies and video games can be extended to animal health. As the authors state: 'If the efficiency of veterinarian medicine can be improved, then more dogs can receive better medical care, letting them live longer, happier lives'. This statement can be extended to other animals in a world requiring the protection of biodiversity.

6.5 OTHER USES OF GAME TECHNOLOGIES IN HEALTH

Technologies such as augmented reality (AR) and virtual reality (VR) are common in serious games [30]. However, their proper use does not imply the creation of a video game. For example, Matu et al. [30] explain a system where a trainer uses two virtual robotic arms, which are superimposed on

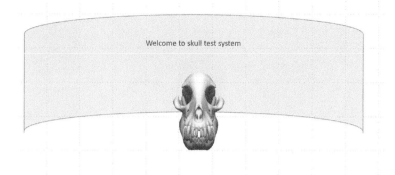

FIGURE 6.11   VR animal anatomy system for veterinaries. A 3D image of the skull is superposed over a 3D virtual curved screen where information is displayed. (Redrawn by Andrés Adolfo Navarro-Newball. For the original image refer to Xu et al. [29], Figure 6.)

a video feed to the trainee using AR. The system allows the demonstration of diverse tasks performed by the trainer to guide the trainee. The trainee can follow and perform the task within a 3D image displayed through a stereoscopic display (Figure 6.12).

Rapetti et al. [31] describe a VR navigation system for prostate biopsy. In this system, the position of the needle and the patient anatomy are tracked by a system which provides orientation and position with respect to the surgical bed. In the operative room, the surgeon is presented with a stereoscopic volumetric rendering of the patient's anatomy and a virtual

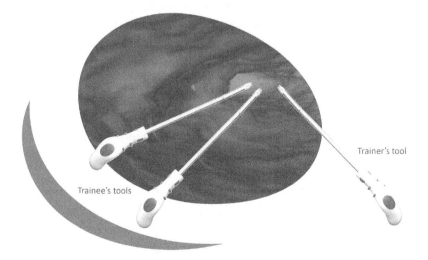

FIGURE 6.12   The trainer guides the trainee using virtual tools. (Redrawn by Andrés Adolfo Navarro-Newball. For the original image refer to Matu et al. [30], Figure 5.)

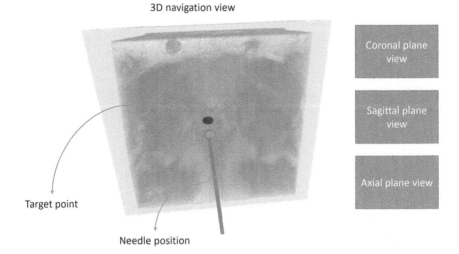

FIGURE 6.13   The position of the needle and the target point are visible during 3D navigation. (Adapted from Rapetti, L., Crivellaro, S., De Momi, E., Ferrigno, G., Niederberger, C., & Luciano, C. (2017). *Virtual Reality Navigation System for prostate Biopsy*. Proceedings of the 23rd ACM Symposium on Virtual Reality Software and Technology (VRST '17). ACM, New York, NY, Article 35, 4 pages. doi: 10.1145/3139131.3139162; Figure 2.)

needle. The idea is to use a virtual reality navigation system where targeted biopsy is performed under the guidance of virtual images (Figure 6.13).

Overall, game technology does not always need to be used to implement a game. Useful health systems can be implemented relying on these technologies. The challenges of creating a game which includes narratives, mechanics, arts and devices are not always required.

6.6 DISCUSSION

Games for health can be useful because they are enjoyable and motivate repeatability. They are usually implemented with available game technology. Additionally, game technology can be used to implement a health system that do not necessarily implement a game and can go beyond human health (e.g. animal health).

The development of games for health is a complex task that should follow most of the games for entertainment principles. However, it is common to focus on simple, measurable tasks that can be implemented on minigames. This way, finding ways to measure performance is easier. Still, automation of games for health generation is a desirable feature. However, in most cases, games are developed to solve specific situations. A SPLE approach could be helpful to make development more efficient. However, the context of the game should be very well understood, and the game engine chosen according to the game's specific needs.

6.7 CONCLUSION

We have briefly presented computer games and their use. We offered a broad classification of games for health systems; these include games for training medical personnel, games for training patients, games for therapy and games for public health policies. However, games for health should not be limited to this categorisation as they may have more diversity. Applications range from mental health, surgery, reproductive health, disaster recovery to veterinary medicine.

REFERENCES

1. Prakash, E. C., & Rao, M. (2015). Gamification in informal education environments: A case study. In *Transforming Learning and IT Management Through Gamification. International Series on Computer Entertainment and Media Technology*. Cham, Switzerland: Springer.
2. El Rhalibi, A., Pan, Z., Jin, H., Ding, D., Navarro-Newball, A. A., & Wang, Y. (2018). *E-Learning and Games*. Proceedings of the 12th International Conference, Edutainment 2018, Xi'an, China, June 28–30, 2018. Springer Nature Switzerland AG 2019. doi: 10.1007/978-3-030-23712-7
3. Andrés,P. M. L., Arbeloa, F. J. S., Moreno, J. L., & Vaz de Carvalho, C. (2014). *TimeMesh: Producing and Evaluating a Serious Game*. Proceedings of the XV International Conference on Human Computer Interaction (Interacción '14). ACM, New York, NY, Article 100, 8 pages. doi: 10.1145/2662253.2662353
4. AlRomi, N. (2015). Human factors in the design of medical simulation tools. *Procedia Manufacturing*, 3, 288–292. doi: 10.1016/j.promfg.2015.07.151.
5. Surgical Science. *Virtual Reality Training Systems for Laparoscopy and Endoscopy*. Retrieved from http://www.lapsim.com/.
6. Sin Era. *LapSim*. Retrieved from http://sim-era.com/product_details/531.
7. Ferracani, A., Pezzatini, D., & Del Bimbo, A. (2014). *A Natural and Immersive Virtual Interface for the Surgical Safety Checklist Training*. Proceedings of the 2014 ACM International Workshop on Serious Games (SeriousGames '14). ACM, New York, NY, pp. 27–32. doi: 10.1145/2656719.2656725
8. Amresh, A., Sinha, M., Birr, R., & Salla, R. (2015). *Interactive Cause and Effect Comic-Book Storytelling for Improving Nutrition Outcomes in Children*. Proceedings of the 5th International Conference on Digital Health 2015 (DH '15). ACM, New York, NY, pp. 9–14. doi: 10.1145/2750511.2750533
9. Romera Sanchez, A. Y., & Kunze, K. (2018). *Flair: Towards a Therapeutic Serious Game for Social Anxiety Disorder*. Proceedings of the 2018 ACM International Joint Conference and 2018 International Symposium on Pervasive and Ubiquitous Computing and Wearable Computers (UbiComp '18). ACM, New York, NY, pp. 239–242. doi: 10.1145/3267305.3267558

10. Guana, V., Xiang, T., Zhang, H., Schepens, E., & Stroulia, E. (2014). *UnderControl an Educational Serious-Game for Reproductive Health*. Proceedings of the First ACM SIGCHI Annual Symposium on Computer-Human Interaction in Play (CHI PLAY '14). ACM, New York, NY, pp. 339–342. doi: 10.1145/2658537.2662983

11. Huang, M.-C., Chen, E., Xu, W., & Sarrafzadeh, M. (2011). *Gaming for Upper Extremities Rehabilitation*. Proceedings of the 2nd Conference on Wireless Health (WH '11). ACM, New York, NY, Article 27, 2 pages. doi: 10.1145/2077546.2077576

12. Lozano-Quilis, J. A., Gil-Gómez, H., Gil-Gómez, J. A., Albiol-Pérez, S., Palacios-Navarro, G., Fardoun, H. M., & Mashat, A. S. (2014). Virtual rehabilitation for multiple sclerosis using a kinect-based system: Randomized controlled trial. *JMIR Serious Games*, 2(2), e12. doi: 10.2196/games.2933

13. Benbouriche, M., Nolet, K., Trottier, D., & Renaud, P. (2014). *Virtual Reality Applications in Forensic Psychiatry*. Proceedings of the 2014 Virtual Reality International Conference (VRIC '14). ACM, New York, NY, Article 7, 4 pages. doi: 10.1145/2617841.2620692

14. Amresh, A., Lyles, A., Small, L., & Gary, K. (2017). *FitBit Garden: A Mobile Game Designed to Increase Physical Activity in Children*. Proceedings of the 2017 International Conference on Digital Health (DH '17). ACM, New York, NY, pp. 200–201. doi: 10.1145/3079452.3079457

15. Bernard-Opitz, V., Sriram, N., & Sapuan, S. (1999). Enhancing vocal imitations in children with autism using the IBM speech viewer. *Autism*, 3(2), 131–147. doi: 10.1177/1362361399003002004

16. Navarro-Newball, A. A., Loaiza, D., Oviedo, C., Castillo, A., Portilla, A., Linares, D., & Álvarez, G. (2014). Talking to Teo: Video game supported speech therapy. *Entertainment Computing*, 5(4), 401–412. doi: 10.1016/j.entcom.2014.10.005

17. de Vasconcellos, M. S., & de Araujo, I. S. (2014). *Video Games and Participation in Health - How Online Games Can Foster Population's Participation in Public Health Policies*. 2014 IEEE 3nd International Conference on Serious Games and Applications for Health (SeGAH), Rio de Janeiro, pp. 1–8. doi: 10.1109/SeGAH.2014.7067095

18. De Paolis, L. T. (2012). *Serious Game for Laparoscopic Suturing Training*. 2012 Sixth International Conference on Complex, Intelligent, and Software Intensive Systems, Palermo, pp. 481–485. doi: 10.1109/CISIS.2012.175

19. Ribeiro, C., Tiago, J., Monteiro, M. & Pereira, J. (2014). *SeGTE: A Serious Game to Train and Evaluate Basic Life Support*. 2014 International Conference on Computer Graphics Theory and Applications (GRAPP), Lisbon, Portugal, pp. 1–7.

20. Ijaz, K., Wang, Y., Ahmadpour, N., & Calvo, R. A. (2019). *Immersive VR Exergames for Health and Wellbeing*. Extended Abstracts of the 2019 CHI Conference on Human Factors in Computing Systems (CHI EA '19). ACM, New York, NY, Article INT043, 4 pages. doi: 10.1145/3290607.3313281

21. Herrera, B. F. J., Navarro Newball, A. A., Marin, T. C. A. (2007). Using an interactive module to enhance and understand 3D cavity navigation: A patient's view. *Journal of Telemedicine and Telecare*, 13(1_suppl), 13–15. doi: 10.1258/135763307781645068

22. Navarro-Newball, A. A., Loaiza, D., Oviedo, C., Castillo, A., Portilla, A., Linares, D., & Álvarez, G. (2014). Talking to Teo: Video game supported speech therapy. *Entertainment Computing*, 5(4), 401–412. doi: 10.1016/j.entcom.2014.10.005

23. Henriksen, B., Nielsen, R., Kraus, M., & Geng, B. (2017). *A Virtual Reality System for Treatment of Phantom Limb Pain Using Game Training and Tactile Feedback*. Proceedings of the Virtual Reality International Conference - Laval Virtual 2017 (VRIC '17). ACM, New York, NY, Article 13, 4 pages. doi: 10.1145/3110292.3110306

24. Guana, V., Xiang, T., Zhang, H., Schepens, E., & Stroulia, E. (2014). *UnderControl an Educational Serious-Game for Reproductive Health*. Proceedings of the First ACM SIGCHI Annual Symposium on Computer-Human Interaction in Play (CHI PLAY '14). ACM, New York, NY, pp. 339–342. doi: 10.1145/2658537.2662983

25. Ushaw, G., Davison, R., Eyre, J., & Morgan, G. (2015). *Adopting Best Practices from the Games Industry in Development of Serious Games for Health*. Proceedings of the 5th International Conference on Digital Health 2015 (DH '15). ACM, New York, NY, pp. 1–8. doi: 10.1145/2750511.2750513

26. Martínez, J., et al. (2018). *Using Software Product Lines to Support Language Rehabilitation Therapies: An Experience Report*. 2018 ICAI Workshops (ICAIW), Bogota, pp. 1–6. doi: 10.1109/ICAIW.2018.8554992

27. Martinez, J., Beltran, E. J. G., Alvarez, G. I., Castillo, A. D., Portilla, A., & Almanza, V. (2019). Video Games to Support Language Therapies in Children with Hearing Disabilities. Presented in Edutainment: *The 13th International Conference on E-learning and Games* (Pontificia Universidad Javeriana Cali, Colombia), 2019.

28. Sierra, M., Pabón, M. C., Rincón, L., Navarro-Newball, A., & Linares, D. (2019). A comparative analysis of game engines to develop core assets for a software product line of mini-games. In Peng, X., Ampatzoglou, A., & Bhowmik, T. (Eds.), *Reuse in the Big Data Era. ICSR 2019. Lecture Notes in Computer Science*, vol. 11602. Cham, Switzerland: Springer.

29. Xu, X., Mangina, E., Kilroy, D., Kumar, A., & Campbell, A. G. (2018). Delaying when all dogs to go to heaven: Virtual reality Canine Anatomy Education Pilot Study. 1–9. *Proceedings IEEE Games, Entertainment, Media Conference (GEM), Galway*, doi: 10.1109/GEM.2018.8516510

30. Matu, F. O., Thøgersen, M., Galsgaard, B., Møller Jensen, M., & Kraus, M. (2014). *Stereoscopic Augmented Reality System for Supervised Training on Minimal Invasive Surgery Robots*. Proceedings of the 2014 Virtual Reality International Conference (VRIC '14). ACM, New York, NY, Article 33, 4 pages. doi: 10.1145/2617841.2620722

31. Rapetti, L., Crivellaro, S., De Momi, E., Ferrigno, G., Niederberger, C., & Luciano, C. (2017). *Virtual Reality Navigation System for prostate Biopsy*. Proceedings of the 23rd ACM Symposium on Virtual Reality Software and Technology (VRST '17). ACM, New York, NY, Article 35, 4 pages. doi: 10.1145/3139131.3139162

III

Game Design, Level Design, and Storytelling

CHAPTER 7

Free to Play Mobile Game Design Fundamentals

Simon Rozner

CONTENTS

7.1   Audience   118
7.2   Genre, Art Style and Casual, Midcore vs. Hardcore Game   118
7.3   Monetization   119
7.4   User Acquisition and Marketing   120
7.5   KPIs   121
7.6   Onboarding, Quality Assurance and Player Support   123
7.7   Live Operations: From Test to Soft Launch to Global Launch   124
Ludography   126
Reference   126

O NE OF THE MOST basic things when it comes to games, is, of course, deciding what kind of game to make. A crucial element, once decided what game to make, is understanding what the essential part of the game is. For most games that is usually the core game, which is the element that usually feels like what most people think of what the game is. If you think of a shooter, the whole set of actions like moving, shooting and destroying opponents is the core game. Some games consist only of the core game, such as chess or *DOOM*. Many if not most digital games today also have a meta game. With a meta game, we mean a game that surrounds the core game with a secondary experience. This can range from everything as a secondary minigame that supports the core, community tools such as a guild to progression mechanics that enhance the core game. Think of *Angry Birds 2*, where players do not just play levels and destroy blocks in the core, but also collect feathers in the meta side of the game via rewards that increase a number multiplier that allows you to gain a bigger score from blocks in the core. Some games go as far as making a meta game so complex and fulfilling, that a game becomes almost entirely about the meta. Games like *Summoners War* can be played primarily in a meta mode, where players manage teams of warriors without having to actively participate in a core battle. As mentioned, many a mobile game has a meta game in additional to the core game, and Free to Play (F2P) games rely heavily on that. It is however crucial for the design of the game to decide where the focus lies. A game must either have a primary focus on the core and be supported by the meta or be mainly on the meta and be supported by the core. If the design tries to make a game about both, neither element will have a focus and ends up suffering. In the words of Sid Meier: "One Good Game Is Better Than Two Great Ones" (Johnson, 2009).

7.1 AUDIENCE

When thinking of what kind of game to build and how to balance core and meta, you need to know WHO you are making the game for. You can basically build the same game, core and all, but have the balance be different—having focus areas in the core and meta be in other places. A great example are RPGs such as *Dungeon Boss* vs. *Star Wars: Galaxy of Heroes*. They are very similar games but where one has a more casual appearance, appealing to players who like quirky stylized fantasy, the other is a more grown-up experience with a strong sci-fi vibe. Knowing who you make the game for does not just help the design of the game and dictate what features make sense, it also helps the visual development about what is the right art style for the game, and it helps user acquisition and marketing in finding the right ways to let your potential players know about your game.

7.2 GENRE, ART STYLE AND CASUAL, MIDCORE vs. HARDCORE GAME

Figuring out your audience is not a trivial problem, and there is no one single solution, nor is it a scientific process. A first step in figuring out where to look is the understanding of what ballpark game genre your game fits in. This might be more than one depending on the features of your game. The visual style of your game is another. Some people like a specific visual style, while others do not like it. And it isn't always the biggest range of appeal that might be good for your game. It makes sense to test your art together with marketing to find what appeal your art has and for whom. Caution is advised, just because people like your art, does not mean they will like your game. The sooner you can test a combination of art and game the better, as it will give you results you can trust and show the relationship between gameplay and art and audience.

When it comes down to audience, knowing how casual or not your game is helps in your strategy. Casual players tend to like games that are less dexterous and not skill heavy, relying on more luck elements and simple game rules. That doesn't mean those games can't have a high level of mastery and require skill to reach the highest levels, but ease players into the game very gently and tend to have a very wide appeal such as *Subway Surfers*. On the flip side, we have hardcore games. These tend to be games of very high skill, even though they can be at times be approached quite easily; highly successful examples are *PUBG: Mobile* or *Game of War*. Many games land somewhere along a range between those two extremes. The middle we call, well, midcore games. Where casual games can have a massive audience, and rely on masses of players, they are relatively easy to build. Hardcore games usually have a much more limited audience size, and cost for user acquisition is much higher and they tend to be harder to build. New teams and companies do well going down a more casual route until working together becomes smooth before attempting the riskier other games. In any case, make sure you have a plan; know WHAT game you make for WHO!

7.3 MONETIZATION

In F2P games, monetization has to come from other ways than selling the game in the same way as traditional game sales. The days are over when the boxed game makes the most money and many of those "premium games" now also employ additional ways to let players spend money on more content. F2P games have to find monetization ways or they won't bring in money for the people behind the game, unless you are an altruistic developer/publisher, you are in this business to make a living. Simply put, there are two basic ways to make money in your game. You have advertisement places in your game or your lock content behind a gate that must be unlocked first. That unlock can happen after some time has passed, by watching an advert, by paying for it or a combination of those. The passage of time is usually coupled with an advert for spending money to reduce or remove said timer. Imagine you lost all your lives in a game, and it takes ten minutes to gain a new life back. You can either wait (the free option) or watch a video advert to gain one life back now or pay $1 to get all your lives back. Paying directly with money is not always desirable, for players or for you, and you can provide players with an intermediary currency that allows players to spend fractions of said dollar without players having to pull out their credit cards every time. Think you want to sell something for $12 in your game? Usually the store you sell something through, like Apple's App Store, has fixed price points that are a hassle to maintain. Imagine further that if you wanted to give a discount on said something, you would have to define a new price point in real money and attach it to said something. Using an intermediary virtual currency makes this a simple task.

7.4 USER ACQUISITION AND MARKETING

All the things you build and plan are nice, but quite useless if you don't get the players who will play your game. The days are mostly over where the old adage "Make it and they will come" holds true. You know who should be playing your game first and foremost. Once you know, you want to put this theory to the test as mentioned earlier. Your two biggest questions should be: Is the user who comes to my game a good user? With good we mean a user who will stay and play, hopefully pay, and how much spending potential does he or she have. And second, how much does it cost to find this player?

Today's marketing specialists can tell you quite a few things about users and where they come from, as well as how expensive a user was and what marketing material was effective—along the lines of click through rate and installs. In essence, getting users requires two parts: marketing creatives and places to show them. The specialist/s can help you in knowing how to visually present your game to potential audiences in the form of an advertising and where to show said advert. How successful an advert is can mostly be measured by the specialists in how many people who saw the advert end up installing the game. This is called the funnel conversion. Now you might think that the better that percentage is, the more successful your game might be. This might be true in some cases, but in the end, remember that most likely you also want to see some revenue coming in from those users. It will all be for nothing if you end up getting a great funnel conversion but end up with users who don't spend a dime in your game.

You want to care about two numbers when it comes to knowing if your user acquisition worked or not.

The first thing you need to know is your Cost Per Install or CPI. This number tells you how expensive it was to get a certain number of users in a specific time period. Say you spend $100 in two weeks with a specific marketing campaign and got 200 users who install the game after clicking your advert. Your CPI is 50 cents for this user cohort.

The second is the lifetime value of the users you have, the LTV. Why not just the revenue per user you might ask. Well, the revenue per user tells you the *overall* health of your business over time, where the LTV tells you how profitable *each* user you get can be. LTV is an estimated value and a true LTV is rarely known until the actual end of the cohort's lifecycle in your game. You will, however, learn how much a group of players will spend over time and you should reflect this back to how much this group cost you to get in the first place. From there you will be able to extrapolate what future LTVs are. The longer the player stays around to play your game, and hopefully keeps buying things you offer, the higher his or her LTV is. So did you get a healthy set of users? You know by seeing the LTV is bigger than the CPI. Knowing LTV and CPI can help you and your User Acquisition (UA) and marketing team in knowing where and how to spend your marketing budget.

On top of these "paid users"—we spent money directly to bring them to our game—there are also "organic users." The organic users are all users we get in all other ways but not by them clicking on your advert. This is the user who, for example, hears from their friends, goes to the app store and installs the game. Those users of course have a CPI of zero, as we can't measure it. What we can try to measure is how many organic users we got for each paid user. This measure of virality is expressed as the k-factor. The bigger the number is, the better for you as you will end up getting more users from your marketing for free, which in turn can have a positive effect on your bottom line.

7.5 KPIs

So you have a game, you have an audience, you have monetization and you managed to get users. How do you now know how healthy your game is? Key performance indicators or KPIs are measurable values that can help you find out. You already learned about CPI and LTV. LTV as we said gets better the longer a user stays around. So you will want to measure a user's retention in your game. This tells you how long a user stays around after starting to play your game. Most users will leave your game within the first week. You also want to know the conversion rate of your users but at what point in time. Finding a balance in retention and conversion is very important. Very casual games, where users leave quickly might benefit from early conversion, especially if the expected LTV is quite low to begin with. Having low retention after a week or two might not be a huge issue as you have a profitable business. Other games, like a 4X strategy title will have quite bad early conversion and low spending overall until players really get into your game. Here you know that the majority of the income is generated maybe weeks after the player started playing. Having as high as possible retention on the long term is absolutely the key to your survival.

Those metrics deal specifically with your money business side but aren't helping you with figuring out specifics about what players actually do in your game. You will want to dig into data to understand the behavior of your players and create KPIs using events players have in your game. If you have a game where players complete levels, you will want to know the pass rate of each level to find if levels are too hard or too easy. There are infinite ways to measure things, and it is easy to try and measure everything. You won't have to: in the end, you *always* want to be able to relate anything you measure to your retention, conversion, LTV and revenue. If a measurement can't help you see how any of these KPIs could be affected, it probably is a waste of your time.

One last piece of advice on KPIs. It is easy to look at your numbers by throwing them all into a pot. This won't tell you a lot, especially when it comes down to optimizing your game. Try to group players together based on playing, spending, retention, UA patterns and so on. Find differences in the behavior and see what works and what doesn't work for a group. Can something be improved without harming another group? Testing your hypothesis is important. Be scientific about it, when you test something, use volumes of players and ensure that your results are statistically significant. Always question your numbers and avoid interpreting and inferring meaning that is not there. Brushing up on your knowledge of statistics is a very useful thing, not just when it comes down to designing games in general, but also in analyzing the business side of them. Additionally, do a qualitative analysis of your game and hear and see what players say and do.

7.6 ONBOARDING, QUALITY ASSURANCE AND PLAYER SUPPORT

When a player first comes to your game, unless it is a game in a series, most likely they know nothing about how to play your game and have, at best, an expectation of how it will work which might or might not match reality. The process of bringing your players aboard and making them feel familiar in the new surrounding is called onboarding.

A good onboarding experience teaches players how to play your game, without feeling overwhelmingly instructional, difficult or challengeless. It is not easy and, unfortunately, there will be no one size fits all solution. It isn't to despair though, as you can make an experience that will be good for the majority of your players. Easing your players into the basics is really the key here, so the most essential thing is to make your game as fun as fast as possible and that the player has a fun challenge in the first few minutes of your game. Onboarding does not end with just teaching the controls or what you might find in many games in the form of an explicit tutorial. It continues for the first few hours of playing, making sure players find their way through all the functions of the game in a structured manner. Some games do a lot of handholding and point things out very directly such as *Puzzles & Empires* and others throw you into the fray quite fast and ease you into all you need to know without you even really noticing it like *Brawl Stars*.

What works best is something you must find out and it will be different for each game, and it will have to match your audience. The better you know your audience, the easier it will be for you to get this right. Service providers such as PlaytestCloud or usertesting.com can help you find players matching your audience criteria, who play your game and record a video along with their comments with it. It is a wonderful tool in your repertoire of testing with your friends and co-workers to get some qualitative feedback. Do not underestimate the power of surveys either, which you can use not just for your game, but also during your audience and marketing research. To set up surveys, get help from professional user researchers so that you do not create questions in a way that could lead your users on and cause them to answer in possible false positives.

Quality assurance (QA) is the other side of the same coin, which helps make sure your product work as intended and helps you find all possible issues that can arise in your game. From running your game on different devices, in different languages and operating system versions to finding the most obscure bugs and simple clarity in your game, a good QA team will throw it all at you and be nitpicky about everything. Go as far as seeing how much they might even enjoy your game. If it looks like they have a blast despite testing the same things over and over again, you can rest assured part of your game is doing just fine. It is easy to dismiss QA as just a process to find your bugs, but it can help you make sure you are making a product that will operate and run as intended when you launch or add new features later on. Keeping a solid record of issues encountered will also help you later once your game is in players' hands.

That is when player support comes in. Player support in an ideal world does more than just help players when they have a technical issue with your game. It can be an integral part in your marketing strategy through community building and be your line to players. When players really like your game, they tend to be quite vocal, especially when something is wrong. Player support can hear and react and even help you keep your sanity when your community has a toxic element. They may be your evangelists and a big reason for some players to stick with your game, when without good player support, they might have left a long time ago. You might even find that very person among your players.

7.7 LIVE OPERATIONS: FROM TEST TO SOFT LAUNCH TO GLOBAL LAUNCH

Making games is always a struggle. There are so many moving parts and few things feel as exciting as when you open the floodgates and players start coming to play your game.

The first time you will have players coming in in droves should be during your technical launch, which should happen a few months before your soft launch, early in your production stage or at the end of your pre-production.

During the technical launch, you want to get a good volume of players to test the stability of your game service, especially if you run your game on a server—learn what happens when many players play and get a baseline of your KPIs. You most likely probably do not want to have any monetization in your game available to players at this stage, especially if you plan on taking the game down again before soft launch. This is the time to make sure your game is functional and does what you tested earlier in small volumes, and in isolated components, such as your funnel or qualitative testing for onboarding, at a much larger scale. During this time, it is still relatively easy to make bigger changes in your game when you find things do not work, where your game economy needs a major rebalance, your onboarding experience, while working well for the people you tested with earlier, needs improvements to work with the majority of your players. You want to hopefully have a few thousand players in your game at this stage to get to that important statistical significance.

You have now completed all the key features your game needs to be fun and engaging for the longer term, have polished your experience and have ways for players to come and play and spend money. It is time to soft launch your game in selected markets. Now you test out how your game resonates with players at a really big scale that is representative of your audience and the countries your players reside in. You will learn what players like to spend money on, how much and where. Now you can optimize the experience and find out what drives players away and remedy it. You can find out what the next few big and small things you need to fix are and add features before you let the whole world see your game. You will now learn how to go about updating your game regularly and smoothly. Your KPIs will tell you some hard truths as well, and it might be that you cannot scale your user acquisition and you will not be able to make a profit. This is the last stage where you have to decide, are you able to launch your game worldwide and have a viable business for the coming months and years? For some games, this is the end, for others, it is the last stage to remove all the breaks and launch.

Time the global launch and you are done. Enjoy the money. It would be nice if it were so easy, for now the hard part of maintaining your game starts. In today's F2P world, "just" shipping your game is not enough. Your players, unless you make a very simple hyper casual game, expect you to provide new updates, bug fixes, content and events. You should make a clear plan and develop tools that let you do that well before you launch your game in soft launch. Imagine you built an ocean liner, you now need to make sure it keeps having customers, the kitchen provides meals, new exciting ports are landed at etc. Your game is a service. Treat it as such and maintain it. Or else the next hot thing will take all your best features and your players away from you. Your customer is not the king and always right, however, he or she is valuable, and it is your job to retain said value until it is time to close doors.

Every game sooner or later, and rather later, will have to say goodbye and close down further development. Most go quietly, losing their luster and their profitability. Knowing when and how to stop is as important as starting in the first place. It is hard for everyone involved, especially when things for you and your team have looked so promising. Stopping for the right reasons and knowing why can make this feel like a success. You might make the most fun game in your opinion, players might even love it, but producing it will cost more money than you have, getting users profitably might turn out to be impossible and, no matter what, sometimes the obstacles cannot be overcome. Realize and accept that this will happen, learn from it, speak with your fellow developers about it and be rational about it, and take it along to the next project where you will already have a better start. Mind you, this all may happen early on when you start a project or after running your game successfully for years.

There are many, many moving parts to making a successful game and many things you need to know. But you don't need to know it all yourself in detail. This primer will hopefully serve you in knowing what topics you should research in more detail as well as getting you going on your journey down the rabbit hole. There are great resources and design authors out there such as Eric Zimmerman, Ernest Adams, Ian Schreiber, PocketGamer, *Gamasutra*, GDC and many more. With the keywords and basic concepts described in this short chapter, googling for more will be a breeze. Good luck!

LUDOGRAPHY

1. *Angry Birds 2*, Rovio Entertainment, 2015.
2. *Brawl Stars*, Supercell, 2017.
3. *DOOM*, id Software Inc., 1993.
4. *Dungeon Boss*, Boss Fight Entertainment, Big Fish Games, 2015.
5. *Game of War*: Fire Age, Machine Zone, 2013.
6. *PUBG: Mobile*, PUBG Corporation & Krafton & Lightspeed Quantum, Tencent Games, 2018.
7. *Puzzles & Empires*, Small Giant Games, 2017.
8. *Star Wars: Galaxy of Heroes*, Capital Games & EA Mobile, Electronic Arts, 2015.
9. *Subway Surfers*, Kiloo & SYBO Games, SYBO Games, 2012.
10. *Summoners War*, Com2uS Corporation, 2014.

REFERENCE

Johnson, S. (2009). Analysis: Sid Meier's key design lessons. *Gamasutra*. Available at https://www.gamasutra.com/view/news/114402/Analysis_Sid_Meiers _Key_Design_Lessons.php.

CHAPTER 8

Evergreen Game Design Principles

Roberto Dillon

CONTENTS

8.1 Introduction 127
8.2 From Retro to Modern 128
    8.2.1 Short Game Sessions and Tight Controls 129
    8.2.2 Using a Familiar Theme 132
    8.2.3 Straightforward Goals 133
    8.2.4 Relying on an Emotional Hook 133
    8.2.5 Teaching, Challenging and Rewarding Players 135
    8.2.6 Mixing Genres 136
    8.2.7 Understanding Technical and Experiential Limitations 137
8.3 Conclusion 138
References 139

8.1 INTRODUCTION

In recent years, retro games have made a comeback that even their most enthusiastic supporters would have thought unimaginable. Thanks to several books on the history of games being published in the last 15 years, covering either games in general (see, for example, Herman (2016), Dillon (2011), Mott (2010), and Loguidice and Barton (2012)) or specific platforms (Weiss, 2018), we witnessed a rising awareness and curiosity for old generations' gaming. Compilations of retro games are now regularly being released on modern platforms, like *Flashback Classics* (two volumes, 2016) or *SEGA Genesis Classics* (2018), remastered or even remade from scratch on completely different technologies like virtual reality (*Doom VFR*, 2018).

Even more surprisingly, hardware devices, from DIY arcade cabinets to a growing list of mini-consoles, including the likes of Atari VCS (Atari Flashback Consoles, 2011), NES (NES Classic Edition, 2016), Sony PlayStation (PlayStation Classic, 2018), and the Commodore 64 (The C64 Mini, 2018), are all met with great enthusiasm by a crowd including people young and old.

Today, in an age where gaming masterpieces like *Red Dead Redemption 2* (Rockstar, 2018) require hundreds of developers and many tens of millions of dollars to be developed, can such primitive playing experiences still have a meaningful role in our entertainment life? Naturally, such old experiences should not be directly compared with AAA titles like the above-mentioned titles but, perhaps, it still makes sense to compare and reference them in the context of the ever-evolving indie, casual and mobile games that are still developed by small teams, often on very limited budgets. These titles today, despite the brutal competition, still manage to be popular among many different audiences by highlighting gameplay and design elements that are actually very similar to the games of 30 or more years ago, making the latter a fundamental resource for studying the theory and practice of game design.

What are then the elements of "good" game design that seem to be forever relevant and should be taken into account by each new generation of game developers? What principles can such old games still teach and remind us in our never-ending quest for designing fun, engaging and immersive games with the potential to be enjoyed for many years to come?

8.2 FROM RETRO TO MODERN

We can start with the consideration that 8-bit gaming became popular thanks to arcades and home gaming systems that aimed at offering a time limited and straightforward bite-sized experience, in some ways not too dissimilar from many modern mobile games designed to be played on the go while commuting. This observation can then help us in identifying and discussing different criteria, illustrating how several retro and modern games successfully managed to replicate particular design features or concepts.

In particular, the importance of the following aspects will be stressed:

- Short game sessions and tight controls
- Using a familiar theme

- Straightforward goals

- Relaying on an emotional hook

- Teaching, challenging and rewarding players

- Mixing genres

- Understanding technical and experiential limitations

8.2.1 Short Game Sessions and Tight Controls

Arcade games, as well as many 8-bit home computer and video games, were simply brutal in terms of difficulty. In particular, arcade games already implemented something that became terribly popular decades later: micro transactions. A quarter to play a game: game over? Continue by inserting another quarter! Very simple and straightforward.

For this to make the game become addictive and, ultimately profitable from a business perspective, a few things had to be done right, since nobody obviously wants to keep crashing into a "Game Over" screen every minute. To avoid frustration, players must always end the game with a strong desire of playing again, which is only possible if their failures won't feel inevitable or unfair: never must the player have an excuse for blaming a fault in the game design but must be forced to admit that failure was due only to his own lack of skills. "Damn! I got it! Next time I will avoid that trap!" must be the implicit thought after the fateful game over message.

The first step to achieve this is to design a tight control scheme that naturally fits the particular platform the game is released on. Games such as *Donkey Kong* (Miyamoto S., 1981) or *Pac-Man* (Iwatani, 1980), as well as most arcade games of the time, only needed a simple directional joystick and, at most, one button, to offer players an engaging gameplay experience that, despite being brutal in terms of difficulty, never felt unfair: players could actually monitor their progress thanks to their high scores and check their increasing mastery game after game. This is an extremely important point because it relates directly to a fundamental concept that was acknowledged in games only in relatively recent times: the concept of "flow." Originally proposed in Csíkszentmihályi, *Beyond Boredom and Anxiety* (1975) and Csíkszentmihályi, *Flow: The Psychology of Optimal Experience* (1990), the flow state is identified as a mental state where a person is completely adsorbed and focused on a specific activity and even the most challenging tasks are performed with apparent ease. The relationship and interdependence between "skill" and "challenge" is the important aspect to determine the mental state of a person engaged in a specific activity, which can fall into more or less positive connotations (Figure 8.1).

Starting with Chen (2007), game designers became increasingly aware of the importance of engaging players effectively from a psychological perspective, so much so that "flow" became a desired state for everyone, not just for the most skilled among players. Proper level design would then allow players of any ability to constantly juggle between boredom and anxiety, surfing within a "flow channel" (Figure 8.2) where the player would remain focused and be challenged in a way to constantly make him feel like a true master, even when still a beginner.

Simple but responsive controls are indeed a core reason for the terrific success of otherwise extremely simple modern game design concepts, like the surprise indie mobile hit *Flappy Bird* (Nguyen, 2013). Despite the game frustrating difficulty level, in fact, the precise and predictable effect of each tap on the touchscreen made the game fair, pushing players to desire mastering the simple yet engaging game mechanic and effectively enter a state of flow from the very beginning.

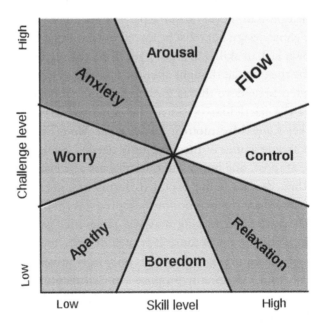

FIGURE 8.1 The original "flow" model as proposed by Prof. Csíkszentmihályi. Different mental states are possible depending on the person's skills and the relative difficulty of the required activity.

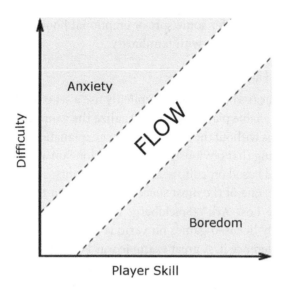

FIGURE 8.2 A simplified version of Figure 8.1, generally adopted by game designers.

Implementing a tight control scheme is even more important in platformers, requiring precise jumping, and shooters where the ongoing action can be extremely hectic. Classic examples for the latter group are the precise geometries of games such as *Tempest* (Theurer, 1981) and *Gridrunner* (Minter, 1982) as well as the chaotic excitement of *Robotron* (Jarvis, 1982), whose successes could not have been possible without responsive and precise controls. The latter game deserves additional discussion as it departed from the traditional joystick-plus-one-button kind of setup for a dual joystick scheme instead, allowing for more freedom of movement and action. Perhaps surprisingly, even such an unconventional approach did pass the test of time. A dual stick control is now common for console games such as *Dead Nation* (Housemarque, 2010) and even for mobile games, with a dual set of virtual sticks making games such as *Minigore* (MountainSheep, 2009) a great joy to play that could have simply been impossible to achieve with less responsive, or floaty, controls.*

With a proper set of controls in place, a game is ready to be played but it still has to capture the player's attention and prick his or her curiosity. Different aspects are of paramount importance here: the game should immediately feel familiar, offer a clearly understandable and intuitive goal

---

* The interested reader can check McAllister (2011) for guidelines on how to effectively implement such a control scheme in the context of mobile games.

as well as be able to offer some sort of emotional hook to engage players from the get-go. Let's start with familiarity.

8.2.2 Using a Familiar Theme

"Familiarity" means being able to implicitly use a set of well-known references that will enable players to contextualize the game and easily understand its settings without the need for further explanations or instructions. This is something that obviously needs to be done on a case-by-case basis and customized based on culture and specific events.

For example, one of the most successful movies in the early 1980s was "Raiders of the Lost Ark" (Spieldberg, 1981) so it was no wonder that, besides officially licensed games on various platforms, other games tried to implicitly reference it. A great example was *Pitfall* (Crane, 1982) which, by presenting a daring explorer jumping across vines in a jungle searching for lost treasures, was not only able to naturally remind the player of the Indiana Jones character but also of the always popular Tarzan story (Burroughs, 1912) (Figure 8.3).

Building a familiar setup was also emphasized by Sid Meier in his postmortem of *Civilization* (Meier & Shelley, 1991) at the Game Developers Conference in 2017 (GDC Vault, 2017). In his talk, the legendary designer stressed the importance for players to interact with well-known historical figures and for the game to rely on common knowledge historical facts taken from primary school level textbooks to draw players into the gaming world. The purpose of the game was not to teach advanced historical

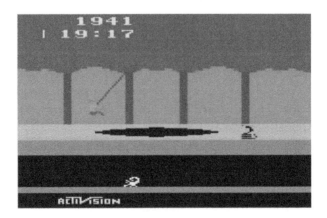

FIGURE 8.3 Indiana Jones + Tarzan = Pitfall Harry! An easy way to make a new character feel instantaneously familiar. (© Activision, 1982.)

material but to use history as a starting point to build a familiar and fun gaming world.

In the mobile space, another modern example that was able to masterfully capitalize on popular events and trends was *Campaign Clicker* (Barnard, 2016), which focused on the highly popular and divisive US presidential elections of 2016 by putting players in charge of the campaigns of either candidate, integrating their original twitter feeds into the game itself.

8.2.3 Straightforward Goals

Not only do the settings need to feel familiar, but it should also be obvious from the first moments of gameplay what the players are actually trying to achieve. It is not by chance that many very successful games, both old and new, manage to explain their goal by showing it without the need for further instructions. Take, once again, the classic *Donkey Kong* (Miyamoto S, 1981): it is clear, even to the most distracted of players, that their character starting at the bottom of the screen needs to climb up all the scaffolding to reach and save the damsel in distress. Infinite runners such as *Temple Run* (Imangi, 2011), besides relying on an "Indiana Jones" type of character like *Pitfall* did decades earlier, make it obvious the player has to keep running and grabbing as may coins as possible by lying a string of them in front of the character while also showing a mob of angry creatures chasing after the character. Also, non-action-oriented games need to take this aspect into account whenever possible, puzzle games in particular. Word games such as *Alpha Bear* (SpryFox, 2015), for example, accomplish this very well not only by clearly laying down the letters on the game board but also by making them look like gummy buttons that are just waiting to be clicked and interacted with to make up the required words. Players know what to do and how they should be doing it without the need to be explicitly told so.

No matter the genre and topic of the game, players must have obvious visual cues to direct them to what they are trying to achieve!

8.2.4 Relying on an Emotional Hook

The last piece of the puzzle to effectively engage players from the very beginning is to offer a strong emotional hook able to grab anyone's attention. The importance of building an engaging experience based on a set of basic emotions is well known, see, for example Dillon (2010), but a core, specific emotion should be stressed above all others to define the experience from the very beginning, hence setting a predominant mood for the entire game. This can be achieved by following a multitude of techniques dependent on the specific emotion desired. Common and highly effective emotional hooks that can be used to build an engaging experience are fear, curiosity, competition, empowerment/greed and the desire of protecting the helpless. Let us briefly discuss a few examples for each of these.

To build a sense of fear, it is possible to set the game in any dark, isolated environment where it is easy to imagine hostile creatures lurking around, waiting for a careless player to step into their trap. Woods worked beautifully yesterday, like in *Forbidden Forest* (Norman, 1983), as well as today in *Slender: The Eight Pages* (Hadley, 2012). Another strategy could be removing vision altogether in favor for an echo-location system like in *Stifled* (Gattai, 2017) where the ability to perceive our surroundings is also going to expose us to the monsters. Essentially, the removal of information, which players need to extrapolate and guess by themselves to proceed in the game, can work very well for creating suspense. On the other hand, if it is knowledge that is missing, instead of sensory inputs, this can help in building a mounting sense of curiosity. This is typical of adventure games, since the days of *Zork* (Infocom, 1977) and its isolated white house in an open field or *Myst* (Miller & Miller, 1993) with its enigmatic and deserted island, quietly waiting for players to unravel its mysteries. A common trope used in countless modern action and RPG games as well.

Competition is another very powerful hook that can work in a multitude of ways. Not only head-to-head battles can make for an exhilarating experience, from the straightforward one-on-one shooting in the Atari VCS launch title *Combat* (Decuir, Mayer & Kaplan, 1977) or the more nuanced confrontations of *Spy vs. Spy* (FirstStarSoftware, 1984) to the modern "battle royale" approach, but even indirect forms of competition can be highly effective. Players were more than willing to struggle for long hours with an objectively difficult control scheme in *Asteroids* (Rains, Logg & Walsh, 1979) to beat their friends and gain bragging rights by showing their three-letter acronym on the game's leaderboard for all arcade goers to see. Also mixing co-op (e.g. having a common goal) and competitive elements (e.g. limited resources or power-ups) can help to originate very interesting gameplay moments, where players have to trust each other and then hope their partner won't suddenly cheat on the agreed co-operation, in ways not dissimilar to common dilemmas reminiscent of academic game theory. *Chip and Dale Rescue Rangers 2* (Fujiwara, 1993) remains a great example until this very day.

Empowering players is another common technique able to arouse strong emotions. Making players feel they are an almighty entity, like in *Populous* (Molyneux & Edgar, 1989) or a powerful mayor, like in *SimCity* (Wright, 1989), who is building a new world, is an excellent starting point, as it is assigning the role of a trader or tycoon who is on his/her way of becoming the richest person in the land. No matter how "virtual" and useless an in-game currency is, players will always love the illusion of become richer.

Last, but clearly not least, the easiest and most overused approach of all: i.e. relying on our instinctive impulse of protecting someone in need. Telling players they are the last remaining hope to save a damsel in distress, never mind if she is kidnapped over and over again, a farrow of piglets threatened by bad wolves (Fujiwara, 1982), the universe or anything in between is, generally speaking, a good starting point to capture someone's attention and long-lasting commitment.

8.2.5 Teaching, Challenging and Rewarding Players

Having captured a player's attention is absolutely necessary but, unfortunately, it is not enough. Such attention must be continuously renewed, ideally by keeping players within the "flow" zone discussed earlier. To achieve this, players should constantly be given suitable opportunities to improve their skills, be introduced to new challenge and rewarded accordingly from the very beginning.

For a beautiful example of how a game can teach players, i.e. introduce them to the most basic game mechanics, challenge and reward them all within the first few seconds of gameplay, look no forward than the original *Super Mario Bros.* (Miyamoto S., 1985) (Figure 8.4).

Here the game starts with the player in the lower left corner of the screen. There is nothing happening yet, and the player is free to start experimenting with the control scheme (i.e. moving around and jumping). As Mario moves toward the right, he will first meet a block with a question mark: beginning players will try to jump on it and hit it from various directions, ultimately finding out how to unlock its secret. A lonely enemy will then show up. The first real challenge in the game. Again, beginners may fail here at first, but the game has just begun so restarting right away won't make players lose any progress. Once the first enemy has been defeated, players will likely keep practicing their newly acquired jumping skills and hit the next question mark blocks. A mushroom will magically appear but, at this stage, the player does not know yet whether that is another enemy or a power up. The trajectory of the mushroom is designed to make

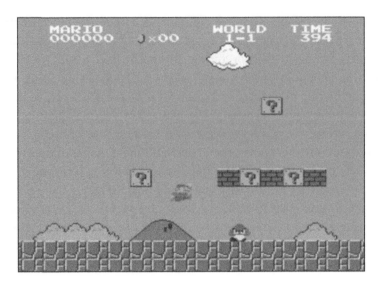

FIGURE 8.4 The beginning of the first level of *Super Mario Bros.* is a masterpiece in level design, showing how to teach, challenge and reward players from the very beginning. (© Nintendo, 1985.)

it difficult to avoid, so beginners will likely collide with it even if they are trying to jump over it (they may be stuck under the blocks) and realize that was a power up and a reward for their jumping efforts!

Within a few seconds of gameplay, the game already managed to teach all the fundamentals, how to defeat enemies, discover secrets and even offered a big reward that made Mario more powerful. Most importantly, it did so without having to explicitly tell players how to do anything: every learning opportunity was naturally integrated in the level itself! Players are now hooked and fully focused on the game, even beginners were likely in the "zone" despite being still close to the origins of the axes in Figure 8.2.

8.2.6 Mixing Genres

As complexity in games increases, it is more and more common to see genres blurring and mixing into each other. This can give birth to original masterpieces or to a disorderly mash-up of ideas. When does it feel one way or the other?

One of the first games that successfully managed to merge different genres and offer an overall cinematic experience was *Impossible Mission* (Caswell, 1984). Besides feeling very familiar to players thanks to obvious 007 references, Caswell's 8-bit masterpiece perfectly integrated a stealth based platforming action with visual and audio puzzles that enriched the gameplay and offered a welcome change of pace when needed. All these, together with state-of-the-art graphics and sound effects, built up an experience that passed the test of time.

For the genre-mixing approach to work, though, it is of fundamental importance to have a strong game design and/or narrative able to integrate each component tightly. The different types of gameplay must support and complement each other by building on the respective strengths. Award winning indie game *Undertale* (Fox, 2015) is great example where traditional RPG mechanics were surprisingly matched with elements from old school shoot 'em ups and rhythm games to form a very innovative way to solve battle encounters.

Games like *Ni No Kuni 2* (Level5, 2018) use a well-written story to bring and tie together in a cohesive unit a set of mini games, as discussed in Reeve (2019) and, indeed, story driven games are a perfect canvas for experimenting with different genres. Titles like *Banner Saga* (Stoic, 2014) tell a compelling story by following a visual novel approach and then successfully switching to strategic turn-based battles to progress it. Every battle integrates with the overall story arc and helps in building a stronger connection between players and each hero in the game. Other titles tried a similar approach but were not as successful. For example, *This is the Police* (Weappy, 2016) tried to support a mature story, told, once again, by following a visual novel approach, with gameplay typical of time/resource management games where the player has to manage all the officers in the department and assign them to suitable cases. Despite the obvious qualities of the game, the result got mixed reviews, as summarized in the corresponding Wikipedia article (Wikipedia, 2020). Several reviewers, in fact, found the latter missions repetitive and the team management aspects unable to effectively integrate with the personal story of the police chief (i.e. the player) being told in the visual novel section of the game.

8.2.7 Understanding Technical and Experiential Limitations

Smart design choices can effectively turn constraints into strengths: in his seminal *Football Manager* game on the ZX Spectrum (Toms, 1982), Kevin Toms took advantage of the computer's sluggish speed (the original game was even written in Basic!) to build up emotional tension as match results were slowly printed out line by line. Today, though, learning how to overcome a system's limitations to optimize and finetune a game may not seem that relevant anymore, given that every single device we use is incredibly more powerful than any 8-bit system the industry used in its early days. By relaying on hardware's raw power, game designers may easily fall into a false sense of security and get the impression that they can finally do whatever they want, without worrying about anything. Nonetheless, players' expectations also keep rising alongside computational power and, if developers are not careful, performance issues can still be found, especially on mobile or handheld devices. In the end, it does not really matter how powerful a platform is: an in-depth understanding of each specific target is always needed to achieve the best possible results. In his 2009 GDC keynote "Making the Impossible Possible,"* Hideo Kojima remarked how he and his team managed to shape the *Metal Gear* game designs to overcome the apparent insurmountable hardware limitations imposed first by the MSX computers and then by the PlayStation and still develop experiences that could match fans expectations (Alexander, 2009). It is important to note, though, that today, with new and emerging platforms like virtual reality (VR), not all problems may necessarily be related to performance but may be even more subtle and experiential in nature. When it comes to games for VR, in fact, we are still learning as we go: developers can identify best practices only thanks to direct experience, via successes and failures. For example, many games are still struggling with annoying side effects such as motion sickness but, even in the unlucky case we cannot find a way to avoid such problems, it does not mean we should give up on the idea of designing an engaging game. The puzzle game *Statik* (Tarsier, 2017) manages to brilliantly avoid such issues by having the player tied to a chair and only able to manipulate the required puzzle elements via his or her hands, which are stuck in a box. It may sound very weird, but the setup will feel perfectly natural once the player's hands are "glued" to the controller.

8.3 CONCLUSION

Hopefully, the examples discussed in this chapter can make us appreciate how old games, despite appearing so distant in time, can still hold valuable design lessons and may actually be quite close, under certain perspectives, to modern games. Students and professionals alike, especially in the fields of casual and mobile games, can still find plenty of inspiration by

---

* The actual video can be watched here: https://www.youtube.com/watch?v=7Pq1Jyr6ffU

analyzing how earlier developers quickly engaged players despite having very little technical means at their disposal.

REFERENCES

Alexander, L. (2009). *GDC: How Kojima Defied the 'Impossible' Throughout Metal Gear's History*. Retrieved from Gamasutra.com: https://www.gamasutra .com/view/news/113883/GDC_How:Kojima_Defied_The_Impossible _Throughout_Metal_Gears_History.php [accessed March 26, 2019].

Atari Flashback Consoles. (2011). AT Games.

Barnard, J. (2016). *Campaign Clicker*. Springloaded Software.

Burroughs, E. R. (1912). *Tarzan of the Apes*. The All-Story.

The C64 Mini. (2018). Retro Games Ltd.

Caswell, D. (1984). *Impossible Mission*. Epyx.

Chen, J. (2007). Flow in games (and everything else). *Communications of the ACM*, 50(4), 31–34.

Crane, D. (1982). *Pifall!* Activision.

Csíkszentmihályi, M. (1975). *Beyond Boredom and Anxiety*. San Francisco, CA: Jossey-Bass Publishers.

Csíkszentmihályi, M. (1990). *Flow: The Psychology of Optimal Experience*. New York, NY: Harper & Row.

Decuir, J., Mayer, S., & Kaplan, L. (1977). *Combat*. Atari.

Dillon, R. (2010). *On the Way to Fun: An Emotion-Based Approach to Successful Game Design*. Natick, MA: A K Peters.

Dillon, R. (2011). *The Golden Age of Video Games*. Boca Raton: CRC Press.

Doom VFR. (2018). Bethesda.

FirstStarSoftware. (1984). *Spy vs Spy*. Beyond Software.

Flashback Classics, 2 Volumes. (2016). Atari.

Fox, T. (2015). *Undertale*. Toby Fox.

Fujiwara, T. (1982). *Pooyan*. Konami.

Fujiwara, T. (1993). *Chip 'n Dale Rescue Rangers 2*. Capcom.

Gattai. (2017). *Stifled*. Gattai Games.

GDC Vault. (2017). Classic game postmortem. *GDC Vault*. Available at https:// www.gdcvault.com/play/1024294/Classic-Game-Postmortem-Sid-Meier.

Hadley, M. (2012). *Slender: The Eight Pages*. Parsec Productions.

Herman, L. (2016). *Phoenix: The Rise and Fall of Video Games*. 4th ed. Springfield, NJ: Rolenta Press.

Housemarque. (2010). *Dead Nation*. Sony Computer Entertainment.

Imangi. (2011). *Temple Run*. Imangi Studios.

Infocom. (1977). *Zork*. Infocom.

Iwatani, T. (1980). *PacMan*. Namco.

Jarvis, E. (1982). *Robotron: 2084*. Williams Electronics.

Level5. (2018). *Ni No Kuni 2: Revenant Kingdom*. Bandai Namco.

Loguidice, B., & Barton, M. (2012). *Vintage Games*. Waltham, MA: Focal Press.

McAllister, G. (2011). *A Guide To iOS Twin Stick Shooter Usability*. Retrieved March 30, 2019, from Gamasutra.com: http://www.gamasutra.com/view /feature/134693/a_guide_to_ios_twin_stick_shooter_.php

Meier, S., & Shelley, B. (1991). *Sid Meier's Civilization*. MicroProse.

Miller, R., & Miller, R. (1993). *Myst*. Broderbund.

Minter, J. (1982). *Gridrunner*. Llamasoft.

Miyamoto, S. (1981). *Donkey Kong*. Nintendo.

Miyamoto, S. (1985). *Super Mario Bros*. Nintendo.

Molyneux, P., & Edgar, L. (1989). *Populous*. Electronic Arts.

Mott, T. (2010). *1001 Games You Must Play Before You Die*. New York, NY: Universe Publishing.

MountainSheep. (2009). *Minigore*. Chillingo.

NES Classic Edition. (2016). Nintendo.

Nguyen, D. (2013). *Flappy Bird*. dotGear.

Norman, P. (1983). *Forbidden Forest*. Cosmi Corporation.

PlayStation Classic. (2018). Sony.

Rains, L., Logg, E., & Walsh, D. (1979). *Asteroids*. Atari.

Reeve, J. (2019). *Overcoming Genre*. Retrieved January 15, 2019, from Gamasutra. com: http://www.gamasutra.com/blogs/JustinReeve/20190115/334347 /Overcoming_Genre.php

Rockstar, S. (2018). *Red Dead Redemption 2*. Rockstar Games.

SEGA Genesis Classics. (2018). SEGA.

Spieldberg, S. (Director). (1981). *Raiders of the Lost Ark* [Motion Picture].

SpryFox. (2015). *Alpha Bear*. SpryFox.

Stoic. (2014). *Banner Saga*. Versus Evil.

Tarsier. (2017). *Statik*. Tarsier Studios.

Theurer, D. (1981). *Tempest*. Atari.

Toms, K. (1982). *Football Manager*. Addictive Games.

Weappy. (2016). *This is the Police*. THQ Nordic.

Weiss, B. (2018). *The SNES Omnibus: The Super Nintendo and Its Games, 2 Volumes*. Atglen, PA: Schiffer.

Wikipedia. (2020). *This is the Police*. Last modified May 14, 2020. Available at https://en.wikipedia.org/wiki/This_Is_the_Police.

Wright, W. (1989). *SimCity*. Electronic Arts.

CHAPTER 9

Architectural Spaces and Level Design in Modern Games

Christopher W. Totten

CONTENTS

9.1	Introduction	142
9.2	Theories of Game Analysis	143
	9.2.1 Single Work Theory	144
	9.2.2 Collected Work Theory	146
	9.2.3 Levels as Unique Works of Game Design	149
9.3	Design Thinking for Games	150
	9.3.1 Empathy and Pre-Design	150
	9.3.2 Architectural Design Thinking as Research for Game and Level Design	152
	9.3.2.1 Design Thinking for Analysis Criteria	152
	9.3.2.2 Design Thinking for Planning Game Design and Art Goals	153
	9.3.2.3 Design Thinking Applied to Non-Architectural Works	154
	9.3.3 Level Design as an Architectural Process	157
9.4	Summary	159
	References	159

9.1 INTRODUCTION

An emerging area of game analysis is that which compares interactive games to works of architecture and urban design. As early as 2002, game designers such as Ernest Adams found comparisons between games and architectural space. In Adams' article for *Gamasutra*, "Designer's Notebook: The Role of Architecture in Videogames," he connects the architectural spaces of games with direct constraints on gameplay, such as providing obstacles or managing exploration, and indirect constraints, things like building atmosphere and storytelling through architectural allusions.[1] In 2007, *Space, Time, Play* offered an overview of contemporary intersections between these fields. The explorations in this text included games where players interacted with environments in novel ways, technologies which added a digital layer to our real, architectural world, and games which used those technologies to create new interactions.[2] In 2008, Michael Nitsche's book *Video Game Spaces: Image, Play, and Structure in 3D Worlds* addressed game worlds and how players perceive them via the structures of screens and input methods. Written for games researchers, this book offers a tantalizing view of how spatial analysis might be used to understand the practical elements of how players interact with the spaces inside games. Game studies scholar Bobby Schweizer does much of the same in studying the urban design of game cities: with promising explorations of how gameplay affects and is affected by players' perceptions of game cities.[3]

In the latter years of the 2000s, a slew of texts appeared written by game industry veterans on *level design*, the organizing of environmental geometry and interactive mechanisms within a game such that the resulting space creates satisfying interactions. While books on the topic had existed before this time, most emphasized the tools used for building levels rather than level design processes or spatial aesthetics. Unsurprisingly, level design was seen as notoriously difficult to write about. Beyond the perceived unavoidability of the tools, Ernest Adams and Andrew Rollings argued that the definition of what made a "good" level changes dramatically based on the needs of individual games.[4]

Rudolf Kremers' book, *Level Design: Concept, Theory, and Practice*, was among the first to challenge this perception. It provides a groundwork for studies of level design based on abstract gameplay factors that can be applied to any genre, such as interactivity, pace, worldbuilding, and sensory perception.[5] While not specifically a work about level design, Anna Anthropy and Naomi Clark's book *Game Design Vocabulary* offers more useful models for understanding how game levels create interesting game-play.[6] Designer and scholar Robert Yang has extensive work on level design and theorized its connections with architectural design. His academic work includes meditations on connections between game and architectural spaces and his industry scholarship is often featured in the yearly Level Design Workshop at the Game Developers Conference (GDC).[7,8]

By 2011, the connections between architecture, game design, and level design were already of great interest in both academic and industry contexts. Having a background in architecture and having done much of my graduate work on the intersections between architecture and games,[9] I started writing about these connections with direct allusions to architectural design theory[10] while also acting as a level designer and artist for several independent games. In 2014, I published a book compiling my experiences and work with level design and architecture, *An Architectural Approach to Level Design*, a second edition of which was published in 2019.[11] Beyond the world of book publishing, level design studies have expanded to include works in the gaming press[12] and popular gaming YouTube accounts,[13] including everything from studies of methods to theory.

While architecture itself is a useful lens for understanding games and the levels within them, the recent emergence of architectural game design theory and level design theory as areas of study may also point to evolving attitudes about how games are viewed. These attitudes are influenced by fan communities which see not only levels as distinct works from the games they inhabit, but also the artwork, music, sound effects, and other multimedia building blocks of games. This chapter will address attitudes towards understanding games as both singular and collected works and how these mindsets lead scholars to integrate knowledge from fields like architecture into their game analyses. It will also address how processes from architecture such as "design thinking" and "pre-design analysis" can be used by game designers to draw inspirations from works outside of games and align their work with the wider art and media landscape.

9.2 THEORIES OF GAME ANALYSIS

For those who attend the gamut of events in the game industry—fan conventions, industry gatherings, and academic conferences—these events hardly seem as though they center on the same medium. At events like the yearly Music and Gaming Festival (MAGFest) or the Penny Arcade Expo (PAX), fans revel in obscure gaming lore, listen to music from famous games, and sell artworks of beloved characters. Industry events are more professionally focused, but they recognize the distinct disciplines that come together to create the media productions that we call games. Conferences such as the GDC or the East Coast Games Conference (ECGC) offer discipline-specific speaker tracks in areas like visual art, programming, sound design, business, production, and so on. Games academia feels dissonant in this way, where games are rarely classified according to anything beyond the ways in which players interact with them. On one hand, this is to highlight the unique aspects of the medium: that a player moves physical components according to rules or uses an input device to affect the game's state. On the other hand, the effect that game artwork, sound effects, music, physics simulations, and so on have on the player's experience of a game are left under-analyzed.

Both of these mindsets have a place in our understanding of games. In many ways, they must both be understood if we are to see how an element of games, such as levels, might be aligned with the work of disciplines outside of games, such as architecture. In this section, we will explore these different mindsets to discover ways in which they shape our ability to place games among the landscape of other media works.

9.2.1 Single Work Theory

In academic contexts, games are typically discussed as whole objects rather than as collections of *assets*, or individual pieces of art or music that are loaded into the game during gameplay, that combine to create interactive experiences. Much of this mindset stems from social science understandings of games, influenced by the works of historian Johan Huizinga,[14] sociologist Roger Caillois,[15] and others who explored the place of play and games in human society during the mid-twentieth century. In these texts and those that have come since, such as James Paul Gee's *What Video Games Have to Teach Us About Learning and Literacy*,[16] games are treated as singular objects that might be applied to transform the player in some way. All of Gee's 12 basic learning principles, for example, orbit around games' interactivity regardless of other elements that might influence a learner such as art or level design.[17]

The influence of these models continues even in works written by game designers that address games as media productions. In their "G/P/S model" of classification for Serious Games, games developed for non-entertainment purposes, Damien Djaouti, Julian Alvarez, and Jean-Pierre Jessel focus on games' "game-related" and "serious-related" characteristics, avoiding elements of the games' productions.[18] Likewise, John Sharp in his book *Works of Game* organizes games with contemporary art-related expressive purposes into *Game Art, Artgames,* and *Artists' Games,* each of which consider games by their relationship with play and interactivity.[19] Some of Sharp's classifications, such as *Game Art,* which uses the tools and visual language of games to make non-interactive media art works, and *Artists' Games,* which subvert the elements of games to make expressive artworks, come closer to acknowledging the assets within games, though the focus of these remains games as singular objects. Even the useful MDA Framework for game analysis classifies "aesthetics," classically defined as the principles and appreciation of beauty as understood by the senses, according to positive effects of interactivity.[20] We will define this focus on games as singular works whose defining characteristic is their interactivity as the *singular work theory* of games criticism.

As we saw with Gee, this is a useful model when considering games as a medium with transformational potential, as with educational, expressive, or "serious" games. It is also employed by museums when exhibiting games: treating them as individual *objects d'art* curated according to a theme as in the yearly Smithsonian American Art Museum (SAAM) Arcade. Singular work game production celebrates the role of individual designers or directors in a game's creation, greatly resembling filmic *auteur theory.*[21] While this applies to many older commercial games from the beginning of the medium (Atari 2600 and early PC game eras of the 1970s and 1980s[22,23]) it presents issues in more modern contexts where game production is a collaborative effort between potentially hundreds of professionals of varied, but equally important, disciplines.

In the context of comparing games to disciplines outside of games, such as art and architecture, single work theory offers an easily understood method for engaging with audiences not deeply familiar with the games medium. In the typical way it is employed, as with the MDA Framework, single work theory in games focuses on the experience created by the game as understood by the game's players. In this way, one might find a useful analogy between the summative effect of playing a game and the holistic experience of being inside a spiritual space such as a church or mosque. An observer in this mindset is evaluating the experience of being inside such a space, and not examining individual three-dimensional sculptures, lighting, or the imagery on surfaces. Single work theory is also at its best when evaluating the expressive goals of games, aligning it with the goals of contemporary art made to communicate abstract ideas. For games such as Anna Anthropy's *Dys4ia*,[24] Nina Freeman's *Cibele*,[25] or Jason Rohrer's *Passage*,[26] single work theory is useful for shifting focus from technical aspects of a game to their personal or expressive goals.

9.2.2 Collected Work Theory

A video game *asset* can be many things. On one hand, they might be several pixel-wide icons integrated into a larger graphical user interface (GUI)—not something that many would notice. On the other, a sweeping piece of orchestral music might also exist in a game's files as an asset. Let us assume that this piece becomes a fan favorite part of the game: maybe it plays during the climactic battle with the game's villain or a moving story moment. Such an asset could find relevance well beyond the game itself: it could be downloaded and listened to by fans of the game, sold as part of a soundtrack album (on vinyl special edition!), or covered by game rock or jazz bands at an event like MAGFest.

Music is just one aspect of this phenomenon: as game enthusiasts regularly pour their enthusiasm and creativity into adapting artwork, design elements, characters, narrative events, and other portions of games into new works. Commercial game studios participate in this phenomenon when they release concept art books and game soundtracks from their most popular games. These products make artists, composers, and designers highly visible to audiences through individual credits, liner notes, and interviews. These elements may even provide unique selling points for games: Studio MDHR's *Cuphead*[27] features visual art made to resemble 1930s American cartoons made with real-world art supplies—ink pens and watercolor. An older but still illustrative example are the competing versions of games based on Disney's *Aladdin* film for the Super Nintendo and Sega Genesis game consoles.[28,29] Despite the popular perception that it had inferior gameplay, the Sega Genesis version had animated characters designed by Disney's artists, giving it a greater visual impact that was even complimented by the director of the Super Nintendo game, Shinji Mikami.[30]

That these elements of games can be enjoyed as separate works or understood as unique selling points by the games' audiences, points to an understanding, even an informal one, of assets as distinct works within a game. We can call this understanding a *collected work theory* of games criticism, as it describes how games are collections of distinct artworks that are juxtaposed (through game engine software and scripting) to create interactive experiences. While uncommon in the world of academic game studies, some analyses inch close to it by acknowledging the craft of how game designers compose the experiences they make, even when treating the game as individual works. In Roberto Dillon's reaction to the MDA Framework, the AGE framework, standing for "actions," "game-play," and "experience,"[31] he uses "experience" to describe how the act of playing games makes players feel a variety of emotions. In focusing on "experience" rather than the vaguer "aesthetics," he provides a metric for addressing the elements of fine art that evoke human emotion such as a work's composition or color palette. In a later article describing a study where observers compared the emotions evoked by games and works of art, participants could describe their engagement with works in terms of both aspects that would apply to a work in general ("immersion"), but which could also apply to individual game elements ("color appreciation").[32]

At first glance, collected work theory is friendlier to game enthusiasts or industry professionals, since they more closely align with how these groups describe games, than audiences unfamiliar with games. However, audio-visual elements games have historically acted as ambassadors for the games medium when enjoyed separately from the games themselves. Concerts of game music from *Final Fantasy* or the *Legend of Zelda* series, for example, are now common at concert halls and have made positive impressions with classical music enthusiasts.[33] Collected work theory is also present in some museum exhibitions of video games. This mindset is very apparent in how design museums such as the Victoria and Albert (V&A) Museum in London show works: their 2018 exhibit *Videogames: Design/Play/Disrupt* showed not only games but also the planning documents, designers' notebooks, office bulletin boards, and assets that went into creating them. The Akron Art Museum in Akron, Ohio, USA, likewise included works that could be said to acknowledge collected work theory in their exhibition *Open World: Video Games & Contemporary Art*. The works *Dataset Diptych 01* and *Dataset Diptych 06* by artist Alan Butler show images of the realistic homeless non-player characters from *Grand Theft Auto V*. The purpose of the work is to highlight the problem of homelessness by showcasing how creating a believable city in a video game requires creating a believable homeless population. The images are accompanied by works showing all of the texture image files, numbering in the dozens, used to create the characters; shown to expose the effort that goes into their creation. While the assets are shown to make a social point according to the affordances of contemporary art, the extraction of game assets shows the potential of collected work understandings of games.

Collected work theory readily provides avenues for studying games in the context of other art and media forms as one would analyze the visual art, music, and other elements of games according to discipline-specific criteria from those fields. In the case of a game like *Cuphead*, the game's animations and visual assets must be evaluated against the principles of animation—anticipation, appeal, timing, and so forth—as laid out by animators Frank Thomas and Ollie Johnson.[34] Collected work theory also makes it easier to find aesthetic precedents for games beyond the games medium itself. The scores of several *Dragon Quest* games, for example, are better appreciated when one considers that among composer Koichi Sugiyama's key influences is Johan Sebastian Bach.[35]

As with any artwork, the collected works within games can be said to singularly evoke emotional responses through color theory, the key of the music, or other aspects of their creation. This is where critics must be cautious with collected work theory and using it to analyze games according to the affordances of other forms of art. Games' interactivity may change how these assets are encountered or juxtaposed, thereby changing their meaning. In *Lissitzky's Revenge* (Figure 9.1a–c), a game based on Bolshevik designer *El Lissitzky*'s 1920 poster *Beat the Whites with the Red Wedge*, players can move the elements of the original poster—a red triangle, white

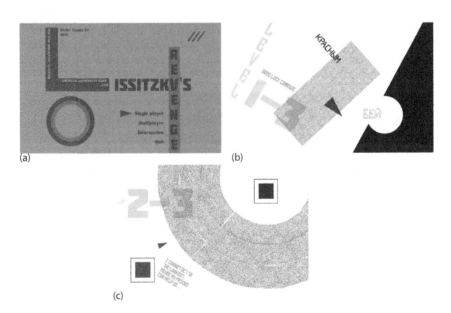

FIGURE 9.1 A screenshot of *Lissitzky's Revenge*, based on a similar artwork by designer El Lissitzky.

circle, and black and gray squares—around the screen. This creates a game where a screenshot may be taken at any time to create a new Constructivist artwork, though not with the poster's original propagandist intent unless its composition is recreated exactly by the player.[36]

9.2.3 Levels as Unique Works of Game Design

The individual levels of video games fall into an unclear area: are they individual assets or holistic works of game design? Should we appreciate them through single work theory or collected work theory? Levels are not singular assets but often a collections of assets, geometry, and *colliders*—invisible masses that perform functions within a game engine's physics system such as create barriers—arranged in such a way that they create interesting gameplay situations and emotional responses.[37] In this way, they are like games, and in fact, many industry observers see level design as a subfield of game design.[38]

Within the file systems of many game engines such as Unity though, levels are also treated as individual *scene* files which can be called and managed like an individual asset. Through efforts such as the GDC Level Design Workshop, World of Level Design,[39] the Level Design Lobby Podcast,[40] and others, practicing level designers are trying to establish the field as a related, but distinct, field from game design itself with its own set of critical discourse and principles. This would seem to point to their appreciation as separate entities from the games with which they are associated.

This is where architecture can be a useful lens for understanding game levels. As with the single work theory of games criticism, a level might be understood as a singular work with a distinct effect as with the metaphor of a church used previously. Like such a church, let us say a thirteenth-century French gothic church, its individual elements can also be appreciated for the way that they contribute to the summative effect. The church's sense of *lux nova*, meant to create an ethereal feeling as though the occupant was encountering God, can be understood through appreciation of the church's rose windows that filter external light through colored glass to create this unique effect. These windows are themselves both individual assets within the church's structural system and contributors to the holistic experience of being inside the structure.

Levels can be seen as merely emblematic of the games of which they are an element, and indeed their design can be a useful metric for evaluating the quality of a whole game design. However, seeing them as unique works within games or even as collected works themselves which use assets to create specific effects allows us to tap into a wealth of knowledge from disciplines outside of games, notably architecture. As a field of design itself, architecture may also have things to teach practicing game designers about approaching their work as products of design. In the next section, we will explore an architectural approach to viewing design problems, and how it might be used to incorporate the knowledge of disciplines outside of games into game works.

9.3 DESIGN THINKING FOR GAMES

While I was in architecture school, my instructor Matthew Geiss described his favorite thing about being an architect: "If I'm doing, for example, a hospital project, I get to learn about doctors and what they do during their day, and how to make it easier."[41] This mindset was similar to what our other professors would describe as *design thinking*, where disparate bodies of knowledge are synthesized by a designer into a product or solution. In the years since, design thinking has as a term become popularized by the Stanford Design School (D.School) and the IDEO Design Consulting Company.[42] The core of their methodology is a toolkit meant to walk students through a process of thinking where they (1) discover facts about a design problem or question (empathy), (2) find the problem (define), (3) conceptualize potential solutions (ideate), (4) build one of the potential solutions (prototype), and (5) evaluate efficacy (test).[43]

Critics of the process have pointed out that it is not entirely a new idea. As Stanford instructor Jonathan Kleiman has admitted, "The ideas, the methodology—they're not that novel. What's radical about design thinking is the way that it's been packaged into something really attractive and accessible."[44] Indeed, the method as presented greatly resemble research-heavy early stages—client meetings, site analysis, definition of the included features that a design must have, and so on—that architects call "pre-design,"[45] followed by an iterative design process that greatly resembles the scrum methodology.[46] Whether a reader is swayed by the buzzwords and branding, a 2018 study found that the method succeeds in improving engagement when used in classroom settings and leads students to become better at identifying design problems, spend more time researching problems, and experimenting with varied solutions.[47]

9.3.1 Empathy and Pre-Design

Digging into Stanford's design thinking literature reveals that it resembles a more formalized version of the architect's design thinking as extolled by my own instructors. Listed among the "8 core abilities" of design thinking are "learning from others," "synthesizing information," and "experimenting rapidly."[48] These greatly resemble the discourse on architectural design thought mentioned early in this section and iterative prototyping of the scrum methodology practiced by many game studios.

Matthew Geiss's notion of learning about a client's daily activities and making decisions based on making a space most usable by them is similar to the "game designer as advocate for the player" mindset championed by game designer Tracy Fullerton.[49] Even interactivity concepts like the *core mechanic*, the "essential play activity players perform again and again in a game,"[50] stem from the player's use of the game. Schell Games designer Sabrina Haskel Culyba, in her book *The Transformational Framework*, places "audience & context," "player transformations," and "barriers for player learning," among the first things designers of educational games must identify in their work.[51]

Regardless of other reasons that a game project is started or its goals— a novel new mechanic, interesting technology, an epic story, real-world transformation, or making money—player experience is (or should be) a central consideration if the game is to create a satisfying experience (Figure 9.2). This client/player-centric approach is key to design thinking and can be utilized to set aesthetic goals for many aspects of a game. For example, a core goal of *Lissitzky's Revenge* was to emulate the art style of

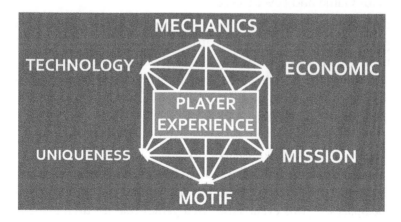

FIGURE 9.2 A graph showing different points from which a designer's initial idea for a game could occur. Lines on the graph interconnect with any other point, showing how most games share several of these criteria. Though many designers highlight one of the outer criteria, player experience must be central if the game is to be satisfying.

Lissitzky's famous poster, but turning abstract art into an understandable game involved a long process of *playtesting*, having your audience play the game, and responding to feedback.

Looking at the process from a macro-level, empathy-based design criteria is one tool among others to help create meaningful gameplay and can be used in concert with the skills of "synthesizing information" to form a rich research base for a game project. Among his pre-design analysis methods for architects, Yatt defines "program analysis" as identifying the spaces that should exist in a building based on the needs of the client's daily activities.[52] For example, most houses likely need a "living room" space for occupants to gather, a kitchen for food storage and preparation, bedrooms, and bathrooms. An architect might find out that their client also makes pottery, and a studio space for the client's wheel and kiln, identified when the architect researches pottery-making, might become a vital aspect of that house's program. Other parts of pre-design analysis also come into play to influence the eventual design of such a house, including zoning laws, fire codes, geographic and environmental site conditions, and other *constraints* that define what the building can be. The resulting structure will reflect all these requirements: empathetic criteria for the client, responses to design constraints, and aesthetic or style goals.

9.3.2 Architectural Design Thinking as Research for Game and Level Design

Used together, collected work theory and design thinking can help game designers form rich project goals that apply to not only a game's high-level interactivity, but also levels and assets. From an analysis perspective, this gives us the ability to define aesthetics for game assets or sections (such as levels) with influences from fields such as architecture for use in game studies works or exhibitions.

9.3.2.1 Design Thinking for Analysis Criteria

This was done for the 2018 SAAM Arcade at the Smithsonian American Art Museum, which featured games with interesting use of the concept "Game Spaces."[53] This event showcased games that featured game levels that included novel game mechanics or which were particularly responsive to player needs, used the space around the game itself in a unique way, or which inspired a social space or community. Despite using a broad definition of "game space" so to include contemporary "serious game" trends, the level design portion of the event allowed organizers to develop a rich system of aesthetic considerations on which to judge game levels. Included in these criteria were use of architectural forms, shape theory, and color theory (among others) to draw player attention and guide them through spaces. Since the event's organizers had focused on an element of games to highlight instead of games as holistic objects, judging criteria could be based on concepts that influenced those elements. Though not explicitly stated in the submission criteria for games, the criteria on which levels would be judged were guided by architectural spatial usability principles.

Mark Mayer's *Desolus*[54] was such a game that exemplified these criteria: players must travel back and forth between different versions of a space in different "dimensions" to progress. Each dimension had different color schemes which contrasted with one another so that, for example, a portal to a purple-colored dimension would stand out when viewed from the orange-colored dimension. Points of interest in these levels were also placed in such a way as to draw player attention, with level geometry used to form sight lines or frame important areas.

9.3.2.2 Design Thinking for Planning Game Design and Art Goals

Such thinking is vital to games with experimental art styles or those with art history inspirations, such as the aforementioned *Lissitzky's Revenge* and the upcoming *Little Nemo and the Nightmare Fiends*.[55] The latter game is based on the public domain comic *Little Nemo in Slumberland*[56] by comic and animation pioneer Winsor McCay and bases its visual style on McCay's original strip. The early design phases for this game therefore included establishing unique criteria for the different aspects of the project: designers identified the experiential goals of the game through defining game mechanics, artists developed the *pipeline* of software processes that would allow them to recreate McCay's artwork, and so forth. Again, design goals could be established down to the asset level and based on pre-design research: character sprites needed to integrate the "art nouveau line" indicative of McCay's drawing style,[57] traditional animation principles, and the half-tone printing look of newspaper comics (Figure 9.3).

Nemo's level design is also the product of design thinking information synthesis. Visually, the environments must resemble McCay's mastery of drawing neoclassical and *beaux arts*-style architecture exemplified by the buildings of the 1893 Columbian Exposition in Chicago. In level design terms, the game's levels must be responsive to the player avatar's movement capabilities and other gameplay mechanics, but also reference the unique layouts of McCay's comics (Figure 9.4a and Figure 9.4b).

FIGURE 9.3 The character model sheet for Nemo from *Little Nemo and the Nightmare Fiends*. This document was used to plan how the sprite for Nemo, an individual game asset, would look. The final design was a product of extensive research into the *Little Nemo in Slumberland* comic, Winsor McCay's drawing style, and other art and design elements from the late nineteenth and early twentieth century. (Original drawing by Christopher W. Totten.)

9.3.2.3 Design Thinking Applied to Non-Architectural Works

This process does not have to be for visual arts alone or even have explicit connections to architecture. Another game, *La Mancha*,[58] was based on Miguel de Cervantes' novel *Don Quixote*[59] and featured gameplay mechanics and player interactions deeply influenced by the original novel (Figure 9.5).

The novel tells the story of Alonso Quijano, an old man who declares himself a knight named Don Quixote after reading too many books about chivalry. The design for *La Mancha* was begun by analyzing the action within the novel to discover what type of gameplay would best allow players to "become" Don Quixote. Don Quixote and his squire Sancho Panza embark on knightly adventures, interpreting the mundane world around them through the lens of chivalric texts. Therefore, the game became one where players compete at telling stories made up of cards with quotes from books of chivalry.

Design empathy was incredibly important in this project, as much of its potential audience, and indeed many of its playtesters might be unfamiliar with the (992 page) original novel. Great care had to be taken to carefully

FIGURE 9.4A The *Little Nemo in Slumberland* episode from June 7, 1909, where Slumberland rises from beneath the ground, was inspiration for a piece of level design concept art for *Little Nemo and the Nightmare Fiends*. McCay's original comic uses the comic's frames to show Slumberland's rise over the course of several seconds of action. The same mindset was used in the concept art where frames are used to show a potential level where a building rises from the ground while players must avoid being pushed off the screen as the action moves over time and the player characters dodge obstacles. Zoomed out, the concept art comic also showcases an elevation drawing of a neoclassical building, based on the Minnesota Building from the 1893 Columbian Exposition. While this exact composition would be difficult to emulate on most 16:9 ratio screens, designing level action and geometry compositions on these comic layouts became a design goal. (From McCay, W., 1909. *Little Nemo*. Available at: https://www.comicstriplibrary.org/display/548.)

FIGURE 9.4B Continued. (Original drawing by Christopher W. Totten.)

write story prompt cards and the game's chivalry cards so they could be clear to players who had not read the book. This process included defining the roles that each player would adopt in each story prompt or providing explanatory text on cards with specific character or place names. Again, empathy for the needs of players, pre-design, and information synthesis were vital for editing individual game elements (in this case cards) and creating an effective overall game.

FIGURE 9.5 An image of *La Mancha*, a storytelling card game based on *Don Quixote* in which design thinking and player empathy was vital for condensing the 992-page novel into a playable and entertaining game.

9.3.3 Level Design as an Architectural Process

This all returns us to architecture and level design. As we have seen, seeing games not only as holistic objects of art and design, and instead as works made up of a collection of other artworks, allows us to focus analyses at different levels of specificity. If we home in on levels as individual works, regardless of whether they are made of specific level assets, we can form a set of criteria for appreciating them. Design thinking is a process through which this can happen. It allows us to see how works of art and design respond to the needs of users and can be the result of information gathering (pre-design research) and syntheses of information from different disciplines into a coherent work.

Games utilize space and architecture in different ways, but primarily as either an asset as in the case of strategy games,[60] as a space "looked into" as in the world maps of Japanese role-playing games, or as inhabitable space. For architecture and level design, it is "inhabitable space" which is the most important.

Focusing on levels as both individual works and as inhabitable space gives us access to a wealth of knowledge from fields like architecture that form classical disciplines for making and appreciating inhabitable space. Indeed, the day-to-day work of a level designer greatly resembles the work of an architect, down to how their tools—game engines, Computer Aided Drafting (CAD), and Building Information Modeling (BIM) programs— render space on a computer screen. The definition for level design given in *An Architectural Approach to Level Design* is "the thoughtful execution of *gameplay* into *gamespace* for players to dwell in."[61] This definition contrasts others, such as Kremers' statement that "level design is applied game design,"[62] by adding the player to the mix. From here, the level designer can look to the work of architectural theorists who focus on human-centric spatial design theory such as Christopher Alexander,[63] Lyndon and Moore,[64] Jane Jacobs,[65] Grant Hildebrand,[66] and others whose work accounts for human activity and perception.

Under design thinking, the design criteria for a level might include the aforementioned aesthetic goals listed in projects like *Lissitzky's Revenge* or *Little Nemo and the Nightmare Fiends*, but may also include memory limits, point-of-view, how engines handle lighting, and other considerations. The level designer practicing design thinking takes the purpose or core mechanic of a level into account as a way to incorporate player empathy into their design: does the level have a theme? Should the placement of level geometry test the player's mastery of their character's movement capabilities by placing objects at the limits of these capabilities or should the level be easier to navigate? Likewise, this designer looks at how individual assets create a system of communication used to help a player through a level and contribute to an overall atmosphere. As with *Desolus*, aspects of individual assets such as shape, form, color, and others allow designers to make objects contrast one another to draw the eye. Lighting and sound can be further added to enhance the atmosphere of a level: friendly, mysterious, dangerous, and so forth.

Finally, such a designer wants to know if any of their designs actually work the way they anticipate. Tracy Fullerton and other game designers champion the process of *paper prototyping* or reproducing digital game environments on paper as though for a board game to test simple mechanics before spending time making them on a computer.[67] This is like the architect's process of sketching and putting ideas quickly on paper so a client can choose from a bevy of concepts before design proceeds. Next is the process of *grayboxing*, where geometry is built quickly with basic forms (often shown in game engines as gray boxes) to test broad level design ideas. This occurs early in the process after a design has been translated onto a computer and allows the designer to further iterate without committing time and effort into producing visually polished scenes. Such testing is a process of putting games in front of players, quietly observing their play, and listening to their feedback after the test. Through this process, the level is further and further refined until the level's intended goals are realized.

9.4 SUMMARY

Beyond merely studying the way in which architecture and space are represented in games, architecture and spatial design have a lot to show game designers. Level design has historically been a challenging area for designers and critics, but this is because a new approach to game criticism that focuses on games as collected works rather than singular works is necessary. Breaking games into their component parts allows understandings such as architectural studies of game levels to exist and unlocks processes, such as design thinking, that come from outside of games. In this chapter, we have investigated perspectives and mindsets that I hope will aid readers in their own work with game design and analysis.

It should be stated that these are connections that I can make, through my training in design thinking, that come from my particular background in architecture. Now I have a challenge for you, dear reader, to find the areas of your own background and expertise that influence games, game design, game art, sound, music, or other works within games. As a relatively young field, we have not yet exhausted the knowledge that, with the right perspective, could be the next breakthrough in our ability to understand our work.

REFERENCES

1. Adams, Ernest W. (2002). Designer's notebook: The role of architecture in videogames. *Gamasutra*. Accessed from https://www.gamasutra.com /view/feature/131352/designers_notebook_the_role_of_.php (accessed July 26, 2019).
2. *Space Time Play*, (2007) (Eds.) Friedrich Von Borres, Steffen P. Walz, & Matthias Böttger. Basel: Birkhäuser Verlag AG.
3. Schweizer, Bobby. (2013). Understanding videogame cities. *DiGRA '13 - Proceedings of the 2013 DiGRA International Conference: DeFragging Game Studies*.
4. Adams, Ernest W. (2009). *Fundamentals of Game Design*. 2nd ed. New York: New Riders.
5. Kremers, Rudolf. (2009). *Level Design: Concept, Theory, & Practice*. Boca Raton, FL: AK Peters/CRC Press.
6. Anthropy, Anna, & Clark, Naomi. (2014). *Game Design Vocabulary: Exploring the Foundational Principles Behind Good Game Design*. Boston, MA: Addison-Wesley Professional.

7. Yang, Robert. (2014). Forced movement. In Rem Koolhas (Ed.), *Elements of Architecture*. Cologne, Germany: Taschen. 1390–1392.

8. Yang, Robert. (2015). *Level Design in a Day: Level Design Histories and Futures*. GDC.

9. Totten, Christopher W. (2009). Masters thesis: Game design and architecture. *Game Career Guide*. Accessed from https://www.gamecareerguide.com/features/705/masters_thesis_game_design_and_.php (accessed July 26, 2019).

10. Totten, Christopher W. (2011). Designing better levels through human survival instincts. *Gamasutra*. Accessed from http://www.gamasutra.com/view/feature/6411/designing_better_levels_through_.php?print=1 (accessed July 26, 2019).

11. Totten, Christopher W. (2019). *An Architectural Approach to Level Design*. 2nd ed. Boca Raton, FL: CRC Press.

12. Parish, Jeremy. (2017). Discovering the (mostly) lost art of mapping. *Retronauts*. Accessed from https://retronauts.com/article/437/rediscovering-the-mostly-lost-art-of-mapping (accessed July 26, 2019).

13. Brown, Mark. *Donkey Kong Country: Tropical Freeze – Mario's Level Design, Evolved*. YouTube video, 12:33. Posted June 16, 2017. Accessed from https://www.youtube.com/watch?v=JqHcE6B4OP4 (accessed July 26, 2019).

14. Huizinga, Johan. (1955). *Homo Ludens*. Boston, MA: Beacon Press.

15. Caillois, Roger. (1961). *Man, Play, and Games*. Champaign, IL: University of Illinois Press.

16. Gee, James Paul. (2007). *What Video Games Have to Teach Us About Learning and Literacy*. London, England: Palgrave Macmillan.

17. Treanor, Mike, Totten, Christopher W., McCoy, Josh, & Tanner Jackson, G. (2018). Merging education, assessment, and entertainment in math games: A case study of function force. *Proceedings of the 2018 International Academic Conference on Meaningful Play*.

18. Djaouti, D., Alvarez, J., & Jessel, J. (2011). Classifying serious games: The G/P/S model. In Felicia, P. (Ed.), *Handbook of Research on Improving Learning and Motivation Through Educational Games: Multidisciplinary Approaches*. Hershey, PA: IGI Global.

19. Sharp, John. (2015). *Works of Game: On the Aesthetics of Games and Art*. Cambridge, MA: The MIT Press.

20. Hunicke, Robin, LeBlanc, Marc, & Zubek, Robert. (2004). MDA: A formal approach to game design and game research. *Workshop on Challenges in Game AI*, 1–4. doi: 10.1.1.79.4561.

21. Brody, Richard. Andrew Sarris and the "A" word. (2012). *The New Yorker*. Accessed from http://www.newyorker.com/culture/richard-brody/andrew-sarris-and-the-a-word (accessed July 25, 2019).

22. Donovan, Tristan. (2010). *Replay: The History of Video Games*. East Sussex, UK: Yellow Ant.

23. Dillon, Roberto. (2010). *The Golden Age of Video Games. The Golden Age of Video Games*. Boca Raton, FL: A K Peters, pp. 25–39.

24. Anthropy, Anna. (2012). Dys4ia. Indie internet browser game.

25. Freeman, Nina. (2015). *Cibele*. Indie game for PC.

26. Rohrer, Jason. (2007). *Passage*. Indie game for PC.
27. Studio MDHR. (2017). *Cuphead*. Indie game for PC and console.
28. Capcom. (1993). *Disney's Aladdin*. Super Nintendo Game.
29. Disney Software. (1993). *Disney's Aladdin*. Virgin Games (developer) and Sega (publisher). Sega Genesis Game.
30. Mackey, Bob., & Gilbert, Henry. Retronauts episode 226: *Aladdin* games. *Retronauts Podcast. Podcast audio*, June 14, 2019. Accessed from https://retronauts.com/article/1224/retronauts-episode-226-aladdin-games (accessed July 26, 2019).
31. Dillon, Roberto. (2014). Towards the definition of a framework and grammar for game analysis and design. *International Journal of Computer and Information Technology* 3 (2): 188–93.
32. Dillon, Roberto. (2016). Videogames and art: Comparing emotional feedback from digital and classic masterpieces. *IOSR Journal of Humanities and Social Science*, 21(7), 79–85.
33. *Smithsonian American Art Museum Indie Arcade: Coast to Coast 2015/2016 Event Book*. (2016). (Eds.) Christopher W. Totten and Lindsay Grace. Self-published museum event booklet.
34. Thomas, Frank, & Johnson, Ollie. (1981). *The Illusion of Life: Disney Animation*. New York: Abbeville Press.
35. Koichi Sugiyama – Developer credits and biography. Moby Games. Accessed from https://www.mobygames.com/developer/sheet/view/developerId,574954/ (accessed July 25, 2019).
36. *Lissitzky's Revenge*. Pie for Breakfast Studios (Christopher Totten). (2015). Indie abstract art game for browser and PC.
37. Totten, Christopher W. (2019). *An Architectural Approach to Level Design*. 2nd ed. Boca Raton, FL: CRC Press, pp. xxxii–xxxiv, 7–8.
38. Kremers, Rudolf. (2009). *Level Design: Concept, Theory, and Practice*. Boca Raton, FL: AK Peters/CRC Press.
39. Galuzin, Alex. (2008, ongoing). *World of Level Design*. Accessed from https://worldofleveldesign.com/ (accessed July 26, 2019).
40. Pears, Max. *Level Design Lobby Podcast*. Podcast audio, September 16, 2017 (ongoing.)
41. Geiss, Matthew. (2008). *Introduction to Architectural Thesis*. Class lecture. Thesis Research from The Catholic University of America, Washington, DC.
42. Tu, Jui Che, Liu, Li Xia, & Wu, Kuan Yi. (2018). Study on the learning Effectiveness of Stanford design thinking in integrated design education. *Sustainability (Switzerland)*, 10(8): 1–21.
43. Tu, Jui Che, Liu, Li Xia, & Wu, Kuan Yi. (2018). Study on the learning Effectiveness of Stanford design thinking in integrated design education. *Sustainability (Switzerland)*, 10(8), 3.
44. Chao, Grace. (2015). What is design thinking? *The Stanford Daily*. Accessed from https://www.stanforddaily.com/what-is-design-thinking/ (accessed July 26, 2019).
45. Yatt, Barry. (2008). *Parti-Planning: A Guide to Pre-Design Analysis*. Morrisville, NC: Lulu Press.

46. Sims, Chris, & Johnson, Hillary Louise. (2012). *Scrum: A Breathtakingly Brief and Agile Introduction.* Accessed from https://www.agilelearninglabs.com/resources/scrum-introduction/ (accessed July 26, 2019).

47. Tu, Jui Che, Liu, Li Xia, & Wu, Kuan Yi. (2018). Study on the learning effectiveness of Stanford design thinking in integrated design education. *Sustainability (Switzerland),* 10(8), 19.

48. About. (n.d.) *Stanford D.School.* Accessed from https://dschool.stanford.edu/about (accessed July 26, 2019).

49. Fullerton, Tracy. (2018). *Game Design Workshop.* 4th ed. Boca Raton, FL: CRC Press, p. 1.

50. Salen, Katie, & Zimmerman, Eric. (2004). *Rules of Play: Game Design Fundamentals.* Cambridge, MA: MIT Press. p. 316.

51. Culyba, Sabrina Haskell. (2018). *The Transformational Framework.* Pittsburgh, PA: ETC Press.

52. Yatt, Barry. (2008). *Parti-Planning: A Guide to Pre-Design Analysis.* Morrisville, NC: Lulu Press.

53. Totten, Christopher, & SAAM Staff. (2018). *SAAM Arcade: Game Spaces.* Smithsonian American Art Museum. July 22, 2018.

54. *Desolus.* (Still in development). Mark Mayers. Indie game on Steam.

55. *Little Nemo and the Nightmare Fiends.* (2021, in development). Pie for Breakfast Studios and Pxlplz. Indie game for PC and console.

56. McCay, Winsor. (1905). Little Nemo in Slumberland. Newspaper comic strip. *New York Herald.*

57. Canemaker, John. (2018). *Winsor McCay: His Life and Art.* Boca Raton, FL: CRC Press, p. 65.

58. *La Mancha.* (2019). Pie for Breakfast Studios. Storytelling card game.

59. Cervantes, Miguel de. (1605). *Don Quixote.* Translated by Edith Grossman. New York. Ecco Press.

60. McGregor, G. L. (2006). Architecture, space and gameplay in world of warcraft and battle for middle Earth 2. *Proceedings of the 2006 International Conference on Game Research and Development,* pp. 69–76. Accessed from http://dl.acm.org/citation.cfm?id=1234354 (accessed July 27, 2019).

61. Totten, Christopher W. (2019). *An Architectural Approach to Level Design.* 2nd ed. Boca Raton, FL: CRC Press, p. xxxii.

62. Kremers, Rudolf. (2009). *Level Design: Concept, Theory, & Practice.* Boca Raton, FL: AK Peters/CRC Press, p. 3.

63. Alexander, Christopher. (1979). *The Timeless Way of Building.* Oxford University Press.

64. Lyndon, Donlyn, & Moore, Charles W. (1994). *Chambers for a Memory Palace.* Cambridge, MA: MIT Press.

65. Jacobs, Jane. (1961). *The Death and Life of Great American Cities.* New York: Random House.

66. Hildebrand, Grant. (1999). *Origins of Architectural Pleasure.* Berkeley, CA: University of California Press.

67. Fullerton, Tracy. (2018). *Game Design Workshop.* 4th ed. Boca Raton, FL: CRC Press.

CHAPTER 10

Encouraging and Rewarding Repeat Play of Storygames

Alex Mitchell

CONTENTS

10.1 Introduction: What is Replaying?   163
10.2 Replaying for Variation   166
10.3 Replaying (As Necessary) for Completion/Closure   170
10.4 Replaying for a Deeper Understanding   174
10.5 Conclusion   178
Acknowledgments   179
References   179

10.1 INTRODUCTION: WHAT IS REPLAYING?

In this chapter, I will be exploring what it means to replay a story-focused game, or 'storygame', and how these types of games encourage and reward repeat play. As Hanson suggests, 'almost all games and the pleasures associated with their play are reliant on the mechanic of repetition and replay' (Hanson, 2018, p. 111). Before discussing how repetition and replay occur in storygames, it is necessary to consider what is meant by 'replaying'. Taken literally, the term seems to suggest 'playing again', the implicit assumption being that there must have been a first, complete 'play' and that a 'replay' takes place after that first, complete playthrough. Interestingly, however, particularly in video games, players often fail to complete a first playthrough, and need to repeatedly try, fail, and try again, gradually improving their skills and their understanding of the game rules and mechanics through this repeated play. This makes the notion of 'replay' a bit complicated, particularly if a game, such as *Tetris* (Pajitnov, 1984), is explicitly designed such that there is very little, or even no, possibility of completion. Instead, all a player can do is constantly restart the game, making more progress, and gaining more skill on each repetition. If a game can't ever be *completed*, can it truly be *replayed*? And yet, at the same time, because many games can't be completed, they almost *have* to be replayed, or at least played again, so that the player can get closer to (but maybe never reach) some form of completion.

One underlying assumption here is that the focus of the player's experience is on the pleasure derived from mastery of the playable system. Each playthrough involves an encounter with the same game system, but the ways in which the player encounters that system allow for variability in the actual sequence of actions taken, and in the resulting play experience, thereby encouraging repeat play due to both challenge and variation. In contrast, games 'built around more linear narratives in which the player may accomplish goals through singular solutions are considered to have low replay value' (Hanson, 2018, p. 119). Similarly, Juul (2002) argues that games that involve a linear progression are 'characterized by the fact that they *can* be completed, and that their replayability is subsequently very low' (emphasis in original). This seems to imply that games with a strong, linear story are *not* replayable.

Further, Hanson suggests that in some games 'player actions… determine their own experiential narrative, resulting in [a] far greater degree of variability on successive plays' (2018, p. 112). This is similar to Juul's notion of games with emergence structures, which 'allow for much variation and improvisation'. However, the trade-off is that games with a linear narrative 'often offer a greater narrative richness and nuance in their initial play, as such game types allow a game designer to more precisely craft the player experience through scripted events and predetermined sequences rather than emergent game narrative produced by the player's play' (2018, p. 120). This suggests that replayability requires an emphasis on variability and system mastery, with an implicit tension between the richness of the play experience and the richness of the narrative.

In this paper what I'm interested in exploring is what it means to replay a specific type of game: *storygames*. Reed defines a storygame as 'a playable system, with units of narrative, where the understanding of both, and the relationship between them, is required for a satisfying traversal'

(2017, p. 18). Examples of storygames include adventure games such as *Zork* (Anderson, Blank, Daniels, & Lebling, 1977) and *The Walking Dead* (Telltale Games, 2012), and computer-based role-playing games such as *Mass Effect* (Bioware, 2007) and *Skyrim* (Bethesda Game Studios, 2011). In contrast, as Reed suggests, abstract games such as *Threes* (Vollmer, 2014), games such as *SpaceChem* (Barth, 2011) where there is no connection between the story and game elements, and even a game such as *Super Mario Bros.* (Miyamoto & Tezuka, 1985), where there are narrative elements but there is no need to understand these elements to progress in the game, are *not* storygames.

With storygames, the tension that Hanson identifies between a rich, playable game system and a rich narrative becomes complicated, as by definition the player's experience is related to developing an understanding of both the playable system and the narrative units, and also an understanding of how these two aspects of the game relate to each other. In a storygame, the player should ideally want to go back to replay or reexperience both the game *and* the story, as the two are intertwined. There are, however, varying degrees to which the game and story are interconnected, depending on the design of the storygame.

To begin to consider how storygames may be able to move beyond the rich gameplay/rich narrative tension, and how this impacts replayability, it is worth considering why people reexperience *stories* (as opposed to games), beginning with non-interactive stories. As Calinescu (1993) argues, there are generally three reasons for people to want to go back and read a story again, which he refers to as partial rereading, simple rereading, and reflective rereading. Partial rereading involves going back in an attempt to complete your understanding of a text, as you may have missed some aspects of the work in your first reading. Simple rereading is an attempt to recapture the experience of the story. Finally, reflective rereading involves stepping back and reading analytically to, for example, understand the way that the text creates its effect on the reader, to explore possible intertextuality, or to look for deeper meaning. In all these cases, the story is *still the same*, so it is clearly not variation that people are looking for when they reread.

In the context of this chapter, the question is: what happens to people's experience of stories when they are *playable*? Mitchell (2012) extends Calinescu's model of rereading to interactive stories, arguing that people initially reread interactive stories for closure, the feeling that they 'get' the way the various possible stories that result from their play relate to their actions as the player. This can be seen as similar to Calinescu's partial rereading. It is only after they reach this understanding that they actually consider what they are doing to be 'rereading', at which point they switch to simple or reflective rereading. What is not clear, however, is what simple or reflective rereading would involve in an interactive story such as a storygame. Simple rereading, as Mitchell (2013) has suggested, is complicated by the very tension that Hanson has highlighted. If the player is replaying for variation, the story will likely not be the same, so is simple rereading possible? And if the player is replaying for the story, and likely making exactly the same choices as in a previous playthrough, is the experience still interactive? Similarly, Mitchell (2015) has suggested that engaging in reflective rereading in an interactive story is problematic, as it likely requires the player to be rereading both to experience the story *and* the playable system. Again, the tension that Hanson foregrounds becomes problematic here, as it suggests that this type of rereading is not possible.

To further explore these ideas, I will now consider three different ways that storygames tend to encourage and reward repeat experience: by encouraging *replay for variation*, by making *replay necessary for completion*, and by encouraging *replay for a deeper understanding* of the game/story relationship that is intrinsic to storygames.

10.2 REPLAYING FOR VARIATION

One way that storygames encourage replay is by signalling, either explicitly or implicitly, that there is something more to be seen once the player reaches the end of the game. This could take the form of additional story content or branches not yet visited, or the suggestion that choices the player makes could lead to some form of procedural variation. Here, for simplicity, I consider the 'end' of the game to be a point at which the player feels there is no longer any possibility for progression without restarting, or possibly going back to an earlier point in the game through some form of rewind mechanics (Kleinman, Carstensdottir, & El-Nasr, 2018; Kleinman, Fox, & Zhu, 2016).

The desire to go back and try different paths tends to harken back to the early forms of (non-digital) storygames, such as choose-your-own-adventure (CYOA) books. In these works, players would literally turn to different pages when they make a choice, making it clear that if they had taken the *other* path, things might have turned out differently. In fact, storygames such as *The Walking Dead* (Telltale Games, 2012) and *Bandersnatch* (Netflix, 2018) directly continue the tradition of CYOA books in their use of branching narrative structures. However, although this form of branching structure and variation allows for some degree of replayability, players quickly reach a point where they 'get it', and no longer feel a need to replay as they can roughly tell where the story will go on a subsequent replay (Mitchell, 2012). This, I argue, is due in part to the illusion of a complex playable system, an illusion that quickly breaks down on repeat play (Mitchell, 2015).

For example, *The Walking Dead* is an adventure game which makes use of a choice-based structure to allow the player to experience some degree of influence over the direction of the narrative. From the start, the game makes it known to the player that her choices will have an impact on the direction of the story. At the splash screen, the player is told that 'This game series adapts to the choices you make. The story is tailored by how you play' (see Figure 10.1, left). This sets up the expectation that your choices are important, and that they are in some way influencing the direction of the story. This is further reinforced by the reminders that appear after certain, seemingly important choices that the player makes, where the player is told that a particular character, such as Kenny 'will remember that' (see Figure 10.1, middle). In addition, at the end of each episode, the player is presented with statistics showing the choices made, and how those choices relate to those of other players (see Figure 10.1, right).

These mechanics clearly highlight the potential for doing something different – for example, what impact did the action that Kenny remembered have on his later responses to the player character? And how might the narrative have changed if the player had followed the choices taken by other players? All of this creates a sense that the playable system within the storygame is in some way adapting to the player's choices, providing some motivation to go back and play again for *variation*. However, as Mitchell (2015) has argued, on replay it quickly becomes evident that, while there is *some* variation, the overall effect is what Cage calls 'bending stories' (Cage, 2006), where the narrative retains its overall shape

FIGURE 10.1   Suggesting the player's choices matter in *The Walking Dead.*

but can be stretched to some extent by the player. Whatever the player does over the five episodes of *Season One*, the final outcome is the result of a single choice made in the final scene, and even that choice simply flavours the final events of the game, changing how the player is likely to feel about the main characters, Lee and Clementine, but not drastically changing their fates. Thus, this 'stretching' of the story allows the player to change some of the events that are encountered on the way towards the end of the story, and allows for some (minor) variation in the ending, but after a small number of playthroughs, the player is likely to have either exhausted all the variations, or reached the point where she has a good idea of which choices may lead to which variations, and no longer has any motivation to replay.

Similarly, *Bandersnatch* is an interactive film that uses choices in a manner very similar to the style used in *The Walking Dead* and other games developed by Telltale Games, such as *The Wolf Among Us* (Telltale Games, 2013) or *Tales from the Borderlands* (Telltale Games, 2014). Much like *The Walking Dead*, gameplay in *Bandersnatch* is preceded by the declaration that 'This is an interactive film where you make choices which alter the story' (see Figure 10.2). Again, this sets up the expectation in the player that choices matter, and that there are variations to be explored. Here, choices take the player through a series of video clips, with choice points leading to potentially quite divergent endings. For example, early in the game the player is asked to choose whether Stefan, the main character, agrees to work on his in-development game, also titled *Bandersnatch*, in the offices of game publisher TuckerSoft. If the player agrees, then Stefan works on the game in the company offices, and it is released to a zero-star review, at which point the playthrough ends, taking the player back to the

FIGURE 10.2   Suggesting the player's choices matter in *Bandersnatch*.

start and suggesting that she should 'try again'. If, instead, the player does not agree, a wide range of other paths become available.

There are two points to note here that differentiate *Bandersnatch* from *The Walking Dead*, other than the use of live-action video rather than cell-shaded animation. First, there clearly *are* a fair number of quite different endings, ranging from getting a bad rating on the *Bandersnatch* game that Stefan creates, to discovering that Stefan is actually a delusional actor on a Netflix sound stage who thinks he is Stefan. This variation in the paths and endings provides a certain amount of motivation for replay, as some players will want to try to reach some sense of completion and satisfaction in the form of 'getting them all'. However, as with *The Walking Dead*, it isn't clear how many times the player would actually want to go back and replay the work, rather than, for example, watching a *YouTube* playthrough of someone else completing the various endings of the work. It is possible that, despite the larger number of endings, as with *The Walking Dead*, the desire to replay for variation is eventually diminished due to the failure of the work to actually implement a strong connection between the playable system and the narrative units. As Mitchell (2015) argued in the context of *The Walking Dead*, this can be seen as an example of the 'Eliza effect' (Wardrip-Fruin, 2009), in which a system initially gives the impression of complexity, but it quickly becomes clear that the system is not as complex as it initially seemed, at which point, as Mitchell argues, the player's interest in going back to re-engage with the playable system is diminished or lost completely (Mitchell, Kway, & Lee, 2020).

The second difference is that in *Bandersnatch*, the structure of the work seems to be designed explicitly for replay. In fact, after many of the 'endings' the player is immediately given options to go back and 'try again' by jumping back to an earlier choice point and skipping over irrelevant choices. For example, as described above, if the player agrees to have Stefan work at Tuckersoft, Stefan's game ends up with a 'zero stars out of five' rating, and the game appears to restart. However, in this second playthrough the game quickly skips ahead to the previous choice, jumping past some earlier, apparently inconsequential choices. This type of 'rewind and retry' happens frequently, often taking the player back to an earlier choice while selectively skipping over previous choices (see Figure 10.3, left). There are only certain endings where an 'exit to credits' option appears, at which point the player can choose to initiate an ending, taking the player back to the Netflix interface (see Figure 10.3, right). There are also a few endings

FIGURE 10.3   Rewinding and exiting to credits in *Bandersnatch*.

where the credits immediately roll, after which the player will have to explicitly start again to replay the work.

This structure raises an interesting question: when exactly is the player *replaying Bandersnatch*? Does going back to 'try again' count as a replay? As mentioned earlier, the question of what it means to replay a game if the game hasn't been completed, and even what it means to complete a game, is not immediately obvious. The 'try again' loops in *Bandersnatch* are more like the rewind mechanics that Kleinman et al. (2018, 2016) describe as explicit meta-game mechanics for moving the story forwards, rather than an actual replaying of the work.

The structure of *Bandersnatch*, and the number of (sometimes incompatible) variations that the player can encounter on repeated replays, also raises the question of whether a player to some extent feels that she *must* replay or rewind in a work like this, otherwise she won't get the 'complete' story. By constantly suggesting that there is more, and hinting, through the repeated use of fourth-wall breaking moments and suggestions of cross-sessional memory (Koenitz, 2014; Mitchell, 2018), where characters are perhaps aware of the player and her attempts to replay the game, the game seems to be deliberately withholding any sense of closure, so as to encourage the player to play again and again in an attempt to make sense of the story. In the next section, I will explore this type of replay in more detail.

10.3 REPLAYING (AS NECESSARY) FOR COMPLETION/CLOSURE

A work such as *Bandersnatch* seems to be designed for replay, foregrounding the possibility of variation and providing explicit mechanics for rewinding and replaying. Going beyond this, there are storygames that seem to *require* replay, either for variation or, more commonly, to reach some sense of completion or closure. Even more so than *Bandersnatch*, these works begin to question what it means to replay a storygame and highlight how this relates to the relationship between the playable system and the narrative.

An example of this can be seen in *Save the Date* (Paper Dino Software, 2013), a visual novel that starts off as a simple story about trying to literally save your date, but then quickly becomes a multi-layered, self-referential story about playing and replaying (Mitchell, 2018). In the first few playthroughs, the player tends to focus on trying to make choices that avoid having the non-player character, Felicia, end up dying for a variety of reasons (including peanut allergies, ninja attack, and a collapsing deck) (see Figure 10.4). Soon, the player starts to realize that the only way forwards is by replaying the game, this time with the goal to convince Felicia that the player character (not just the player) is actually replaying a game and trying to figure out how to stop her from dying.

This shift in goal alters the process of replay, essentially unwinding the replay loop into a single, continuous play session. This is another way that the notion of what it means to 'replay' can become problematic – if the player is constantly 'dying' and then restarting the game, much like in a game of *Tetris*, but begins to see this as part of a longer process of progressing, both in terms of the playable system and the narrative, in what

You're not really surprised when the ashen-faced medical technician comes to tell you what you already basically know: Felicia had a severe peanut allergy, and it killed her.

FIGURE 10.4   One of many ways that Felicia dies in *Save the Date*.

sense is the player 'replaying'? It is important to note here that, unlike in *Tetris*, the repeated restarts are not just providing the player with an opportunity to better understand the playable system and therefore make progress towards the 'ending', but the player is also developing a better understanding of and making progress in the *narrative*. In this sense, the fact that *Save the Date* is a storygame becomes important to understanding the process of replaying.

Interestingly, it eventually becomes clear to the player that the only way to actually 'end' the game is to realize, as Felicia says, that it's better to stop playing before the inevitable death of the character, thereby 'saving the date' from death, but at the same time failing to reach the end of the game, as the play session is prematurely terminated. However, at this point it is still possible to restart one more time, with a change to the original option to not go on the date, which was previously presented as failure to go on the date, but is now presented as a somewhat positive outcome (see Figure 10.5). Here, the player has realized that the system works in such a way that it is possible to move from one set of puzzles to the next (save Felicia from the first restaurant death, save her from the second restaurant death, save her from the meteor death on the hilltop, and realize that the only way to save her from the final death is to quit), and has also realized that the narrative

FIGURE 10.5   Playing beyond closure in *Save the Date*.

of the game is not so much about saving the date, but about reflecting on the process of saving the date. This implies that the player has both reached what Mitchell et al. (2020) call *system closure*, similar to Murray's electronic closure, which 'occurs when a work's structure, though not its plot, is understood' (Murray, 1998), and *narrative closure*, the 'phenomenological feeling of finality that is generated when all the questions saliently posed by the narrative are answered' (Carroll, 2007).

This approach to replay, which requires the player to repeatedly restart the game to progress in the story, is something that Kleinman et al. (2018, 2016) refer to as a 'metagame mechanic', a mechanic that sits above the standard in-game mechanics but is a necessary part of progression in the game. It is important to stress here that this is not necessarily a new phenomenon. Similar strategies of requiring repeat play of the same sequences, either within a play session or across play sessions, have appeared in classic storygames, such as *Spider and Web* (Plotkin, 1998). It is also similar to the mechanism seen in *Eternal Darkness: Sanity's Requiem* (Miyamoto, 2002), which, according to Hanson (2018), 'prompts its players to replay the entire game several times, with each iteration revealing more of the game's backstory and recasting its conclusion, culminating with a final true ending that explains and encapsulates each iterative play-through'. As Hanson says, this is perhaps a somewhat dubious approach to replay as it essentially defers the 'real' ending as a way to encourage players to replay, requiring extensive replay to reach completion. However, in *Save the Date*, what is perhaps different is that there is an attempt to reframe the narrative at the level of the individual playthrough in terms of the larger set of replays, creating a higher-level narrative that incorporates the need to replay as part of its internal logic. There is a reframing and what could be considered a 'twist' in the narrative, but this twist is not limited to the story – it also changes what the player is doing as they replay. Rather than replaying to save Felicia, the player is replaying to solve the larger puzzle of how to convince Felicia that they are in a game. Later this shifts again to replaying once again to save Felicia, but now across rather than within play sessions. It is worth considering whether this change in what the player is doing as she replays is similar to the shift in what the reader is doing during rereading as described by Mitchell (2012). According to Mitchell, 'rereading actually involves *doing something different*' (2012, p. 74) (emphasis in original), either unconsciously in the case of simple rereading, or consciously in the case of reflective rereading. As the player goes back and shifts goals during these repeated play sessions, initially it would be safe to assume that she is involved in partial rereading, but possibly, both due to the changing goals in the playable system, and also the meta-fictional nature of the narrative, the player may also be engaging to some extent in reflective rereading.

A similar strategy can be seen in *Doki Doki Literature Club* (*DDLC*; Team Salvato, 2017). Here, the player completes one playthrough of the game, but then goes back through the story, with each playthrough increasing the degree to which the characters break the fourth wall (Roe & Mitchell, 2019). It eventually becoming apparent that, rather than restarts, these are actually 'pseudo-restarts' that are unwinding the series of replays, much as in *Save the Date*, into a single, extended narrative. An interesting, extreme example of extended play can be seen in *Nier Automata* (Taro, 2017), in which the player needs to play through the game multiple times, often changing perspective and encountering radical reframings of the narrative, before she has 'completed' the game. Also appearing in earlier games in the series, the approach taken in *Nier Automata* requires extreme dedication from the player to actually 'complete' the game given the length of each playthrough, as Gerrish (2018) and Jacevic (2018) both discuss in detail.

This strategy of repeated restarts and extended play can take many forms, either in the form of pseudo-restarts, as is the case with *DDLC* and other games such as *The Stanley Parable* (Galactic Cafe, 2013), the use of persistent data that leads to a new game actually continuing from the previous game unless the player explicitly deletes the save game, as in *Save the Date* and *Undertale* (Fox, 2015), or a 'new game plus' mode which, as in *Oxenfree* (Night School Studio, 2016), leads to the player eventually discovering that each replay is actually a continuation of a previous playthrough. All of these examples tend to tie together the player's motivations to both progress in the playable system and also advance their understanding of the narrative, and they do this by requiring repeat play as a means of progression. At the same time, they throw some doubt on the notion of replay, as the repeated play involved in these games seems to actually be part of a larger, single play session moving towards a broader sense of an 'ending'.

10.4 REPLAYING FOR A DEEPER UNDERSTANDING

The above discussion suggests that although some storygames are designed so as to *require* replay, it eventually becomes clear that what is happening in these games is not so much a replay as a continuation of the previous or current play session, focusing much more on the inclusion of additional narrative units rather than revisiting previous aspects of the narrative. *Nier: Automata* is an extreme example of this. Once this extended, linear narrative is complete, there is likely to be little reason for the player to *actually* replay the game, particularly in cases such as *Nier: Automata* where the length of the game is potentially somewhat prohibitive. There are, however, some storygames where the player is encouraged to replay not simply to complete the extended narrative, but rather to attempt to come to some understanding of the game *as a storygame*, for example, to understand both the playable system and narrative, and the relationship between the two. This can arguably be seen as similar to Mitchell's (2015) concept of reflective rereading in interactive stories, as the player is not just looking to complete their understanding, but instead is looking deeper into the work, possibly at both the system and narrative level.

One example of this approach can be seen in *Cultist Simulator* (The Weather Factory, 2018), a 'rogue-like card game' that requires the player to repeatedly fail and play again, so as to both uncover the narrative and also develop an understanding of the various layers of game mechanics and how those mechanics relate to the story. *Cultist Simulator* involves the player working to manage a number of 'timers' that consume 'cards' and produce other 'cards', in the process uncovering a narrative about a character who is working to uncover occult mysteries and build a cult (see Figure 10.6).

The game is extremely unforgiving, with no explicit 'save' mechanism, and a 'permadeath' mechanic, such that failure requires a complete restart. The game also does not provide any information as to how to play the game, much like other permadeath games (*Don't Starve* (Klei Entertainment, 2013) comes to mind), forcing the player to replay many times to simultaneously uncover the workings of the game world and the related story. In fact, at the start of the game the player is explicitly told that 'You won't always know what to do next. Keep experimenting, and you'll master it' (see Figure 10.7). This tends to retain the player's focus on both the playable system and the narrative units. It also draws attention to the possible relationship between these two elements, both at a metaphorical level (both the player and the player character are trying to understand 'how the world works' and to dig into the system under the surface of the world, either in terms of game mechanics or occult mechanics) and at a mechanical level (unlocking narrative units and unlocking gameplay tend to coincide). Unlike a game such as *Bandersnatch*, where the connection between

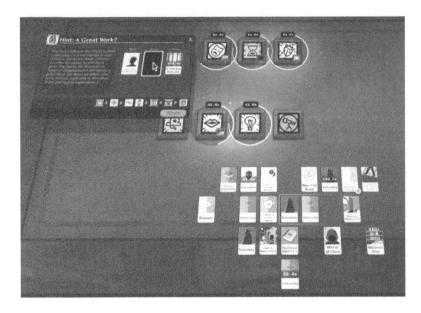

FIGURE 10.6 Game mechanics and narrative units are closely connected in *Cultist Simulator*.

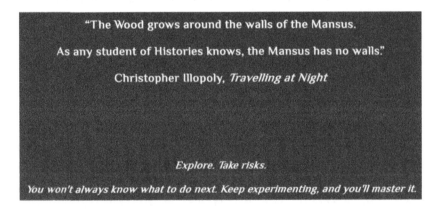

FIGURE 10.7 Encouraging the player to explore in *Cultist Simulator*.

playable system and narrative is not particularly strong, leading to a loss of motivation for replay, in *Cultist Simulator*, the player needs to continue working to understand both aspects of the work, and how they relate to each other (Mitchell et al., 2020). This helps to sustain the player's desire to replay.

Similarly, *Blood and Laurels* (Short, 2014), an iPad-based story built on the now-defunct *Versu* (Evans & Short, 2014) system, closely ties the playable system to the unfolding narrative. In *Blood and Laurels,* the player actions, conveyed through dialogue choices, change the underlying state of the storyworld, with available actions determined by a set of 'social practices' that model what conversational moves would be appropriate for the player character to take in the current situation (see Figure 10.8). A similar model is used to determine what actions non-player characters have available, and which actions are selected to move the story forwards. The actions the player takes, the potential directions the story can move as represented by the display of each character's mental state, and the actions taken by NPCs, all represent a complex playable system which generates

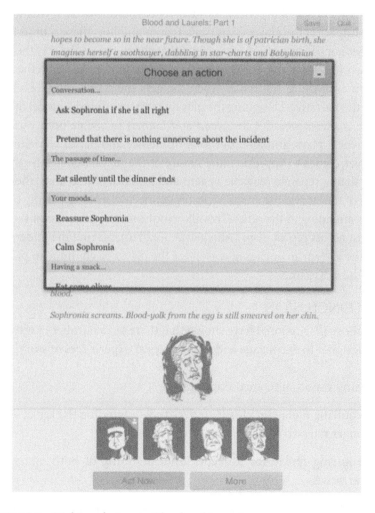

FIGURE 10.8   Making choices in *Blood and Laurels.*

the narrative units. These narrative units, in turn, help to determine how the player makes sense of what she has done, and what she can do next to move the story forwards. As with *Cultist Simulator*, in *Blood and Laurels*, the ongoing process of play, and the resulting progression, requires the player to keep all the elements of the storygame, both the playable system and the narrative units, in mind while playing the game.

As Mitchell (2015) describes, the complexity of the playable system and the resulting narrative in *Blood and Laurels* allows for repeated playthroughs, with each playthrough not following on from the previous playthrough, and not representing a 'branch' in a predetermined set of paths, but instead representing an emergent narrative as determined by the player's actions and the authored set of social practices. As such, repeat play involves trying to work out the impact of the player character's actions and how these actions fit into the larger 'social physics' (Murray, 1998) that characterizes the way the storyworld works. This allows for repeated plays that do not end when the player has 'seen everything', but rather when she 'gets' the system, and its relationship to the narrative. Designing the playable system around a model of social practice makes it possible for *Blood and Laurels* to enable both variability across repeat plays, and a deeper level of nuance and narrative richness, as the player comes to appreciate the nature of the playable narrative system. Rather than a separate playable system and set of narrative units, these two aspects of the storygame are inextricably connected, making playing one the same as attending to the other. This allows for the *storygameness* of the work to persist across repeat plays (Mitchell et al., 2020), making the understanding of the system an engaging reason for the player to continue to play, and replay, the storygame.

10.5 CONCLUSION

In the above discussion, I have shown that there are a number of ways for a game designer to encourage and reward repeat experiences of storygames:

- using variation to encourage replay;
- requiring replay for closure (effectively unwinding the replays into a longer narrative); and
- requiring replay for a deeper understanding of both system and narrative.

Each of these approaches has advantages and disadvantages. Replay for variation is satisfying to some extent, as is replay for closure, but both tend to require a lot of content, and eventually the player's interest in replaying will be exhausted either once the content is exhausted, or (more likely) once the player 'gets it', and no longer feels the need to actually see new content, instead feeling that she can predict what the content will be based on the previously encountered variations. Replay for a deeper understanding, in contrast, requires a much more complex playable system, and it can be very challenging to effectively tie this playable system closely to the narrative. However, this approach potentially leads to a much more replayable storygame, creating an experience in some ways closer to traditional replayability of non-narrative games, due to the incorporation of the story *into* the game mechanics, rather than seeing the narrative and the playable system as separate types of experience. This merging of replay of a rich playable system and the experience of a rich narrative closely tied to the playable system may be one way to move beyond the tension Hanson (2018) identified between a rich, replayable game system and a rich, but ultimately linear, narrative experience.

ACKNOWLEDGMENTS

This research is funded under the Singapore Ministry of Education Academic Research Fund Tier 1 grant FY2018-FRC2-003, 'Understanding Repeat Engagement with Dynamically Changing Computational Media'.

REFERENCES

Anderson, T., Blank, M., Daniels, B., & Lebling, D. (1977). *Zork* [computer game].
Barth, Z. (2011). *SpaceChem* [computer game]. Zachtronics.
Bethesda Game Studios. (2011). *Elder Scrolls V: Skyrim* [computer game]. Bethesda Softworks.
Bioware. (2007). *Mass Effect* [computer game]. Electronic Arts.
Cage, D. (2006). *Postmortem: Indigo Prophecy. Gamasutra.*
Calinescu, M. (1993). *Rereading.* New Haven, CT: Yale University Press.
Carroll, N. (2007). Narrative closure. *Philosophical Studies*, 135(1), 1–15. doi: 10.1007/s11098-007-9097-9
Evans, R., & Short, E. (2014). Versu – A simulationist storytelling system. *IEEE Transactions on Computational Intelligence and AI in Games*, 6(2), 113–130.
Fox, T. (2015). *Undertale* [computer game]. Toby Fox.
Galactic Cafe. (2013). *The Stanley Parable* [computer game]. Galactic Cafe.
Gerrish, G. (2018). NieR (de)automata: Defamiliarization and the poetic revolution of NieR: Automata. *Proceedings of Digra Nordic 2018.*
Hanson, C. (2018). *Game Time: Understanding Temporality in Video Games.* Bloomington, IN: Indiana University Press.
Jacevic, M. (2018). 'This. Cannot. Continue'. Ludoethical tension in NieR: Automata. *Philosophy of Computer Games Conference 2017.*

Juul, J. (2002). The open and the closed: Games of emergence and games of progression. *Proceedings of the Computer Games and Digital Cultures Conference*, pp. 323–329.

Klei Entertainment. (2013). *Don't Starve* [computer game]. 505 Games.

Kleinman, E., Carstensdottir, E., & El-Nasr, M. S. (2018). Going forward by going back: Re-defining rewind mechanics in narrative games. *Proceedings of the 13th International Conference on the Foundations of Digital Games*, pp. 32:1–32:6. New York, NY: ACM. doi: 10.1145/3235765.3235773

Kleinman, E., Fox, V., & Zhu, J. (2016). Rough draft: Towards a framework for metagaming mechanics of rewinding in interactive storytelling. *Interactive Storytelling: 9th International Conference on Interactive Digital Storytelling, ICIDS 2016*, Los Angeles, CA, November 15–18, 2016, Proceedings, pp. 363–374.

Koenitz, H. (2014). *Save the Date – Cross-Session Memory, Metanarrative and a Challenge to Endings*. Retrieved January 29, 2018, from http://gamesandnarrative.net/save-the-date-cross-session-memory-metanarrative-and-a-challenge-of-endings/

Mitchell, A. (2012). Reading again for the first time: Rereading for closure in interactive stories. *NUS Graduate School for Integrative Sciences and Engineering, National University of Singapore*.

Mitchell, A. (2013). Rereading as echo: A close (re)reading of Emily Short's 'A Family Supper'. *ISSUE: Art Journal*, 2, 121–129.

Mitchell, A. (2015). Rereading and the SimCity effect in interactive stories. In H. Schoenau-Fog, L. E. Bruni, Louchart, & S. S. Baceviciute (Eds.), *8th International Conference on Interactive Digital Storytelling, ICIDS 2015.*

Mitchell, A. (2018). Antimimetic rereading and defamiliarization in save the date. *DiGRA '18 – Proceedings of the 2018 DiGRA International Conference.*

Mitchell, A., Kway, L., & Lee, B. J. (2020). Storygameness: Understanding repeat experience and the desire for closure in storygames. *DiGRA 2020 – Proceedings of the 2020 DiGRA International Conference.*

Miyamoto, S. (2002). *Eternal Darkness: Sanity's Requiem* [GameCube game]. Nintendo.

Miyamoto, S., & Tezuka, T. (1985). *Super Mario Bros* [NES game]. Nintendo.

Murray, J. H. (1998). *Hamlet on the Holodeck: The Future of Narrative in Cyberspace*. Cambridge, MA: The MIT Press.

Netflix. (2018). *Bandersnatch* [interactive film].

Night School Studio. (2016). *Oxenfree* [PC computer game]. Night School Studio.

Pajitnov, A. (1984). *Tetris* [computer game]. Alexey Pajitnov.

Paper Dino Software. (2013). *Save the Date* [PC computer game].

Plotkin, A. (1998). *Spider and Web* [Inform 6 game].

Reed, A. (2017). *Changeful Tales: Design-Driven Approaches Toward More Expressive Storygames*. Retrieved from http://escholarship.org/uc/item/8838j82v.pdf

Roe, C., & Mitchell, A. (2019). 'Is this really happening?': Game mechanics as unreliable narrator. *Proceedings of DiGRA 2019.*

Short, E. (2014). *Blood and Laurels* [iPad app]. Versu.

Taro, Y. (2017). *Nier: Automata* [PlayStation 4 game]. Square Enix.

Team Salvato. (2017). *Doki Doki Literature Club!* [computer game]. Team Salvato.

Telltale Games. (2012). *The Walking Dead: Season 1* [computer game]. Telltale Games.

Telltale Games. (2013). *The Wolf Among Us* [computer game]. Telltale Games.

Telltale Games. (2014). *Tales from the Borderlands* [computer game]. Telltale Games.

Vollmer, A. (2014). *Threes* [iOS/Android game]. Sirvo.

Wardrip-Fruin, N. (2009). *Expressive Processing: Digital Fictions, Computer Games, and Software* Studies. Cambridge, MA: The MIT Press.

The Weather Factory. (2018). *Cultist Simulator* [computer game]. Humble Bundle Inc.

IV

Game Development and Technology

CHAPTER 11

How We Make Mobile Work

An Indie Perspective

James Barnard

After 15 years of corporate game development I went indie, built a studio and made many games. I made many mistakes and had many successes. How did I balance the idea of making art versus making a business? What would I do differently and how can people not make the same mistakes? This chapter will be an overview of the differences between indie games in mobile and corporate game development, and how we can still find ways to make money despite not having the tools that the bigger studios have.

OK – welcome to my chapter! Like any good game pitch or steam product page, I am going to try and 'sell you' on the benefits of my chapter, and if it is not for you then skip ahead… no hard feelings. I have to first accept that what I write isn't for everyone, just like a hardcore JRPG fan isn't going to buy my Arcade-Prison-Sim, no matter how pretty I make the screenshots, or how many months I spend refining that trailer. Everything is not for everybody, which is probably partly why I now run an indie studio – but more on that later.

The synopsis: Well, this chapter is about how triple A works and why that contrasts with indie. The processes used by big studios draw parallels with a lot of creative industries, and even some uncreative ones. How do these processes help in the creation of games, and why do they exist? I have seen people apply AAA methodologies to indie often with disastrous results because they did not understand what certain processes were designed for, they just see it as a part of 'how you make games'. Processes are there as tools to help us, but we need to understand them, just as a brain surgeon uses a drill to open your skull, he probably should not use the same drill when trying to cure you of the flu.

Understanding the way big and small studios work is an opportunity to give yourself a better chance of success in the deadly world of indie game development. In this chapter you might realise some of the reasons AAA companies are amazing places to work, and also some of the reasons many people decide to strike out on their own, just like I did around seven years ago.

Before we get going, a little bit about me – I have been making games for over 20 years, and throughout that time I have been lucky enough to work as a producer, artist, musician and programmer. However, my main job has always been design and creative direction. I worked on several franchises you may have heard of, like *The Sims*, *Star Wars* and *Pac-Man*. I also have shipped just over 50 games. Entertainingly, while that all sounds great as a LinkedIn profile, when we pull back the curtain a bit, the sheen quickly falls away.

Most games are not glamorous: I worked on *SimCity 2000*! But, no, not 'that' *SimCity 2000*, I was writing music and testing the Gameboy Advance (GBA) version. Porting a game to an inferior platform is never going to be the best job in the world. For one, we were porting the game to a console with barely any processing power so people hoping to get 'a portable version of that game they love on PC' were only ever going to be disappointed. No matter how hard we tried, it wasn't going to be possible to perfectly recreate *SimCity 2000* on a Gameboy. As a game designer, even if you have an idea that could make the game better, you can't actually do anything with it. Because, of course, the game is a port, and all the design has already been done. So making a change that isn't required due to technical limitations would be a deviation and, therefore, not what players would be expecting. This feeling of general uselessness is not as terrible as it might sound, the experience of building something with a team, overcoming technical challenges and eventually seeing the game on a shelf in a store (this was a long time ago!) is still something that can be relished. But ultimately no one gets into the games industry to do ports of existing games, you get into it to create new worlds and new experiences that delight players. What may surprise you is that the further I got in my career, the more and more I realised that the experience of working on a port like *SimCity* was not that dissimilar from being the creative lead on the next *Star Wars* game.

That may sound like a stretch, but bear with me. I am going to try to explain the structure of corporate games (and probably any large company with shareholders), and what it means to you as a creative individual working within a large company.

First, why did *SimCity* on the GBA exist? Well, clearly EA made the game to make money, but why that? Well I am sure it's obvious, *SimCity* is a well-known game, no doubt Toys 'R' Us alone would have pre-ordered enough copies to ensure that the COGS (cost of goods – i.e. manufacturing the cartridges with Nintendo) and development costs would be covered. Therefore, by starting development with zero financial risk, EA could guarantee a small profit for them and their shareholders. As a business you would be stupid not to do this wouldn't you? Who cares about the game designer in his mid-20s feeling like he is wasting some of his life? As a game developer he is just a tiny component in this whole machine, in which the only measure of success is profit.

It is important that we stop and think about this, a company is not usually altruistic by nature. Even if perhaps they appear to be, it is probably just good PR that in some way is expected to pay off as profit in the long term; 99% of the time, the people at the top of a big company are no longer involved in the creative process, their responsibility is to their shareholders and, to a lesser extent, keeping their employees gainfully employed. Therefore, when you walk into an executive's office and tell them about your amazing game idea, they do not really care about the idea at all. They mostly care about two things. One – will this game make money? And two – do we have the ability to actually make it, whether that means people on hand in the studio, or a production plan that factors in working with a third-party vendor such as Virtuous or any number of work for hire companies that have sprung up over the last couple of decades.

So point one, 'Will the game make money?' How can this be answered in a meaningful way that eliminates as much uncertainty as possible. I think as game designers we often just believe in our ideas so much that we just know people will be falling over themselves to play it. 'Look – you play as a sentient spaceship with giant tanks for arms! What's not to like!?' Unfortunately, that is not going to work. Your passion will really help with point number two (do we have the people to make this), but no one is going to drop potentially millions of dollars on your idea, just because you think it is great. Imagine if you were a president of a large company, and you invest in a game just because you think it sounds 'cool'. Now imagine that game fails at launch and endangers the entire company's future. The first thing someone will ask you is 'why did you approve this game?' If you managed to reach the level of company-president, you probably need to know more about business than you do game design, and answering your shareholders 'The designer seemed to really like the idea, so I thought why not!' is probably going to get you fired.

So in order to actually put a game into production you would probably go through several steps. First, you would have done a P+L (profit and loss summary). In this, your most overpaid experts will do everything within their power to predict the future. This starts with some accuracy when the team thinks about what might happen if the game was going to be released tomorrow, but then proceeds to become less and less accurate as your team tries to imagine what the market will be like in two or three years' time when this game finally launches. So they look at trends, are games of this genre becoming more popular year over year? Do we see multiplayer as a safer bet because it has a longer tail (the period of time that it continues to sell after launch) as opposed to single-player story games that tend to crash in price quickly after launch due to sales of pre-owned copies and other factors (because once someone has experienced the story, they don't need to play anymore). If we are making a single-player game, how can we counter the negative sales impact inherent with that type of game? Perhaps release some DLC, so people need to hang onto their games for longer to get the whole story, or sell a season pass that not only makes people hold on to their games, but also gives the opportunity for boosting the bottom line revenue. Based on today's knowledge, how are sci-fi games generally selling against other genres, perhaps we should suggest that the game be a fantasy game instead, as these tend to sell 15% more on average. And if the main character is a white male, we will sell 32% more than if the character is a woman from a non-Western country, however, there seems to be a trend in breaking that norm, which may be bringing about a new norm. So yes, perhaps a white female with slightly revealing attire would sell better, let's focus test it and see how potential players react, and map their reactions on top of predictions made by market analysts and so on. You get the idea. Almost every decision has to be validated against the current market, which is used as a barometer to test potential sales and profit, which then eliminates risk. When the president is answering those hard questions, they will have a big pile of data to back them up 'it should have done well because of all these predictions, we didn't know at the time that 100 player battle royale games were going to become so popular and destroy the market, we just went on the information we had to go on at the time'.

So, if you understood my waterfall of words, you may have realised a problem with this approach? Yes, innovation becomes the victim on the side of the road to sustainability, predictability and profit. Because our designer wanted to make a game about spaceships with tanks for arms, the marketing department couldn't find enough similar products to bench-mark against. Which then resulted in the game being too much of an unknown entity to green light into production.

There are ways to lessen this risk (for example, building prototypes and market testing them), but generally this is how things work. Why does EA make *FIFA* games year after year? Because they know almost exactly how many copies they will sell before they even start making the game! How many totally new IPs do we really see from big companies? Sticking with EA and their one new IP *Anthem*, they want to do their best to guarantee success, 'Let's make a game a bit like *Destiny*, even if it costs 150 million dollars, at least we have an example in the market that we can look at and measure ourselves against'. The fact the game failed spectacularly is not really the point. It was a sound plan, backed up by predictions and calcu-lations that eventually failed due to unforeseen circumstances. But don't worry, they spent so much money on the thing, that I am sure there will be a sequel that does ever so slightly better than the first game.

It's a real shame that things are this way, it perpetuates stagnation in the types of games we play and reinforces stereotypes and a whole host of other terrible things (why is almost every Ubisoft game set in an open world full of fetch quests?), but it makes sense. Indie companies die every day, they release game after game that doesn't sell. When you are Namco, and your monthly burn rate is probably 30 million dollars, it doesn't take too many failures to empty your cash reserves and sink your company. Of the many indie games that fail, a small percentage go on to become huge hits, rewarding their creators with unimaginable fortunes. It is fair to say that if all indie games were released by one company, their '*Minecraft*' would not make up the shortfall of all the other games that fail. It's very fair to compare making indie games to gambling, you know that the odds are stacked heavily against you, but you still want to do it anyway. Just like people that play poker who say it is a game of skill, no doubt indie developers (like me), think we have some magic edge that puts us ahead of everyone else and increases our chance of 'winning', but really, we probably sound like those scrawny sleep deprived gambling addicts in Vegas who will tell you they have a 'system' and that it's all going to work out eventually.

In 2018, the average return on an indie game was less than US$30,000. Seeing as most games are made by multiple people, and take more than a year to build, the return on these games is generally worse than working a minimum wage job a few hours a week. And this is only part of the picture, the way sales are distributed means that the top games make the majority of the money, so the games at the bottom aren't making US$30,000, they are probably making double digits in sales. A report on Steam stated that in 2017 the top 0.5% of games on the store accounted for 50% of all revenue spent. And historically this is a trend that is getting more and more pronounced, meaning that it's harder than ever to make a living as a game developer. This pushes big companies to take fewer risks than ever and rely on existing known IPs to generate sales, so the aforementioned spaceship-tank-arms game is looking even more unlikely than ever.

In their search for profit, larger companies have begun to follow the successes of smaller indie companies very closely. In that one in a billion chance that an indie game does become successful, large companies are increasingly taking inspiration from those titles and building their own similar product. When *Minecraft* became a huge hit, it wasn't too long before people started following them with games like *Lego Worlds*, or the somewhat unlikely *Dragon Quest Builders*, eventually it felt that the building things your way was permeating into almost everything from *Fallout* to indie ultra-hit *No Man's Sky*. The time it took for *Minecraft*'s influence to go through the industry could be measured in years. The next game to have a similar impact was *PUBG*, which spawned *Fortnite* and *Apex Legends* not long after. *Fortnite* was a very different game originally, but it was reshaped in the image of *PUBG* and released into the world, where it generated a staggering US$2.4 billion in 2018, while *PUBG* still made a respectable US$1.08 billion that same year. It wasn't too long until Activision got in on the action, and launched their very own take on the genre, with *Apex Legends*. The time frame in which these big budget clones appeared was substantially shorter than the time it took for *Minecraft* to end up rebuilt as a *Dragon Quest* game under the Square Enix umbrella. Fast forward to the indie game/mod sensation known as *Auto-Chess* and it took only six months for both Valve and Activision to launch their own fairly shameless takes on the genre (they both released within the same week!).

So what does all of the above mean? It means that when working in a large videogame company, the chances of you getting to 'Make your dream game' are technically zero. Even if your concept gets through to production, the marketing team may well shift your design pillars so violently that it doesn't feel anything like the game you wanted to make anymore. You perhaps have read some of the stories surrounding production of large games like *Anthem* and *Destiny*, and how they went wildly off the rails. To me this is endemic in AAA games, because no one really has a final say, even when you think the creative director is the final person in the decision chain, that person can be entirely undermined if a marketing test does not go to plan and the game needs to be changed to increase the probability of success.

Earlier on, I mentioned that the company-president was looking at two main factors when agreeing to start developing a game. The first was profit potential, the second was being sure that the company could make it. In many ways this ties into the profit, because even if you have the greatest product idea, the truth is that if you do not have the people to make it, you will not get very far. So how does a big company ensure it has the team to actually build a game? There are a couple of factors, one is having the right people leading the project, these directors need the passion and drive to push the team through the tough times and deliver the game. This group of people need to solve day-to-day problems, while keeping everyone on track to deliver the game that matches the original risk assessed product description. Usually, once this leadership group is in place, their job is to break down the next few years of work in as realistic way as possible. This is about as scientific as you can imagine and is just a big list of random guesses and gut instincts. The more games you make the better you get at guessing what it will take to make one, but really there is no way to accurately predict how long anything will take in game development, which is partially why most games are late. So with a schedule in place, the team will start making things. Despite the pretence of 'Agile' development, there is almost always a target end date for the project. This means that while you can explore different ideas and concepts, you still need to do them within a certain time box. And better yet, those explorations still need to line up with the product the marketing department thinks they can sell.

In simple terms, a project has an estimated sales potential, which in turn means there is maximum budget that the company should spend, which finally means you need some kind of schedule and timeline in order to try to ensure that the game will make money.

As you can imagine, predictability is a very important part of this process. If a game is going to go over budget or over time, you would want to know as soon as possible. Either can clearly have such drastic impacts on the game that it might need to be cancelled. If the game is going to be late, perhaps a new console will have been released which might affect your sales negatively (compounding the fact that the longer timeline probably pushed your budget up too). So how does a company deal with predictability in the unpredictable world of game development? The answer is a combination of micromanaged schedules, milestones deliveries and expected redundancy.

A milestone is your big delivery. Often a milestone is viewed as a possible cancellation point for a game. For example, delivery of a vertical slice (a section of gameplay that is expected to be representative of the final product) might represent the first time external people get to play the game. If it does not meet expectations in focus tests, the game could easily be canned. When milestones are late, or do not achieve all their objectives, it is usually a sign that things are not going to plan. If milestones start to slip, it is usually impossible for a team to make back up the time. From there, it is possible to get a prediction of how late the game might be and decide the future accordingly.

The idea of redundancy is a harder one to explain, but it hit me several times in my career. I would be working on something and get to the end of my task list. I would then want to use that extra time to add something extra to make the game more awesome, only to be told not to. To me that did not make any sense at all! Why wouldn't we want more stuff in the game!? Well, the issue is that if I add something else, I might make more bugs, and that would have a knock-on effect for the rest of the project, this extra content would have to be tested and maintained until we shipped. Equally, I might overload myself and shift from being ahead of schedule, to dropping behind, and as we know, the most important thing is that we stay on schedule, and ship the thing that we set out to make in the first place. Perhaps my awesome new idea is slightly out of line with the original vision for the project? I can see the logic behind a producer thinking: it's probably best to not take the risk and just find something else to do to fill my time. Finally, everything in games is always late so, when we make a schedule, it is a good idea to add a whole heap of contingency time in. If a programmer says something will take him a day, write down two. Anyone who has made any number of games will agree, nothing ever goes to plan, so this kind of practice is fairly standard.

In general, from my personal experience, everything really starts to go wrong when the game starts coming together. That design idea where the robots tank arms would detach and be controlled by other players on the internet is too complicated to make work well, or maybe it is just not as fun as we imagined. Whatever the issue is, it usually results in something getting changed, and that redesign means suddenly there is a lot more work, and there isn't space in the schedule for it. So either some of that redundancy gets taken up, or if there isn't enough left, you have to cut something from the game. This regimented drive towards delivering games on time and on budget almost always affects the quality of the product you are working on. And it is something almost all teams have to deal with at some point or another.

Task micromanagement exists in many teams but not all. The concept is that you have a set of tasks to complete, you may have a set order in which they are to be done, or you can just pick whatever you fancy doing from a bucket of tasks. When you take on a task you set it as in progress, so everyone knows you are doing it, and then set to complete or 'ready for review' as soon as you are done. In general, this is considered to be a great way for the team to see what other people are working on or easily see the history of a task so they know how to find out more information. The task itself should have all the required information written down to make achieving it possible. This is all very efficient. The reality is that this inter-team efficiency is really only a very small part of the picture. Task tracking software like Jira or Hansoft is very good at generating graphs and reports, that in turn make it very easy to see whether a team is working to their schedule. If you drop behind by just one hour every day, the compounded nature of this constant slippage can be brought to light quickly within the project management reports. This information can then be used to correct the path of development by adding more people or cutting content.

As far as I know, a variant of this kind of tracking is used at every major games company. I personally despise this system. When a valuable programmer is typing in task information, forwarding tasks to other people, reviewing someone else's tasks or a host of other project management related activities, they are not programming. In my career, I have seen companies that assign as much as 25% of a day's working hours to administrative tasks such as Scrum meetings, task planning, progress reviews and so on. When we are making games, the worst thing we can do is do something that does not directly contribute to putting something on the screen. These admin tasks exist mostly to alleviate concerns in management by building a predictable record of the team's progress. So by having such a detailed history we can attempt to predict the future! Even if 25% of the games budget (at least) is spent making sure that the company knows whether or not to stop development it's worth it. In a game that costs US$100 million, if US$30 million in you can see that it might actually cost double that amount, the corporation can cut their losses easily. Equally, if you start realising that the game will be late, perhaps pull the plug on that US$10 million-dollar marketing campaign you had lined up for this year's E3 convention.

When I started my company, I did some very high-level milestone style scheduling, and that was about it. I quickly realised that by keeping the team small, we did not need to have complicated communication channels. I also know that realising a game will be late is not going to change anything! Unlike a big company, most indies don't have the money to cancel a project and move on to something else, we simply have to do our best to finish it. If we do it ahead of time, then great! But if it takes longer, then every second we spent pushing tasks around on virtual whiteboards is a second earlier we could have finished. For people exiting AAA and going to indie, this is usually the biggest mistake I see happen time and time again. I often think when people are in AAA development, they do not question the systems around them. They just accept that this is how things are done in game development. For me, the most important thing to remember is, 'If I am doing something that isn't directly contributing to the game, or selling the game, then maybe I shouldn't be doing it'.

Another thing that happens when AAA developers become indie, is that their confidence can undermine them. In a big company there is a huge support structure all around you, you take it for granted that when the network goes down, someone from IT will fix it. Or if your PS4 dev kit needs updating, someone else will do it for you. When you go indie, you realise that no one is going to do things for you, you have to do it all yourself! This sudden influx of additional responsibilities can result in people being able to do a lot less work than they anticipated. Going back to the rule that everything takes longer in game development than you anticipate, sometimes the switch to being a solo developer can make you feel so unproductive that the pressure mounts and you become even less productive. It's a kind of psychological stacking: where you hit a roadblock and there is no one there to help you over it, you just throw your hands up in despair. To succeed, you have to forget the life of AAA, you are now the same as anyone else and have to fight to make it by pushing yourself to be productive each and every day. The fact that you were a lead engineer on *GTA VI* means nothing now, and you will have to do all those boring uninteresting tasks that you used to just pass off to junior programmers.

On the flip side of this, there are people who become indies without ever having worked in a games company. The kind of mistakes these developers make are often similar, but many new developers lack the sense of urgency that the endless grind of AAA teaches you. If you are in this situation, it makes sense to step back and envision what success means for you. To do this, you have to know a bit about the industry, watch YouTube videos from developers who cover their own experiences and have discussions within your local games dev community. It is easy to trawl the internet and read about the success stories of Toby Fox with *Undertale* or Eric Barone with *Stardew Valley*. Believing you can replicate the success of these people is like buying a lottery ticket and putting a down payment on a house because you are convinced you will win. If you study a broader range of developers you will realise fairly quickly that success is a rarity, not the norm. Once you understand that, try to set out a plan that aligns with a more informed version of reality.

Don't assume you will do any better than the average, in fact many of the people who make up that average will have things over you such as experience and industry connections.

So 'what does success look like for you' is an important question, and when I was first asked it by my publisher Kongregate, I didn't fully grasp just why it was so important. My first answer was probably something like 'To make crazy money and make whatever games I want to for all eternity'. That was clearly unrealistic. Knowing the things I know now about the industry, I think obtaining *'crazy money'* in mobile requires 'crazy investment', large teams of people making sense of the data collected on your players, lots of money to spend on UA (user acquisition), along with teams of people who can actually optimise your UA strategy so it can return a positive ROI (return on investment). On top of that, you need people managing customer support and ensuring that your ad networks are optimised for the biggest profits. If I wanted to make as much money as possible, I should probably get some investment, and move away from actually writing code on a daily basis, and create products for the demographics with the highest spending power and so on, essentially running my business like a AAA studio. The other part 'make whatever games I want to' is just a contradiction to the first part.

If I break down my answer to this question today, it would be something like 'Have a sustainable income, creative freedom and have fun every day'. Looking at my business, I can break down the ways that this can be done. We do not earn a lot from our existing games, and I see the trend of new games not getting the big sales spikes that they once did. So in order to make enough money to survive, we just need more games. Looking forwards and thinking that the next game will be a huge hit, is just wishful thinking. Therefore, each game I make, I try to think about whether the idea is simple enough to make in a reasonable amount of time and what monetisation potential it has. This sounds cold, but it is not. It's just sensible. I find it easy to come up with ideas, so if an idea does not fit my plan, then I just scrap it and think of another one.

The point is, when you have a more realistic vision of what success means for you, you can work backwards and determine a plan that makes that possible. If your plan does not result in that success, then you need to try a new plan! I have met too many developers who think vast success is easy to obtain, and so far, only one developer I know has managed to become successful in true fairy tale fashion.

The other thing that almost all new indie developers do is procrastinate and over scope. If you think your game will take a year, double it, Hell, maybe even triple it. Your first game will fail, and probably your second one too, so it is probably best to make something very small as your first game and save the 'big dream project' for later. I still have not started on the game I dream of making, and I probably never will. The experience of launching something will teach you so much, and if you have a community in place (like Reddit/Discord) you can start building a small following. My company really started using Discord about a year ago, and when we added links to our most recent game, the community started to grow. If you are selling premium games, having a community or a mailing list is really important because with premium games it doesn't take too many sales for it to be meaningful. But the most important thing is just to release things, don't make it perfect, don't rebuild an entire system in the game unless you really know it's worth it. A question we ask ourselves is 'what is the value of this feature?' By 'value' we mean 'will this translate into more sales? Will this get the game to generate more traffic on social media?' We then compare that value with how long it takes to make the feature (which really means how much it will cost). Even though sometimes it is hard to estimate what small details will do for the overall experience, it's important to be critical and look at your game as a business otherwise your company will fail pretty quickly.

Also, never stop learning. Chances are your team are going to let you down at some point (or you will let them down) so unlike AAA development, it always pays to know enough about every discipline so you can get by. Perhaps you will need to fix a small bug and upload a new build to the App Store or open a file in Photoshop and move the layers around so you can create that new image that Sony requested. Successful indie developers are usually doers, they work hard at making the actual content of the game, rather than being managers or 'ideas-guys'. This isn't totally isolated to indie games, Naughty Dog (makers of *Crash Bandicoot* and *Uncharted*) employ the same approach, and have publicly stated that they don't have producers on their teams (producers do schedules and management tasks, not actual development of the game).

Reading back over this chapter, I see I painted a fairly bleak picture, but I think it's important to understand the realities behind the 'fun creative world of videogame development'. I personally would never do anything else, making games brings me fulfilment like no other creative endeavour. Whichever path you decide to take, the road is a hard one. To me, the safest bet is to work for a big company and learn enough to take the leap into your own games when you have an honest and realistic plan. Or make games on your weekends for fun while you hold a game development job during the week. My very first indie release was actually made in my evenings while I was still working at LucasArts. While that went against the contract I had signed with them, it was an opportunity for me to prove to myself that I had what it takes to actually build and launch a game on my own. Without that experience, I am pretty sure I would still be working for someone else.

LUDOGRAPHY

1. *Anthem*, Bioware/Electronic Arts, 2019.
2. *Apex Legends*, Respawn Entertainment/Electronic Arts, 2019.
3. *Auto Chess*, Drodo Studio/Chengdu Dragonest, 2019.
4. *Crash Bandicoot*, Naughty Dog/SCEA, 1996.
5. *Destiny*, Bungie/Activision, 2014.
6. *Dragon Quest Builders*, Square Enix Business Division 5/Square Enix, 2016.
7. *Fortnite*, Epic Games/Epic Games, 2017.

8. *Lego Worlds*, Travellers Tales/Warner Bros, 2017.
9. *Minecraft*, Mojang/Mojang, 2010.
10. *No Man's Sky*, Hello Games/Hello Games, 2016.
11. *PUBG*, PUBG Corporation/Bluehole, 2017.
12. *SimCity* 2000, Maxis/Mindscape, 1993.
13. *Stardew Valley*, ConcernedApe/Chucklefish, 2016.
14. *Undertale*, Toby Fox/8–4, 2015.
15. *Uncharted*, Naughty Dog/SCEA, 2007.

CHAPTER 12

The Development and UI Design of an Interactive Game Map

Tomasz Zawadzki, Korneliusz Warszawski, Slawomir Krezel and Slawomir Nikiel

CONTENTS

12.1	Creating Virtual Cities	200
	12.1.1 Developing UI, City Layers and Simulations in Unity: An Example of the BCD project	201
12.2	Terrain: An Asset for a 3D Game Map	207
	12.2.1 Terrain Representation	207
	12.2.1.1 Height-Field	207
	12.2.1.2 Voxel-Map	208
	12.2.2 Array to Vector Conversion	208
	12.2.2.1 Elevation Model	209
	12.2.2.2 Volumetric Model	209
	12.2.3 Terrain Geometry	209
12.3	Creating Procedural Assets in Unreal Engine 4	210
	12.3.1 Interactive Tree Creator	211
	12.3.1.1 Main Concepts	212
	12.3.1.2 Root, Branch and Sub-Branch Placement	212
	12.3.1.3 Branch Intersection Blending	214
	12.3.1.4 Leaf Placement	215
	12.3.1.5 Fruit Placement	217
	12.3.1.6 Wind Weighting	218
	12.3.1.7 Automatic Billboard Generation	218

12.3.1.8   Preparing the Trees for Use   220
12.3.1.9   Force Reaction and Dynamic Wind   220
12.3.1.10 Tree Chopping, Falling Fruits, Leaves and
             Debris   222
12.3.2 Smart Spline Generator   224
12.3.2.1   Main Concepts   224
12.3.2.2   Recursive Surface Align Algorithm   225
12.3.2.3   Vert Count Optimization with *Spline Thicken*
             Function   226
12.3.2.4   Merging to Static Mesh   227
12.4 Game Level Design   228
12.4.1 Game Level Construction: "Presence" Approach   228
12.4.1.1   Presence and the Concepts of Space   229
12.4.2 Level Design: Game Genres and Levels   230
12.4.3 Components of a Level   232
12.4.3.1   Geometry of the Level   232
12.4.3.2   Game Level Description   233
12.4.4 Aesthetics   236
12.4.5 Elements of Good Level Design   240
Acknowledgements   242
References   242

12.1 CREATING VIRTUAL CITIES

In 1980, a virtual model of the entire Los Angeles basin was built. The model was used to interactively fly, drive or walk through the city. A virtual scene was constructed by combining aerial photographs with street level imagery and three-dimensional (3D) geometry to create a realistic visual simulation of the dense Los Angeles urban environment, detailed enough for the graffiti on the walls and signs in the windows to be legible (Jepson, 2006).

The Helsinki City Simulator contains a virtual model of the Helsinki city center and a powerful multi-channel display system for real-time simulation on a large screen. The purpose of the simulator project was to build a realistic vision of the future city center as it is planned today. For architects and planners, a virtual model is a platform to test and improve their design. For city residents and politicians, the simulator is an easy and very illustrative way to walk and fly through the future city. It provides a good basis for exchanging opinions on a future design (Suomisto, 2001).

Virtual London was produced using GIS8, CAD and a variety of new photorealistic imaging techniques including photogrammetric methods of data capture. The core model is aimed to be distributed via the Internet utilizing techniques to optimize large urban data sets for broadband distribution. There are several vendors who have contributed money and data or donated software to this big project, including CASA, Greater London Authority, Ordnance Survey, Infoterra, ESRI, London Connects (Batty et al., 2000).

The idea of the VR Beirut 3D project was to develop an interactive urban design tool which could be used to consider a building footprint and massing options, as well as maintaining a record of floor space and the proposed land use by parcel, block and sector (Horne, 2004).

12.1.1 Developing UI, City Layers and Simulations in Unity: An Example of the BCD project

The *Building City Dashboards* (BCD, 2016) project, shortly called *BCD*, is currently under development in the *Department of Geocomputation* at *Maynooth University* in Ireland. A desktop version of the project was built in the Unity game engine and it can be accessed by launching an executable file from the build. There were a few stages in project development including: importing the 3D model (in .FBX format), adding orthophoto map and city layers, developing the *User Interface* (UI), including buttons, sliders, checkboxes, real-time simulations, navigation modes and other interactive elements. The Dublin 3D city model was imported to the project and placed in the center of the scene (0,0,0). The same was done with orthophoto which let the buildings correspond with the map. City layers were exported in .FBX format from *City Engine* [2] and imported into Unity [3] in the same place (0,0,0). During export, it was not possible to keep attributes joined with the mesh and we proposed a parser to read .CSV data attributes directly in Unity. Each city layer group node contained all the objects assigned to it. To recognize whether the user clicked on one particular 3D object, it was necessary to assign a script called *MapClickDetector* which was based on IDs provided in the mesh name (Mesh Filter) and displayed corresponding attribute IDs from the row of the CSV file (Figure 12.1).

To make it work, *Mesh Collider* had to be added to each game object (single mesh). In addition to that, highlighting would only work when the mouse was over the mesh. It was important to uncheck *Convex* parameter, otherwise an invisible box was drawn over the shape and despite the

FIGURE 12.1 The view from the project and parser window in Unity.

mouse not touching the shape, it still highlighted. This small fix helped to sort it out (Figure 12.2).

The BCD project contained few types of interactive UI menu elements. Buttons were created to facilitate interaction with 3D Dublin city. The most used script called *Enable_Disable* was facilitating showing and hiding game objects in the scene by use On Click () events (Figure 12.3). Based on this approach, it was possible to control all the 3D objects and city layers in the scene.

For planning purposes, it was important that we could hide and show the roads, rivers, bridges, trees, lamp posts, including access to underneath city layers. Objects were grouped into those five groups and controlled by the Development button. Another issue was to add some buildings to the scene which could be activated in runtime. Two free 3D models were loaded into Unity and hidden by default. In planning mode, you can activate them and place in the scene, with their position fixed. Planning mode

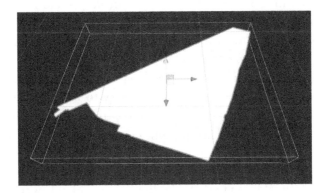

FIGURE 12.2 Random shape with *Convex* parameter checked (dark gray line outside the shape).

Runtime Only	‡	GameObject.SetActive	‡
3D Objects	⊙	☐	

Runtime Only	‡	InteractiveToggle.SetState	‡
Button1 (Intera	⊙	☐	

Runtime Only	‡	GameObject.SetActive	‡
ROADS	⊙	☑	

Runtime Only	‡	InteractiveToggle.SetState	‡
Button2 (Intera	⊙	☐	

Runtime Only	‡	GameObject.SetActive	‡
RIVER	⊙	☑	

Runtime Only	‡	InteractiveToggle.SetState	‡
Button3 (Intera	⊙	☐	

Runtime Only	‡	GameObject.SetActive	‡
TREES	⊙	☑	

+ −

FIGURE 12.3   An example of an On Click () event with *Enable_Disable* script loaded.

can be utilized by switching between two viewpoints modes added to the scene from the top menu (Figure 12.4).

BCD WebGL [4] has two navigation modes: *FPP* (first-person perspective) and *Bird's-eye View*. *FPP* mode uses *Character Controller*—a default Unity component where you can set up your avatar size, speed and other parameters for locomotion. The second mode—*Bird's-eye View* explores the city from a higher distance—it uses *Mouse Orbit* script which refers to a center pivot and has 360 degrees rotation with zoom in and zoom out. It is only possible to switch between the two modes (Figure 12.5).

Real-time simulations were added to the project: day and night simulation—correlated with shadow and sun trajectory simulations in a day

FIGURE 12.4   Planning mode in early stage. Left: empty zone. Right: proposed utilization for investment areas.

FIGURE 12.5   Two modes for navigation.

cycle. By attaching *Directional light* to the *Slider* component (default Unity component), we could control the position of the *Sun* in the scene. The initial value on the Slider was set up to 0 and *Min* and *Max* values ranging from −90 to 90 degrees. *RotateWithSlider* script with *adjustRotation* function was necessary to update the *Sun* position based on the current cursor position on the *Slider*.

The *Flood Resilience (FR)* controller works in a very similar way but instead of attaching *Directional light* to the *Slider*, we attached the *Visualization Controller (VC)*—a game object. The *VC* contains the following: *Water plane, Water Height Slider* and *Water Height UI*. From *Water Height Slider* we refer to the slider in the *FR* game object. In the *Slider*, we added the *Flooding script* with the *AdjustHeight* function enabled and a Min starting value equal to 0 with a Max value equal to 5 meters. *Water Height UI* refers to *Dynamic Label* where we added the *Text Mesh Pro UGUI* component to be able to display the water level in a text box (Figure 12.6).

On the left side there is access to the *Main menu* which can be shown and hidden at any time. The menu was created from a set of standard

FIGURE 12.6   Left: shadow simulation based on sun day and night cycle. Right: water level simulation.

buttons and image components in Unity. Only this element is animated in the scene. The menu contains eight categories of data which store city data layers (originally. SHP files, but now in .FBX format). Each data category only contains a few sub-categories of data sets and is in early stages of development.

Project logotypes and navigation info were added using Image components. Navigation info changes in real-time based on a user's interaction and has three main descriptions in the bottom-right of the project. Two of them are related to navigation modes (*FPP* or *Bird's-eye View*) and one to the Viewpoints. In Viewpoint mode, there is no movement and it is to be only used to showcase planning purposes.

Another useful feature was to add a *Compass* to the project. Only one part of the *Compass* is animated (*Arrow*), the rest staying as a background. The *Arrow* has its own pivot point in the center of the *Compass* and by default it was set up to the *North*. To make it work we had to add a *Button* component to the *Arrow* image component and an On Click () event assigned to the *Main_camera* which the *Compass* refers to. Another step to finally connect it was to select *Compass* script from the list with the *SetNorthDirection* function assigned by default.

BCD WebGL contains some icons to enhance the user experience: hide all icons to close all the open windows by a single click and an exit icon—to close the application. On the bottom window, the real-time date and time component was added (Figure 12.7).

Nowadays, game engines like Unity can be used to build games like viewing experiences, even if they do not refer to the game industry, as

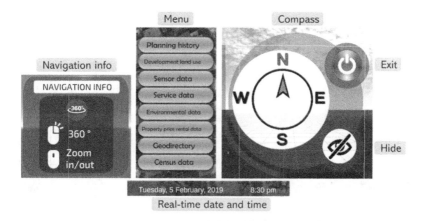

FIGURE 12.7 Menu and other *BCD WebGL* UI components.

with the BCD project (Figure 12.8 and Figure 12.9). The characteristic of the project does not change how the UI interface and other interactive elements should be built. However, we are still expected to use game objects, but now for other purposes.

FIGURE 12.8   BCD WebGL project with an interactive UI FPP (*First Person View*).

FIGURE 12.9   BCD WebGL project – Dublin city layers overview BEV (*Bird's-eye View*).

12.2 TERRAIN: AN ASSET FOR A 3D GAME MAP

The terrain asset used in open world environments is responsible for maintaining an appropriate scale and proportion of objects placed in the scene. A more accurate terrain model increases the visual acceptability and leads to better immersion.

Since the works of Mandelbrot (Mandelbrot, 1982), procedural methods have had a very important function in computer-assisted terrain modeling. Those methods range from basic fractal algorithms to complex techniques producing structures that include erosion influence, rivers, canyons and coastlines (Smelik et al., 2009; Galin et al., 2019).

The manual preparation of a terrain asset is time consuming and in large projects is totally ineffective. A better way is to support it by one or several procedural methods. In this section, we focus on the general preparation of the terrain asset for further use by terrain generation techniques.

12.2.1 Terrain Representation

Terrain models can be categorized into two main types with advantages and weaknesses. The simplest is a model based on elevations, which is referred to as a height-field or height-map. Elevation models can define the geometry of the terrain surface but in general form cannot be used to describe the internal structure of geological materials. Models are also limited to terrains without arches, rock shelves or caves, which cannot be described by height structures. The complex terrain models without these restrictions are based on volumetric representation and are referred to as voxel-map. The voxel models can define both the geometry and the subsurface structures of landscapes. Unfortunately, the methods based on the volumetric model are expensive in memory demands and computational complexity. Hybrid models can also be isolated by trying to accumulate positive aspects of both main representations, while minimizing their weaknesses (Benes and Forsbach, 2001; Smelik et al., 2009; Galin et al., 2019).

12.2.1.1 Height-Field

The common structure to represent the terrain asset in the memory of the computer is to use a height-field (Smelik et al., 2009; Galin et al., 2019). It is defined as a discrete two-dimensional (2D) model over a regular grid and consists of a collection of heights records of the landscape (Figure 12.10). The structure is also used in Geographic Information Systems (GIS) – referred to as the Digital Elevation Model (DEM).

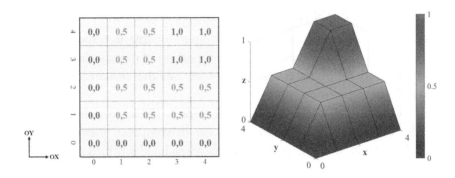

FIGURE 12.10   Sample height-field data and render.

12.2.1.2 Voxel-Map

The complex landscape is represented in computer memory by a voxel-map (Galin et al., 2019). It is defined as a 3D model over a regular grid and consists of a collection of terrain data such as materials, hardness, density and so on. In the simplest form, it takes the form of a Boolean array, where 1 means a solid material and 0 means the air or water (Figure 12.11).

12.2.2 Array to Vector Conversion

In practical implementation, the array representation can be described as a one-dimensional vector in both elevation and volumetric models. In general, the vector notation is faster, and mostly it requires only one loop to process the model in the steps of the terrain generation procedure.

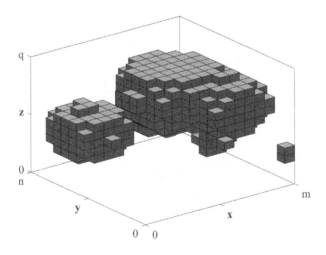

FIGURE 12.11   Sample voxel-map render.

12.2.2.1 Elevation Model

Conversion between dimensions can be performed by the following procedures.

Let us assume that H is a m-by-n height-field, where m is the number of columns and n is the number of rows. Let us also assume that H is represented as a vector in column-based notation.

When k is an index of H, then indexes of the column (i) and row (j) can be acquired as follows:

$$i = k \bmod m$$

$$j = \mathrm{floor}\left(k/m\right)$$

In the opposite direction, the cell data pointed by column and row indexes can be acquired as follows:

$$H[i,j] = H\left(i + j * m\right)$$

12.2.2.2 Volumetric Model

Let us assume that V is a m-by-n-by-q voxel-map, where m is the number of columns, n is the number of rows and q is the number of pages. Let us also assume that V is represented as a vector in column-based notation.

When k is an index of V then indexes of the column (i), row (j) and page (k) can be acquired as follows:

$$i = a \bmod m$$

$$j = \mathrm{floor}\left(a/m\right)\bmod n$$

$$k = \mathrm{floor}\left(a/m * n\right)$$

In the opposite direction, the cell data pointed by column, row and page indexes can be acquired as follows:

$$V[i,j,k] = V\left(i + j * m + k * m * n\right);$$

12.2.3 Terrain Geometry

In game design, the procedural methods for terrain geometry are faster and in general a better way to generate data for terrain assets than simulation-based techniques. In most cases, the reconstruction of real geological formation is not the goal of projects.

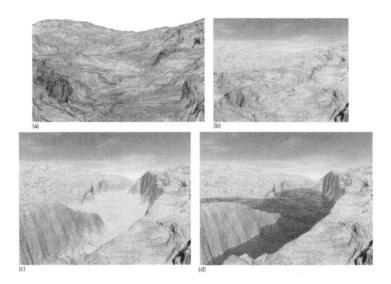

FIGURE 12.12   Preparing the terrain asset, step by step.

There are many forms and variants of landscape modeling procedures, starting with noise or fractal geometry (Smelik et al., 2009; Galin et al., 2019) and ending with genetic algorithms (Saunders, 2006) or machine learning techniques (Guérin et al., 2017).

We would urge readers to experiment with the techniques, adjust parameters and adapt results to the needs of your projects.

Finally in the process, terrain assets obtained by procedural methods (Figure 12.12a) look fine, but should be textured (Figure 12.12b) and adding some lighting effects should increase the realism of the scene. Next, the asset can be extended by valleys (Figure 12.12c). The valley can be simply painted over the terrain surface. Now, the terrain looks better but it can still be improved. As an option, some of the terrain valleys can be filled with water, which makes the scene feel better (Figure 12.12d).

12.3 CREATING PROCEDURAL ASSETS IN UNREAL ENGINE 4

Incorporating procedural asset creation into the development pipeline allows the achievement of large-scale environments and diverse 3D model libraries, without the need for a dedicated team of artists working on each aspect during scene iterations. Procedural assets are also more convenient to modify and iterate on when using parameterized asset properties. After defining procedural generation rules, it is easy to change an asset's look and swap its elements, which, for example, allows the reuse of the same asset in different projects, even with totally different art styles.

This section will concentrate on describing two procedural asset generation tools which were made in Unreal Engine 4, using the Blueprint visual scripting system.

12.3.1 Interactive Tree Creator

Trees are one of the most common assets that can be encountered in games, especially when it comes to open world titles. Many game projects need a set of different 3D tree models – and sometimes, depending on game mechanics, there is a need for things like tree chopping, smoothly changing wind strength/direction, falling leaves or other dynamic features. It is especially prevalent in survival games or projects where interactive nature objects play an important role in the game loop.

Interactive Tree Creator is a tool that allows the user to create interactive 3D trees, all inside the Unreal Engine 4 (UE4) editor, using procedural generation logic made in the UE4 Blueprint system. It is available on the UE4 Marketplace, along with a video preview for more insight (Figure 12.13).

The user can define many tree properties and immediately see the updated 3D tree preview. Parameters are grouped into separate sections for tree trunks, branches, leaves, sub-trunks, roots and fruits. The default preview scene contains a wind preview object that controls the wind direction and strength – this shows how the generated tree will react to different wind conditions. User can tweak this by changing the *Wind Weight Falloff* parameter.

FIGURE 12.13   Fragment of tree editor in the Unreal Engine viewport.

12.3.1.1 Main Concepts

The tree generation process is based on using UE4 Spline Components to define the shape and placement of roots, trunk, branches and sub-branches. Spline points are controlled by an extensive set of parameters that are exposed for the end user to tweak.

All the parameters can be randomized based on seed values, which can result in a different tree each time a seed value is changed. It is also possible to control the spline points individually by hand, so full artistic control can be retained despite the procedural nature of the tool.

12.3.1.2 Root, Branch and Sub-Branch Placement

Spline Component allows the user to specify a set of subsequent points in 3D space to create curves with controllable tangents. It also provides *GetLocationAtSplinePoint* and *GetLocationAtTime* functions that allow the user to access location coordinates along a specified spline distance – this is used to place branches along the trunk and add sub-branches on parent branches.

By default, roots are placed on the lower section of the trunk spline, but that can also be overridden if there is a need for surrealistic tree types.

Branch orientation is also based on spline data, in this case on trunk spline direction at a specified distance. By combining the obtained location and rotation values, the system spawns another spline that is used for roots, branches or sub-branches (Figure 12.14).

Spline Mesh Component is used to generate 3D mesh geometry along a specified spline. For the trunk and branch generation, a modular uncapped

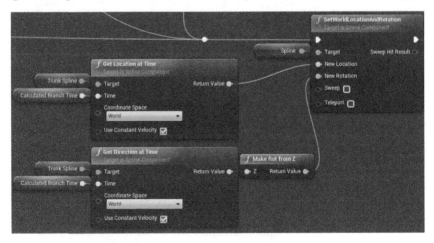

FIGURE 12.14   Example of branch placement setting for location and rotation.

cylinder mesh is used to distribute it along the spline while respecting all the spline tangents and scale values (Figure 12.15).

Besides the spline-based placement, the user can control the branch number and other placement rules, for example, the yaw rotation method (Figure 12.16).

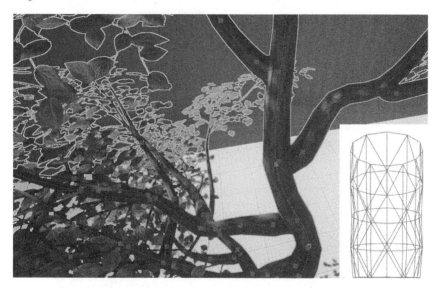

FIGURE 12.15   Wireframe view of modular trunk mesh with an example along-spline distribution.

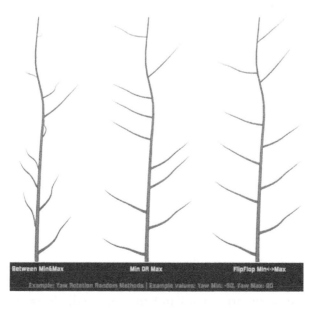

FIGURE 12.16   Examples of default yaw rotation methods for branches.

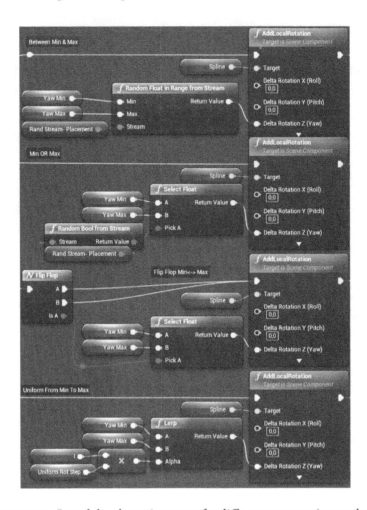

FIGURE 12.17   Branch local rotation setup for different yaw rotation methods.

There are also parameters for limiting the individual rotation axis (*Roll*, *Pitch* and *Yaw* values), so it is possible, for example, to generate trees that do not follow the natural growth behavior rules and have branches facing downwards or twisted in a specific way.

It works by getting a main parent branch spline direction, using it to rotate the child-branch rotation vector around it and converting the result to a regular *Rotator* value type, so it can be used with the final *Transform* value for a branch (Figure 12.17).

12.3.1.3 Branch Intersection Blending

Each branch has a special start section, where the mesh is scaled at its base to align to the parent branch or trunk more naturally. This solution helps to improve the look of the trunk – branch transition, but the intersection area is still visible due to the 3D meshes that intersect with each other and have different vertex normals.

To solve this issue, branches are vertex colored at the base. Then, the bark material applies a dithering effect on that region, using the *DitherTemporalAA* material function. Dithered opacity is better for performance than regular transparency (it also works better under certain specific lighting conditions), since it uses a checkerboard-like pattern with 0–1 values to determine if a pixel should be opaque or not, instead of a more costly alpha blending (Figure 12.18).

This creates an effect where branches visually blend with trunk and parent branch textures at the intersection area. It eliminates the harsh intersection and from a certain distance it looks like a naturally developed transition (Figure 12.19).

The difference is especially prominent when using bark textures with strongly visible patterns. Scaling the UV coordinates can also lead to more or less visible seams and a stronger or lesser transition blending effect.

12.3.1.4 Leaf Placement
Location and rotation values for leaves are calculated using the same spline functions for getting spline point location/direction. Every branch can have a user-specified number of leaves, using a custom leaf layer system that allows for different leaf layers if there is a need for more leaf types growing on the same tree (Figure 12.20).

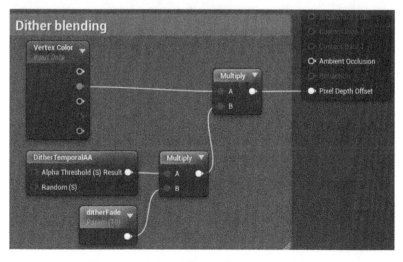

FIGURE 12.18   *DitherTemporalAA* blending inside bark material graph.

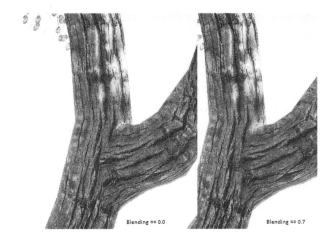

FIGURE 12.19   Branch intersection blending example.

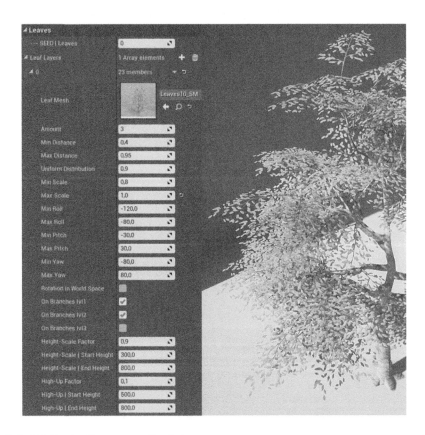

FIGURE 12.20   Fragment of leaf placement parameters.

By default, the leaves are distributed along the parent branch spline with uniform spacing to achieve a natural leaf coverage. The user can override this by using many parameters for leaf placement.

Any mesh can be used as a leaf. The standard approach is to use simple plane-like meshes with alpha-tested material to reduce the vertex count on the final tree asset. One of the drawbacks is increased shader complexity in scenes with many trees, caused by overdraw (many alpha-tested meshes overlapping each other through their transparent areas). To minimize this, leaf meshes are trimmed in a way that they fit leaf texture as closely as possible, without increasing the vertex count too much. The goal is to reduce the transparent area (coming from the assigned leaf texture alpha channel or opacity mask) on the mesh (Figure 12.21).

There are more leaf growth behavior settings in the ITC tool. For example, leaves can grow smaller at the top of trees or be more up-facing the higher they grow – this is useful for creating certain tree types, for example, some conifer trees.

12.3.1.5 Fruit Placement

Procedural placement methods can also be utilized to add fruits on generated trees in the correct places. The system calculates fruit locations by getting mesh data from leaf planes and offsetting mesh surface points by fruit mesh pivot points. The final effect is approximated (especially when looking at leaves during GPU wind simulation in the vertex offset shader), but from a certain distance it looks convincing enough for use in most cases (Figure 12.22).

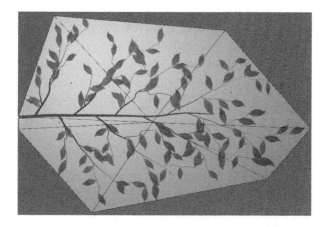

FIGURE 12.21   Example leaf mesh plane with visible wireframe.

FIGURE 12.22   Example fruit mesh placed on a tree.

12.3.1.6 Wind Weighting

Wind is simulated using a GPU vertex offset inside the leaf and branch shader. To make the trees behave realistically, vertices need to be weighted for different wind intensity values, depending on height along the tree and progress along the parent branch. This way, tree branches can sway differently based on their location when affected by the wind.

The system writes this data into vertex colors of branches and leaf meshes, using 0–1 value, where 0 means no wind effect and 1 corresponds to full strength wind effect. Then, the material can read it via the *Vertex Color* node and apply the correct vertex offset for current wind strength and direction, using the *Lerp* node (linear interpolation) (Figure 12.23).

12.3.1.7 Automatic Billboard Generation

Billboard is a term used to describe a simple version of an asset that can be used to mimic mesh geometry when viewed from a great distance – usually it is a flat plane mesh with assigned texture representing the original asset

Default wind weighting for branches

FIGURE 12.23   Wind weights visualized with vertex colors.

model. It is important to reduce vertex count in more complex scenes (e.g. dense forest scenarios) and using billboards as distant mesh versions at largest LOD (level of detail) helps with that.

The Interactive Tree Creator allows the generation of billboards automatically for each created tree. The system measures tree dimensions in all three axes (XYZ), comparing each result and based on maximum bound extent it applies proper dimensions for the billboard mesh plane. This way the tree billboard plane matches the true tree geometry.

The tree image is captured via the *Scene Capture 2D* component that writes the result into a *Render Target* texture. The capture component needs to be located at an accurately calculated position, in a way that it encompasses the whole tree in its camera view, using orthographic projection. The component is also tweaked to capture only the specified objects, in this case only the tree that needs to be captured. The rest of the scene is discarded in the scene capture rendering (Figure 12.24).

Scene lighting is altered before capturing the subject to eliminate as much lighting information as possible. Evenly lit, neutral billboard texture is required to make it usable under different lighting conditions.

There is also a possible improvement for that which requires generating dedicated normal maps for each billboard. Having normal maps on billboards can help to achieve realistically lit distant trees with an additional sense of depth.

FIGURE 12.24   Example billboard meshes compared with regular trees.

12.3.1.8 Preparing the Trees for Use

Procedurally created trees can be converted to regular static meshes, which allows them to be used with UE4 instanced mesh foliage tools. This is necessary to achieve good runtime performance and to be able to place trees in 3D scenes in a convenient way, either by hand (by using the Unreal Engine 4 Foliage tool) or procedurally.

Using the *Merge Actors* tool, procedurally generated trees can be saved as static meshes while retaining all the necessary data like vertex colors.

12.3.1.9 Force Reaction and Dynamic Wind

Trees generated with the Interactive Tree Creator contain additional information (stored, for example, in vertex colors) that is used by the main tree shader to apply different forces and make the trees react accordingly (Figure 12.25).

The default system allows for control of the dynamic wind speed and direction, point impulse forces and constant radial forces. Besides dynamic, smoothly changing weather conditions, these features also allow for things like bomb shockwaves or helicopters flying over trees while affecting the branches and leaves in a convincing way.

FIGURE 12.25   Point force example, affecting trees within a specified radius.

The system knows where to apply force points through the global material parameter collection. Location, radius and strength of a force is passed from tree Blueprint logic to the global parameter collection, then it is accessed by the main tree material shader (Figure 12.26).

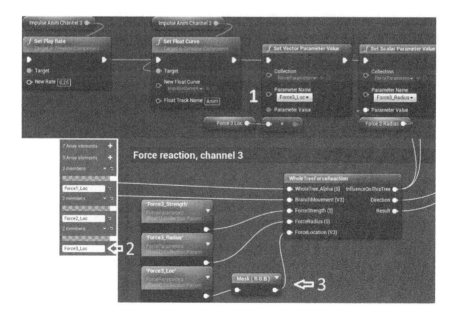

FIGURE 12.26   Force reaction logic flow.

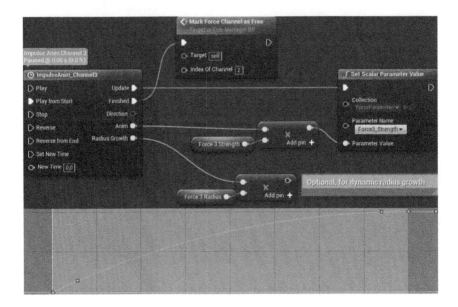

FIGURE 12.27   Impulse animation logic with timeline curve.

Blueprints also control the duration of forces, and when it is time to turn one off, they gradually decrease the force strength value via Timeline with custom curve (Figure 12.27).

12.3.1.10 Tree Chopping, Falling Fruits, Leaves and Debris

Each procedurally created tree is assigned to a custom Foliage Component, where all the tree specific data is stored. This allows the implementation of additional game mechanics like tree chopping or wood and fruit gathering.

The tree chopping system supports many chopping progress stages, where each tree type can have a different *HP* (*Health Points*) value. Based on that, the developer can set these values in a way that each chopping hit will gradually carve in the tree surface, resembling a real chopping process. To achieve that, tree Blueprint generation logic saves a separate set of data: top tree part, bottom tree part and parameters for trunk area where chopping should occur. Then the Foliage Component swaps the tree mesh to chopped version and adjusts the chopping area to match current tree HP value (Figure 12.28).

If the *HP* value reaches 0, the tree is marked as chopped and it starts simulating tree fall, using the Unreal Engine 4 physics engine. Falling trees are controlled by dedicated Blueprints where the system waits until it hits any surface by checking current tree velocity and comparing it with the previously recorded value. If it is drastically different, then it can

FIGURE 12.28   Tree chopping in game.

assume that the tree landed, and it is the right time to play impact animation (Figure 12.29).

Upon impact, the tree can spawn other physics objects defined by the user, for example, bark parts, little twigs, leaves or fruits. There is also a slot for a particle system that can be used to add dust particles to enhance the tree impact effect.

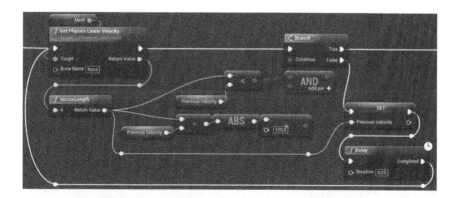

FIGURE 12.29   Logic for checking if the falling tree hits the ground.

Besides the fall impact, trees can also drop leaves while being in an idle state or while a player chops the trunk. These effects (for idle leaf falling) are calculated only when a player is near a tree for performance reasons. The simulation cull distance is controllable.

Another way to make leaves, fruits or debris fall from a tree is to use the included force effect Blueprints. When impulse force is deployed near a tree and it is strong enough, it will make it drop a specified amount of leaves, debris and fruit (if the tree has any fruits).

12.3.2 Smart Spline Generator

Some game assets are meant to be used only in specific level locations, conforming to unique scene geometry. For example, vines or other plants that hang from point A to point B. Assets like these can be cumbersome to create, especially when there is a need to modify the underlying level geometry or add a new element that interferes with current asset design.

Smart Spline Generator is a tool that allows the user to procedurally generate assets that automatically align to level geometry. The user can use any custom mesh, so the generator can produce vines, fences, ropes, cables, walls, drainpipes and more. It is available on the UE4 Marketplace, along with a video preview for additional insights (Figure 12.30).

12.3.2.1 Main Concepts

Procedural surface-aligning asset generation works with any collision enabled surface. The user can drag an asset preset from the Unreal Engine 4 editor content browser and drop it into a 3D scene to immediately see the effect. The generator detects surface in a specified direction, over a specified distance, using many parameters exposed from the Blueprint system.

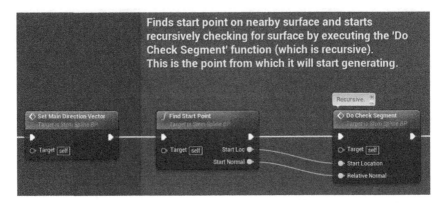

FIGURE 12.30 Example assets created with Smart Spline Generator.

12.3.2.2 Recursive Surface Align Algorithm

A custom algorithm was created in order to implement the surface align feature. After setting the main direction vector and finding the start point using *Line Trace* functions, it executes a recursive function for surface detection in a previously calculated direction (Figure 12.31).

SetMainDirectionVector allows the user to specify in what direction the asset should generate. The main direction vector is saved as a variable inside the main generator class, so the other functions inside it can access it later. The variable is also used in other parts of the tool, so the value is not passed through the function outputs in this case.

FindStartPoint function performs a *Line Trace By Channel*, where it detects a starting point from near the surface in a specified direction. It also returns the normal vector of a detected surface, so the next function can use it to align the detection points properly.

DoCheckSegment: most of the surface detection logic is contained in this function. It is recursive, in this case it executes itself if a specified condition is not met yet, for example, if the user wants to generate X amount of spline segments along the surface, it will keep generating until the desired number of segments are created.

After each execution, the function passes new calculated values for inputs *StartLocation* and *RelativeNormal* when calling itself from inside. This way, it can use the last calculated point as a new starting point to detect and generate points one after another, progressing through the detected surface.

FIGURE 12.31   Initial logic for surface detection.

Surface detection relies on *LineTrace* functions from calculated locations to check the hit location and normal values to determine further generation steps. In general, the algorithm works as shown in Figure 12.32.

Additionally, the algorithm checks if the specified point amount is already reached. If that is true, it does not execute the function, breaking the recursive execution chain.

The set of points calculated in the *DoCheckSegment* recursive function are passed to the next function which creates *Spline Mesh Component* along the points.

12.3.2.3 Vert Count Optimization with Spline Thicken Function

Using modular cylinder meshes as *Spline Mesh Component* sections will provide good results for most cases, but for larger assets, it introduces a significant vertex count increase. To reduce the vertex amount, the system uses the *Spline Thicken* function inside the main material. This function is a part of the Unreal Engine 4 toolset and it allows the use of simple polygon strips instead of cylinders while retaining the cylindrical look (Figure 12.33).

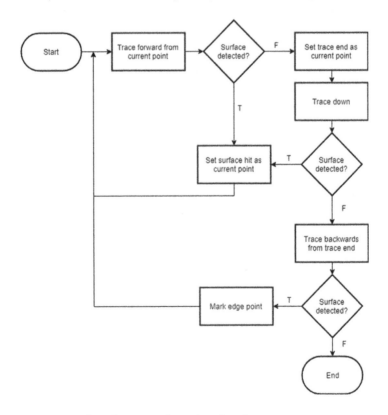

FIGURE 12.32   Surface detection algorithm flowchart.

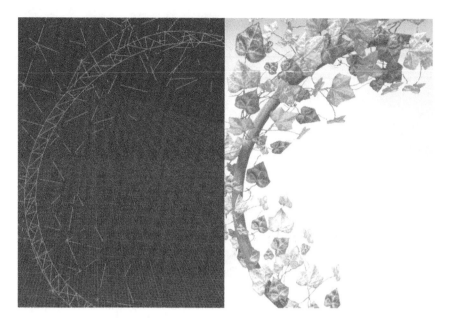

FIGURE 12.33 Wireframe and regular view of polygon strip with the *Spline Thicken* function applied.

Thickness is controlled inside the material by getting vertex color values from polygon strip mesh. The mesh is painted with the *PaintVerticesLerpAlongAxis* function with 0–1 value that represents thickness. It is saved into the *Red* channel of vertex color. This way the user can control the thickness along surface aligned points, usually it is used to taper vine stems at the end or set the overall volume of stems, cables, ropes and so on (Figure 12.34).

Controlling the stem look via vertex colors also allows to add more visual tweaks inside the material. There is also room for more features that can be controlled using other vertex color channels (green and blue).

12.3.2.4 Merging to Static Mesh

Assets generated with Smart Spline Generator are ready to use immediately, but it is recommended to merge them into a regular static mesh as a final step. This significantly reduces the draw call amount for each asset by combining all spline mesh sections and, for example, many leaves mesh into one object. It can be achieved with the Merge Actors tool that is available in Unreal Engine 4, under the Developer Tools menu.

Merging an asset into one static mesh also provides a way to easily save generated assets and export them in FBX or OBJ format to external 3D applications for further editing.

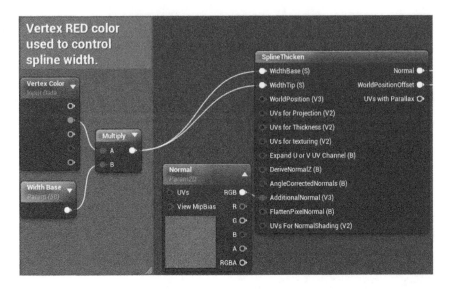

FIGURE 12.34   Vertex color used to control stem thickness inside material graph.

12.4 GAME LEVEL DESIGN

Game level is the arena for both players' avatars and non-playable characters (NPCs). It gives the game player a sense of "Presence" to immerse her/him in the gameplay. Game design includes the planning and integration of various 3D assets that form the entire game "world." Terrain, buildings, foliage, lights and other elements including HUDs (Head Up Displays) should be thoughtfully composed to ensure maximum playability and fun for the player. This section provides hints on successful game level design.

12.4.1 Game Level Construction: "Presence" Approach

The synthetic environment of the first-person perspective (FPP) game level is created to give the impression of "being" in the multisensory three-dimensional space. The phenomenon of immersion is closely related to the quality of experiences experienced by means of sight, hearing and touch. In recent years, there has been a rapid development of computer graphics techniques enabling hyper-realistic depiction of the visual space. The introduction of emotional visuals and narratives increases the sense of "Presence" or immersion of the game player. The aims of this section are:

- to understand the potential to use ideas from "Presence" space and place when considering immersion of the game player;

- to understand different properties of visual space which can impact upon game level design; and

- to learn about a specific method of evaluation.

12.4.1.1 Presence and the Concepts of Space

For the first time, the term "Presence" was mentioned by Minski (Minsky, 1980) as an experience of being in a remote environment. In literature, "Presence" is most often given as "behaviour in a virtual environment as in the real world" and refers not only to spatial relations but also to non-physical elements of perception and interaction (Riva, 2003). The definition of "Presence" as a phenomenon gives it as "an effective replacement or enrichment of reality perception by virtual stimulation" where efficacy is confirmed by user behavior analysis in physiological, psychological and behavioral aspects and comparison of results obtained without stimulation (EU FP6 PRESENCCIA). Effectiveness depends on the quality of interaction and information transfer along with its context. Another definition of "Presence" as a research area is focused on understanding and controlling the "experience" (in the perceptual and emotional sense) of being "somewhere." "Somewhere" is understood as a Place and Space and time or as another person. "Experience" is provided through technologies such as VR (virtual reality), AR (augmented reality), and Telepresence. Other definitions of "Presence" (abridged version of the remote presence of Telepresence) include a psychological state or a subjective perception in which, despite synthetic stimulation, the user is unable to partially or completely recognize the use of technology in contact with the environment. The environment is observable, stochastic, sequential, dynamic and is inherently a continuous process (ISPR: International Society for Presence Research: http://ispr.info/). Space is an ontology for three dimensions, taxonomy and linguistics that organize it. The American researcher Edward T. Hall dealt with determining how we behave in various socially and culturally defined spaces-distances (Hall and Pellow, 1996).

Proxemics define the invisible personal space of a man whose reach is shaped by a culture specific to a given person. It determines not only distances, but also the boundaries that divide us from others (intimate, personal, social, public). For example, Jandt (see Table 12.1) specifies the dimensions and method of interpersonal communication in these spaces (Jandt, 2007).

TABLE 12.1 Distances in Interpersonal Relations

Space category	Distance	Description	Sound volume
Intimate	Up to 45 cm	Highly emotional experiences incorporating touch and body contact	Whisper
Personal	From 45 cm to 1.2 m	Distance of a handshake	Silent
Social	From 1.2 m to 3.6 m	Customer and seller relations, co-workers	Loud
Public	More than 3.6 m	Teacher/speaker in the classroom, concerts	Very loud/amplified

Several researchers tried to define the relationship between the concepts of space and the feeling of presence/immersion. According to Slater and Wilbur we can be immersed within the movie, game or virtual reality to the extent that displays can deliver an extensive, surrounding and vivid illusion of reality to our senses (Slater, 1997). The more we forget about the medium delivering stimuli, the more immersed in this environment we are. Then, we experience a high feeling of presence when we have a more vivid memory "as if we were there." Based on the results of research related to IP City and Benogo projects (McCall, 2008), it is possible to determine how places are perceived in both real and fully synthetic environments. The "place" is characterized by several properties, the most prominent is the association of space and meaning. The place is interesting when it has a certain function. The places can be connected to form environments. We are particularly interested in highly responsive environments, since they are the backbone of good game level design. Such environments are characterized by permeability (usability), variety (of associated actions), robustness (multiple actions and uses), visual appropriateness (we can easily recognize type of the place), aesthetics and visual richness (with consistent style) and legibility (we can recognize all assets).

12.4.2 Level Design: Game Genres and Levels

The definition of "game level" varies greatly according to the game type. It usually refers to the game world of arcade side-scrollers, puzzles, adventures, flight and car simulators, FPS (first-person shooters) and RPGs (role-playing games). These games have distinct playing areas which are referred to as "game levels." These areas can be constrained by geography (maps), by geometry (arenas) or by amount of gameplay that must be completed before the player is granted access to the "next" (usually more "demanding") levels. Some games (retro/arcade) take place entirely on one level, other have some variations of the game area, and they can be linked into maps, mazes or tracks (for racing games). There are also so-called "building" games where the level is designed and built by the player (*Minecraft* and *Fortnite* are the most popular examples). The base levels for such games are usually randomly generated and it is the player's responsibility to construct the level during her/his playing. This chapter deals primarily with games that use pre-built levels that have a great impact on user experience and gameplay.

Different types of games use different visuals. Table 12.2 illustrates different viewing approaches (and level construction paradigms) according to game imaging technology. The chapter contents are mostly devoted to 3D games, although some ideas can be relatively easy ported to 2.5 and 2D games (Rogers, 2014; Rouse, 2001).

TABLE 12.2   Visuals, Types of Games and Camera Narrations

Game engine	Typical Games	Description	Camera
2D	Arcade/retro	Flat images, that can be arranged in different layers. The main visual tools are sprites and image textures.	Flat, orthogonal. No perspective applied.
2.5D	Ecosystem simulations, RPGs, strategies, combat arcade	"3D"-like looking images put on a plain background. The driving technology is still sprites/impostors and textures.	Isometric camera with "God's eye" perspective, other perspectives can be applied (cavalier, etc.)
3D	First-person shooters, fighting, sports, simulations, RPGs	Fully 3D assets, the game is displayed on a flat screen. The underlying game engine operates on a plethora of graphic object, including 3D meshes, 3D sprites, particle systems, textures and lights.	Moving/floating camera, first-person perspective, third-person perspective. Cinematic quality requires "camera operation" as it is done in classical movies.
3D XR	RPG, first-person shooters, puzzle/ escape rooms, music/rhythm games	Fully 3D assets, the game is displayed in on head-mounted displays or VR goggles. The underlying game engine operates on a plethora of graphic objects, including 3D meshes, 3D sprites, particle systems, textures and lights.	Usually first-person perspective only. Stereoscopic imaging is necessary to realistically depict the game "universe."

Different types of games require different approaches to game level design. The underlying visual technology (performed by the game engine and reflecting the gamer's point of view) determines the level flow. There are basically two groups of games: linear (action/adventure, puzzle solving, role-playing and racing) and non-linear (strategy/simulation, sports and shooters/death-match). Whether it is a linear or non-linear game, various game level components will be arranged in a different manner (Costikyan, 2015).

12.4.3 Components of a Level

Once the idea of the story describing the game and the type of game have been decided in, the next task is to actually design and create the game levels. The goal of each level is to provide a highly engaging experience and maximum fun for the player. In this pre-production stage, we need to remember that each level should be played differently from others. Before construction of the level, the team/designer should break down the various gameplay components of the game. One of the approaches is to break down the components of a level into elements associated with geometry, actions, asset and sounds (Rouse, 2001).

12.4.3.1 Geometry of the Level

Physical space consists of various elements that give meaning (functionality) to the place (Figure 12.35). When applied to the game level, appropriate use can enhance playability of the game and clearly state the objectives of game design.

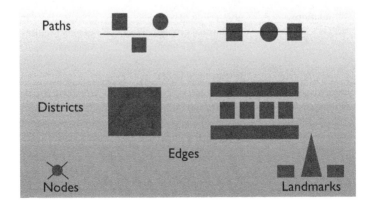

FIGURE 12.35   Different geometry elements of physical space.

All elements can be composed to a game level map (see next section) and illustrate game narratives visually. Paths declare, then, routes for possible movement of a player's avatar and NPC, Districts offer exploration areas and can also serve as a duel arena, Edges funnel the player to the predetermined goal, Landmarks offer memorable visual clues and help with player's orientation and Nodes are goals and assets to be completed/collected during gameplay.

12.4.3.2 Game Level Description

Before placing all assets on the game level scene, it should be thoughtfully designed. Time spent on design pays off during final composition and saves effort in the further game testing phase.

12.4.3.2.1 Description of a Place   Concept of the game level design can be outlined by several means, including text, storyboards, concept arts and mood boards. Game documentation agreed upon at the previous game development stages usually contains names of Section/Level/Scene and its textual description including physical and audio appearance. A sketch of the background, or mood board are very useful (Figure 12.36). Foreground objects and characters (see Section 12.4.3.2.3) may be depicted too (Schwartz, 2005).

12.4.3.2.2 Level map   Level maps help to clarify the definition of the landscape and playable areas/districts. They include positions of all-important assets and (simplified/iconized) physical elements. A simple legend

FIGURE 12.36 Sample moodboard for the post-apocalyptic game. (Created by Anna Wieszczeczynska as a part of student's project at the University of Zielona Góra, Poland, 2014. All permissions granted.)

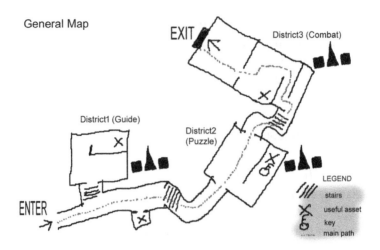

FIGURE 12.37   Sample general map of a level.

attached to the map can help with understanding the construction of the level (Figure 12.37). Additional descriptions of action paths and asset roles (Section 12.4.3.2.3) is welcome too.

12.4.3.2.3 Assets   Digital assets are all elements of the game. Most of them are defined by geometry, however, they include digital sounds and AI algorithms. Speaking of geometry, digital assets are graphic elements that can be 2D or 3D meshes, with or without rigs (internal skeleton). Graphic elements also include textures/materials that define their appearance, lights/shading (responsible for spatial properties of the scene) and various special effects (fire, smoke, explosions, water etc. where we cannot strictly determine underlying geometry). We can generally define different types of assets specifying their role in the game and position (node) or path on the game level map. While placing active elements on the map we can use the distances defined in Table 12.1 to evoke desired emotions (Freeman, 2003; Koster, 2013). A sample description of assets is provided in Tables 12.3 and 12.4.

12.4.3.2.4 Sounds   Music and sounds add mood and sense of physical reality to the game level. While music and generally background sounds are omnidirectional and add some "spice" to the scene, action sounds are tightly connected to physical assets and their performance. When you shoot a shotgun, you should hear the explosion and the sound of hitting pellets. When you walk on the broken glass, you should hear cracks and so on. Such sounds are directional, have location and limited range.

TABLE 12.3   Action-Type Definitions of Active Assets

Color category	Cost	Player/AI control abilities	Combat	Speed	Lifespan	Hitpoints
Green	Low	Scout and errand. Can use few weapons.	Low	Fast	Medium	Low
Gray	Medium	Medium combat skills. Can use some weapons. Can transfer health to humans.	Medium	Medium	High	Medium
Yellow	High	Good combat ability. Can use all weapons. Strong defense.	High	Medium	Low	High
Black	Very high	Strong combat, detect and disable traps and ambushes. Seek and destroy abilities.	Very high	Slow	Medium	Low

TABLE 12.4   Sample Asset Classification Based on the Narratives

Asset category	Action	Location	Description
Monster	Eat	Jungle	Teeth
	Growl	Trees	Horns
	Hide	River	Scales
	Run	Meadows	Claws
	Sleep		Tail
	Hunt		Eyes
	Scratch		
	Scare		
Fairy	Sing	Trees	Wings
	Hide	Bush	Fur
	Sleep	Meadows	Eyes
	Help		

12.4.3.2.5 Technical Design Specification   When the early prototype of the game level is about to be ready, it is worth documenting technical details. This saves time and money, especially in cases where the game project is shared with other developers or gamedev team members allowing many people to work at once. If we document further details of assets (type and size of meshes, rigs and textures, definition of data structures and interfaces, parameters of procedural design) and pseudocode describing actions and interactions, it forms a solid background for game development.

12.4.4 Aesthetics

Visual emphasis greatly influences "Presence" of the player and her/his gameplay. The way the game is emotionally perceived is strongly related to a level's appearance. Even if the game is visually gorgeous, we must remember that all elements should support the player in game, help him/her to navigate, engage AI powered NPCs and comply to hardware specification in order to make the game engine run efficiently. To do so, the level designer should balance the appearance of the level with its functionality. The ideal compromise is when the level looks great, actions are smooth and all renders quickly and fit in the narratives of the game. The level designers "collect" their experiences with a given game engine or level editor and make a "workbench" of "tricks" to be applied. Some solutions are not very realistic but they are good enough to be plausible. If the player cannot tell what elements of the game level are "fake" it is okay. This is the basic principle of VFX (visual special effects), to create something that looks like something when it is actually different. The level designer job is similar to a VFX artist! The visuals of the game level have a big impact on the game perception and immersion of the player, it holds especially for the XR (eXtended reality) games including virtual reality and mixed reality games. Plenty of time can be spent on the aesthetics of a game level. The time spent in the creative process is directly proportional to the complexity of the underlying game engine and the given level editor. Some elements like lighting can be endlessly adjusted (the lighting of the scene is beyond the scope of this chapter, we suggest following the rules of digital photography guide books, for example (Donati, 2009). We can, however, use several "tools" and rules to make the game level design process easier, including: motion, location, size, shape, padding (HUD), rule of thirds, leading lines, rhythm-actual, implied, psychical, contrast, hue, saturation and humans/face/eyes. See following examples. Motion and movement are great methods for getting players' attention guiding their actions. Dynamic elements of the level highlight points of interest and can also serve as "landmarks" (Figure 12.38).

Location and size. Sometimes it is useful to funnel the player through narrow areas when you want to orient her/him towards the goal. By funneling the player's avatar, you know where the player will be looking. It is particularly useful in VR games and for guiding the player after navigating through open areas (Figure 12.39).

FIGURE 12.38   Illustration of dynamic elements of the level. (fire draws the player's eye attention). (Chernobylite © 2019. With permission from The Farm 51 Group SA. All rights reserved.)

FIGURE 12.39   Illustration of funneling (the only way out is through the footpath). (Chernobylite © 2019. With permission from The Farm 51 Group SA. All rights reserved.)

Shape. Characteristic shape can serve as a landmark or grab attention of the gameplayer. The shape should create visual contrast between it and the rest of the environment (Figure 12.40).

Padding (HUD). Head up displays provide current information (status, time, compass, life, ammo etc.) to the player. HUD should be legible in any

FIGURE 12.40   Illustration of shape role in the level flow. (Chernobylite © 2019. With permission from The Farm 51 Group SA. All rights reserved.)

level/lighting conditions and should not obscure the game arena during the action (Figure 12.41).

Leading lines. Some visual patterns suggest directions and movement to the game player. The leading lines are the most straightforward approach (Figure 12.42).

FIGURE 12.41   Illustration of proper HUD padding. (Chernobylite © 2019. With permission from The Farm 51 Group SA. All rights reserved.)

FIGURE 12.42   Illustration of guiding lines. (Chernobylite © 2019. With permission from The Farm 51 Group SA. All rights reserved.)

Rhythm. Repeated elements of the scene can help to guide the player through the level. (Figure 12.43) Contrast and lighting also help with depicting possible targets to the game player. (The floor in Figure 12.43 is clearly lighter than the surroundings.)

Hue and Saturation. Careful use of hue and saturation is necessary in the design of open spaces (Figure 12.44). So-called atmospheric effects (clouds, fog, smoke) highly influence the mood of the game.

FIGURE 12.43   Illustration of rhythm-guiding repeated elements (toys with similar size). (Chernobylite © 2019. With permission from The Farm 51 Group SA. All rights reserved.)

FIGURE 12.44 Illustration of hue and saturation influence on the level mood. (Chernobylite © 2019. With permission from The Farm 51 Group SA. All rights reserved.)

Humans/face. The appearance of humans, in particular, their faces, has a very strong impact on the mood of the game. While humanoid characters are the most demanding assets (requiring rigging, skinning and nowadays motion and performance capture) they certainly pay off during the game. First of all they add a "human" touch to the scene and define proportions of assets, evoke different emotions and moreover they can serve as a guide in helping the game player to complete all the tasks assigned in the game (Figure 12.45).

12.4.5 Elements of Good Level Design

A good game level must balance several things. The game level designer is not only a VFX expert but should balance aesthetics, action, storytelling and technical requirements (texture sizes, meshes, simulations) to make everything work smoothly. All elements are interdependent, and the decisions made are always a kind of trade-offs. There are common measures that can form a "checklist" to test completeness of the game level. Every designer will have her/his own list of "dos" and "don'ts" that is kept in mind. A collection of typical "design rules" which can be applied virtually to any project is presented here.

Player cannot get stuck. The player's avatar should never become stuck when playing the level. The routes should be designed with no holes to be fallen into without the possibility of climbing out, no objects can block

FIGURE 12.45 Illustration of human presence influence on the level design. (Chernobylite © 2019. With permission from The Farm 51 Group SA. All rights reserved.)

the way both for the avatar (always) and NPCs (unless they can be placed and removed by the player) and no doors that fail to open under certain conditions. This requirement should be obvious, but to make it happen, it needs a lot of time to design and test paths and actions on the given level. The best way to achieve game flow in such situations is either to end the game instantly in case of a wrong sequence of actions (if the key is needed to open the door and the player destroyed the key with dynamite…) or to provide alternative solutions/actions. The level must end despite any actions of the game player.

Sub- and side-tasks. As the player plays the game level, she/he should clearly understand how to accomplish some larger goal. To do so, the level should consist of various clearly defined sub-tasks to be completed to archive the main goal. This can be done through various sub-quests, funneling the player through some level areas and hints/positive feedback after the completion of certain tasks.

Milestones and Landmarks. The more levels are "completed" by the player, the harder it becomes to complete them. The player should not be confused while navigating even more complicated levels. The best way to help him/her is to use memorable visual landmarks, characteristic to the level. A good landmark is any unique visual object in the level that the player recognizes next time she/he sees it. As far as exploration is considered, when the player returns to (respawns at) the landmark, she/he will know it is the location previously visited.

Critical paths. In cases of non-linear level flow, the game needs critical paths to give the player the sense of direction she/he can go in order to complete the level. This can be a physical direction, signs or some more ambiguous goals. The player should have a clear idea of the possible routes in the level. We can use various visual clues as illustrated in the previous sections to help the player move around the level and find the tasks.

Limited backtracking is necessary in games where the game covers a geographically large area. If the player has already explored some extent of the game, it would be a bad idea to force him/her to go through large sections of the level to continue the game.

Multiple choices. Good levels give the game player choices of how to accomplish tasks. Choices do not always mean multiple paths through a level; we can use different assets or alternative game logic to extend available options. We can provide alternative ways to complete the level taking into account, for instance, the easiest and toughest situations that can be faced on the level.

Estimated time to complete the level. The best way to control the level flow is to control the time to complete it. Varying time can induce different "hardness" levels and may force the player to perform faster actions or the opposite, get some rest and explore the district both for "fun" (so-called "Easter eggs") or to collect necessary assets useful at further levels.

ACKNOWLEDGEMENTS

This publication has emanated from research conducted with the financial support of Science Foundation Ireland (SFI) under Grant Number 15/IA/3090.

REFERENCES

Batty, M., Dodge, M., Jiang, B., & Smith, A. (2000). *For Urban Designers: The VENUE Project.* ISSN:1467–1298. CASA/UCL.

Beneš, B., & Forsbach, R. (2001). Layered data representation for visual simulation of terrain erosion. *Proceedings of Spring Conference on Computer Graphics (SCCG '01)*, Budmerice, Slovakia, pp. 80–85. ISBN: 0-7695-1215-1.

Building City Dashboards. (2016). Retrieved July 1, 2019, from https://dashboards.maynoothuniversity.ie/.

Costikyan, G. (2015). *Uncertainty in Games*. MIT Press.

Donati, J. (2009). *Exploring Digital Cinematography*. Cengage Learning Inc.

Eleftheriou, O. (2018, May 12). Creating Procedural Meshes. Retrieved July 2, 2019, from https://orfeasel.com/creating-procedural-meshes/.

Epic Games. (2018, October 4). Building Better Blueprints. Retrieved from https://www.youtube.com/watch?v=WA8ihra87cM.

Freeman, D. (2003). *Creating Emotion in Games: The Craft and Art of Emotioneering™*. New Riders Publishing.

Galin, E., Guérin, E., Peytavie, A., Cordonnier, G., Cani, M.-P., Beneš, B., & James, G. (2019). A review of digital terrain modeling. *Computer Graphics Forum*, 38(2), 553–577. ISSN: 1467-8659.

Guérin, E., Digne, J., Galin, E., Peytavie, A., Wolf, C., Beneš, B., & Martinez, B. (2017). Interactive example-based terrain authoring with conditional generative adversarial networks. *ACM Transactions on Graphics*, 36(6), 228.

Hall, E. T., & Pellow, D. (1996). *Setting Boundaries: The Anthropology of Spatial and Social Organization*. Greenwood International.

Horne, M. (2004). Visualization of Martyr's Square, Beirut. *Conference on Construction Applications of Virtual Reality, ADETTI/ISCTE*, Lisbon, Portugal.

Jandt, F. J. (2007). *Intercultural Communication*. Sage Publications Inc.

Jepson, W. B. (2006). *The UCLA Urban Simulation Lab and the Complete Virtual L.A. Model(s)*.

Koster, R. (2013). *A Theory If Fun for Game Design*. O'Reilly Media.

Krezel, S. (2016, June 29). Smart Spline Generator. Retrieved July 2, 2019, from https://www.unrealengine.com/marketplace/en-US/slug/smart-spline-generator.

Krezel, S. (2017, September 26). Interactive Tree Creator. Retrieved July 2, 2019, from https://www.unrealengine.com/marketplace/en-US/slug/interactive-tree-creator.

McCall, R. (2008). *Place Probe, BENOGO*. FET EU FP6 Programme.

Mandelbrot, B. B. (1982). *The Fractal Geometry of Nature*. 2nd ed. San Francisco, CA: H.W. Freeman and Co. ISBN: 0-7167-1186-9.

Minsky, M. (1980). *Telepresence*. Omni.

Riva, G. (2003). *Being There: Concepts, Effects and Measurement of User Presence in Synthetic Environments*. Ios Press.

Rogers, S. (2014). *Level Up! The Guide to Great Game Design*. Wiley.

Rouse, R. (2001). *Game Design Theory and Practice*. Wordware Publishing, Inc.

Saunders, R. L. (2006). *Terrainosaurus: Realistic Terrain Synthesis Using Genetic Algorithms*. Master's thesis, Texas A&M University.

Schwartz, L. (2005). *Adobe Photoshop for VFX Artists*. Thomson Course PTR.

Slater, M., & Wilbur, S. (1997). A framework for immersive virtual environments (FIVE): Speculations on the role of presence in virtual environments. *Presence: Teleoperators and Virtual Environments*, 6(6), 603–616.

Smelik, R. M., Kraker, K. J. de, Tutenel, T., Bidarra, R., & Groenewegen, S. A. (2009). A survey of procedural methods for terrain modelling. *Proceedings of CASA Workshop on 3D Advanced Media In Gaming And Simulation (3AMIGAS '09)*, Amsterdam, The Netherlands, pp. 25–34.

Suomisto, J. (2001). Urban simulation in Helsinki city planning. *KeyNote Presentation at ECAADE 2001 Conference*, Helsinki.

Unreal Engine 4 Documentation. (n.d.). Retrieved July 2, 2019, from https://docs .unrealengine.com/en-US/index.html.

CHAPTER 13

Challenges in Designing and Implementing a Vector-Based 2D Animation System

Jie Jiang, Hock Soon Seah, Hong Ze Liew, and Quan Chen

CONTENTS

13.1 Introduction 246
13.2 Background 248
  13.2.1 Vector-based Versus Raster-based Techniques 248
  13.2.2 System Architecture Supporting Traditional Animation 249
  13.2.3 Stroke Inbetweening 250
  13.2.4 Coloring 251
13.3 Inbetweening 251
  13.3.1 Linear Interpolation 253
  13.3.2 Non-Linear Interpolation 253
  13.3.3 Stroke Connectivity 254
  13.3.4 User Interactions 256
    13.3.4.1 Feature Point 256
    13.3.4.2 Motion Path 256
13.4 Occlusion 257
  13.4.1 High-Level Information 258
  13.4.2 Region and Region Analysis 259

13.5 Color Management   260
    13.5.1 Coloring   260
    13.5.2 Region Types   261
    13.5.3 Automatic Color Updating   262
    13.5.4 Gap Closing   262
    13.5.5 Vector Flood Fill   264
13.6 Results   265
    13.6.1 Feature Points- and Motion Path-Assisted Inbetweening 265
    13.6.2 Occlusion Handling Based on Boundary Strokes 267
    13.6.3 Vector Flood Fill with Gap Closing   268
13.7 Conclusion and Future Works   268
Acknowledgements   269
References   269

13.1 INTRODUCTION

Since "flipper books," or kineographs, were patented in 1868 (Woodcroft, 1872), 2D animation or hand-drawn animation has grown as a popular art form appreciated by adults and children alike. By 2D animation, we tend to mean 2D "character animation" (Catmull, 1978). With the simplest tools possible, i.e., pencil and paper, artists could draw and show pictures sequentially and make audiences believe that a character is alive on screen (Thomas, Johnston, & Thomas, 1995). However, the cost of this art form is the need for a tremendous amount of drawings. Winsor McCay took two years to create 25,000 drawings for his cartoon, *The Sinking of the Lusitania*, in 1918 (Richard, 2002). In an effort to alleviate the problem, the concept of engaging artists to create "inbetween drawings" was invented in the 1920s (Richard, 2002). But even with assistant animators and inbetween artists, a typical Disney 2D animation feature film needed an average of over a million inbetween drawings (Thomas et al., 1995), which required considerable time and cost to complete.

Besides feature films and TV cartoons, animation is ubiquitous in games as well. Despite some differences in the processes of making animation, game development also aims to create lively characters and motion for players and faces the same difficulty of having to create large quantities of drawings. The use of 2D digital puppetry or skeletal animation tools is a popular solution to get around this problem, with many different software packages available in the market today (Gamefromscratch, 2018). The number of drawings created is reduced as the drawings of character components can be attached to skeletal structures (typically as texture meshes) and reused for multiple animations.

The compromise is that the movement tends to be stiff and perceived to be inferior in quality, as the audience can visually identify the same drawings being transformed over time, hence the animations look less realistic. This is a reason why in the fighting game genre, bone animations or "component-based animations," are not widely used (Rantala, 2013).

The emergence of 3D modeling and animation tools brought a change to this production problem, where animators manipulate virtual 3D puppets rather than having to create drawings frame by frame. However, the look and feel of 3D model rendering is very different from traditional cartoons based on line art, which many people think have lost the essential style of 2D cartoons. Multiple 3D-based cel-shading rendering methods have since been developed to re-capture this quality of the hand-drawn animation aesthetic (Nilsson & Lundmark, 2017). Among various methods, Arc System Works' UV-Aligned method seems the most visually impressive and closest to mimicking the 2D art style. However, the downside is the need for a large number of bones in the 3D model's animation rig (GDC, 2015). It also requires additional manpower experienced in the 3D animation pipeline.

It is our thinking that 2D vector line art allows the 2D animator to work in the same way as they are used to, by drawing lines. The mathematically generated nature of vector line art allows for the potential for targeted embedding of data. At the same time, the need for the animator to learn a totally new set of tools and workflows is greatly reduced and the original aesthetic and sensitivity of the drawn image can be retained.

Only the "animation" and "inbetweening" components of the process require improvement in the productivity aspect. However, suitable interpolation of drawn line art is a formidable task, due to the problem of missing information (Catmull, 1978). VPaint, which was developed based on Vector Animation Complex (VAC) (Dalstein, Ronfard, & Van de Panne, 2015), is revolutionary in that it attempts to connect multiple dissimilar line drawings in time. However, these connections have to be made manually by the user.

In this chapter, we propose that conceptually two key drawings can be considered as two different renditions of the same character and that by analyzing the changes in the existing information of both drawings and minimal input from the user, the missing information can be adequately inferred to suit the purpose of the animator in generating inbetween drawings. We want to work towards a user-centered stroke-based drawing and inbetweening system.

Readers can refer to some relevant publications by our research group and collaborators (Qiu, Seah, Tian, Chen, & Melikhov, 2003; Wu, Seah, Tian, Xiao, & Xie, 2004; Seah, Wu, Tian, Xiao, & Xie, 2005b, 2005a; Q. Chen et al., 2006; Qiu et al., 2008; D. Liu et al., 2011; Yu, Liu, Tao, & Seah, 2011; Zhang et al., 2015; Ao et al., 2018; Yang, Seah, Chen, & Liew, 2018).

13.2 BACKGROUND

To produce 2D animation in the traditional way, artists usually need to draw key frames to depict the starting and ending of the main character poses in a motion. Subsequently, more frames are inserted between these starting and ending poses to make a smooth animation. This process is called inbetweening, which is a key step in animation production. Even for a short animation, many inbetween frames are needed. Thus, 2D animators need to create a large number of drawings, which is a problem for game animators as well.

A vector-based 2D animation system needs to help artists to manage their drawings like stroke, region, layer and color management, and so on. The artists can then efficiently create, modify and reuse their drawings, and freely express their creative ideas through their drawings. Most existing animation systems build their architectures based on the concepts developed in the traditional cel (hand-drawn) animation.

13.2.1 Vector-based Versus Raster-based Techniques

With the development of computer graphics and software technologies, computer-assisted animation techniques have been proposed to reduce the tedious and labor-intensive inbetweening process. Generally, there are two categories, raster-based (de Juan & Bodenheimer, 2006; Sỳkora, Dingliana, & Collins, 2009a; Mahajan, Huang, Matusik, Ramamoorthi, & Belhumeur, 2009) and vector-based (Seah et al., 2005b; Whited et al., 2010; Yang, 2017; Ciccone, Öztireli, & Sumner, 2019). The most significant differences are that vector-based techniques, unlike raster-based techniques, are resolution independent and support user interactivity as strokes can be modified easily. In this chapter, we will mainly focus on vector-based 2D animation systems, where artists can draw directly on a computer with digital input devices such as a drawing pad and stylus. Researchers have developed methods to automate some steps in traditional animation production, such as inbetweening, frame coloring, etc.

13.2.2 System Architecture Supporting Traditional Animation

Figure 13.1 shows a simplified architecture of a vector-based 2D animation system. Traditionally, artists draw different characters or objects, or part of them, in different layers in a frame. In this way, it is easier for them to reuse or loop certain parts of the drawings. For example, a still character with its hair blowing in the wind. In the motion, only the hair is moving and the rest of the character stays still. If the entire character is drawn on one single layer, artists need to repeatedly draw the entire body, which is unnecessary and inefficient. So, artists may draw the hair, face, body, etc. in separate layers. In this way, artists only need to focus on drawing the hair motion in the hair layer and the rest of the layers can be reused.

In the system architecture shown in Figure 13.1, a cel comprises one or more layers that contain different parts of a drawing. For each layer, "transparent" sheets are placed on the layer and strokes are drawn on these sheets. The strokes may be corresponded across the sheets in the same layer. As each layer is independent of another, it may be offset to the left or right. Also, the layer sequence can be reordered, i.e., shifted up or down. Although not shown in the figure, there can be multiple cels. Vertically placed sheets under a frame number are composited to become a complete drawing, which is similar to traditional animation. By displaying these drawing sequentially, an animation is created.

The setup operates like a "Microsoft Excel" spreadsheet for strokes that can be corresponded across each layer and interact with strokes within the same sheet and with other strokes across sheets in other layers, with the additional function of generating inbetweening. Hence, it is important to

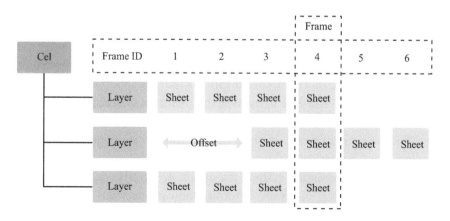

FIGURE 13.1   Architecture of a vector-based 2D animation system.

design operations that will work not break when a layer is shifted or reordered, or when a stroke is modified.

13.2.3 Stroke Inbetweening

In 2D animation production, some steps are preferred to be done by computer (Catmull, 1978), among the steps is the labor-intensive and time-consuming inbetweening. Computer-assisted automatic inbetweening helps artists to reduce tedious work and focus on key frame drawing (Kort, 2002). We follow the same terminology that each drawing comprises stroke chains, which have one or more connected strokes. A shape or character is described by one or more stroke chains.

Automatic inbetweening is very complex and formidable due to many problems, such as stroke correspondence, interpolation and occlusion resolution, and so on. Stroke correspondence, i.e., to find the matching between strokes in consecutive key frames, is a challenging part in stroke-based inbetweening. Two key frames may have a different number of strokes and stroke sequences. When strokes are corresponded across two or more key frames, intermediate strokes can be computed with an interpolation function. Many existing vector-based 2D stroke interpolation methods are usually developed under an assumption that the strokes in the key frames are correctly corresponded. Nevertheless, there are some works (Whited et al., 2010; Yang, 2017; Yang et al., 2018) that provide semi-automatic ways to correspond strokes with user interactions.

The interpolation method is another key problem in automatic inbetweening. Generally, interpolation methods indicate how intermediate strokes or shapes should be interpolated. However, inbetweening is not a simple interpolation of key frames (Kort, 2002). For inbetweeners, they need to obey, bend, or ignore the physical rules according to the desired animation. From artists' point of view, although automatic inbetweening is efficient, the more important thing is that the inbetweening results should be natural and able to express the intention of artists. Computer-generated intermediate strokes tend to be too rigid.

Besides the stroke correspondence and interpolation method, stroke occlusion is another critical problem in automatic inbetweening. In a 3D model-assisted animation system, the use of 3D models can easily resolve occlusion. However, in a pure 2D animation production, the occlusion problem cannot be easily resolved due to the lack of complete models and depth information.

Figure 13.2 is a drawing with partial occlusion. In Figure 13.2(a), the contour lines of the hand are depicted using solid lines which we call normal strokes. However, some strokes should be occluded, and the drawing should be like Figure 13.2(c). In order to manage occlusion, we allow artists to specify occlusion by setting hidden lines as indicated in Figure 13.2(b). We use solid and dashed lines to represent normal strokes and hidden lines, respectively.

13.2.4 Coloring

Coloring is another basic function in vector-based 2D animation systems. In raster-based coloring, a closed region consists of pixels and can be colored via a flood fill method. Similarly, in vector-based coloring, closed regions have to be detected before coloring them. We call the region detection, region analysis. Vector-based systems often cannot detect closed regions due to the presence of gaps between strokes. Manual gap closing is very time-consuming and tedious because there could be a large number of gaps in a drawing. Thus, how to automatically search for gaps and close gaps are two problems that we need to face.

Furthermore, artists may want to color regions formed by strokes in different layers. As mentioned before, artists may draw different parts in different layers. This increases the difficulty in color management. Deciding how to represent and where to store the color information for uniform region coloring and handling non-uniform coloring are other challenges, which are beyond the scope of this chapter.

13.3 INBETWEENING

Automatic inbetweening is a very hard problem for computer-assisted animation systems (Catmull, 1978). Boundary shape interpolation is a

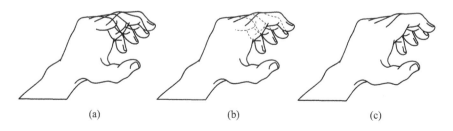

(a)   (b)   (c)

FIGURE 13.2 Hand example with partial occlusion. Black strokes are normal strokes. Dashed lines are hidden lines. (a) All the strokes are visible. (b) Occluded lines are set to be hidden lines. (c) Hand without rendering hidden lines. (Courtesy of Yovanny Ramirez.)

method to interpolate intermediate shapes by sampling two given shapes into two sets of vertices. A straightforward way is to correspond these vertices and linearly interpolate them. However, it introduces many problems as mentioned in Sederberg and Greenwood (1992). A boundary shape interpolation method usually follows three steps, shape description, quantity interpolation, and quantity-based shape reconstruction (R. Chen, Weber, Keren, & Ben-Chen, 2013). Some geometric values, such as edge length, exterior angle (Sederberg, Gao, Wang, & Mu, 1993; Dym, Shtengel, & Lipman, 2015), and curvature (Saba, Schneider, Hormann, & Scateni, 2014; Hirano, Watanabe, & Ishikawa, 2017) are investigated and implemented. We refer readers to Hirano et al. (2017) for comparisons of aforementioned methods.

Different from boundary shape interpolation, stroke-based interpolation mainly focuses on the interpolation of individual strokes instead of boundary shapes. To represent a stroke, interval spline can be a way to simulate artistic brushstrokes (Su, Xu, Shum, & Chen, 2002). Disk B-Spline Curve (DBSC) (Wu et al., 2004; Seah et al., 2005b, 2005a) is a good representation of strokes based on B-Spline basis (Piegl & Tiller, 1995) and disks (Lin & Rokne, 1998) due to its ability to model strokes with varying widths (Seah et al., 2005b). In this section, we will mainly discuss challenges in single-pixel-wide stroke inbetweening. For varying width strokes, an additional width parameter needs to be taken into account.

FIGURE 13.3 Feature point- and motion path-based interpolation. (a) and (c) are the first and second key frames; (b) is a linearly interpolated inbetween frame of (a) and (c); (d) shows the corresponded hair strokes in the first and second key frames. Each dashed line connects a pair of feature points and indicates the motion path of the point. (e) The updated inbetween frame based on feature points and motion paths. (Courtesy of Hong Ze Liew.)

13.3.1 Linear Interpolation

A simple stroke-based inbetweening method is linear interpolation (Burtnyk & Wein, 1975) that linearly interpolates the parameters of two corresponded strokes. However, it faces many problems. Figure 13.3(a) and (c) are two key frames and (b) is an inbetween frame generated based on (a) and (c) via linear interpolation. As we can see in both key frames, there are some sharp corner points on the hair strokes. However, linear interpolation only interpolates parameters without considering the shape of the stroke. It is obvious that the shape of the hair stroke is not preserved as shown in Figure 13.3(b). The ideal interpolation result should be like Figure 13.3(e). Thus, linear interpolation, in general, does not produce realistic motion.

13.3.2 Non-Linear Interpolation

To generate more natural and realistic inbetweening results, non-linear interpolation methods have been proposed. Similar to linear interpolation, cubic interpolation also interpolates parameters but with a different interpolation function. The motion trajectory of a point becomes a non-linear curve instead of a straight line. More function-based spline interpolation methods can be found in Erdogan (2014). Sederberg et al. (1993) presents an algorithm to determine paths along corresponding vertices. Intermediate shapes are generated via an intrinsic interpolation method in which edge angle and length are considered. A semi-automatic tight inbetweening system BetweenIT is proposed in Whited et al. (2010). The interpolation method is inspired by the basic principle of action arcs (Thomas et al., 1995). The motion path of each endpoint is represented by a logarithmic spiral vertex trajectory from calculating spiral parameters. For strokes incident on a point, individual stroke trajectories are composited by averaging parameters. To compute interpolated strokes, strokes are first represented by edge lengths, vertex angles, and thicknesses. Interpolated shapes are constructed by linear interpolation of intrinsic definitions. Then, curve fitting and tangent alignment are applied to maintain inter- and intra-stroke continuity. This method works well for tight inbetweening. If the shapes in both key frames are very different, this method would fail.

As pure stroke-based interpolation methods often suffer from a shape distortion problem, some mesh-based methods like Sumner, Zwicker, Gotsman, and Popović (2005) and Fu, Tai, and Au (2005) have been proposed to preserve local shapes of intermediate strokes. They interpolate local properties like vertex Laplacian coordinates and edge deformation-gradient features. Yang (2017) proposes a context-aware inbetweening method. It constructs sub-features by detecting feature points and each sub-feature represents a curve segment in certain degrees. Curve segment information is recorded with respect to a local parametric coordinate system specified by a corresponding sub-feature. Subsequently, a context mesh is modeled based on the sub-features and a k-neighborhood method. After that, intermediate context meshes are interpolated and strokes are recomputed based on intermediate sub-features. Though it is able to interpolate shapes with less distortion, it would fail under large 3D rotations.

Another non-linear inbeweening method is Vector Graphics Complex (VGC) (Dalstein et al., 2015). It is a novel method to create space-time continuous inbetweening results by introducing VAC (Dalstein, Ronfard, & Van De Panne, 2014). It allows splitting and merging of points, edges, and faces. Before inbetweening, topology structures are created for key frames to combine points, edges, and faces. The topology structure gets updated every time a user interaction is applied. Different from traditional stroke-based interpolation methods, topology keyframing is done by interpolating topology information instead of interpolating strokes directly. Finally, edges are interpolated accordingly.

13.3.3 Stroke Connectivity

In automatic inbetween frame generation, a big issue is how to maintain stroke connectivity. Many stroke-based methods focus on how to interpolate a stroke while stroke connectivity is usually ignored. Figure 13.4 shows a linear interpolation-based inbetweening result of two strokes in which the connectivity between stroke 1 and stroke 2 is lost. In both key frames, the upper endpoint of stroke 2 is connected to stroke 1. Both strokes should remain connected in the inbetween frames. However, as we can see in the inbetween frames in Figure 13.4, stroke 2 crosses stroke 1, resulting in artefacts.

We can classify the stroke connectivity problem into three different types according to the observations shown in Figure 13.5. In Figure 13.5(a), in the first key frame, both strokes form a "T" junction. However, in the second key frame, both endpoints are connected to form a "V" connection. In Figure 13.5(b), the "T" junction formed by stroke 1 and 2 is reversed in both key frames. In Figure 13.5(c), stroke 3 connects to different strokes in both key frames.

To the best of our knowledge, previous works only partially solve this stroke connectivity issue. Whited et al. (2010) treat every junction point

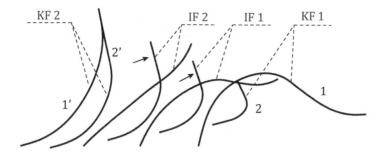

FIGURE 13.4 Stroke connectivity lost. "KF" and "IF" stand for "Key Frame" and "Inbetween Frame." Stroke 1' and 2' are the corresponded strokes of stroke 1 and 2. Two inbetween frames (IF 1 and IF 2) are generated via linear interpolation. In both key frames, the upper endpoint of stroke 2 (2') is connected to stroke 1 (1'). In the inbetween frames, the upper endpoint of stroke 2 crosses stroke 1 as indicated by arrows. (Courtesy of Hong Ze Liew.)

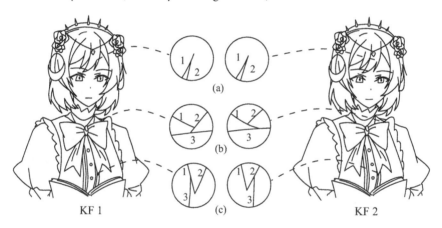

FIGURE 13.5 Stroke connection types. The left and right images are two key frames; (a), (b), and (c) are three local areas in both key frames. In (a), (b), and (c), corresponded strokes are labeled with a same number. (a) "T" junction to "V" connection. (b) Reverse "T" junction. (c) Stroke 3 connects to different strokes in both frames. (Courtesy of Oldman Rabbit.)

as a salient point and the correspondence between salient points in key frames should be detected before generating inbetweens. However, when the topology changes significantly, it may fail. Dalstein et al. (2014) consider points of each "T" junction as feature points that they are involved in sub-feature detection. Because the curve reconstruction method is based on context mesh interpolation that interpolates sub-features, the connection points are maintained. However, it also cannot handle significant topology changes like those Figure 13.5(b) and (c). VAC (Dalstein et al., 2015) is able to keep stroke connection by inheriting topology from key frames to inbetween frames. A connection point in the drawing splits stroke into sub-edges, which are connected via the connection point in the graph. However, it cannot handle the case in Figure 13.5(c) as well. We will be able to handle this case if we know that it is due to occlusion by the ribbon as it moves across the dress. This is an example where higher-level information, such as shape semantic, is required.

13.3.4 User Interactions

When drawing inbetween frames, an inbetween artist needs to use the knowledge of physical rules of the world. However, sometimes they may need to bend or ignore the rules (Kort, 2002). While an inbetweening method is to create motion, there is no perfect interpolation method that caters to all kind of motions, for example, wave or rotation. Thus, in order to generate the desired inbetweens, user interactions should be available for artists to achieve the resulting outcomes. We will discuss them from the following two aspects.

13.3.4.1 Feature Point

Shape distortion is frequently seen in computer-assisted inbetween generation. As most parameter-based interpolation methods simply interpolate parameters without considering stroke shape, stroke shape cannot be correctly preserved all the time. An example is shown in Figure 13.3. If we directly interpolate based on the two key frames shown in Figure 13.3(a) and Figure 13.3(c), the corner points are not preserved as shown in Figure 13.3(b), resulting in unacceptable shape distortion. The correct inbetweening result should be like Figure 13.3(e) in which the corner points are preserved. Thus, feature points play a very important role in inbetweening. Feature points are defined as points with high visual saliency. For example, the points circled in Figure 13.3(d). They commonly include stroke endpoints, stroke connection points, and points with a large curvature change. Related studies can be found in Q. Chen et al. (2006), Whited et al. (2010), and Yang (2017).

13.3.4.2 Motion Path

An interpolation method may interpolate points along certain trajectory, for example, a straight line, a cubic curve, or a logarithmic spiral curve. However, sometimes the motion of a point or stroke cannot be simply represented by a function. Thus, motion path is frequently used to improve inbetweening results. Some methods (Kort, 2002; Whited et al., 2010; Yang, 2017) improve inbetweening results by specifying point-to-point motion path. In Ciccone et al. (2019), motion paths can be assigned to skeleton points. The trajectory, orientation, and timing can be altered with the help of motion paths.

In Figure 13.3(d), each dashed line represents a manual specified motion path for a pair of corresponded points. During interpolation, points will move along the artist-specified motion path. By using motion paths, artists are able to better manipulate the stroke interpolation.

13.4 OCCLUSION

A 2D drawing comprising vector strokes is the projection of a 3D scene as visualized by an artist (Catmull, 1978). Due to incomplete information, occlusion is a tough and unavoidable problem, which is still very challenging today.

Figure 13.6 shows two examples where occlusion happens. Figure 13.6(a) is a region occlusion example in which the stroke and circular region move closer and the region occludes the stroke. The left stroke is entirely visible in the first key frame and partially occluded in the second key frame. Thus, strokes can be occluded by closed regions. Figure 13.6(b) is an eye-closing example. In the animation, the eyelid is gradually occluding the eyeball. In the drawing, the eyelid is simply drawn using one single stroke. Therefore, occlusion can occur even if there is no closed region.

Different from 3D animation systems that are able to detect occlusion from the provided 3D models, 2D animation systems can only obtain 2D

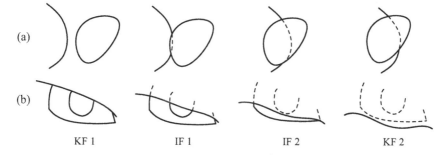

| KF 1 | IF 1 | IF 2 | KF 2 |

FIGURE 13.6 Examples with occlusion problem. Dashed lines represent hidden lines. "KF" and "IF" stand for "Key Frame" and "Inbetween Frame." (a) Region occlusion. The circular region occludes the stroke. (b) Stroke occlusion. The eyelid occludes the eyeball. (Courtesy of Hong Ze Liew.)

information like coordinates, curvatures, stroke connection, and so on. Occlusion problems can be easily resolved by human as we can visualize the original model of the drawing in our mind. However, it is very difficult for a computer to understand the model (Catmull, 1978) based on only 2D information. Catmull (1978) mentioned some possible approaches to the occlusion problem such as inferring 3D information, layering, providing missing information, and so on. In this section, we will discuss how to manually input or infer high-level information from a 2D drawing other than from pure 2D information.

13.4.1 High-Level Information

One way to handle an occlusion problem is to provide more high-level information to a 2D drawing. The most straightforward way is to allow artists to provide 3D information manually. In some systems like Adobe AE, they provide a 2D drawing canvas as well as a "Z" axis (*Use 3D layers in After Effects*, 2017). It allows artists to convert a 2D layer into a 3D layer by adding a "Z" value. Some other systems like Whited et al. (2010) and Yang (2017) require artists to specify hidden lines when generating inbetweens. Hidden lines provide missing information and facilitate stroke matching. Apart from specifying 3D information by user interaction, many works have been done to detect depths from 2D drawings. In our context, the depth of a point, stroke, or region is defined based on a virtual "Z" axis that is perpendicular to the 2D drawing and points towards viewers. If A is higher than B, A has a larger depth value or Z value, i.e., A is closer to viewers along the "Z" axis.

Different from the simplicity in obtaining high-level information from 3D models in 3D animation systems, 2D drawings only consist of a collection of strokes and they provide very low-level information like point coordinates, curvatures, and so on. How to detect high-level information from 2D visual clues is a major problem. Sketch-based modeling (SBM) is a 3D construction system that relies a lot on 2D visual clues. The most frequently used visual clues include junctions and cusps. To a certain extent, they carry information about stroke depth, occlusion and surface curvature change. In Karpenko and Hughes (2006), Miao, Hu, Zhang, Chen, and Pajarola (2014), and Yeh, Jayaraman, Liu, Fu, and Lee (2014), visual clues are used to reconstruct simple 3D models. More sketch-based methods can be found in Kazmi, You, and Zhang (2014) and Ding and Liu (2016). In X. Liu, Mao, Yang, Zhang, and Wong (2013), depth is inferred from junctions and cusps and assigned to regions. Regions are ordered by depths to overcome occlusion. However, animation drawings have much more intrinsic semantics than conveyed by sketches input to the modeling systems. Though junctions and cusps do provide useful depth information, they are still limited.

As described in Section 13.2, layers are used to organize strokes. Sometimes, layer ordering can be a way to resolve occlusion when all strokes in one layer are higher or lower than all those in another layer (Kort, 2002). However, the shortcoming is that the layering order is invariant (cannot be reordered). Rivers, Igarashi, and Durand (2010) is an automatic stroke layering method that detects depth information for each stroke from three views of the same character. Different from X. Liu et al. (2013), it integrates depth information to strokes instead of regions. However, it only supports uniform depth for each stroke, which is not sufficient to animate an object with varying depth. Besides, it requires multiple-view inputs, which increases the cost of animation production.

13.4.2 Region and Region Analysis

To handle occlusion problem, region information is very crucial. In our context, a region is a closed area formed by strokes. We call the process to detect regions from 2D drawings, region analysis, where efficiency is a key problem.

Since an animation may contain a huge number of frames, c.f. Figure 13.1, how to detect regions efficiently from each frame is critical to an animation system. The sweep line algorithm (Bartuschka, Mehlhorn, & Näher, 1997) is an efficient method to find intersections of a 2D drawing with low complexity. It may be adapted to find regions as well. For a single frame with multiple layers, a region can be formed by strokes from the same layer or different layers as shown in Figure 13.7(b). Thus, region analysis is applied to each individual layer of the frame as well as a composite drawing with all the strokes compressed into a single layer. Due to the sweep line algorithm, every time a user modifies any of the strokes, the region information of affected layers has to be recomputed.

Figure 13.8 shows some statistics of the region analysis in our implementation. Experiments are conducted on a platform with a 64-bit Window 10 Professional system, an Intel(R) Xeon(R) CPU (E5-1650 v4 @3.60 GHz 3.60GHGz) and 16GB RAM.

Since a drawing may contain multiple layers, we only apply region analysis to the composite layer of each drawing. Case (a)–(f) has fewer than 200 strokes and a small number of intersections and regions. As we

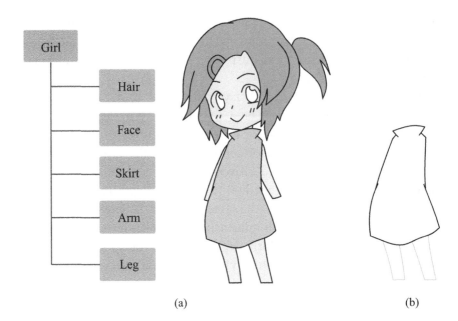

(a)   (b)

FIGURE 13.7   Region types. (a) Original drawing and the layer structure. All the strokes are drawn in five layers as shown in the chart. (b) The 'skirt' region and two 'leg' regions. The black and gray strokes are from the "skirt" layer and the "leg" layer. The "skirt" region is formed by strokes from the "skirt" layer. Both "leg" regions are formed by strokes from the "skirt" and "leg" layers. (Courtesy of Zirong Low.)

can see, the time spent in analyzing such drawings is usually short, which can be neglected. However, when a drawing is complicated like case (g), which has many intersections and regions, it takes a longer time in region analysis. Note that these statistics are only for the composite layers. For multiple-layer drawings, it usually needs extra time in processing each individual layer. For example, a drawing has six layers. There are around 1000 strokes and 1600 intersections and 800 regions in the composite layer. According to our test, it usually takes 0.6s to finish all the layers. If a modification is made to a layer or layers, sometimes it takes > 0.5s to update (re-analyze) the region information depending on the affected layer(s). If the region analysis is slow, it keeps the artist waiting until it is done, which adversely affects the user experience.

13.5 COLOR MANAGEMENT

13.5.1 Coloring

Coloring is a basic function in all computer-assisted drawing systems. For vector-based coloring, a user usually assigns colors to closed regions. In traditional raster-based drawing systems, to color a region, it only needs to

[55, 104, 54, 14]
(a)

[37, 63, 32, 16]
(b)

[101, 133, 48, 19]
(c)

[195, 228, 55, 25]
(d)

[80, 179, 114, 35]
(e)

[165, 243, 94, 36]
(f)

[930, 1234, 403, 96]
(g)

FIGURE 13.8   Region analysis statistics. (a)–(g) are drawings that may have multiple layers. Our timing test is conducted based on the composite layer of each drawing. The first three integers inside brackets indicate the number of strokes, intersections, and regions of the composite layer. The last integer denotes the time (in ms) spent in analyzing it. ((a) Courtesy of Hong Ze Liew; (b) courtesy of Martina McKenzie; (c) and (f) courtesy of Eugene Babich; (d) courtesy of Sergio Cajazeiras; (e) courtesy of Yovanny Ramirez; (g) courtesy of Oldman Rabbit.)

assign colors to the pixels forming the region via flood fill (Rogers, 1986). However, in vector-based systems, region coloring and color management differ from the traditional raster-based ways.

13.5.2 Region Types

Figure 13.7 is a simple example in which the hair, the face, the skirt, the arms, and the legs of a girl are drawn in different layers. As we can see from Figure 13.7(b), the skirt is formed by strokes from the skirt layer. We call it a self-layer region. However, if we look at both legs in Figure 13.7(b), they are formed by the gray strokes and one of the skirt strokes. In this case, we call such regions cross-layer regions. Due to these two types of regions, color management becomes more involved. To color the "leg" regions in systems that do not support cross-layer coloring, artists need to add additional lines in the leg layer to make it region closed. In this way, artists need to spend extra efforts to form closed regions.

In Adobe Illustrator, when coloring a cross-layer region, all the segments forming the region are grouped and transferred to a single layer.

Then, a color is assigned to the corresponding region. Therefore, it is a layer-dependent color management, which does not support reordering of layers. In a layer-independent coloring scheme, an additional layer is used to store cross-layer region information internally. In this way, self- and cross-layer region color information can be stored separately. Such a layer-independent coloring scheme supports the reordering of layers.

13.5.3 Automatic Color Updating

Automatic color updating is how to update region colors of drawings in the entire animation sequence if any modifications are made. In Asente et al. (2007), Live Paint is a graph- and topology-based method, which allows planar-map-based coloring. However, as addressed in the paper, it fails to handle cases like interwoven shapes and stacked art from non-closed paths as shown in Figure 13.9. Region correspondence detection (Qiu et al., 2003) is another solution to the color updating problem. The region correspondence between the drawings before and after modification is detected and corresponding region colors are transferred.

13.5.4 Gap Closing

When coloring in a vector-based system, artists may face coloring problem caused by gaps. Gaps, intended or unintended, are seen frequently in drawings as shown in Figure 13.10. We call each dangling stroke endpoint a gap point. When creating drawings, artists usually focus on aesthetic aspects and may not care about stroke connectivity. Besides, due to the floating-point precision of stroke representation, gaps could be produced unknowingly during drawing. Although the integer values of the visible points are the same, their floating-point values could be slightly different. Hence, the two points are not actually connected. The gaps may be visible when the strokes are rotated or scaled. Due to the presence of gaps, some areas that should be closed are open, and hence cannot be painted

FIGURE 13.9   (a) Stacked shapes. (b) Interwoven shapes.

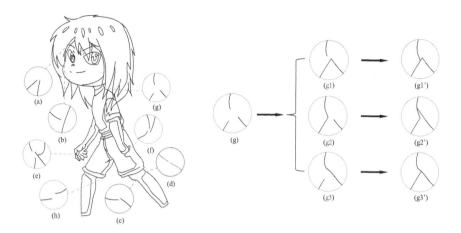

FIGURE 13.10   Gaps in a drawing. (a)–(h) are gaps in the drawing; (g) is a gap with three gap points and different gap-closing results are shown. (Courtesy of Hong Ze Liew.)

correctly. In order to color properly, artists need to clean up all the gaps manually before proceeding with the coloring process.

There are two ways to prevent gaps from happening. The first way is to require artists to draw carefully. This results in more time to complete a drawing since artists need to pay attention to stroke connectivity. The second way is to close all the gaps manually after finishing all the strokes. Artists may need to draw a new stroke or edit existing strokes to close the gap. For a drawing with hundreds of strokes, there can be tens or even hundreds of gaps in the drawing. Therefore, manual gap closing is a tedious and time-consuming step.

For efficiency, gap closing should be done by computer instead of by artists. Although many of the current vector-based 2D animation systems are able to close gaps automatically, the results usually do not look desirable aesthetically. The main problem is how to generate gap-closing results that are as close to the artists' intention as possible. An automatic gap-closing method was first proposed in Gangnet, Van Thong, and Fekete (1994). It considers each gap point individually and the gap point is directly connected to a nearest point. Though this method is simple, it often generates undesired results with sharp bends. In Seah and Chua (1997), angle and distance are introduced as two constraints in gap closing to prevent sharp bends. Besides sharp bends, handling gap point individually is a cause of undesired results. In a drawing, some gap points can be very close to each other and they are very likely to form certain shapes. For example, if two gap points are very close, they may form an end-to-end "V" connection. Though some works like Schmidt, Wyvill, Sousa, and Jorge (2006), Sandhya, Agarwal, Rao, and Wankar (2009), Huang et al. (2013), and Sasaki, Iizuka, Simo-Serra, and Ishikawa (2017) are able to detect "V" connections, they fail to handle multiple-point end-to-end connections. In addition, the number of nearby gap points is another factor that increases the difficulty in automatic gap closing. Generally, more gap points mean more possible gap-closing results. As shown in Figure 13.10(g), there is a gap involving three gap points with three possible gap-closing results. Thus, how to handle gaps with multiple gap points is a very challenging under-constrained problem.

13.5.5 Vector Flood Fill

As mentioned earlier, in vector-based 2D animation systems, regions may not be painted correctly due to the presence of gaps on the region boundaries. LazyBrush (Sỳkora, Dingliana, & Collins, 2009b) is a raster-based coloring method, which is able to color regions with gaps. It implements graph theory to compute region boundaries regardless of gaps and provides artists with a gap-aware coloring tool, which does not require gap closing before coloring. For a raster image, a flood fill algorithm is able to search a region from a starting pixel without analyzing the entire drawing. However, vector-based 2D animation systems do not have such property. To color a region in vector-based systems, all the closed regions need to be analyzed before coloring. Thus, a more efficient vector flood fill approach is needed.

We implemented a vector flood fill using sweep lines to construct a 2D drawing into a graph. Theoretically, the sweep lines can be oriented arbitrarily. In this section, we use horizontal scan lines for illustration.

The first step is to detect all the key points in the drawing. We define key points to include local extreme points and intersections. In Figure 13.11(a), the nearest iso-height points (points on the same horizontal scan line) of each key point are detected. Then, each key point is linked to its nearest iso-height points via scan lines. The second step is to find adjacency between scan lines. If two scan lines share the same key point, for example, 1 and 2, or directly connected, for example, 1 and 11, they are treated as being adjacent. Thus, in the graph, nodes corresponding to the key points are connected. In this way, we are able to convert a 2D drawing into a graph as shown in Figure 13.11(b). If we look at the graph, there are two independent node clusters. Each cluster represents a region. To search for a region

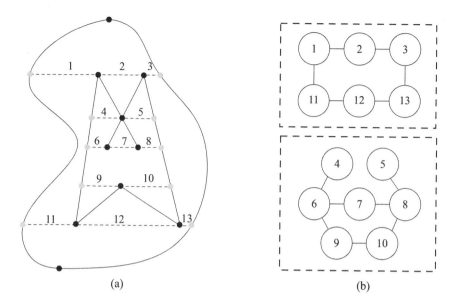

FIGURE 13.11   Graph representation of a 2D vector drawing for vector flood fill. (a) The black points are the key points. The gray points are iso-height points. Each dashed line is a scan line connecting a key point and a horizontal neighboring iso-height point. Scan lines are labeled from 1 to 13. (b) Each node represents a scan line in (a). The edge between two nodes indicates that the corresponding scan lines are adjacent.

in a 2D vector drawing, we only need to search the graph to look for independent node clusters.

Such a graph-based vector region searching method is able to handle regions with gaps. To determine if we have met a gap point during graph searching, we only need to check both endpoints of a scan line. Once a gap is filled, we only need to update the graph accordingly instead of reanalyzing all the regions of the entire drawing.

13.6 RESULTS

In this section, we will show some results of the implementations of our solutions to the three aforementioned challenges. It includes three parts, inbetweening, occlusion handling, and gap-aware coloring.

13.6.1 Feature Points- and Motion Path-Assisted Inbetweening

Figure 13.12 shows an example on how to use feature points and motion paths to manipulate inbetween results; (a) and (b) are the first and second key frames—(c1) is one of the inbetween frames generated via linear

FIGURE 13.12 Girl crouching animation. (a) and (b) are the first and second key frames. (c1) An inbetween frame by linear interpolation. In this frame, the shapes of the lower hair and the character's left arm are distorted. (c2) Improved inbetweening result by adding feature points. (c3) Improved result by specifying the motion path for the character's left arm. The gray dashed line is the motion path. (c4) Improved result with both feature points and motion path. (d1) Specifying feature point correspondence between corresponded strokes (the hair stroke) in both key frames. The black and gray strokes are from the first and second key frames, respectively. (d2) Specifying the motion path for the character's left arm. (Courtesy of Zirong Low.)

interpolation. Obviously, the result looks unrealistic. The "hair" stroke near the right cheek of the girl is distorted because the corner points are not preserved. Thus, we provide a feature point-based inbetweening scheme. Feature points of the "hair" stroke are specified according to (d1). In (d1), there is the same "hair" stroke in the two key frames. A dashed line connects a pair of corresponded feature points; (c2) is the inbetween result with feature points preserved. Compared with (c1), the shape of the hair stroke is well preserved.

Another distortion problem in (c1) is the character's left arm. Because it is generated via linear interpolation, the trajectory of the arm is a straight line. The arm is shortened, hence it is unnatural. To handle this, we

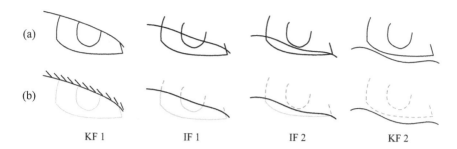

FIGURE 13.13 Eye-closing example. "KF" and "IF" stand for "Key Frame" and "Inbetween Frame." (a) Inbetweening result without setting hidden segments. (b) Black and gray strokes represent boundary and occluded strokes. In the first key frame, the eyelid is set to be a boundary stroke whose upper side (the shaded side) to be a "hidden" side. The rest of the strokes are set to be occluded strokes. These settings are transferred to other frames and occluded lines are properly detected. (Courtesy of Hong Ze Liew.)

implement motion path as shown in Figure 13.12(d2). The motion path is added to guide how the arm should move; (c3) shows the updated inbetweening result with manually specified motion path. The motion of the arm follows the motion path and the length of the arm is well preserved.

13.6.2 Occlusion Handling Based on Boundary Strokes

Figure 13.13 is an eye-closing example with an occlusion issue. In order to properly generate the motion, all the strokes illustrating the eye should be present in both key frames as shown in Figure 13.13(a), where all the strokes are visible. However, as the eyelid stroke moves down, the segments above the eyelid should be occluded.

In order to detect occlusion, we introduce two concepts, boundary stroke and occluded stroke. Both boundary and occluded strokes are used to specify occlusion information. Occluded strokes will be entirely or partially occluded by other strokes or regions. Boundary strokes have side visibility and affect the visibility of occluded strokes. In this example, the eyelid is occluding the eyeball. Thus, we set the "eyelid" stroke to be a boundary stroke whose upper side (the shaded side) is "hidden" as shown in the first key frame in Figure 13.13(b). The rest of the strokes are set to be occluded strokes. Then, these boundary and occluded stroke settings are transferred to other frames. For each frame, if an occluded stroke is partially or entirely on the "hidden" side of the

(a) (b)

FIGURE 13.14 Vector flood fill with gap closing. (a) An uncolored drawing with gaps. (b) Shaded drawing with gaps properly closed. (Courtesy of Zirong Low.)

boundary stroke, its segments on the "hidden" side are set to be hidden as shown in Figure 13.13(b).

Boundary stroke allows artists to use simple stroke settings to input occlusion information to key frames or inbetween frames. These settings can be transferred to other frames and utilized to resolve occlusion, which greatly reduces the time in tweaking frame by frame.

13.6.3 Vector Flood Fill with Gap Closing

In our implementation, we integrate vector flood fill-based gap closing with coloring function. Figure 13.14(a) is the same drawing as Figure 13.12(c4). It has gaps around the ponytail, body, and legs, which prevent various regions from being correctly colored. When an artist picks a color and clicks to paint, our vector flood fill searching method starts from the clicked point and it automatically searches for gaps and closes them. Figure 13.14(b) is the final colored drawing of Figure 13.14(a) with gaps properly closed. As can be seen, our coloring method produces smooth gap-closing results.

13.7 CONCLUSION AND FUTURE WORKS

Vector-based 2D animation is more flexible than raster-based 2D animation as it can be rotated or scaled without any loss to the quality of the image. It also provides greater user interactivity as the vector graphics can be refined easily. However, they pose more challenges than their raster-based counterparts do. Instead of just manipulating pixels, strokes need to be modeled and manipulated with regard to their geometric and topology properties.

From the point of user experience, 2D animation systems should provide user friendly tools to help artists to easily and efficiently guide the inbetweening generation process and refine the inbetweening results. Due to the varied complexity of motion expected, even non-linear inbetweening methods cannot handle all the situations. Thus, some user interactions are needed to improve the inbetweening results. We try to reduce such interactions to the minimum, and if possible, to eradicate them entirely. Occlusion is another critical challenge to be solved. Pure 2D animation lacks high-level information like depth. Coloring is another issue that requires consideration attention. We have presented only some solutions. Overall, there are still many challenges to be resolved.

Ultimately, we are working towards the scenario that, once the key frames are drawn and prepared with minimum user interaction, the resulting inbetween frames and color would not need additional user intervention to "repair" them.

ACKNOWLEDGEMENTS

We would like to thank the artists for their lovely drawings: Yovanny Ramirez; Hong Ze Liew; Oldman Rabbit; Zirong Low; Martina McKenzie; Eugene Babich; and Sergio Cajazeiras.

REFERENCES

Ao, X., Fu, Q., Wu, Z., Wang, X., Zhou, M., Chen, Q., & Seah, H. S. (2018). An intersection algorithm for disk b-spline curves. *Computers and Graphics*, 70, 99–107.

Asente, P., Schuster, M., & Pettit, T. (2007). Dynamic planar map illustration. *ACM Transactions on Graphics (TOG)*, 26, 30.

Bartuschka, U., Mehlhorn, K., & Näher, S. (1997). A robust and efficient implementation of a sweep line algorithm for the straight line segment intersection problem. *Proceedings of Workshop on Algorithm Engineering.*

Burtnyk, N., & Wein, M. (1975). Computer animation of free form images. *ACM Siggraph Computer Graphics*, 9, 78–80.

Catmull, E. (1978). The problems of computer-assisted animation. *ACM Siggraph Computer Graphics*, 12, 348–353.

Chen, Q., Tian, F., Seah, H., Wu, Z., Qiu, J., & Konstantin, M. (2006). DBSC-based animation enhanced with feature and motion. *Computer Animation and Virtual Worlds*, 17(3–4), 189–198.

Chen, R., Weber, O., Keren, D., & Ben-Chen, M. (2013). Planar shape interpolation with bounded distortion. *ACM Transactions on Graphics (TOG)*, 32(4), 108.

Ciccone, L., Öztireli, C., & Sumner, R. W. (2019). Tangent-space optimization for interactive animation control. *ACM Transactions on Graphics (TOG)*, 38(4), 101.

Dalstein, B., Ronfard, R., & Van De Panne, M. (2014). Vector graphics complexes. *ACM Transactions on Graphics (TOG)*, 33(4), 133.

Dalstein, B., Ronfard, R., & Van de Panne, M. (2015). Vector graphics animation with time- varying topology. *ACM Transactions on Graphics (TOG)*, 34(4), 145.

de Juan, C. N., & Bodenheimer, B. (2006). Re-using traditional animation: Methods for semi-automatic segmentation and inbetweening. *Proceedings of the 2006 ACM Siggraph/Eurographics Symposium on Computer Animation*, pp. 223–232.

Ding, C., & Liu, L. (2016). A survey of sketch based modeling systems. *Frontiers of Computer Science*, 10(6), 985–999.

Dym, N., Shtengel, A., & Lipman, Y. (2015). Homotopic morphing of planar curves. *Computer Graphics Forum*, 34, 239–251.

Erdogan, K. (2014). Spline interpolation techniques. *Journal of Technical Science and Technologies*, 2(1), 47–52.

Fu, H., Tai, C.-L., & Au, O. K.-C. (2005). Morphing with laplacian coordinates and spatial- temporal texture. *Proceedings of Pacific Graphics*, pp. 100–102.

Gamefromscratch. (2018, November 10). *2D Bone Animation Software for Game Developers*. Retrieved from https://www.youtube.com/watch?v=TLU8H PBBwAc.

Gangnet, M., Van Thong, J.-M., & Fekete, J.-D. (1994). Automatic gap closing for freehand drawing. *ACM Siggraph*, 94.

GDC. (2015, May 21). *GuiltyGearXrd's Art Style: The X Factor Between 2D and 3D*. Retrieved from https://youtu.be/yhGjCzxJV3E?t=1836.

Hirano, M., Watanabe, Y., & Ishikawa, M. (2017). Rapid blending of closed curves based on curvature flow. *Computer Aided Geometric Design*, 52, 217–230.

Huang, H., Yin, K., Gong, M., Lischinski, D., Cohen-Or, D., Ascher, U. M., & Chen, B. (2013). 'Mind the gap': Tele-registration for structure-driven image completion. *ACM Transactions on Graphics (TOG)*, 32(6), 174–1.

Karpenko, O. A., & Hughes, J. F. (2006). Smoothsketch: 3D free-form shapes from complex sketches. *ACM Transactions on Graphics (TOG)*, 25, 589–598.

Kazmi, I. K., You, L., & Zhang, J. J. (2014). A survey of sketch based modeling systems. *2014 11th International Conference on Computer Graphics, Imaging and Visualization*, pp. 27–36.

Kort, A. (2002). Computer aided inbetweening. *Proceedings of the 2nd International Symposium on Non-photorealistic Animation and Rendering*, pp. 125–132.

Lin, Q., & Rokne, J. G. (1998). Disk bézier curves. *Computer Aided Geometric Design*, 15(7), 721–737.

Liu, D., Chen, Q., Yu, J., Gu, H., Tao, D., & Seah, H. (2011). Stroke correspondence construc- tion using manifold learning. *Computer Graphics Forum*, 30(8), 2194–2207.

Liu, X., Mao, X., Yang, X., Zhang, L., & Wong, T.-T. (2013). Stereoscopizing cel animations. *ACM Transactions on Graphics (TOG)*, 32(6), 223.

Mahajan, D., Huang, F.-C., Matusik, W., Ramamoorthi, R., & Belhumeur, P. (2009). Moving gradients: A path-based method for plausible image inter-polation. *ACM Transactions on Graphics (TOG)*, 28, 42.

Miao, Y., Hu, F., Zhang, X., Chen, J., & Pajarola, R. (2014). Sketch-based reconstruction of symmetric 3D free-form objects. *Siggraph Asia 2014 Posters*, 42.

Nilsson, M., & Lundmark, A. (2017). *2D Aesthetics with a 3D Pipeline: Achieving a 2D Aesthetic with 3D Geometry (Dissertation)*. Retrieved from http://urn .kb.se/resolve?urn=urn:nbn:se:uu:diva-324678.

Piegl, L. A., & Tiller, W. (1995). *The Nurbs Book*. Springer.

Qiu, J., Seah, H., Tian, F., Chen, Q., Wu, Z., & Melikhov, K. (2008). Auto coloring with enhanced character registration. *International Journal on Computer Games Technology*, 1–7. https://doi.org/10.1155/2008/135398

Qiu, J., Seah, H. S., Tian, F., Chen, Q., & Melikhov, K. (2003). Computer-assisted auto coloring by region matching. *Proceedings of the 11th Pacific Conference on Computer Graphics and Applications, 2003*, pp. 175–184.

Rantala, T. (2013). Animation of a high-definition 2D fighting game character (Bachelor's thesis, Kajaani University of Applied Science, Kajaani, Finland). Retrieved from http://urn.fi/URN:NBN:fi:amk-201305148471

Richard, W. (2002). *The Animator's Survival Kit*. Faber & Faber.

Rivers, A., Igarashi, T., & Durand, F. (2010). 2.5D cartoon models. *ACM Transactions on Graphics (TOG)*, 29, 59.

Rogers, D. F. (1986). *Procedural Elements for Computer Graphics*. McGraw-Hill, Inc.

Saba, M., Schneider, T., Hormann, K., & Scateni, R. (2014). Curvature-based blending of closed planar curves. *Graphical Models*, 76(5), 263–272.

Sandhya, B., Agarwal, A., Rao, C. R., & Wankar, R. (2009). Automatic gap identification towards efficient contour line reconstruction in topographic maps. *Proceedings of the 2009 Third Asia International Conference on Modelling and Simulation*, pp. 309–314.

Sasaki, K., Iizuka, S., Simo-Serra, E., & Ishikawa, H. (2017). Joint gap detection and inpainting of line drawings. *Proceedings of the IEEE Conference on Computer Vision and Pattern Recognition*, pp. 5725–5733.

Schmidt, R., Wyvill, B., Sousa, M. C., & Jorge, J. A. (2006). Shapeshop: Sketch-based solid modeling with blobtrees. *ACM Siggraph 2006 Courses*, p. 14.

Seah, H. S., & Chua, B. C. (1997). A skeletal line joining algorithm. *Insight Through Computer Graphics-Proceedings of the Computer Graphics International 1994 (Cgi94)*, p. 62.

Seah, H. S., Wu, Z., Tian, F., Xiao, X., & Xie, B. (2005a). Artistic brushstroke represen- tation and animation with disk b-spline curve. *Proceedings of the 2005 ACM Sigchi International Conference on Advances in Computer Entertainment Technology*, pp. 88–93.

Seah, H. S., Wu, Z., Tian, F., Xiao, X., & Xie, B. (2005b). Interactive free-hand drawing and in-between generation with DBSC. *Proceedings of the 2005 ACM Sigchi International Conference on Advances in Computer Entertainment Technology*, pp. 385–386.

Sederberg, T. W., Gao, P., Wang, G., & Mu, H. (1993). 2-D shape blending: An intrinsic solution to the vertex path problem. *Siggraph*, 93, 15–18.

Sederberg, T. W., & Greenwood, E. (1992). A physically based approach to 2-D shape blending. *ACM Siggraph Computer Graphics*, 26, 25–34.

Su, S. L., Xu, Y.-Q., Shum, H.-Y., & Chen, F. (2002). Simulating artistic brush strokes using interval splines. *Proceedings of the 5th IASTED International Conference on Computer Graphics and Imaging*, pp. 85–90.

Sumner, R. W., Zwicker, M., Gotsman, C., & Popović, J. (2005). Mesh-based inverse kinematics. *ACM Transactions on Graphics (TOG)*, 24(3), 488–495.

Sỳkora, D., Dingliana, J., & Collins, S. (2009a). As-rigid-as-possible image registration for hand-drawn cartoon animations. *Proceedings of the 7th International Symposium on Non-photorealistic Animation and Rendering*, pp. 25–33.

Sỳkora, D., Dingliana, J., & Collins, S. (2009b). Lazybrush: Flexible painting tool for hand- drawn cartoons. *Computer Graphics Forum*, 28, 599–608.

Thomas, F., Johnston, O., & Thomas, F. (1995). *The Illusion of Life: Disney Animation*. New York: Hyperion.

Use 3D Layers in After Effects. (2017, October 23). Retrieved from https://helpx .adobe.com/after-effects/using/3d-layers.html.

Whited, B., Noris, G., Simmons, M., Sumner, R. W., Gross, M., & Rossignac, J. (2010). BetweenIT: An interactive tool for tight inbetweening. *Computer Graphics Forum*, 29, 605–614.

Woodcroft, B. (1872). *Chronological Index of Patents Applied for and Patents Granted*. London, UK: G.E Eyre and W. Spottiswoode.

Wu, Z., Seah, H., Tian, F., Xiao, X., & Xie, X. (2004). Simulating artistic brushstrokes using disk b-spline curves. *Conference on Multimedia Arts Asia Pacific, Maap*.

Yang, W. (2017). Context-aware computer aided inbetweening. *IEEE Transactions on Visualization and Computer Graphics*, 24(2), 1049–1062.

Yang, W., Seah, H. S., Chen, Q., & Liew, H. Z. (2018). Ftp-sc: Fuzzy topology preserving stroke correspondence. *Computer Graphics Forum*, 37(8), 125–135.

Yeh, C.-K., Jayaraman, P. K., Liu, X., Fu, C.-W., & Lee, T.-Y. (2014). 2.5D cartoon hair modeling and manipulation. *IEEE Transactions on Visualization and Computer Graphics*, 21(3), 304–314.

Yu, J., Liu, D., Tao, D., & Seah, H. (2011). Complex object correspondence construction in 2D animation. *IEEE Transactions on Image Processing*, 20(11), 3257–3269.

Zhang, T., Wang, X., Jiang, Q., Wu, Z., Zhou, M., & Seah, H. (2015). An extension algorithm for disk b-spline curve with g2 continuity. *Computer-Aided Design and Applications*, 12(5), 519–525.

CHAPTER 14

Best Practices
for Pixel Art

Cindy Lee

W HEN TALKING ABOUT PIXEL art, most still continue to think that it's retro and mainly used in 'old' games. Contrary to belief, it's more modern than ever before. No longer limited to software or hardware capabilities, new and popular games have adapted to new and creative forms of pixel art from incorporating shaders and gradients (e.g. *Hyper Light Drifter*) to even 3D planes (e.g. *Octopath Traveler*) (Figure 14.1).

The relevance of pixel art to the game industry continues to boom as both the indie and AAA companies continue to produce pixel art games to cater to not only the people who grew up with pixel art games, but the new generation of people who can see the beauty in its surface simplicity. This chapter discusses the techniques and guidelines on how to approach pixel art and how to go about animating it.

The 'rules' of pixel art originated from the restrictions of the hardware which could only display 8-bit or 16-bit graphics in the past. If a game wished to display any graphics, pixel art was the only option. Artists had to think of creative ways to utilize the limited colours and canvas size in order to produce sprites that render as the graphics in the game. Today, with technology so advanced, pixel art has now become a choice of style instead, artists are no longer constricted by colours or size of sprites. So what really is the pixel art of today? The 'rules' of pixel art have evolved through its growth. No one can really state if a piece of art is good or bad

FIGURE 14.1   Background art for game in development, *Tiny Dice Dungeon 2* (© Springloaded, 2019. With permission.)

because ultimately, all art, including pixel art, is subjective. However, there are still some fundamental practices of pixel art are respected throughout its evolution. Before we proceed, do not get me wrong! I personally feel that artists should always be free to break the 'rules' in search of new, creative and original art styles. However, in this chapter, we will be focusing on a slightly more traditional outtake on pixel art. There are some guidelines that differentiates 'good' pixel art from 'bad' ones, read on to find out more!

Before we get started, you have to find a program to draw in! There are many available programs that support drawing pixel art today, some of which are even free editors that allow you to save your work online (for example, PiskelApp and Pixie). For me personally, I use Adobe Photoshop as I require the flexibility to do more than just pixel art in my line of work, however, feel free to experiment with different software or programs. It is important to find the one you are most comfortable to work with!

Now, getting down to the technicalities. First thing I would like to bring up is respecting the number of colours used in pixel art. To preserve the origins of pixel art where the number of colours are limited due to hardware, pixel art has generally evolved to still contain a limited number of colours per sprite or per art even though we are no longer limited by selective colours. Best pixel practices make use of as little colours as they can to still produce the balance of depth, perspective and content, depending on what is required. It is best to never use two colours too similar together in an artwork or a sprite. It will create a seemingly 'dirty' effect when viewed from far compared with a clean, easily distinguishable contour that reflects the purity of that pixel art. Since one of the difficulties of pixel art is ensuring that the viewer understands what it is you have drawn (especially if your sprite is really small), the cleaner the sprite, the easier it is to comprehend what that object is. Depending on what your sprite looks like, it might be better to completely remove a colour tone if it is too similar to another. Otherwise, you can choose to increase its contrast to make the two colours more distinguishable from each other.

In the example on the left, exhibit A contains more shading and colours compared with exhibit B (Figure 14.2).

This results in B are much easier to read compared with A as the leaves of the plant in A are all lost in the mess of pixels. Especially when placed in a bigger scene, the cleaner the individual object, the less messy the image will look as a whole. Unless it is a purposeful art choice, you should consider being prudent about the number of colours you use in your sprites.

Some skilled pixel artists even use unexpected colours in the shading within their sprites, using complementary colours to produce an enticing artwork. Though this probably sprouted from the fact that they had only certain colours to choose from due to the hardware, nevertheless, the result is pleasing to the eyes and it is definitely worth considering to implement in your artwork. Complementary colour shading is not only used in pixel art, but is also widely used in 3D lighting, movies and so on. However, unlike the others, it might be slightly trickier when using it in pixel art. While complementary colours produce a high contrast, vibrant look, it might look too jarring, especially since there are limited pixels to work with, and we cannot use gradients to blend the colours naturally. So do exercise caution when shading and ensure that your pixel art works as a whole!

FIGURE 14.2 Exhibit A contains more shading and colours compared with exhibit B, making it more difficult to read.

Shading smaller sprites are simple enough to understand, but what about shading large areas, like the sky? When drawing large scale pieces of pixel art (for example, pixel concept art or pixel backgrounds in games), shading becomes a little trickier, and requires a very different approach compared with shading smaller sprites. As mentioned before, to keep true to the origination of pixel art, the number of colours and tones should be used sparingly to preserve the simplicity of the image. And yet, there comes a point in time when you would want to give an effect of a smooth transition colours. How does one make nice colour gradients with a limited number of colours and in pixel art to boot?

To create smooth colour gradients, pixel artists use a method called dithering. There are many types of dithering an artist can use, depending on the size or style the art piece has. Dithering is basically implementing a pattern of dots so as to create an illusion of two colours merging smoothly to one another (Figure 14.3).

I would say that the method of dithering is similar or perhaps even inspired by the traditional art style of Pointillism. Pointillism is an art method developed in 1886 in the era of Impressionism. Using Pointillism, artists created whole masterpieces of scenery and images, yet upon closer inspection, they are merely just patterns of dots of colours. Sounds like the basis of pixel art doesn't it! (Figure 14.4 and Figure 14.5).

Dithering is a useful skill to blend your colours or even give the illusion of a new colour, similar to mixing two different colours of paints on your palette. This makes dithering extra valuable as you can use existing

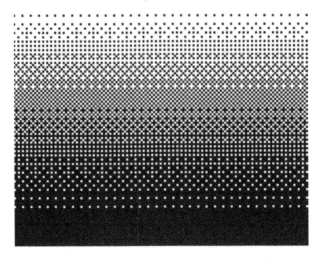

FIGURE 14.3   Some examples of different dithering.

FIGURE 14.4   A simple colour pattern.

FIGURE 14.5   Paul Signac, 1909, *The Pine Tree at Saint Tropez*. (From Wikipedia, n.d., *The Pine Tree at Saint Topez*. Last modified 5 April, 2020. Available at https://commons.wikimedia.org/wiki/File:Paul_Signac,_1909,_The_Pine_Tree_at_Saint_Tropez,_oil_on_canvas,_72_x_92_cm,_Pushkin_Museum,_Moscow.jpg.)

colours in your art to create seemingly new ones, and that allows for a smarter management of your palette, especially since pixel art is about respecting the number of colours (Figure 14.6).

For purposeful blending, like shading skies, do make sure that you try your best to maintain the same pattern throughout the dither. Should there be a mistake in your dithering, it will 'pop' in the viewer's eyes,

FIGURE 14.6   Adding two colours via dithering.

negating the results we are trying to achieve, which is to create a smooth gradient of colour (Figure 14.7).

The mistake in the dithering will cause a disturbance in the viewer's perceived pattern and it will be very evident in the end results.

Also, do take note that dithering requires more pixel space. This is why dithering is usually not used in small sprites, but in large background pieces like sky or cliffs.

On the topic of dithering, you can also use dithering to produce different surface materials of objects. Depending on whether you want a wooden box or a metal one, you can use different techniques of dither to create different textures on the object. Dithering more shades creates the illusion of a rougher texture. For example, when it comes to shading metal surfaces (which tend to be smoother), less dither should be used to shade it compared with the rougher surface of a wooden texture. A metal texture should also have more highlights to simulate light bouncing off its edges. To make wood textures more organic, you can also choose to go with a 'messy' dithering with fewer patterns to make it seem more natural. Depending on the texture of your object, dithering them right can give the viewers a more enhanced 'feel' of the objects in your art, if that is what you aim to achieve (Figure 14.8).

Each material has their own characteristics that you can differentiate through their individual dithering and shading. Once you understand what those are, you will be shading and creating different textures in no

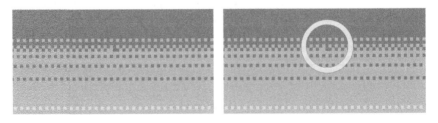

FIGURE 14.7   Make sure you maintain the same pattern throughout the dither: Mistakes will be easily spotted!

FIGURE 14.8 Dithering can also be used to effectively enhance textures.

time! If you are new to art or pixel art, I would recommend looking at how other artists dither or shade their art as a reference starting point and learn from them that way. Practice is king!

The next point I would like to talk about would be edging. If you haven't already realized from our discussions above, pixel art is more mathematical than most people perceive. It is all about simplicity and patterns. In general, we should draw the edges of our pixel art in a pattern, for example, diagonals should be drawn in an equal number of pixel lengths (refer to Figure 14.9).

As for curves, they should follow an ascending or descending length of pixels (refer to Figure 14.10).

In following these steps, the pixel art as a whole will look cleaner and more consistent. This is important as it makes it easier for people to decipher the shapes and therefore the content of the pixel art, especially in a bigger picture.

Sometimes it is not always possible to achieve drawing in equal pixel lengths when dealing with diagonals, especially when you intend to produce a smooth animation of a diagonal. In the example of an animation of a swinging stick, good pixel artists come up with creative ways to counter

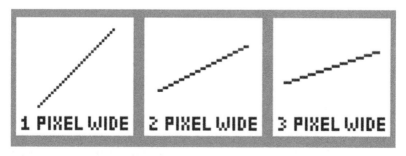

FIGURE 14.9 Edges should be drawn in a pattern.

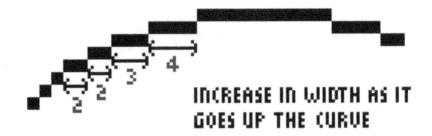

FIGURE 14.10   Curves should follow an ascending or descending length of pixels.

this issue. One method would be to reduce the number of frames of animation. This method is not as recommended as it forces a quicker animation (Figure 14.11).

Depending on the requirement of your sprites, it might turn out snappy due to less tweening between the key frames. But hey, whatever works does the trick! It can work for some cases of an animation where framerates are fast enough to get away with a small amount of snappiness. This method should be considered on a case-by-case basis.

Another more commonly practiced method is to use action blurs to cover up the pixel edges as the stick makes its swing. In using action blurs, you are still able to achieve a smooth animation without worrying about

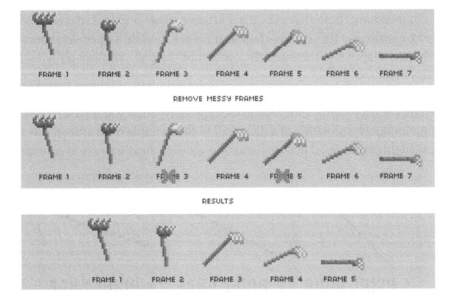

FIGURE 14.11   It is not always possible to achieve drawing in equal pixel lengths when dealing with diagonals. Reducing the number of frames may solve the issue but it will produce a quicker animation.

pixel ratios for the diagonal in each frame – you only need to animate the action blur to follow through its direction. This method is also used not just in pixel art, but in 2D art sprites. By using action blurs, you can further exaggerate the action by making it look bigger than it should be and without tweening a large number of frames between the animation. If you want a powerful swinging-weapon action, such as swinging a sword, you may want to consider using this form of animation! Many pixel art games, such as *Scott Pilgrim vs the World*, utilize this method to give their art a clean and polished look (Figure 14.12).

One other method would be to 'cheat' by using slight colour differences to still have the prominent pattern yet still contain the movement of a swinging stick (refer to Figure 14.13).

This method, once again, should be used subjectively. Since you have to respect the number of colours used in the pixel art, it might be tricky to utilize a new colour for the purpose of a smooth animation. If the new colour used for the animation is already present in the rest of the scene, one can consider this method to avoid breaking the pixel ratios during tween frames. Usually for this method of implementation, it will work better on animation with a stiller silhouette, such as falling water or molten lava, where the movement or animation is more prominent within its area of art.

However, there are games that implement code to produce a clean rotation in pixels. Some people would argue that this method breaks

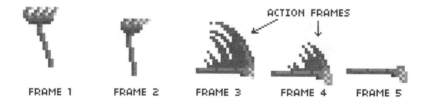

FIGURE 14.12   An example of 'action blur'.

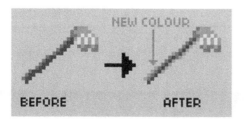

FIGURE 14.13   Changes in colour can also be used to emphasize animations.

traditional pixel art; whether it was a development choice (so less animation had to be manually curated) or an art style, it works in the case of the mobile game *Crusader's Quest*. Using pixel limbs and weapons rotating smoothly through code around joints of hero sprites, they made it look endearing, with smooth movements of their characters prancing around the battlefield.

Still, these are merely guidelines. Artists are constantly thinking of new and stylized ways to draw and animate their art, and this stems to stunning masterpieces all over the world. One particular piece of pixel artwork gained considerable popularity due to the interesting way it had been animated. A beautiful scenic waterfall drawn by one of the pioneers of pixel art, Mark Ferrari, gives the illusion of an animated, moving waterfall. However, the twist was that he did not animate his pixels individually. It is in fact produced by colour cycling each pixel of the water, resulting in a wave of smooth transiting colours that resembles a life-like, realistic waterfall.

Once you understand the basic technique of pixel art, you can explore more modern and creative fusion of the art styles, like using gradients or overlays to further enhance the art. In Figure 14.14, the sky colour is a smooth gradient and there are alpha glows in the light of the giant machine.

This method has become more common and prevalent in pixel art games that have been released in recent years. Unconventional though it may be, it nevertheless still produces a wonderful effect when done right!

FIGURE 14.14   In-game art for a game in development, *Obelus*.

Ultimately, pixel art, like any other art, is subjective. Despite the rules and guidelines, people all over the world are still coming out with new and innovative ways to make pixel art look attractive without fully conforming to the norm. I personally recommend using the guidelines and theories to be your starting point if you are new to pixel art. But once you get comfortable with pixels, you should embrace your inner artist and just go crazy with anything you can come up with to create new techniques and masterpieces! Who is to say what is right or wrong when it comes to art: in the end, it boils down to people appreciating it on your canvas or in a game! I must stress though, that practice is the most important key to get good at pixel art (or anything else for that matter!). Keep learning from other artists, adapt to new techniques and maybe even new software to keep improving your skills. Practice makes perfect!

LUDOGRAPHY

1. *Hyper Light Drifter*, Heart Machine, 2017.
2. *Octopath*, Square Enix, 2018.
3. *Tiny Dice Dungeon 2*, Springloaded, 2019.
4. *Obelus*, Springloaded, in development.

CHAPTER 15

Making Sound Decisions in Game Audio

Gwen Guo

CONTENTS

15.1 What Is Game Audio? 287
15.2 Where Is Game Audio in the Production Pipeline? 288
15.3 Elements of Game Audio 290
    15.3.1 Music 290
    15.3.2 Sound Design 291
    15.3.3 Voice 293
    15.3.4 Implementation 295
    15.3.5 Examples of Game Audio Implementation 298
Ludography 301

15.1 WHAT IS GAME AUDIO?

Ever found yourself humming to a memorable music riff in-game or found yourself being unable to play first-person shooters (FPS) with the audio muted? In the discipline of game audio, it is both creative and technical, and both an art and for functionality. There are three common objectives for audio in games – to provide non-visual aesthetics, to build the world and to provide feedback to the player. Many other games have included audio as part of their core gameplay design, not limited to rhythm games.

The main difference between game audio and linear audio for films, TV and podcasts is its interactivity; if one watches a film, both the audio and visuals will play out exactly as intended at the exact timecode it was told to play at. In games, however, multiple permutations of player actions can affect its journey, thus also directly affecting the way audio behaves as part of this journey.

15.2 WHERE IS GAME AUDIO IN THE PRODUCTION PIPELINE?

Whether the audio person is based in-house or outsourced, it is recommended that they enter the conversation from pre-production. A common saying goes in the film industry, 'Sound is 50% of the film'. In the case of games development, we can safely say that it is 33.33% of games alongside visuals and gameplay. As generalized as it sounds, the main point of this quote is to emphasize how sound is as essential as visuals and is just as capable of conveying meaning, narrative and world-building. To some, this is stating the obvious, yet many game studios still only involve sound in the middle of the production cycle, or worse, at the end.

To understand why the audio team needs to be involved early, we must first understand what exactly goes into audio pre-production (Figure 15.1).

As with all creative disciplines, time needs to be allocated for the conceptualization of audio direction, whether it's music or sound design. This could come in the form of designing sound to a linear screen capture of the game or a game design document. References can come from either the audio person or developers if they have something specific in mind; sharing audio clips and videos with audio is often clearer than describing sounds using words as the interpretation of mere words can often be subjective. A strong, solid foundation of audio direction will ensure that the game sounds cohesive throughout.

The audio department must also contribute to the discussion if the project needs additional tools such as audio middleware or engine plugins

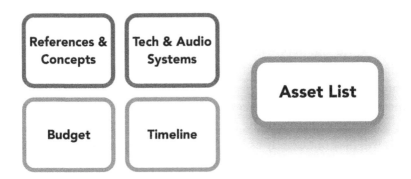

FIGURE 15.1   Audio pre-production. (© Imba Interactive. With permission.)

and it's essential that their perspectives play a major role in making the purchase decision. Creating customized audio tools will be necessary with or without audio middleware. As different projects have their own unique tech structure, the audio department would need to have constant discussions with the programmers and designers on customizing these audio tools starting from pre-production. This will vastly improve the work pipeline as the team journeys deeper into production.

If the audio department has an audio director, the latter's responsibility is to ensure that the audio team has adequate resources, tools and information from the development team to do the work, lead creative ideation and brainstorming (this does not mean that ideas come solely from the audio director), solidify creative direction, look out for their co-workers' well-being and mentor their co-workers if needed. They will also be the main liaison for game developers to speak with as a representative of the audio department.

With adequate time given to the audio pre-production, the team can also more accurately scope and negotiate for the timeline in conjunction with the entire game development timeline and therefore cost for budget, effort and time. Some larger game projects assist with the scope by having the production team work on a vertical slice. This is an ideal milestone and structure for the audio team to best put their creative concepts to the test as well as iron out any pipeline-related kinks which could arise along the way, ensuring a smoother experience during the production phase for the main game later on.

An example of a game audio production pipeline is shown in Figure 15.2.

After pre-production, the audio department can dive deep into production. Figure 15.2 illustrates a typical production pipeline within the audio department. Production is only a portion of the audio department's responsibilities – implementation and play testing are another huge part in the development cycle.

Depending on budget and the size of the company or game, some game studios may delegate the implementation task to a programmer from the development team. If so, it's recommended that the audio department at minimum has access to a build where they're able to hear the game in its entirety and suggest implementation improvements.

The audio department needs to have ownership of the game – having access to the build is essential to ensuring that the audio is at its best quality. Any sound asset created from production, no matter how great by itself, will not shine in-game if the implementation is poorly done.

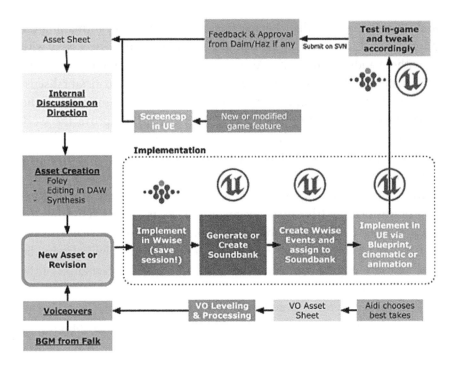

FIGURE 15.2   Audio production pipeline. (© Imba Interactive. With permission)

15.3 ELEMENTS OF GAME AUDIO

15.3.1 Music

There are two main ways of composing game music: using software instruments and live recordings.

Software instruments are plugins which can be used within a digital audio workstation (DAW) such as Logic, Cubase or Reaper. While recordings manifest as waveforms in these DAWs, software instruments follow the MIDI notation format, or for specific DAWs such as Sibelius, music notation.

Samplers and synthesizers are the two main types of software instruments. Synthesizers mimic the capabilities of analogue synths, manipulating basic tones such as sine, square, sawtooth and white noise, subsequently running them through oscillators and editing their attack, decay, sustain, release (ADSR). After manipulation, the composer obtains their desired instrument. Synthesizers typically produce sounds which can be found in electronic genres of music.

Samplers contain pre-recorded waveforms which are triggered by MIDI – they can be looped or played as a one-shot sample, depending on the instrument. Some samplers allow for more variety and advanced features. For example, a violin sampler can have different common violin expressions such as legato, pizzicato, tremolo, etc. Samplers can be used for all genres of music from orchestral to hip hop.

Although samples are able to achieve some degree of expression, no sampler can accurately mimic a live sessionist, especially if it's a solo instrument. In a world where it still takes a considerable amount of effort to get software instruments sounding exactly like an acoustic instrument, this is where live recordings come in – live recordings are used when the song calls for a more naturally expressive performance than software can ever perform. However, live recordings require a professional recording space with decent microphones, a recording engineer and a seasoned sessionist. That being said, the result is almost always better than attempting the same genre and expression using software instruments.

Most game composers use a combination of both software and live recordings in their arsenal of wonderful composition tools. Many composers would argue that it's often not just about the tools; building an identity with their music is often valued more than the gear and tools used.

In the context of games, building a brand and thematic identity for the project is one of its core functions, alongside the ability to influence how the player should feel. A great example would be the music of Thumper, with its music described as 'rhythm violence' – it is aggressive, intense and gripping. Even as a standalone OST (Original Sound Track), listeners are immediately able to discern the theme of the game that this music is written for.

Composing for interactive music requires composers to think like live mixing from a DJ, except that the player of the game is the DJ while composers provide the intro, outro, loops and stingers. The composer will have a big picture of the arrangement of the track, but ultimately the player actions will determine when the music transitions to its next intended destination.

15.3.2 Sound Design

Similar to the methods of production used in music, sound design also involves both synthesis and live recording, but they differ in materials being recorded.

Based on the introduction to synthesis written in the music section, sound designers may use synthesis to produce and manipulate basic electronic tones to their desired complexity. Some may choose to work on plugins running on DAWs or visual programming software such as Pure Data, MaxMSP or Kyma (these can also be used for music). Essentially, the sounds are moulded by numerical and mathematical data, although they are presented in graphical format. An example of a sound synthesiser which uses purely algorithmic functions even in its presentation is Supercollider. The audio generated from these synths used in the context of sound design are typically used for non-organic ambiences and sound effects such as for the sci-fi genre of games, digital user interface (UI) sounds or magical effects. Organic sounds which can be mimicked using synthesis are sounds which are similar to white noise and its variants such as rain, wind, whooshes and simple impacts.

Pertaining to organic sounds, sound designers will most likely record the sounds using a microphone and sound interface setup – the two main types of live recording for sound effects are foley recording and field recording.

Foley recording is popular in film sound where the foley artist performs in sync to picture while the sound engineer records. In the case of game audio, foley artists sync to a recorded screen capture of the game animation, but for delivery format, the recording is separated into single one-shot sounds for implementation. Foley artists have a range of props and tools to help them create the sounds they need. The point of foley recording is to only capture a single source of sound in isolation; they're recorded in a controlled space – a room which is heavily padded to prevent reflections and is silent. Examples of foley recordings in the context of game audio include footsteps on various surfaces, cloth movement, water splashes, physical object impacts and whooshes.

Field recording is almost exclusively used as ambiences or sound effects recorded outdoors if it's quiet enough; if the prop is based outdoors or is too large to fit into the controlled space (i.e. a pool of water, large rock). Due to the nature of audio implementation, it's important for the recordist to have an initial vision of what they'd like the final product to sound like in-game, then break them down into layers – those layers will be recorded separately. To illustrate, imagine that the player is standing in the middle of an open field – they hear a cacophony of birds constantly chirping, some wind rustling through the grass, occasionally a bee would fly past the player and a distant waterfall. The recordist will record each of these elements separately – a recording of birds chirping WITHOUT any other sounds including wind, JUST the sound of grass rustling in the wind, a bee buzzing in isolation and finally just a waterfall.

Recording these elements separately provides the audio integrator more flexibility when mixing for the game. The integrator will be able to pan the bee buzz from left to right, or right to left however they want without affecting the panning of any backing track. They will also be able to place a point source of the waterfall at where it should be – the waterfall model in the game engine. About to enter an ominous situation? Simply attenuate the birds and keep the grass rustling.

As with music, sound designers often use a combination of synthesis and physically recorded sources to create their final asset. Often, there are also musical elements within a sound effect, so the principles of music can also be applied to sound design.

It's also common practice to use sample libraries to design a sound the same way a painter uses a palette of paint. Sample libraries are pre-recorded material which can be bought online or accumulated by the sound designer over years of recording. There is absolutely no shame in using sample library sounds as a layer for your sound creation. There are a couple of things the sound designer needs to take note of: the licensing model for assets obtained from the sound library and the overall original-ity of their work. Where relevant, the sound designer may not want their sounds to resemble anything else out there in the market and also achieve a unique identity for their game sounds, therefore sufficient processing and manipulation to the sample is recommended.

Sound design is not limited to simply playing the supporting role in games. It can achieve aural identity the same way music does. A collection of sound effects will be able to best convey the overall theme for the game rather than a single sound effect in isolation, yet there are examples where sound effects are memorable; the alert chime in the *Metal Gear Solid* series is unmistakable, or the ascending synth when Sonic spins before travelling.

Thinking like a game designer sets us apart from film sound designers – we predict player choices, prepare for differing permutations on top of aes-thetic intention. This influences our work process from the way we record and compose our audio assets to how we export our files.

15.3.3 Voice

In the realm of indie game audio, voice is often regarded as a tertiary con-sideration in comparison with music and sound design. However, good voice acting can make or break a game. Whether it's about using voice as a narrative element or creature design, the voice talent in question needs to be suited for the function. Voice performance can't be fixed in post, so it's essential that team and/or their voice director finds the most suitable talent via voice casting.

For voice casting, several factors need to be considered. What's the personality of the character in question? What circumstances are they faced with? What emotions and energy do they portray in the game? Is the voice talent able to achieve the intended performance naturally? Does the personality of the voice match that of the game character? Having voice talents submit an audition would be ideal in the casting process. A well-cast voice talent and a voice director with a clear vision will ensure a smoother recording as they're able to perform with minimal revisions, maximizing the time and budget spent in the recording room, as well as representing the game character accurately.

Before entering the actual voice recording process, it's important for the script to be confirmed and formatted for easy reading and marking. It's not recommended to make changes to the script on the spot, or worse, change the script after the recording is done. Again, this is to avoid situations where the voice talent will have to re-record the lines which will incur costs in both time and money. Furthermore, the filenames should be consistent, especially when localization is involved. This will ensure an efficient process for the implementation of localized dialogue.

During the recording process, having a professional studio with a qualified sound engineer is ideal. A well-padded, quiet recording space and an engineer who's able to listen out for audio discrepancies while organizing takes and files is well worth the money. However, for those on a budget and can't consider a professional space, setting up a non-reverberant space in a quiet location could be an option. For example, a walk-in closet surrounded by plenty of clothes or a makeshift vocal recording booth covered by a heavy blanket. Unless having a reverberant voice recording is the intended effect, the voice recording should be as clean as possible. Remember that voice is produced with the physical body so do remember to hydrate and set a maximum time limit for each recording (recommended two to three hours per session); ensure that the voice talent is not overworked as it may affect the consistency of their voice, their morale and energy.

For gear, those on a tight budget should minimally consider a USB condenser microphone as it's able to capture a good dynamic range from the voice without it sounding too washed out or tinny. Overall, a good, clean recording will minimize the time needed for clean-up later on. As the famous saying in film sound goes, 'Not everything can be fixed in post'.

In reference to the previous statement, there are some things which can be fixed in post. Light, consistent background noise can be fixed in post. If you're recording in a makeshift space, that space may pick up low industrial hum or noise wash from a distant air conditioner. The voice editor can then use denoiser hardware or software in their DAW to remove the noise. Examples include the Izotope RX series or Cedar products. However, a noise floor which is too high will be tedious or impossible to be removed, even with the best tools; an attempt to do so in a noisy recording may result in a voice recording that has missing frequencies or artifacting. Dialogue levelling ensures consistent dialogue volume levels where a whisper can be audible in-game and a scream doesn't hurt the ears. Mouth clicks are a bane in dialogue editing, but they would have to be edited out nonetheless. Some popular methods which sound engineers recommend voice talents who often have unintended mouth noises is to eat an apple or suck a Tums tablet before recording.

Generally, the work required in post-production for dialogue can be minimized if adequate preparation is done before recording takes place; from good microphones, suitable voice talents and a decent recording venue to finalizing the script before recording and having a streamlined voice and localization pipeline. Once you have your clean, levelled voice recording, you can use plugins to manipulate the voice if the character is not entirely human to enhance the identity of your character.

The addition of voice to your game project can hugely add to your game theme and identity. In narrative-heavy games such as games from Bioware, a great voice performance is essential to player immersion. Competitive games such as *Quake* and *DOTA* hugely benefit from voice as players gain immense satisfaction whenever they receive vocal feedback for their achievements such as 'Double Kill!'. *Overwatch* not only uses voice to give their characters deeper personalities, their voices are also important for player and enemy feedback. Even casual games such as *Candy Crush* benefit from celebratory vocal gestures.

15.3.4 Implementation

Determining the behaviour of sound playback in-game is a core role of implementation and also an integral part of game audio in general. Closely intertwined with game design and programming, good audio implementation ensures that all possible scenarios in the game are accounted for. Something as simple as footsteps involve implementation, and can also be as complex as you'd like, depending on the level of detail.

In many games, footsteps are a sound effect you'd hear almost through-out the game, so it's important that there are variations of footsteps to pre-vent it from sounding unnaturally monotonous. The sound designer and foley artist may provide a range of footsteps which cover different surface materials and different performances between run, walk and jump. The audio implementer ensures that these footsteps are randomized as they playback to prevent repetition, with the footstep assets changing based on material the player's feet collide with in-game and also whether the player is running, walking or jumping. The sounds may even randomize in pitch or be separated according to heel and toe for greater variation.

Another example; it's common in match-three puzzle games to play an ascending success tone if players consecutively achieve combo chains – the longer the combos are strung together, the higher the pitch of the sound plays up till a max success of combo chains. Similar to randomization, these sound assets are exported as variations, but they are played in a fixed sequence instead, so players develop familiarity that their success is grow-ing with ascending notes.

Interactive music behaviour is also done by the audio implementer. Apart from simple crossfading between music tracks as a player travels between locations, exporting your music track as stems provides more flexibility for implementation. For example, when the player pummels a boss until its health reaches 20%, a one-shot stinger plays and a new drum loop plays perfectly in sync with the existing loop, informing the player that the boss is weak and it's a crucial moment for the player to finally beat it.

When it comes to tools, most game engines already have a native audio engine – Unity 5 onwards have the audio mixer to be used in tandem with the audio sources, and Unreal Engine has its own powerful audio func-tions. If the audio implementer is well-versed in programming, or there is a dedicated audio programmer, or if the project requires a heavily custom-ized audio solution, and adequate time has been factored into the game production pipeline to include the construction of audio tools, perhaps the audio team may choose to work with the native audio features of the game engine.

Another powerful solution for audio implementation is audio middle-ware. Popular tools such as Wwise, FMOD and Fabric are commonly used by both AAA and indie developers alike. They're the key to efficient audio implementation without the audio implementer needing to directly code. These tools export audio events instead of audio files; within these events, not only can the implementer determine an audio asset to play back, stop or pause, they can also set mix presets (volume changes), determine which effects to play and randomize as many sounds in a single event.

Although some audio implementers work exclusively on the audio middleware, having access to the game engine build is still essential. Most audio implementation can be best previewed and tested in the game engine itself, because the build takes 3D positioning, actual player response and gameplay triggers/collision boxes into consideration.

Three-dimensional positioning of a physical object within the game engine determines where the sound will play and how it transmits the signal within the 3D space. We will discuss two main factors in positional audio – volume and panning.

For example, an audio source will be attached to a large waterfall, but because it's a large feature, it can't just be a single point source – if the player is able to travel from the top to the bottom of the waterfall, multiple audio sources will need to be considered, or a spline that creates a single audio source following the player can also be implemented. Also, to simulate real life, an audio source with too extreme panning would be unnatural, so implementers will explore this audio feature called 'spread', which determines how directional the sound should be. An audio source from a 3D space would also attenuate accordingly in volume – the further you are from the object emitting sound, the softer it will be and vice versa.

In film sound, the overall mix is done at the final mix stage with a huge console of faders and knobs. The same can be applied to games, except that the mix is done in the audio middleware or game engine. The concept of volume faders still applies. Because player response is unpredictable and non-linear, it's important to test out every possible scenario in the game to ensure that the audio plays back in a balanced manner. Similar to DJing, the volume controls of sounds in a game are controlled by player interaction and therefore code instead of a human DJ.

Apart from volume and panning, there are other more customized effects which can be used in various situations in the game project. Reverb will allow players to feel the space with sound – a footstep playing in a cathedral sounds very different from being in the bedroom. Typically for positional sounds, reverb implementation comes in the form of collision boxes – when the player enters the collider box, it will switch to a reverb preset. Sounds which aren't positional and therefore won't take its 3D position into consideration may have its effects either baked into the audio file or implemented within the event. Another popular effect would be the low-pass filter, an effect which muffles sound when you're underwater or behind a wall, to cite from many other examples.

A major feature which sets us apart from film sound is the need for optimization. For game audio, it's always a tough balance between disk space and memory usage. An audio file which is compressed will require less disk space but add to the memory used to uncompress it, whereas audio which is uncompressed will require hardly any memory but will take up loads of disk space. A general rule of thumb is to export short but frequently triggered one-shot sound effects as uncompressed sounds while long, occasional sounds like ambiences and music be compressed, and, of course, there are exceptions.

The best practice for audio file compression is to take place within the audio middleware (if you're using middleware) or engine. Therefore, audio assets should be exported in its uncompressed .wav or .aiff format as it's more efficient and flexible to compress files later on than to bounce and re-export already compressed files, with the latter potentially leading to double work if the audio team realizes that it's not the ideal format.

There are also additional loading options for audio, like streaming and preloading, enabling programmers and audio implementers to have more choices for memory optimization. Also be aware that optimization is different across all platforms – it's important that the audio team gets a chance to test the game on all the platforms that it's being released on.

15.3.5 Examples of Game Audio Implementation

For music implementation, there are several basic music transitions the audio implementer can explore – branching allows phrases to simply transition to the next start of the phrase. It is similar to the transitions of pop songs where a verse, chorus and bridge are discrete phrases. The implementer may choose to transition immediately or in the next bar/beat (Figure 15.3).

Crossfading is another common transition where the current track fades out the same time the incoming track fades in. The audio implementer may choose to define the duration of the crossfade and the types of fade curves – it could be a straight line or a logarithmic curve of varying steepness.

Choosing whether to use branching or crossfading depends on the genre of music and intended aesthetic. Tracks with a regular beat like dance music within an energetic portion of the game may prefer to use branching because the entry of the next track needs to be impactful and

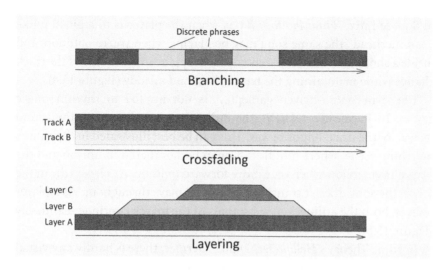

FIGURE 15.3   Music transitions. (© Falk Au Yeong, soundtrec. With permission.)

be introduced with a punch. Other tracks like ambient music or situations which are less impactful might want to explore crossfading as a transition option.

Another transition is layering, here the composer exports stems (layers of instruments) instead of a full track, allowing the audio implementer more flexibility for transitions. This allows for all the stems to play at the same time, but the system decides which stems are audible. An example

FIGURE 15.4   *Final Fantasy XV.* (© Square Enix.)

in Square Enix's *Final Fantasy XV* is when the player is in a pit stop like 'Hammerhead', the same song may be playing when you're outdoors and inside a shop, yet when player enters the shop, the instruments of the track change while maintaining the tempo, beat and melody (Figure 15.4).

The term 'audio-driven gameplay' is not limited to rhythm music games. In Playdead's *INSIDE*, the animations are synced to the sound instead of the usual opposite way. This can be best illustrated in the game's marching scene, where mindless human bodies march in unison and the player has to follow when they move forward or jump. As players die in the scene, the song doesn't transition or cut – it plays throughout. As a player revives, both the animation and sounds of the march continue seamlessly (Figure 15.5).

In Ninja Theory's *Hellblade: Senua's Sacrifice*, there is hardly any visual 2D HUD to indicate the player's health or how they're feeling, therefore the game relies largely on sound to convey these gameplay aspects (Figure 15.6). Voice is a huge aspect of the character, Senua, where her thoughts do not simply play a single narrative sentence – short voice snippets often play back in her mind, very similar to how we think and be conscious of the 'voices in our head'. To achieve the latter effect, the voices were recorded using a binaural microphone and implemented to be sparse or crowded with thoughts depending on her state of mind.

In conclusion, the basic understanding of non-linear audio in the context of games will hopefully encourage sound designers and game

FIGURE 15.5   *INSIDE*. (© Playdead.)

FIGURE 15.6 *Hellblade: Senua's Sacrifice.* (© Ninja Theory.)

developers to think about elegant, clever and creative audio solutions for their game projects regardless of platform and scope.

LUDOGRAPHY

1. *DOTA* (*Defense of the Ancients*), IceFrog, 2003.
2. *Final Fantasy XV*, Square Enix, 2016.
3. *Hellblade: Senua's Sacrifice*, Ninja Theory, 2017.
4. *Inside*, Playdead, 2016.
5. *Overwatch*, Blizzard Entertainment, 2016.
6. *Quake*, id Software, 1996.

CHAPTER 16

Making It Real

Andre Pong and Justin Ng

CONTENTS

16.1 Introduction	304
16.2 Types of Virtual Reality	304
16.2.1 VR: Virtual Reality	305
16.2.2 AR/MR: Augmented Reality/Mixed Reality	305
16.2.3 XR: Extended Reality	305
16.3 Key Traits of VR	305
16.3.1 Depth Perception	305
16.3.2 Tracking Degrees-Of-Freedom	305
16.4 Challenges and Solutions	306
16.4.1 Environmental Hazards	306
16.4.1.1 Digital Boundaries	306
16.4.1.2 Going All In	306
16.4.1.3 Designing for Safety	306
16.4.2 Nausea (Vection)	307
16.4.2.1 Avoidance	307
16.4.3 Tricking the Eyes, Ears and Brain	307
16.4.3.1 Teleport (X/Y Movement)	307
16.4.3.2 Snap Turn (Z-Rotation)	308
16.4.4 Blurring the Line between the Artificial and Natural	308
16.4.4.1 Arm Swing Movement	308
16.4.4.2 Head-Oriented Movement	308
16.4.5 General Aids	309
16.4.5.1 Simplify Your Visuals	309
16.4.5.2 Variable Peripheral Vision	309
16.4.5.3 Add a Stabilising Factor	309

16.5 Giving Options   309
    16.5.1 Uncanny Valley   310
        16.5.1.1 Scale   310
        16.5.1.2 Stylisation   310
        16.5.1.3 View Change   310
    16.5.2 User Interfaces   311
16.6 Future Possibilities   311
16.7 Conclusion   312

16.1 INTRODUCTION

The idea/term of virtual reality (VR) has existed for many decades already with Nintendo being the 'first to market' and also to failure with a consumer-level game device called the Virtual Boy.

The technology faded into history until 2012, when the Oculus Kickstarter blasted it back into prominence. That built a huge hype around the tech which has mellowed out over the years, but one cannot deny the power of VR as a platform and a medium.

When video game graphics technology made the leap from 2D to 3D, the range of new digital experiences it enabled developers to create advanced the medium significantly. VR is poised to do the same by advancing spatial immersiveness through depth perception and new interaction models.

Despite all this, the tech in its current implementation still faces many challenges when it comes to widespread adoption. These challenges range from cost, hardware limitations, content design and user-experience issues. On top of all that, the term 'virtual reality' is often poorly defined or understood, making in-depth discussions tough.

Through this chapter, we hope to define the space around VR, highlight common challenges and solutions, as well as look at possibilities yet to be explored.

16.2 TYPES OF VIRTUAL REALITY

In order to facilitate discussion, let us first review the common terms and definitions of VR technology and the variations they refer to.

These definitions may vary depending on who you talk to, and when you talk to them, but these serve as a reasonable starting point in understanding and discussing some distinctions in the space.

16.2.1 VR: Virtual Reality

The user is effectively isolated from the real world. You cannot see your surroundings and are transported into an entirely different world. Some well-known examples are the Oculus Rift, HTC VIVE and PlayStation VR.

16.2.2 AR/MR: Augmented Reality/Mixed Reality

Often used interchangeably, both terms generally refer to having a digital world 'overlaid' onto the real world.

This is most commonly experienced through wearable headsets, glasses-like devices like the Magic Leap and Hololens or through the screen of your smartphone or other handheld devices equipped with a camera.

16.2.3 XR: Extended Reality

This is a catch-all term that refers to all of the above, and potentially future additions. You will quickly notice that all forms of 'reality' share a lot of common attributes, and XR is a convenient way of referring to them as a whole.

With these clarifications out of the way, let us move on to some key traits that define the experience of Virtual Reality, and the terms used to discuss them.

16.3 KEY TRAITS OF VR

The things that set VR apart from conventional 2D experiences.

16.3.1 Depth Perception

Depth perception is arguably the biggest distinction between digital content presented on a flat screen and through the lens of a VR headset. By delivering a stereoscopic image to the user (a slightly offset view of the content to each eye), the depth perception we get in reality is recreated in a headset.

This sense of depth makes everything we see in the digital world feel an order of magnitudes more tangible, giving us that increased sense of realism. Hence the term, virtual reality.

16.3.2 Tracking Degrees-Of-Freedom

The other critical aspect of the VR experience is the way we interact with the virtual world. Our various limbs' change in positions and orientations are tracked and translated into the virtual world via headsets and controllers. This tracking is what immerses not just our sight and hearing but our bodies into the virtual world.

The scope of tracking being done is referred to as the Degrees-of-Freedom (DoF); 6DoF is the most common standard, with tracking rotation and translation on three axes each, for a total of six. Some older or simpler platforms may track only rotation and are thus described as 3DoF devices.

The different DoF enable different levels of interaction. For example, 3DoF headsets only allow players to turn and look around themselves, without being able to move closer, farther or to the sides when looking at the virtual world; 3DoF controllers only allow players to point, without being able to reach out or draw back their hands.

Now that we have a common understanding of how VR is different from conventional 2D mediums, we can move on to discussing the issues that plague VR, as well as the ways we can potentially alleviate them.

16.4 CHALLENGES AND SOLUTIONS

16.4.1 Environmental Hazards

This is by far the greatest risk that VR poses to the end user. While engaging with VR content, the headset makes the user effectively blind to his real-world surroundings, and there is a real risk of colliding into objects in his/her vicinity if allowed to wander too far off the starting or ideal position.

16.4.1.1 Digital Boundaries

Most existing headsets already allow users to demarcate safe zones and boundaries that will be visible in the headset, allowing the system to warn them when they get too close to those boundaries.

16.4.1.2 Going All In

Embrace the hazard and build around it. Companies like The VOID go all out and build digital experiences with matching physical facilities that are only playable at said facilities. Every in-game wall, door, chair or table is mapped to a real-world proxy. Awesome, but out of reach for most developers.

16.4.1.3 Designing for Safety

Developers can subtly anchor players to the centre of their playspaces, well away from danger, through simple environmental contexts. For example, the PSVR game *Blood & Truth* puts players in a variety of fixed locations, behind a desk for cover or in the passenger seat of a car. These scenarios encourage the player to stay mostly on one spot in the real world, away from hazards.

16.4.2 Nausea (Vection)

VR is great at transporting us into a different world. And moving around the world also feels really good, as long as you are doing it with your own two feet. Artificial (input-drive) movement, however, creates quite a bit of dissonance. Your eyes tell you you're moving, but your ears say no. That makes the brain nervous and escape to puke town!

16.4.2.1 Avoidance

The simplest solution here is to remove artificial movement altogether, and many popular VR games like *Superhot* and *Beat Saber* do this. While this is a simple and effective solution, not all games (or content) can or should be played without artificial movement. So, where does this leave us?

16.4.3 Tricking the Eyes, Ears and Brain

If there's a need/want to give players the freedom of movement, we can 'fake' it using the following techniques.

16.4.3.1 Teleport (X/Y Movement)

Remove the perception of movement by using a teleport function instead of smooth movement. If your eyes don't see movement, they won't argue with the ears. That said, this mode of movement creates a lot of edge cases to consider.

- Is this a valid teleport location?

- Will I fall off the edge if I teleport just a tiny bit too close to it?

- Does teleporting even make sense for my game/character?

Sometimes teleportation gets in the way of achieving certain gameplay experiences or emotions, and as such is not always suitable for all games.

We opted against teleport in *Stifled* (a sound-based stealth thriller) because we felt it took away from the slow and deliberate stealth gameplay. However, we are using it for our latest game, *KungFucious* (a VR Kung Fu simulator), because it is action-driven, and teleporting around makes you feel like a bad-ass Kung Fu master!

16.4.3.2 Snap Turn (Z-Rotation)

While users of VR are usually able to simply turn their heads and body to look around, they are often discouraged by the possibility of getting the headset cables tangled, or are limited by frontal sensor setups like PSVR and Oculus Rift. Here is where artificial, input-based rotation is required, and like movement, it has a high possibility for causing motion sickness.

In the same manner that we converted smooth movement into discrete teleportation steps to minimise the sense of vection, we can also divide rotation into discrete steps of fixed intervals, which is what we refer to as *Snap Turns*.

This rotation can be done instantly to completely remove the sense of motion or have small easing motions at the start and end to help orientate users to the view that they are rotating towards.

In a conventional flat 3D game, this locking of rotation intervals would be extremely limiting, but in VR it is easily compensated physically with a slight shift and rotation of the players' heads or bodies.

It is also preferable to choose a rotation interval that adds up to a full 360° to minimise confusion.

- $16 \times 22.5° = 360°$

- $12 \times 30° = 360°$

- $8 \times 45° = 360°$

- $4 \times 40° = 360°$

16.4.4 Blurring the Line between the Artificial and Natural

As the most common reason for nausea is the conflict between what the eyes see and the body perceives, another way of mitigating it is by introducing a little body movement to match what the eyes see.

16.4.4.1 Arm Swing Movement

By having players mimic the arm swinging motion from jogging and walking to move their in-game character, the perception of moving is then associated with the arm swing movement and reduces the disconnect between what the player sees and what their body feels.

16.4.4.2 Head-Oriented Movement

The phrase 'look where you're going' best describes this movement scheme. When the forward/back input is activated, the in-game character moves towards/away from where the user is looking. This is in line with our natural tendencies to look towards where we're going, hence creating a more comfortable experience.

16.4.5 General Aids

The following are some tips that can be used to mitigate nausea in a wide variety of situations.

16.4.5.1 Simplify Your Visuals

One thing we noticed is that across the same quality of movement, games with stylised aesthetics and a lower level of visual details tend to be less likely or take longer to cause nausea in players.

Even though VR is immensely immersive, you very quickly realise that visual fidelity is not the most important thing that draws players in. It is instead the ability to interact naturally with the world that gives you a deep sense of immersion. Simplifying your visuals (may) also have the beneficial side effect of giving you a more optimised, smoother and hence more comfortable experience.

16.4.5.2 Variable Peripheral Vision

Peripheral vision is a big factor in helping us recognise and feel movement. This increases the sense of immersion, but also the likelihood of us becoming nauseous.

There is a balance to be maintained here between immersion and comfort. As developers we can clean up, simplify or temporarily block off your peripheral vision through the use of depth of field visual effects, motion blur and even vignetting.

These options should be used sparingly and reserved for moments of extreme movement. During more tranquil moments, we can afford to let players be immersed fully with little risk of nausea.

16.4.5.3 Add a Stabilising Factor

This is often seen in vehicular-based games, where players are confined to the cockpit of a spaceship or a mech. In this visual context, the brain attributes any artificial movement to the vehicle and not the self, helping it to resolve the argument between the eyes and the ears.

16.5 GIVING OPTIONS

We'd like to end this chapter by saying that these are merely ideas on what can be done.

Traditional wisdom will ask you to avoid overloading the player with options but with the nascent state of VR, options will always be a welcome addition. This allows players to customise the game to best fit their personal limitations.

What works best varies wildly with each player, and thus it is good to give players the freedom to choose the mix of solutions that best suit them.

16.5.1 Uncanny Valley

This term generally refers to the zone where the appearance of digital human characters approaches full realism, but the few minor imperfections that remain create a sense of eeriness, discomfort and occasionally full out revulsion in viewers.

This phenomenon is more intense in VR and arguably applies to non-human objects as well. The additional depth perception and realism makes users more sensitive to the subtle flaws and inconsistencies that may otherwise be passed over in flat 3D media.

There are a few simple tips to mitigate this effect.

16.5.1.1 Scale

Because of the additional depth perception in VR, discrepancies in scale are more apparent and they stick out like a sore thumb. In flat 3D games, it is possible to distort/exaggerate the size of objects/props to improve usability; for example, making a doorway wider and taller so it's easier to walkthrough. Doing this in VR will break immersion as the doorway will seem humongous.

During the development of *Stifled*, we actually went around our house and office measuring items to make sure they were modelled to scale to minimise this problem.

16.5.1.2 Stylisation

Another option is to sidestep the uncanny valley entirely by using a stylised, non-realistic aesthetic. This breaks the users' preconceived notions of how things should be represented, making immersion easier. This immediately signals players' minds to not expect photorealism, making it easier to ignore flaws and maintaining the suspension of disbelief and immersion becomes easier.

16.5.1.3 View Change

Similar to stylisation, we can disconnect the user from their usual understanding of the world by placing their 'eyes' elsewhere, like in the body of a rat, bird or a floating disembodied being. By eliminating the sense of 'body', we have a more difficult time judging the scale of the items that we see in VR.

16.5.2 User Interfaces

Our eyes can only focus at one focal length at a time. While this is all well and good in conventional 2D flat experiences, where UI and content are experienced through a screen. The addition of depth perception in VR introduces some challenges.

Imagine all the HUD you need for your virtual experience printed on a piece of glass, providing information by hovering in front of your users' vision. That piece of glass, stuck too close to your users' eyes, will cause them to go cross-eyed, unable to make out any text. Push it too far away and it starts to frequently collide with and be occluded by the world around it.

Because of this, there is a need for UI implementations in VR to actually 'exist' in the virtual world to allow the user to focus at different depths. These types of interfaces are generally categorised in the following manner.

- **Spatial:** Interfaces that have a 3D position in the virtual world, but are not necessarily seen by the characters within said virtual world. For example, the highlights that show up when a user looks at an interactable item in *Stifled* is a UI element that aids in the users' understanding but does not exist in the game world.

- **Digetic:** Interfaces that are described as diegetic exists in the game world and are perceivable by both the player and characters in the virtual world. An example of a diegetic UI is the inventory menus of *Dead Space*. In *Dead Space*, the inventory menu is presented as a digital hologram projected by Isaac's suit that is visible to both the player, Isaac and other characters in the game.

An added benefit of having diegetic user interfaces that 'exist' in the virtual world is that it provides a more immersive experience by being grounded and behaving in a natural/familiar manner. This reduces the need for pop-up buttons, prompts and instructions that can often be jarring.

16.6 FUTURE POSSIBILITIES

At the time of writing, the majority of VR content is designed and built around the human body and experience. This is, in our opinion, born out of practicality/limitations and ease of understanding for the end user.

VR setups are commonly made up of three major components:

- **Headset:** head tracking and display unit

- **Hand controllers:** hand tracking/input

- **Tracking cameras:** to track headset and hand controllers

With the interaction driven by the headset and hand controllers. Anything more than this baseline raises the barrier of entry and limits the potential audience.

Second, building around the human body is also an excellent way of creating intuitive controls by playing to the users' natural tendencies. This paradigm is well and good, but there's nothing stopping us from exploring the unique experiences the platform can provide by putting ourselves in non-human bodies. To that end, there are some existing examples out there in the market. Some put users into the bodies of birds and another as a robot with the ability to customise/swap out limbs.

But there is still room for exploration. Could we replace our arms with virtual tentacles? Give ourselves four arms instead of merely two? Additional hardware that simulates the sensation of non-human/additional limbs? We could simulate the experience of learning to use prosthetics, perhaps for science, perhaps for fantasy. The possibilities are seemingly limitless.

16.7 CONCLUSION

Throughout this chapter, we have gone over the issues plaguing VR experiences today and a variety of mitigation strategies. We have also briefly touched on possibilities with the medium that have yet to be explored and the future challenges we might face in that regard.

As the medium continues to evolve rapidly (the industry went from cabled headsets to its first mass-market, standalone, 6DoF enabled headset, Oculus Quest, while we were writing this book), the content in this chapter will likely be obsolete in no time. However, we hope it will still come in handy for budding VR developers making their first foray into the medium and grappling with the fundamentals.

CHAPTER 17

Player Locomotion in Virtual Reality Games

Andrey Krekhov and Katharina Emmerich

CONTENTS

17.1 Presence and Cybersickness		314
17.2 VR Locomotion Landscape		316
	17.2.1 Stationary Approaches	316
	17.2.1.1 Traditional I/O Approaches	316
	17.2.1.2 Teleportation	317
	17.2.1.3 Gestures	318
	17.2.2 Walking-Inspired Techniques	319
	17.2.2.1 Natural Walking	319
	17.2.2.2 Walking in Place	320
	17.2.2.3 Physical Treadmills	321
	17.2.2.4 Redirected Walking	321
	17.2.2.5 Multiscale Navigation	322
17.3 Design Implications		323
Bibliography		325

CURIOSITY AND THE THIRST for exploration are an important part of human nature. It is not surprising how easy we tend to lose ourselves in large, open game worlds, spending countless hours on roaming around unknown terrain. Hence, locomotion ever since had an important role in game design. And while this challenge is solved to a large extent in common digital games, locomotion techniques in virtual reality (VR) remain a large obstacle to this day.

This chapter discusses the challenges of VR locomotion and outlines a number of available solutions that allow the exploration of fictional worlds. We begin by looking at two important components of VR that one might also call the curse and blessing of such immersive setups: cybersickness and presence. In particular, we explain why common locomotion approaches, such as mouse and keyboard, are not viable in VR, and how the high degree of immersion allows the players to experience a feeling of being in the virtual world.

The main part of this chapter focuses on classifying the past and ongoing research on VR locomotion. We discuss a broad spectrum of possibilities to move in VR, ranging from stationary approaches relying on gamepads to advanced redirected walking techniques that trick our perception to enable unrestricted natural walking in a limited space. Finally, we propose a set of design guidelines to simplify the implementation of player locomotion in future VR games.

17.1 PRESENCE AND CYBERSICKNESS

At present, VR technology is considered mainstream, and more and more manufacturers are putting effort into creating head-mounted displays (HMDs) at affordable prices. Such HMDs are capable of rendering stereoscopic images at HD resolutions for each eye while maintaining a high refresh rate (90 Hz or above). The hardware also tracks the head orientation, which allows players to look around in VR like in the real world and gather close-up experiences during gaming.

Players usually describe such impressions as a feeling of "being there" (Heeter, 1992; Lombard & Ditton, 1997). Other popular wordings often include the two terms *presence* and *immersion*—sometimes in an interchangeable manner. Throughout this chapter, we utilize immersion (Cairns, Cox, & Nordin, 2014) when focusing on the technical quality of VR hardware (Biocca & Delaney, 1995; Sherman & Craig, 2002). In contrast, we use presence to describe how immersive setups affect our perception to make us believe that we are indeed in the virtual environment (Slater, 2003). Hence, (game) researchers and developers often target the increase of presence when coming up with novel VR approaches, and VR locomotion is a prominent advocate for such presence-enhancing research (Slater, Usoh, & Steed, 1995). To measure presence, the most common methods include the Presence Questionnaire (PQ) (Bob G. Witmer & Singer, 1998; Bob G. Witmer, Jerome, & Singer, 2005) and the Igroup Presence Questionnaire (IPQ) (T. W. Schubert, 2003; T. Schubert,

Regenbrecht, & Friedmann, 2018). In addition, the Immersive Tendencies Questionnaire (ITQ) (Bob G Witmer & Singer, 1998) can be administered before the actual survey to check participants' individual tendencies to get immersed in an activity or fiction.

Unfortunately, the increase in a players' perceived presence is not the only thing that an immersive setup entails. The produced realism imposes high demands on VR software and hardware regarding human perception. Minor faults or technical issues, such as slightly offset locomotion or a sudden frame rate drop, can have severe consequences regarding the players' well-being and result in *cybersickness* (Stanney, Kennedy, & Drexler, 1997; LaViola Jr, 2000). Other prominent terms often used in this context are simulator sickness (Kolasinski, 1995) and motion sickness (Money, 1970; Lawrence J Hettinger & Riccio, 1992; Ohyama et al., 2007). In contrast to the manifold reasons of cybersickness, the main cause of simulator sickness is an incorrectly adjusted simulator (Kennedy, Lilienthal, Berbaum, Baltzley, & McCauley, 1989) and can be regarded as a rather technical problem.

Cybersickness involves symptoms such as nausea, eye strain, and headaches. Roughly spoken, the main reason behind that negative phenomenon is a mismatch in our vestibulo-ocular system. Our vestibular system senses acceleration that ideally matches the visual input. When these signals do not match, the aforementioned symptoms are likely to occur (Reason & Brand, 1975). There exist three popular explanations (LaViola Jr, 2000) for such an unwanted body reaction: poison theory, postural instability theory, and—the most prominent—conflict theory.

Lawrence J. Hettinger, Berbaum, Kennedy, Dunlap, and Nolan (1990) also mentioned vection as a possible reason behind cybersickness. Vection describes the feeling of movement that relies only on our visual system and can be experienced when, e.g., we sit in a standing train and observe another train that is currently accelerating. Vection is influenced by several factors, including the field of view (FOV), the alignment and proximity of moving objects, and the optical flow rate. For instance, the combination of a large FOV and fast objects that account for a large proportion of players' view amplify the perceived vection and smooth the way to cybersickness. Hence, limiting the FOV is one of the possible approaches to reduce cybersickness (Fernandes & Feiner, 2016; Lin, Duh, Parker, Abi-Rached, & Furness, 2002).

To conclude, we suggest keeping cybersickness in mind and to avoid cognitive mismatches where possible—however, not at all costs, as "sickness-save," stationary scenes without any locomotion would potentially miss out on a wide range of benefits that VR has to offer. And sometimes, as shown by Von Mammen, Knote, and Edenhofer (2016), games might even benefit from an artificially induced cybersickness.

17.2 VR LOCOMOTION LANDSCAPE

We have seen that locomotion in VR is not just a way of transporting the player from A to B. Rather, locomotion strives to provide realistic, immersive experiences that increase the player's presence while working around cybersickness. In recent years, research (Boletsis, 2017) and the game industry (Habgood, Wilson, Moore, & Alapont, 2017) created a plethora of varying locomotion approaches. As often is the case, there is no "right" answer which one must pick for your upcoming VR game. Hence, the main purpose of the following sections is to provide a rough overview and classification of available approaches and to serve as a starting ground for further research and development. In particular, we start by considering locomotion approaches that do not involve a physical movement of the player, before moving on to techniques that evolve around the idea of natural walking in VR.

17.2.1 Stationary Approaches

Although HMDs can track head movements, only a subset of them are capable of tracking the global position of a player in the room. One also says that such setups support room-scale tracking. One common approach is to utilize a set of base stations that emit infrared pulses, which are captured by the HMD to estimate the global position. Conversely, there is a considerable number of HMDs that come without room-scale support. The main reasons to omit such tracking are the lower costs and the increased portability. As such, devices do not support the physical movement of the player, stationary locomotion techniques are required to allow the exploration of game worlds. Another reason for stationary approaches is reduced fatigue, as players might even remain seated during a gaming session.

17.2.1.1 Traditional I/O Approaches

Existing games are sometimes ported to VR, be it to promote the title or to build on the success of the original game. In such cases, developers tend to take over the controls, including locomotion, to reduce the turnaround time and keep the familiar game UI. Hence, VR players are pushed towards a desktop I/O, be it a keyboard (Argelaguet & Maignant, 2016), a joystick (Bozgeyikli, Raij, Katkoori, & Dubey, 2016a) or a gamepad (Fernandes & Feiner, 2016). The advantage of the method is, without doubt, its simplicity regarding implementation and the familiarity to experienced players.

However, as we pointed out before, a cognitive mismatch between our vision system, i.e., seeing the motion via the HMD, and our vestibular system, i.e., remaining stationary or even seated, can easily lead to cybersickness when using such approaches. Hence, we recommend paying close attention to this issue when relying on traditional methods. As a partial remedy, developers might want to reduce the FOV, as, e.g., was done in *Skyrim VR* (Bethesda Softworks LLC, 2017). Another way would be to limit or disable continuous in-game player motion in favor of quick or discrete player movements (Habgood et al., 2017) to reduce vection. The work of Medeiros et al. (2016) and Yao et al. (2014) also confirmed the benefits of short, fast movements with no acceleration as one measure to combat cybersickness in such cases.

17.2.1.2 Teleportation

If we take the idea of fast and short movements to the extreme, we will end up with a technique called the point and teleport locomotion approach (Bozgeyikli, Raij, Katkoori, & Dubey, 2016b). Players select a destination using a pointing device, e.g., a controller (Xu, Murcia-López, & Steed, 2017), and are instantly teleported to that place, thus entirely removing the vection issues. Regarding cybersickness, this technique is more robust than traditional gamepad locomotion (Frommel, Sonntag, & Weber, 2017) and is being strongly encouraged by the majority of established VR systems such as the HTC Vive. The targeting is often visualized by an arc that starts at the controller or the virtual hand representation and ends at the planned destination. On the one hand, the targeting is considered intuitive and robust. On the other hand, however, such implementation limits the travel distance to visible places that are not far away, and certain virtual environments might further limit the travel distance by exposing obstacles, such as trees or walls, that prevent players from targeting more distant locations. In addition, the displayed teleportation arc itself is a rather obstructive interface element that covers parts of the game world and might decrease players' perceived presence if it does not blend in well with the setting. Another issue to be considered is the limited precision when teleporting to very close areas, as the displayed arc gets too compressed and is not very helpful for predicting the outcome.

This uncertainty often results in numerous relocation attempts until the desired position is finally achieved.

The last drawback of teleportation is the reduced spatial orientation of players, which might also impact their experienced presence. Players need to reorient themselves after a relocation, which imposes an additional cognitive load. To overcome this obstacle, researchers propose to render previews of the destination area, or, as proposed by Bruder, Steinicke, and Hinrichs (2009), utilize such previews as virtual portals where players have to pass through to reach their target.

The described arc-based teleportation, although being recommended by hardware manufacturers, is still relatively uncommon in VR games. A more widespread variation of the technique is known as node-based teleportation (Habgood et al., 2017). This technique is based on predefined points of interest that could be represented by, e.g., an icon. In contrast to the arc-based method, players cannot pick their destination freely and can only travel between such nodes. The node selection is usually implemented by looking at a node and pressing a button. The subsequent teleportation process is often accompanied by a fading animation. This feature, in combination with a clever choice of node locations, allows a reduction in player disorientation, but obviously limits the perceived freedom of exploration.

17.2.1.3 Gestures

Ever since the introduction of the Microsoft Kinect, gesture-based interaction finally became mainstream and also entered the gaming area. In general, gestures are often considered natural and intuitive, which is likely to have a positive influence on the player experience and the perceived presence in VR. Accordingly, we can rely on gestures to perform locomotion—still not as intuitive as physical walking, but often more natural than steering one's avatar via a gamepad while remaining seated.

For mainstream VR setups, i.e., HMDs including tracked controllers, the number of supported gestures is usually limited to head and arm/hand movements. When we talk about head gestures, we refer, of course, primarily to gaze-based locomotion: players rotate their heads in the direction they want to walk (Kitson, Hashemian, Stepanova, Kruijff, & Riecke, 2017; Cardoso, 2016). The actual walking speed can be either predefined or controlled by leaning the head forward or backward. This kind of locomotion has the crucial advantage of not requiring any additional interaction devices. Hence, this approach is often utilized in VR setups based on low-cost smartphone head mounts, such as Google Cardboard, that have no alternative ways of gathering user input rather than tracking the head orientation. On the downside, gaze-based locomotion is less suited for games that require simultaneous interactions, e.g., aiming and shooting while moving. Accordingly, we often find this approach in exploration-only scenarios like virtual tours through exhibitions. Instead of moving the head only, one could also use the whole body as a kind of human joystick (Harris, Nguyen, Wilson, Jackoski, & Williams, 2014) and lean into the desired direction. However, such approaches require additional sensing hardware, e.g., a Wii balance board.

One straightforward way to support player multitasking is to control the locomotion by arm or hand gestures. Two prominent examples for such gestures include tap and push as proposed by Ferracani, Pezzatini, Bianchini, Biscini, and Del Bimbo (2016). Tapping (Piumsomboon, Clark, Billinghurst, & Cockburn, 2013) is performed by pointing with the index finger, i.e., players show the direction they would like to walk. Pushing resembles more the control of a machine, i.e., one grabs a virtual lever by closing the hand and triggers the locomotion by translating the hand forward. In terms of performance, tapping turned out to be more efficient regarding collision avoidance. A physically more expressive way to control locomotion is to swing our arms (Wilson, Kalescky, MacLaughlin, & Williams, 2016; McCullough et al., 2015) to initiate translations in VR. In contrast to delicate finger recognition required for the aforementioned tapping gesture, such arm swings can be easily tracked via mainstream VR controllers.

17.2.2 Walking-Inspired Techniques

We started our exploration of the locomotion landscape by looking at traditional I/O approaches and transitioned to more natural user interaction in the form of gestures. However, the most natural way for us, humans, to explore our environment is to walk. If you have ever witnessed a kid putting on a VR HMD for the first time, you have noticed that this kid will start moving right away, because that is our "out of the box" locomotion technique. Hence, we dedicate the second part of our overview to approaches that are based on natural walking—be it physical treadmills, redirected walking, or just walking in place.

17.2.2.1 Natural Walking

Without doubt, the most realistic movement in VR is based on physical walking, as this approach copies our real-world locomotion one to one.

A significant amount of research has confirmed the resulting superior realism and the positive effect on the perceived presence (Slater et al., 1995; Usoh et al., 1999; Ruddle & Lessels, 2009; Waller & Hodgson, 2013; Ruddle & Lessels, 2006). Furthermore, natural walking positively influences the cognitive map in large environments, as shown by Ruddle, Volkova, and Bülthoff (2011). As our real and virtual movements can be perfectly matched using natural walking, the risk of cybersickness is also minimized.

Unfortunately, unrestricted natural walking is hardly achievable for various reasons. First, the physical location of the player has to be estimated, i.e., additional tracking is necessary. Second, even if we can track the player, the physical room size imposes an insuperable obstacle: sooner or later, you will end up against a wall. And while the tracking issue is solved to a large extent in modern VR setups, the room limitation still persists. Later in the text, we will see diverse solutions to that problem that rely on tricking our perception or modifying and rescaling the virtual environment to "fit" the game world into our living room.

In its pure form, natural walking is mainly used in combination with teleportation or other stationary locomotion. Players perform large transitions via teleport and then walk a small distance, e.g., one or two steps, to their precise destination. On paper, this combination removes the excessive number of relocations that happen in pure teleportation approaches. However, researchers and developers also noticed that teleportation plays the dominant role and players often tend to forego the option of doing some real steps, as switching and combining multiple locomotion approaches produces an increased cognitive load. Another possibility to apply natural walking without further modifications is to design game worlds that are smaller than our living rooms. It sounds too restrictive, but certain games work surprisingly well under such conditions—above all, we point readers to the popular genre of escape room games.

17.2.2.2 Walking in Place

One possible way to bypass the room-scale limitation is to walk in place. Being based on natural, walking-like motions, this approach also enhances presence (Slater et al., 1995; Tregillus & Folmer, 2016) and is easy to learn (Usoh et al., 1999). According to Usoh et al. (1999), walking in place is less immersive than natural walking, but both solutions outperform virtual locomotion approaches such as teleportation regarding the achieved feeling of presence.

Walking in place is usually implemented by tracking the leg movements of the player, either with built-in tracking or via additional sensors (Templeman, Denbrook, & Sibert, 1999). More sophisticated approaches are capable of deriving the correct walking speed by utilizing gait principles (Wendt, Whitton, & Brooks, 2010) to respond to variations in step frequency.

17.2.2.3 Physical Treadmills

One variation of in-place walking are treadmills that allow the players to move in a physical way. Combined with an HMD, players usually cannot distinguish such installations from real walking experiences. However, in contrast to a fitness studio, virtual worlds are hardly ever built in a linear way and players need the ability to change the walking direction.

Hence, VR games require omni-directional treadmills (Darken, Cockayne, & Carmein, 1997) or variations such as the omni-directional ball-bearing disc platform (Huang, 2003). Due to their spatial requirements and high costs, commercial omni-directional solutions such as the *VirtuSphere* (Skopp, Smolenski, Metzger-Abamukong, Rizzo, & Reger, 2014) did not find their way into our living rooms. A viable alternative is a stepper machine (Bozgeyikli et al., 2016a), which is cheap, small, and easy to use. However, the walking direction has to be extracted from additional input, such as head orientation, potentially increasing the cognitive load.

17.2.2.4 Redirected Walking

In contrast to walking in place techniques, which address the room-scale limitation by completely avoiding the player moving through the real room, other approaches enable natural walking by applying redirection or reorientation. The idea of redirected walking is to manipulate the player's movement in the virtual world by creating a mismatch between real-world locomotion and the translation in the game world. As a result, the perceived movement in the virtual world is more extensive than the player actually moves in the real-world space (Razzaque, Kohn, & Whitton, 2001; Razzaque, 2005; Steinicke, Bruder, Jerald, Frenz, & Lappe, 2010). While players do not notice the manipulation, they unconsciously compensate the offset by slightly repositioning and reorienting themselves. Hence, by manipulating translation, path curvature, and rotation, reorientation techniques can be used to keep players inside the boundaries of the tracked space without making them aware of the fact that they are actually walking in circles.

Nescher, Ying-Yin Huang, and Kunz (2014) and Paris, McNamara, Rieser, and Bodenheimer (2017) discuss different redirection methods and algorithms, providing further information how such techniques can be applied to VR games.

Redirection and reorientation techniques maintain the advantages of natural walking regarding high perceived presence, intuitiveness, and a low risk of cybersickness. However, though current approaches tackle the issue of space limitation to some extent, they still require a much larger space than is given in common living rooms and, thus, require further adaptations in that regard (Grechkin, Thomas, Azmandian, Bolas, & Suma, 2016; Engel, Curio, Tcheang, Mohler, & Bülthoff, 2008; Langbehn, Bruder, & Steinicke, 2016; Bruder et al., 2009). The demands of such techniques in terms of VR setup and implementation are considerably high.

17.2.2.5 Multiscale Navigation

Until now, the approaches we considered usually perform on a 1:1 ratio between the physical and the real world. In other words, the traveled distance in the physical room roughly corresponds to our virtual footprint. An alternative way to deal with the room-scale limitation is rescaling of players and/or their motion (Bhandari, Tregillus, & Folmer, 2017). Note that world rescaling is equivalent to player rescaling. However, we strongly discourage altering the world size, i.e., the size of all objects, due to obvious performance reasons and, in the worst case, floating point precision issues.

In research, the dynamic scaling of virtual environments is mostly used within multiscale virtual environments (MSVEs) (Zhang & Furnas, 2002). For instance, such approaches can be utilized to explore the inner organs of virtual human representations (Kopper, Ni, Bowman, & Pinho, 2006). Hereby, the current scale can be set either manually by the player or computed automatically based on current task or location. As shown by Argelaguet and Maignant (2016), automatic scaling is often more predictable for developers and allows the optimization of rendering parameters to reduce diplopia or cybersickness.

In games research, a recent example of player rescaling is a locomotion technique called GulliVR (Krekhov, Cmentowski, Emmerich, Masuch, & Krüger, 2018). The approach allows players to turn into giants on demand and cover large distances in just a few steps. At first glance, the idea is similar to a common flying approach, as both variants share the same camera position and velocity. However, flying is known for its severe cybersickness due to the cognitive mismatch of physical and virtual movement speeds. In contrast, GulliVR increases the interpupillary distance as part of the whole-body rescaling process, which has two effects. First and foremost, the cybersickness is removed as players feel like they are walking as giants (no mismatch) and not like they are artificially floating or flying. Second, players perceive the environment from above as a miniature world, which opens up novel design possibilities (Cmentowski, Krekhov, & Krueger, 2019).

17.3 DESIGN IMPLICATIONS

Locomotion in VR has a huge impact on the failure or success of a game. A well-chosen technique is able to enhance the player experience and help players to immerse even more in the fictional worlds. On the downside, technical issues or cognitive mismatches can easily render a game unplayable due to a significant amount of introduced cybersickness. Not surprisingly, our high-level recommendation is to design locomotion in a way that minimizes the risks of cybersickness and maximizes the perceived presence. Ideally, we would choose natural walking for most cases, but, unfortunately, the room-scale limitation forces us to consider alternatives and handle respective trade-offs.

For that reason, we recommend enforcing a decision regarding locomotion quite early in the development process, as certain approaches have a considerable interplay with other game mechanics, such as object interaction, quest locations, world size, and so on. As a starting point for such decision making, we summarized the mentioned locomotion methods in Figure 17.1. Please note that such overviews rely on certain over-generalizations, e.g., not all gamepad-based techniques causre cybersickness.

However, we feel that a condensed summary might be helpful, especially when designing a VR game for the first time. Furthermore, we propose the following questions to be asked during the VR game design process with respect to locomotion.

- **What is my target audience?** The canonical question for almost any kind of decision making. We emphasize three aspects of this question. First, how exhausting is the locomotion allowed to be? This depends on age and the overall target group, as well as the type of the game, i.e., it might be an exergame or something meant for relaxation/recovery. Second, how long are the players meant to play the game at a time? This aspect also determines how physically straining the locomotion is allowed to be. Third, what hardware setups do our

	natural motion	cybersickness	intuitiveness	hardware reqs	short distances	long distances	fatigue
traditional I/O	-	-	o	+	+	o	+
teleport/node	-	+	-	+	o	+	+
gestures	-	o	o	o	+	o	o
natural walking	+	+	+	o	+	-	-
walking in place	o	o	+	o	+	o	-
treadmills	+	+	+	-	+	o	-
redirected walking	+	+	+	-	+	o	-
multiscale nav	+	+	o	o	-	+	-

FIGURE 17.1 An overview of VR locomotion techniques including their benefits and drawbacks. Dark gray (+) means that this attribute is a known advantage of the technique, light gray (O) stands for limited value, and medium gray (-) is rather a disadvantage.

players have? In other words, are we designing for Google Cardboard that only tracks head orientation or can we assume room-scale tracking? In particular, we are limited to stationary approaches if we do not have access to the player position.

- **How important is exploration?** In general, games with a heavy focus on exploration and player movement benefit a lot from realistic, well-constructed locomotion approaches that allow a free and natural journey through the virtual world. Conversely, if the main emphasis of the game is on aiming and shooting, a node-based teleportation technique with carefully predefined locations might be more efficient. Furthermore, the overall size of the virtual world should be considered, as some of the techniques excel at short distances, whereas other approaches are designed to cover large distances in a short amount of time. Taken to the extreme, certain game genres, such as escape rooms, might even consider relying only on natural walking by fitting the virtual environment completely into the living room.

- **What else happens during locomotion?** This question is also related to the main focus of the game. Certain techniques, such as gaze-based locomotion, limit the amount of concurrent activities and are less suited for games in which players need to perform additional interactions while walking. The overall effort required for locomotion—be it mental or physical—also impacts the general pace of the game. In other words, fast-paced games might rather benefit from an instant, node-based teleportation rather than forcing players to physically run through their living rooms or spending precious seconds while aiming with the arc-based teleportation approach.

Again, these questions are meant as a starting point. In combination with the overview in Figure 17.1, this kind of reasoning might be helpful in establishing a well-suited locomotion technique early on to take full advantage of virtual reality gaming.

BIBLIOGRAPHY

Argelaguet, F., & Maignant, M. (2016). Giant: Stereoscopic-compliant multi-scale navigation in VEs. *Proceedings of the 22nd ACM Conference on Virtual Reality Software and Technology*, pp. 269–277. ACM.

Bethesda Softworks LLC. (2017). *Skyrim VR*. Game [SteamVR]. Rockville, MD: Bethesda Softworks.

Bhandari, J., Tregillus, S., & Folmer, E. (2017). Legomotion: Scalable walking-based virtual locomotion. *Proceedings of the 23rd ACM Symposium on Virtual Reality Software and Technology, VRST '17*, pp. 18:1–18:8. Gothenburg, Sweden: ACM.

Biocca, F., & Delaney, B. (1995). Communication in the age of virtual reality. In F. Biocca & M. R. Levy (Eds.), *Immersive Virtual Reality Technology*, pp. 57–124. Hillsdale, NJ: L. Erlbaum Associates Inc.

Boletsis, C. (2017). The new era of virtual reality locomotion: A systematic literature review of techniques and a proposed typology. *Multimodal Technologies and Interaction*, 1(4), 24.

Bozgeyikli, E., Raij, A., Katkoori, S., & Dubey, R. (2016a). Locomotion in virtual reality for individuals with autism spectrum disorder. *Proceedings of the 2016 Symposium on Spatial User Interaction*, pp. 33–42. ACM.

Bozgeyikli, E., Raij, A., Katkoori, S., & Dubey, R. (2016b). Point & teleport locomotion technique for virtual reality. *Proceedings of the 2016 Annual Symposium on Computer-Human Interaction in Play*, pp. 205–216. ACM.

Bruder, G., Steinicke, F., & Hinrichs, K. H. (2009). Arch-explore: A natural user interface for immersive architectural walkthroughs. *2009 IEEE Symposium on 3D User Interfaces*, pp. 75–82. IEEE.

Cairns, P., Cox, A., & Nordin, A. I. (2014). Immersion in digital games: Review of gaming experience research. *Handbook of Digital Games*, 337–361.

Cardoso, J. (2016). Comparison of gesture, gamepad, and gaze-based locomotion for VR worlds. *Proceedings of the 22nd ACM Conference on Virtual Reality Software and Technology*, pp. 319–320. ACM.

Cmentowski, S., Krekhov, A., & Krueger, J. (2019). Outstanding: A perspective-switching technique for covering large distances in VR games. *Extended Abstracts of the 2019 CHI Conference on Human Factors in Computing Systems (LBW1612)*. ACM.

Darken, R. P., Cockayne, W. R., & Carmein, D. (1997). The omni-directional tread- mill: A locomotion device for virtual worlds. *Proceedings of the 10th Annual ACM Symposium on User Interface Software and Technology, UIST'97*, pp. 213–221. Banff, Alberta: ACM.

Engel, D., Curio, C., Tcheang, L., Mohler, B., & Bülthoff, H. H. (2008). A psycho-physically calibrated controller for navigating through large environments in a limited free-walking space. *Proceedings of the 2008 ACM Symposium on Virtual Reality Software and Technology*, pp. 157–164. ACM.

Fernandes, A. S., & Feiner, S. K. (2016). Combating VR sickness through subtle dynamic field-of-view modification. *2016 IEEE Symposium on 3D User Interfaces (3DUI)*, pp. 201–210. IEEE.

Ferracani, A., Pezzatini, D., Bianchini, J., Biscini, G., & Del Bimbo, A. (2016). Locomotion by natural gestures for immersive virtual environments. *Proceedings of the 1st International Workshop on Multimedia Alternate Realities*, pp. 21–24. ACM.

Frommel, J., Sonntag, S., & Weber, M. (2017). Effects of controller-based locomotion on player experience in a virtual reality exploration game. *Proceedings of the 12th International Conference on the Foundations of Digital Games*.

Grechkin, T., Thomas, J., Azmandian, M., Bolas, M., & Suma, E. (2016). Revisiting detection thresholds for redirected walking: Combining translation and curvature gains. *Proceedings of the ACM Symposium on Applied Perception [SAP '16]*, pp. 113–120. Anaheim, CA: ACM.

Habgood, M. J., Wilson, D., Moore, D., & Alapont, S. (2017). Hci lessons from playstation VR. *Extended Abstracts Publication of the Annual Symposium on Computer-Human Interaction in Play [CHI PLAY '17 Extended Abstracts]*, pp. 125–135. Amsterdam, The Netherlands: ACM.

Harris, A., Nguyen, K., Wilson, P. T., Jackoski, M., & Williams, B. (2014). Human joystick: Wii-leaning to translate in large virtual environments. *Proceedings of the 13th ACM Siggraph International Conference on Virtual-Reality Continuum and Its Applications in Industry*, pp. 231–234. ACM.

Heeter, C. (1992). Being there: The subjective experience of presence. *Presence: Teleoperators and Virtual Environments*, 1(2), 262–271.

Hettinger, L. J., Berbaum, K. S., Kennedy, R. S., Dunlap, W. P., & Nolan, M. D. (1990). Vection and simulator sickness, *Military Psychology*, 2, 171–81.

Hettinger, L. J., & Riccio, G. E. (1992). Visually induced motion sickness in virtual environments. *Presence: Teleoperators and Virtual Environments*, 1(3), 306–310.

Huang, J.-Y. (2003). An omnidirectional stroll-based virtual reality interface and its application on overhead crane training. *IEEE Transactions on Multimedia*, 5(1),39–51.

Kennedy, R. S., Lilienthal, M. G., Berbaum, K. S., Baltzley, D., & McCauley, M. (1989). Simulator sickness in us navy flight simulators. *Aviation, Space, and Environmental Medicine*, 60(1), 10–16.

Kitson, A., Hashemian, A. M., Stepanova, E. R., Kruijff, E., & Riecke, B. E. (2017). Comparing leaning-based motion cueing interfaces for virtual reality loco-motion. *2017 IEEE Symposium on 3D User Interfaces (3DUI)*, pp. 73–82. IEEE.

Kolasinski, E. M. (1995). *Simulator Sickness in Virtual Environments*. Alexandria, VA: Army Research Inst. for the Behavioral and Social Sciences.

Kopper, R., Ni, T., Bowman, D. A., & Pinho, M. (2006). Design and evaluation of navigation techniques for multiscale virtual environments. *Virtual Reality Conference*, pp. 175–182. IEEE.

Krekhov, A., Cmentowski, S., Emmerich, K., Masuch, M., & Krüger, J. (2018). Gullivr: A walking-oriented technique for navigation in virtual real-ity games based on virtual body resizing. *Proceedings of the 2018 Annual Symposium on Computer-Human Interaction in Play [CHI PLAY '18]*, pp. 243–256. Melbourne, VIC: ACM.

Langbehn, E., Bruder, G., & Steinicke, F. (2016). Subliminal reorientation and repositioning in virtual reality during eye blinks. *Proceedings of the 2016 Symposium on Spatial User Interaction*, pp. 213–213. ACM.

LaViolaJr, J. J. (2000). A discussion of cybersickness in virtual environments. *ACM SIGCHI Bulletin*, 32(1), 47–56.

Lin, J.-W., Duh, H. B.-L., Parker, D. E., Abi-Rached, H., & Furness, T. A. (2002). Effects of field of view on presence, enjoyment, memory, and simulator sickness in a virtual environment. *Proceedings of Virtual Reality, 2002*, pp. 164–171. IEEE.

Lombard, M., & Ditton, T. (1997). At the heart of it all: The concept of presence. *Journal of Computer-Mediated Communication*, 3(2), 0–0.

McCullough, M., Xu, H., Michelson, J., Jackoski, M., Pease, W., Cobb, W., Williams, B. (2015). Myo arm: Swinging to explore a VE. *Proceedings of the ACM Siggraph Symposium on Applied Perception*, pp. 107–113. ACM.

Medeiros, D., Cordeiro, E., Mendes, D., Sousa, M., Raposo, A., Ferreira, A., & Jorge, J. (2016). Effects of speed and transitions on target-based travel tech-niques. *Proceedings of the 22nd ACM Conference on Virtual Reality Software and Technology*, pp. 327–328. ACM.

Money, K. E. (1970). Motion sickness. *Physiological Reviews*, 50(1), 1–39.

Nescher, T., Huang, Y.-Y., & Kunz, A. (2014). Planning redirection techniques for optimal free walking experience using model predictive control. *2014 IEEE Symposium on 3d User Interfaces (3DUI)*, pp. 111–118.

Ohyama, S., Nishiike, S., Watanabe, H., Matsuoka, K., Akizuki, H., Takeda, N., & Harada, T. (2007). Autonomic responses during motion sickness induced by virtual reality. *Auris Nasus Larynx*, 34(3), 303–306.

Paris, R. A., McNamara, T. P., Rieser, J. J., & Bodenheimer, B. (2017). A comparison of methods for navigation and wayfinding in large virtual environments using walking. *2017 IEEE Virtual Reality (VR)*, pp. 261–262.

Piumsomboon, T., Clark, A., Billinghurst, M., & Cockburn, A. (2013). User-defined gestures for augmented reality. *IFIP Conference on Human-Computer Interaction*, pp. 282–299. Springer.

Razzaque, S. (2005). *Redirected Walking*. University of North Carolina at Chapel Hill.

Razzaque, S., Kohn, Z., & Whitton, M. C. (2001). Redirected walking. *Proceedings of Eurographics*, 9, 105–106.

Reason, J. T., & Brand, J. J. (1975). *Motion Sickness*. New York, NY: Academic Press.

Ruddle, R. A., & Lessels, S. (2006). For efficient navigational search, humans require full physical movement, but not a rich visual scene. *Psychological Science*, 17(6), 460–465.

Ruddle, R. A., & Lessels, S. (2009). The benefits of using a walking interface to navi- gate virtual environments. *ACM Transactions on Computer-Human Interaction (TOCHI)*, 16(1), 5.

Ruddle, R. A., Volkova, E., & Bülthoff, H. H. (2011). Walking improves your cognitive map in environments that are large-scale and large in extent. *ACM Transactions on Computer-Human Interaction (TOCHI)*, 18(2), 10.

Schubert, T., Regenbrecht, H., & Friedmann, F. (2018). *Igroup Presence Questionnaire (IPQ)*.

Schubert, T. W. (2003). The sense of presence in virtual environments: A three-component scale measuring spatial presence, involvement, and realness. *Zeitschrift für Medienpsychologie*, 15(2), 69–71.

Sherman, W. R., & Craig, A. B. (2002). *Understanding Virtual Reality: Interface, Application, and Design*. Elsevier.

Skopp, N. A., Smolenski, D. J., Metzger-Abamukong, M. J., Rizzo, A. A., & Reger, G. M. (2014). A pilot study of the virtusphere as a virtual reality enhancement. *International Journal of Human-Computer Interaction*, 30(1), 24–31.

Slater, M. (2003). A note on presence terminology. *Presence Connect*, 3(3), 1–5.

Slater, M., Usoh, M., & Steed, A. (1995). Taking steps: The influence of a walking technique on presence in virtual reality. *ACM Transactions on Computer-Human Interaction (TOCHI)*, 2(3), 201–219.

Stanney, K. M., Kennedy, R. S., & Drexler, J. M. (1997). Cybersickness is not simulator sickness. *Proceedings of the Human Factors and Ergonomics Society Annual Meeting*, 41, 2, pp. 1138–1142. Los Angeles, CA: SAGE Publications.

Steinicke, F., Bruder, G., Jerald, J., Frenz, H., & Lappe, M. (2010). Estimation of detection thresholds for redirected walking techniques. *IEEE Transactions on Visualization and Computer Graphics*, 16(1), 17–27.

Templeman, J. N., Denbrook, P. S., & Sibert, L. E. (1999). Virtual locomotion: Walking in place through virtual environments. *Presence*, 8(6), 598–617.

Tregillus, S., & Folmer, E. (2016). VR-step: Walking-in-place using inertial sensing for hands free navigation in mobile VR environments. *Proceedings of the 2016 CHI Conference on Human Factors in Computing Systems*, pp. 1250–1255. ACM.

Usoh, M., Arthur, K., Whitton, M. C., Bastos, R., Steed, A., Slater, M., & Brooks Jr., F. P. (1999). Walking> walking-in-place> flying, in virtual environments. *Proceedings of the 26th Annual Conference on Computer Graphics and Interactive Techniques*, pp. 359–364. ACM Press/Addison-Wesley Publishing Co.

Von Mammen, S., Knote, A., & Edenhofer, S. (2016). Cyber sick but still having fun. *Proceedings of the 22nd ACM Conference on Virtual Reality Software and Technology*, pp. 325–326. ACM.

Waller, D., & Hodgson, E. (2013). Sensory contributions to spatial knowledge of real and virtual environments. In *Human Walking in Virtual Environments*, pp. 3–26. Springer.

Wendt, J. D., Whitton, M. C., & Brooks, F. P. (2010). Gud wip: Gait-understanding-driven walking-in-place. *2010 IEEE Virtual Reality Conference (VR)*, pp. 51–58. IEEE.

Wilson, P. T., Kalescky, W., MacLaughlin, A., & Williams, B. (2016). VR locomotion: Walking> walking in place> arm swinging. *Proceedings of the 15th ACM Siggraph Conference on Virtual-Reality Continuum and Its Applications in Industry- Volume 1*, pp. 243–249. ACM.

Witmer, B. G., Jerome, C. J., & Singer, M. J. (2005). The factor structure of the presence questionnaire. *Presence: Teleoperators and Virtual Environments*, 14(3), 298–312.

Witmer, B. G., & Singer, M. J. (1998). Measuring presence in virtual environments: A presence questionnaire. *Presence*, 7(3), 225–240.

Xu, M., Murcia-López, M., & Steed, A. (2017). Object location memory error in virtual and real environments. *2017 IEEE Virtual Reality (VR)*, pp. 315–316. IEEE.

Yao, R., Heath, T., Davies, A., Forsyth, T., Mitchell, N., & Hoberman, P. (2014). Oculus VR best practices guide. *Oculus VR*, 4, 27–39.

Zhang, X., & Furnas, G. W. (2002). Social interactions in multiscale CVEs. *Proceedings of the 4th International Conference on Collaborative Virtual Environments [CVE '02]*, pp. 31–38.ACM.

CHAPTER 18

Working Everywhere and Nowhere. A Practical Guide to the Virtual Office

Allan Simonsen

CONTENTS

18.1 Why Would You Go to an Office Every Day?   331

    18.1.1 Serve the Underserved   332

18.2 Longitude and Latitude   333

    18.2.1 How Do You Know That They Are Working   333

    18.2.2 Yes, Mum… I'm At Work   334

    18.2.3 The Heartbeat   335

18.3 Insiders and Outsiders   335

    18.3.1 Throughput vs Permanence   336

18.4 Infrastructure in the Virtual Office   337

18.5 Lessons Learned   338

18.1 WHY WOULD YOU GO TO AN OFFICE EVERY DAY?

There are many reasons why a company, especially a startup, might start thinking about going virtual. Cost is an obvious one; office space in the various development hubs around the world is anything but cheap and carry risky binding terms that lock you in for several years, and come with a seemingly unending parade of paperwork for fittings, electricity, broadband, power and water coolers. Conversely, the total infrastructure effort involved in starting a virtual development studio involves rolling out of bed and turning on your existing computer. If you for some reason lack the necessary software licenses, your vendor of choice will happily supply them for you in the five minutes it takes the teakettle to boil. After a life lived largely online, encountering the world of Brick and Mortar feels like going from fiber to a dial-up modem.

But more important than the setup cost is the daily cost to your staff and yourself. The hours each day spent jammed into a train or sitting bumper-to-bumper on a highway. The missed family dinners when crunch hits or missed graduations because an office culture has convinced you hours spent in the office hours equaled productivity.

The games industry historically suffers from a tremendous brain drain past 35; many of our best staff pack up and leave a job they love because the hours are not compatible with being a father or mother. I once hired an amazing engineer who told me he had never, in a year of unending crunch, seen his nine-month-old daughter in daylight. At some point he broke and quit without another job. Which I guess was their loss, and our gain; he quickly became one of our lead engineers and loved the work–life balance the virtual office afforded him.

There has been a big move throughout tech companies, especially among the most desirable employers, to reimagine the office as a playful experience complete with beanbags, foosball tables, offices named after whiskies and gourmet cafeterias onsite. None of that alleviates the fact that it is basically a pale copy of the home office. That Herman Miller Aeron chair won't be as comfortable as your old, worn-in, gamer chair, no fancy canteen will ever match the meals you eat with your kids, and no Casual Friday will compete to an office environment where pants are optional.

18.1.1 Serve the Underserved

While, in theory, game development can happen anywhere, the bulk of development happens across approximately ten metropolitan areas, none of which are particularly cheap. When staffing up an office in Singapore, Tokyo or San Francisco, you are often dragging prospective employees into a situation with very high rents and general cost of living. If it is tempting, as an employer, to consider that it is not your problem, you should also remember that you're pulling them into an extremely competitive environment where other studios can out-bid you for key talent.

Many of our staff have historically been in the local equivalent of fly-over country. Often, they have returned to their hometown to be close to family or to raise children. Cost of living is lower, and unlike development hubs like San Francisco, Seattle or London, housing prices are low enough that young professionals can afford to purchase their own home. In fact, the only thing missing are good job opportunities, which is what the virtual office aims to solve. There are of course downsides to this; rural infrastructure, especially internet access, can be spotty. If you are dealing with the developing world, you can extend that to the occasional blackout or flood, and in one memorable event, a volcanic eruption.

The lack of an office community can be a challenge. Fresh graduates, often single and expecting the office to provide the community they had in college, often struggle with the transition. Married staff, on the other hand, especially with children tend to thrive; they already have the social network they want, and the additional time with family is valued.

18.2 LONGITUDE AND LATITUDE

We once used to say the sun never set on Boomzap; with staff in Japan, Southeast Asia, Russia, Finland and the United States, there was always someone who had daylight. It was a terrible idea.

With a virtual office, distance by and large does not matter. Once you design processes for dealing with it, the difference between different cities and different countries is largely academic. But time zone matters, greatly. Whether it is scheduling meetings, asking for technical help or discussing game design, being able to bring everyone working on a project together is critical. For us, we have found one hour plus or minus works fine. Once it gets past four hours from the early to the later time zones, parts of the day will have points where people are unable to find someone when they need, and anything beyond that rapidly gets unfeasible.

18.2.1 How Do You Know That They Are Working

In an office environment, we often consider someone's presence in a chair proof that they are busy working. A question that often gets asked is "how do I know that my staff are actually working in a virtual office"? To be "at work" in our case is to be online on Slack and responding to questions. There is no real way of knowing if the person is busy coding, or busy playing *World of Warcraft*, but as long as they are online and responsive, it does not really matter.

What does matter is that you track output, which is a very different thing than hours. You know roughly what a good programmer, artist or designer can perform in 40 hours of solid work. If the weekly output meets that, and people can easily communicate with the staff, it is less important that the work was done between 10 and 17. It is largely the same case for physical offices; between the internet and their phone, people have access to more distractions than a mere eight hours of sitting in a chair will exhaust. Track output, not hours.

One aid here is the Daily Report. Each staff writes a one paragraph "what I did today" at the end of each working day. Artists post work-in-progress art to the channel twice a day, and the programmers build a new version of the game each night, complete with the latest code and assets. The key is to have this in a format where you can easily track individual task lists over time; an underperforming staff will often list the same task repeatedly, or pad their daily reports with tiny tasks to make it seem like they are more productive than they actually are.

That kind of behavior is hardly limited to the virtual office, though; I once had a co-worker that would strive to be at the office first every day. He would sit down, turn on the lights and the computer, and send out some emails to prove that he was "in and working." After which he would promptly head to a nearby cafe to have a two-hour breakfast, having proved his productivity for the day. Always track output: that is a lot harder to fake.

18.2.2 Yes, Mum… I'm At Work

Most people in a virtual office want to succeed and want to be productive. We are lucky enough to be working in an industry where most people genuinely love what they do. A greater impediment to productivity can be family. They can sometimes struggle to understand that someone sitting in their gaming chair, doing game-looking things on their gaming PC, is actually busy at work.

It is worth having a dedicated space to work, and a process that mentally makes it clear that you are "at work." Treat it like work, avoid the thousands of distractions a well-stocked gaming den provides. Make it clear to the people around you that you are just as much at work as someone in a physical office, and your ability to walk the dog, babysit your nephew or pick up your remote cousins from the airport is subject to the same restrictions as anyone else with a fulltime job. Conversely, without those processes, it is really easy to fall into the trap of always being "at work." Between work, games, social media and the internet at large, many of us spend far too much time in front of a screen. Without having clear delineation between work and play, it is far too easy to stagger from your PC at midnight, feeling you've spent 14 hours working, even though most of that time was spent surfing the web or playing games.

Setting clear boundaries between your home office and the virtual office is one of the key challenges in the virtual office, and one that is often ignored by both staff and management.

18.2.3 The Heartbeat

It is a common misconception that a virtual office is one devoid of processes; the opposite is true. We internally refer to this as the Heartbeat of the studio; the things that happen daily, weekly, per review or per project to drive things forward.

Each day we expect staff to play the game; we do a daily build, encompassing all new assets and code that has changed. We often say that if something is not in the build, it does not exist. At the end of each day, each staff writes up their Daily Report, and the lead programmer tells the Build Server to create the daily build. Some teams also do daily "standup" meetings, to make sure everyone is aware of what the rest of the team is doing.

Each Virtual Studio will develop their own rhythm, but it is critical that something builds a cadence. Without it, it is really easy for teams to slide out of alignment, and for problems to fester unaddressed.

One problem that is rarely talked about when discussing the virtual office is mental health. The games industry, as a rule, is not great at dealing with these issues. Common problems, like stress, long hours, unhealthy eating and bad exercise habits are further exacerbated by isolation and lack of human contact. A strong heartbeat helps; the rhythm gives some structure to the days, having clear beginning and end rituals to the day help to separate work from life, and daily reports help managers spot problems early and have a sit down talk.

18.3 INSIDERS AND OUTSIDERS

Companies that have dabbled in the virtual office often start by having some outsourcers, or a satellite office somewhere. Often, they will later discard it as a failed experiment, with common reasons cited being lack of collaboration, bad communication and lack of performance.

A common trend in these cases of "going virtual" is that the core team remains a physical unit, with communication and processes designed to facilitate that. Meetings are organized over lunch, ideas pitched over the watercooler, and communication often verbal and impermanent. In effect, that creates a first- and second-class employee; those at the physical office who have processes designed for them. And those in the virtual office, who find themselves out of the loop, unable to contribute and often blindsided. While it is possible to combine a physical and a virtual studio, it is significantly harder. It requires the physical office to become more organized in terms of communication, that things are documented and accessible online and that discussions happen in a forum where everyone can contribute. Failing that, a hybrid physical/virtual office will grow to resemble a smaller company with an attached insourcing unit, which is not good for morale or collaboration.

18.3.1 Throughput vs Permanence

When talking about communication it is useful to think of a graph over two axes: throughput and permanence. Throughput measures the speed and ease of distributing the information; permanence refers to the ease of accessing the information after the fact. (See Figure 18.1.)

On the far left (optimizing for information throughput), screen sharing video calls are a great way for a single person to distribute a lot of information to listeners quickly. We frequently use this for project reviews, design briefs and document overviews. It is inherently one-to-many; someone is sharing their screen—they are in the driver's seat. Once that call is over, that information lives only in memories; anyone not in the call having no

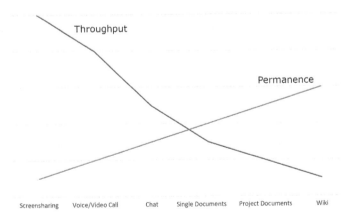

FIGURE 18.1 Throughput vs performance.

way of accessing the information, and inside the week, it will be lost to memory.

As we work our way left to right; chat is inherently egalitarian. Anyone with access to the chat channel can contribute equally, and the data is accessible to people who might have missed a voice call and can be updated later as people think about the implications of the information discussed. While in theory, the Chat Logs last forever, in practice finding a conversation more than a week or two ago is hard. Chat systems do not have good systems for tracking key decision points and search is not an adequate replacement. To deal with that, information that has been nailed down gets upgraded to a document system.

Almost always the first pass at that will be some form of shared document; for us usually a Google Slide or Google Doc. They are simple to access, easy to share and inherently informal. One aspect of the graph is that as we progress left to right on the graph, communication becomes more formalized and writing it becomes less of an impulse action. For projects of any size you will quickly need some system to organize that. In recent years, we have used Basecamp, which works great from an asset centric pipeline, and Trello, which works well from a process tracking standpoint.

Finally, for documentation where we value permanence above all things, we use formalized document management systems, in our case, a company Wiki. This tracks company handbooks, code and tool documentation, build processes and other information that rarely changes and needs constant referencing. A trend is that we go from easy to write and informal language (the average under 30 is happier chatting than talking) to technical and formal writing, which largely is only written under duress. Permanence at the expense of throughput.

One of the key aspects of running a Virtual Studio is to understand when and how to use the various forms of communication. Too far to the left, and you will create a fluid but chaotic environment where people feel empowered but confused. Too far to the right, and you will stifle creativity and the exchange of ideas, leaving innovation to whoever is most dedicated to editing documents. Once a consensus has been found, designate someone to document it for posterity.

18.4 INFRASTRUCTURE IN THE VIRTUAL OFFICE

We will split the infrastructure requirements into things that help the company itself and things that help your workers be productive.

With no physical location you will be reliant on the cloud to a greater extent than a physical studio. It is probably best to accept, and embrace, that from day one. For dedicated applications (like Source Control and dedicated server executables) a hosted server remains an option, but most Virtual Studios will end up embracing the cloud. For us, that has meant embracing Google Docs and Gmail, using Dropbox extensively to distribute assets across often fragile networks and cloud-based communication platforms like Slack and Trello. We have also moved the build pipeline into the cloud using a dedicated server and a leased virtual OSX machine, which allows us to free up the programmer's development machine during the daily build.

Sometimes, it is useful to help sponsor staff hardware. It is highly situational what will make a difference, but depending on what the pain-points are for your remote staff, it can be useful to reimburse or provide rebates to solve them. In our case, a lot of staff dealt with sporadic internet blackouts, so we helped reimburse a backup mobile broadband connection. We also found that many staff only used a single monitor, so we provided a rebate towards purchasing a second monitor. Finally, we provided rebates towards things like gym memberships and health insurance; unlike a physical office, it is hard to organize corporate memberships, but it is still worthwhile to encourage staff to get health insurance and exercise.

18.5 LESSONS LEARNED

Structure and communication are the two keys to a successful virtual office. Work hard to include everyone in the discussions and make sure you transition finalized information to a more permanent form. The virtual office requires more discipline than a physical office, and frequently works better with older developers who already have routines and a family around them. Distance does not matter, but time zones do; it is hard to collaborate across widely spaced working hours. Ultimately, the virtual office is about balancing the benefits to cost, talent pool and quality of life against the additional process and communication overheads involved.

V

Game History, Society, and Culture

CHAPTER 19

A Short Summary of Mobile Games' History

Simon Rozner

CONTENTS

19.1 Paving the Way: Original Handheld Games   341
19.2 First Phone Games   342
19.3 The Advent of the iPhone   346
19.4 In-App Purchases   348
Bibliography   356

19.1 PAVING THE WAY: ORIGINAL HANDHELD GAMES

We all love our games, from ages past, we did, and as long as we are around, we will. And the games we liked the most are those we could put into our pockets and carry with us. It is a natural extension that when digital games came about, sooner or later someone would figure out how to make them small enough to carry about. It is rather a small surprise that Mattel would, as so often with toys, beat others to the punch with the release of *Auto Race* in 1976. All digital, crude by today's standards for sure, it nevertheless started a rather successful business for Mattel, with their digital games repeatedly selling out.

The competition wasn't sleeping either though, as more portable games saw the light of day with the Milton Bradley MicroVision in 1979. Famous for great handhelds was the newcomer Nintendo in 1980 with the *Game & Watch* series. We know the rest of that story with the Game Boy (1989) and then Sega's Game Gear with a fabulous 32 simultaneous colors displayed on screen in 1990. Yes, business was good, but it was not to last forever.

19.2 FIRST PHONE GAMES

Something else started to happen in the 1990s. Where mobile phones were a luxury for the rich, the eccentric or the government before the last decade of the 20th century, in this last ten years of the millennium, the mobile phone turned into a commodity. Pagers were definitely out and mobile phones were in. And with Nokia & Co. having not just affordable and cool looking phones for calling, SMS and so on, well, the games were part of the fun.

It did not happen overnight however, and the first games were still rather an obscurity by engineers who well, who wouldn't, code a game into the device. Siemens arguably was the first on their S1 device in 1993 with a *Tetris* clone called *Klotz* (German: Block) that was hidden away behind an obscure key combo, apparently because they never got a license to actually publish it. IBM had their own on the IBM Simon, also in 1993, with *Scramble*. The real kicker though came in 1997 when Nokia released *Snake* on the Nokia 6110. Subsequently, Nokia released it on all their phones and with the Nokia 3110 in 2000, it was an established fact that Nokia phones had a Snake game. From a business perspective however, phone games hadn't really been big business.

Although independent developers started making games for phones around the millennium, and games could be downloaded to a device through a service such as NTT DoCoMo's I-Mode platform in 1999, many games were either preloaded on a device with a publishing contract with a telephone carrier or only available for download with a contract, again with a carrier via WAP—full browser access to the internet was years away. WAP was quite a problem for many developers. And still, no free market whatsoever existed, and if you wanted your game on a phone, well either deal with a carrier or go bust.

Another limitation that wasn't solved until about 2002 was that the software environment to develop games was basically a mobile house of horrors. J2ME (Java 2 Micro Edition) hailed an end to such barbaric conditions and hardware quality improved at the same time. However, despite J2ME, most devices on the market were still monochrome and games, even with improvements, couldn't even keep up with what a Game Boy could do 13 years earlier. While J2ME phones could give more "action" due to more powerful computing, their display quality was lagging behind. Thus, devices that were less powerful but had better graphics, providing games via WAP won out for the time being.

However, one must admire the brave companies that despite such an uphill battle, still managed to generate a proper income. The golden goose hadn't appeared that would allow mobile to compete with PCs and consoles and the ones who profited from games weren't the developers but the operators.

Mobile games—games for phones—excluding the handhelds business, have accounted for very little of the global yearly revenue generated by games. True enough, if we include handheld games, Nintendo has won that game over the competition. Nintendo, from the end of the 1990s, keeps generating a good income all the way from the Game Boy days to the latest incarnation of the Nintendo DS. However, even that grand master of game creation was sent packing for good during that fateful day when the Apple and Android App Stores introduced in-app purchases (IAPs). It would take Nintendo until *Super Mario Run* in 2016 to catch up and release its first true mobile title (Nintendo has released other third-party titles before, initially developed for other platforms).

We are getting ahead of the curve though. To understand the business of 2019, we have to head back again to the year, wait for it, 2000. And there were plenty of good games on mobile, even before the Apple revolution, but until 2008, the mobile games industry was mostly dominated by outrageous attempts of innovation and attempts to make it into a business that could compete with its big brothers on PC and console.

By the end of 1999, considerable success had been expected with the boom in mobile phone ownership, but dreams remained dreams for the time being. We all survived the millennium transition—not really a surprise—and hope for the future was abundant. So it came to pass that two companies were established that caused a stir in the years to come. Just at about 23:59 and some seconds before we could hail the year 2000, Michel Guillemot, one of the co-founders of Ubisoft, founded Gameloft in Paris. Here was a guy who knew how to make big games and had plenty of financial support. He had an entire catalog of games licenses from Ubisoft and more to bring to mobile audiences. Thus, it comes as no surprise that most titles in the early years had their PC/Console counterpart produced by Ubisoft. This fact is surely a big reason as to why Gameloft has stayed around long enough to be part of the later rise in mobile games. Experience does count for quite a bit in order to make steady progress and keeping heads above water.

Shortly after the start of Gameloft in Europe, JAMDAT was founded by ex-Activision executives Scott Lahman and Zack Norman in March 2000.

JAMDAT was a developer and publisher of mobile phone games in the US in partnership with the operator Sprint. They released, for example, the *Lord of the Rings* mobile titles, *Bejeweled* and had exclusive rights to *Tetris* on mobile. JAMDAT was later acquired by EA for a staggering US$680 million, catapulting EA Mobile to the number one position in games publishing on mobile. What is notable is that JAMDAT's business was evaluated as so big when profit margins on mobile were very competitive and development rather expensive. Obviously though it was lucrative enough for the long haul.

Regardless of the start of these two big studios, many smaller outfits made their debuts in these early years: HandyGames (Handy is German slang for Mobile) in Germany, Sorrent (now Glu) in the US, Picofun in Sweden, Rapture Seekers aka. Relude and what would ultimately become Rovio Entertainment and Riot-E in Finland, just to mention a few.

Riot-E deserves a little special mention here as for how much the pot of gold at the end of the rainbow could be, just to end up being a colossal disaster. Riot-E had a lot of investment, the license to create the *Lord of the Rings* mobile games and the license for the Marvel catalog. However, the hype around the company was just talk the talk, not walk the walk, and investors ended up having to write off their investments. It wasn't all bleak, by the time Riot-E was finally able to turn a profit, all trust in the company was eroded and by 2002 its doors closed. The legacy and learning that remained however would benefit the mobile games business in the years to come, as well as learning how to mature into a multibillion dollar business. (The rise and fall of Riot-E can be watched in the documentary *Riot On!*)

Let's fast forward and look at the advent of Nokia's N-Gage. Finally, a phone came along that boasted a mobile phone with a color screen and the power to beat a Game Boy. It was not to be however. The high retail price and clunky design didn't appeal to anyone but the geeky gamer, and not enough of them could afford it. Even a redesign to make it look more appealing didn't work, and so, the chance was missed as the competition wasn't sleeping. Devices started to get ever more powerful, a good thing for the games to come.

Notably, Trip Hawkins invested in mobile games after 3DS went bankrupt and launched Digital Chocolate in 2003. Although it eventually died as well with its Barcelona studio sold to Ubisoft and its Helsinki studio closed in 2013. It did however develop some great original mobile games that sustained its business through that time.

Despite the limitations of hardware, Namco released a fabulous demo of *Ridge Racer 3D* on mobile with impressive 3D quality. Gamevil released a series of stunning games such as *Skipping Stone, Super Boom Boom* and *Nom*. The last being especially innovative as it required the user to rotate his phone to leap over the craziest of objects, something not possible on a console or a PC and taking full advantage of a mobile device. To top it off even more, in *Nom 2* you could send a message to outer space by beating the whole game via a Ukraine Space Agency satellite.

JAMDAT also got in on the fun by releasing a multiplayer version of *Bejeweled*. Unfortunately, due to high data costs, multiplayer games, even asynchronous, still didn't take off on mobile.

In 2004, EA finally entered the mobile market, giving up licensing only for mobile, and instead planned to fully jump into bed with its partner Digital Bridges (later I-Play and acquired by Oberon Media) to build a full mobile studio. This, however, never really transpired into a success for EA, despite releasing games like *The Fast and the Furious* and *Colin McRae Rally 2005*. In the end, EA bought JAMDAT in 2005 and formed EA Mobile. This was a lucky break for EA as just earlier JAMDAT acquired Blue Lava Wireless, and along with it, the *Tetris* license. *The Sims 2, Need for Speed, Burnout, Dakar 2007,* etc. were soon to follow and EA Mobile established itself as a major mobile mover and shaker, albeit with varying success, for example, the sloppy attempt of bringing *Command & Conquer 3: Tiberium Wars* to mobile. EA in particular was heavily pushing big brands on mobile, from *Sims* and *SimCity* to *The Simpsons, Harry Potter, Wolfenstein, Monopoly, Tetris* and *Tomb Raider*. However, EA despite being a long-term developer of mobile games, major breakthrough successes were still waiting.

Other developers were not sleeping however, and during the 2004 and 2005 mobile investment craze, Gameloft and Glu established themselves, while others went under. It is notable that racing games, casual puzzle games and card games are as appealing then as they are now.

From 2006 onwards, we see quite a few ups and downs, but there was a steady trend to bring 3D to mobile games. Gizmondo even brought a new device for this reason, just to spectacularly crash and burn, figuratively and literally, when then director Stefan Ericcson crashed his Ferrari, which started a criminal investigation.

Glu in particular followed up through clever contacts and mergers like iFone to publish hit games like *Lemmings, DiRT, Crash Bandicoot: Mutant Island* and *Project Gotham Racing: Mobile*.

Clouds started to appear on the horizon quite quickly, with devices springing up like weeds making porting and maintaining games across devices a nightmare. Having moved into games in 3D didn't help either. This chaos stifled innovation right when it was really taking off with publishers focusing on having titles on as many phones as possible instead of investing in new games. Licensed games were the thing, and it wasn't about to end. Some curious games did show up though, such as *Paris Hilton's Diamond Quest* in 2006. Gameloft must have had a licensing bash too, and many went down that path, and if history is anything to not learn from, Rovio Entertainment tried similar shenanigans with a Shakira inspired Match 3 game called *Love Rocks* in 2015, however, it was not successful.

Despite the usual industry mayhem, and mobile did get its fair share of IPOs, bankruptcies and crappy as well as great games, it was to persevere in the good old habit until the fateful day on January 9, 2007. Time was ripe to give the status quo a good kick up the ole butt.

19.3 THE ADVENT OF THE IPHONE

All changed overnight when Apple gave the boot to the carrier middleman who decided what goes on a phone and what doesn't and the big publishers who sucked up to carriers like a bad wart. Why should developers give all that revenue to a carrier and a publisher? The manufacturer of the device doesn't really benefit from applications made for the phone beyond just selling the device in the first place. Also, why burden developers to make their games work on hundreds of devices, instead of just one?

So the iPhone arrived in 2007, with the AppStore in 2008 as part of the iPhone OS 2.0. For a small fee, anyone could start developing applications for a phone, all the tools to start provided with support and if you made something cool, free promotion on top of it. Give your app for free or charge a little and share your income, 70% for you and 30% with Apple. Boom! If you think that is a bad deal, try selling art at a gallery.

Anyway, suddenly with entertainment devices in millions of peoples' pockets, anyone could create stuff to sell without having to bother with the carrier dinosaurs. Nokia, Sony and so on got hit by a proverbial truck out of left field and they wouldn't recover until Googles' brilliant Android OS was the bitter pill the rest of the industry had to swallow as their own endeavors for a proper phone OS couldn't keep up. A few of the established device manufacturers did not recover from this blow, in turn giving rise to new behemoths in the smartphone sector like Samsung and Huawei. And make no mistake, this shift in paradigm gives the manufacturer billions in revenue each year, on top of the billions they make selling the hardware. Not a bad business one would argue.

It wasn't all a new device stunt. What the Apple iPhone did was revolutionize the mobile business not just in terms of a better store, but with great hardware, an actually usable touch screen, responsive apps, a design that made your head turn and fueled by the great reputation of Apple all contributed to the success.

Suddenly, making games for phones looked like a lucrative business beyond the few players who tried to get crumbs of the ever-growing games entertainment business of which phone companies were the only real big money makers on mobile. Here was a possible motherload coming. Before all that money really started flying like confetti, one crucial invention still needed to happen. The hockey stick moment that really allowed game developers to join the feeding frenzy. But we are getting ahead of ourselves.

In July 2008, the AppStore arrived and developers now could get any app they wanted (pending Apples approval) published and download by anyone owning an iPhone. The sheer ease of accessibility and curated apps helped customers find apps in a meaningful way and developers could finally reach their end user with little hassle. This was quite apparent in the top rated games on the iPhone in 2008, where the top ten iPhone games only had three games by major publishers: EA at rank seven with *Spore Origins* and Gameloft at ranks five and ten with *Hero of Sparta* and *Asphalt 4: Elite Racing* respectively, according to PocketGamer. The power of the iPhone brought a plethora of great games for our mobile enjoyment, all in wonderful color and smooth graphics; 2008 and 2009 really was the year for that and all genres were represented. From *Tap Tap Dance* to *Zynga Poker, World of Goo, Need for Speed: Undercover, Zenonia* and many more. *Edge* deserves a special mention as it arguably heralded the modern mobile minimalist puzzle platformer.

2009 also was the beginning of the first of many, although maybe not quite as big, phenomena that without mobile games, and the iPhone in particular, wouldn't exist today. Unarguably, the biggest hit from 2009 was *Angry Birds* by mobile developer Rovio Entertainment. And it almost wasn't going to happen either as Rovio, after years working mostly as a gun for hire to make quality games for mobile, was close to closing shop after 51 game projects. It needed a success and fast. Rovio or as it was called in the "days," Relude, had been around for YEARS on the mobile scene with a reputation of tech excellence and roots in the foundation of the Finnish demo scene.

Though as luck has it, *Angry Birds* became a smash hit. It was so big in fact, that well, everyone, except maybe folks in Japan, who to this date barely know *Angry Birds*, knew about it. When the iPad launched that same year, Steve Jobs even had it installed and visible on the home screen during the big unveiling. Yeah, that happened. But how is this significant. Well for one, *Angry Birds* was the first massive game on mobile. By now it has way north of 3 billion downloads. Second, it was the last of its kind on mobile.

When *Angry Birds* finally cracked open the gaming market on mobile, bringing tens of millions in revenue to the developer, it was also at the same time the end of mobile as we knew it—2009 also marked the end of the premium games market on mobile. The final nail in the coffin was struck and it was a long time coming.

19.4 IN-APP PURCHASES

Oh what a magical wonderful word. IAPs, in-app purchases, the magic bullet, the holy grail, the whatchamacallit of printing money faster than we can spend it and with it the free to play (F2P) business model. Free to play wasn't a new invention. It was around since the late 1990s, but it was basically tied to your PC with an internet connection. Notable early F2P games were *RuneScape* and *Maplestory*. The premise was quite easy, play for free, pay for premium content.

With games that "anyone" could make and publish on a device millions were carrying in their pockets every day, wherever they went and download for free and pay for all sorts of extras in the game, it was just a matter of time before it would explode. It took about one second. Well almost, but the moment IAPs became available on mobile in 2009, revenue from mobile games skyrocketed. The rest is not quite history. F2P found a lot of popularity in web games in the late 2000s, and with the help of the likes of Facebook and MySpace, it was even easier to get players into the games and use social mechanics to get people to spend.

Today, in 2019, the revenue from mobile games worldwide is about US$68 billion of the US$152 billion of all game revenue. Noteworthy is that the United States and China are almost on par in revenue from all games.

Monetization is a big deal in mobile games and nowhere is this as true as in F2P games on mobile, which account for the majority of income. Clever game design, triggers of the players psychological buttons and application of behavioral economics bring a range of monetization methods to the table, from the obvious as buying an extra life to the unethical and outright illegal like complete gacha.

Apart from different legal challenges games have faced in the past few decades, one might argue that the current somewhat justifiable witch hunt against loot boxes is the biggest threat to the F2P model and games in general. What most people don't understand is the entire premise of RPGs, for example, depends on loot tables to begin with, be they packed in a box or a drop from a monster, and making random loot boxes illegal, well, sort of opens Pandora's Box of litigation well beyond just selling gacha boxes but any random system in a game. However, the ethical aspect of this is a topic for another time.

Nevertheless, nobody can deny that loot boxes have brought significant revenue from F2P games and are a valid and lucrative income stream as well as a fun way to get content for players. Gacha is not the only big money maker for F2P games. Every piece of new content and events can provide regular ways for players to spend and customizations ways for players to express themselves. We digress, the nitty gritty of this topic is big enough to discuss somewhere else.

We mentioned earlier that *Angry Birds* was first as well as the last really big premium mobile game. As we know now, the AppStore came about and allowed for IAPs, unfortunately for Rovio, the company didn't really manage to jump on the bandwagon of F2P, despite numerous attempts, until *Anrgy Birds 2* launched in 2015 and even then struggled until around 2016 to really accept the fact that F2P was here to stay. That is not to say that the company didn't try, but too many people came from a premium mindset, didn't understand F2P and didn't know how to make F2P games and all the shebang that accompanies it. It managed to turn the ship around though and it is a thriving company with F2P at its heart.

F2P in any case was here to stay, and it was BIG, so big that by 2011, the top 100 F2P games on the Apple AppStore generated more money that the store's premium games. By 2018, F2P games were estimated to make around 80% of video game revenue, with almost two-thirds coming from mobile alone.

It wasn't quite such a huge bonanza by 2010. And we start to see that great games do last. So while the shift to IAPs happened in 2009, the charts in 2010 were still dominated by our friends the premium games. *Angry Birds* was leading the pack, closely followed by *Plants vs. Zombies* developed by then PopCap, which was acquired by EA in 2011, with about half the revenue that Rovio was pocketing. And the stores were full of innovative games that year, as mobile games had a habit of being, with *Cut the Rope* and *Fruit Ninja* joining the party. *Cut the Rope* and its follow-ups are physics-based puzzle games, and it is noteworthy that the original game came in a free version lite version as well, making it the most downloaded app of 2010 and the fastest selling app according to Chillingo of 2010. Surely having a free "demo" with such massive downloads (about 9.7 million) helped the downloads for the paid app (about 3.5 million)? Interestingly enough, the long-time crowd pleaser *Tetris*, continued to be owned by EA, was still around, and even *Scrabble*, *Need for Speed* and *Battlefield* from EA made appearances. Electronic Arts wasn't the only old-time mobile company to still be kicking, Glu and Gameloft were along for the ride with plenty of titles in the top 100 grossing chart. Maybe one fun game to mention is *Flick Kick Football* by Australian developer PikPok. It reached rank 20 that year with an estimated US$350,000 in revenue. Not bad for a simple sports game. Interestingly enough, Nordeus, a Finnish developer released *Golden Boot 2019* in, you guessed it, 2019, with exactly the same core mechanics, now as a F2P game and pocketing about US$210,000 in revenue. Not quite as much, but then it is a much more competitive market than it was in 2010. One thing becomes staggeringly clear: "good games last." And what is really meant by that is "well designed and built game mechanics last." Plenty of games have great gameplay, sometimes they simply can't be found. This is the reason why a plethora of similar games with proven cores simply last and keep coming back. *Angry Birds* wasn't the first physics based, slingshot game, nor the first successful one. Remember games like *Worms* and even *Artillery Simulator*? Although very different in flavor, the basic idea of the core mechanics, throwing something in 2D along a trajectory to make the target go "boom," is as true and fun today as it was in the 1970s.

In 2011, as mentioned before, the inevitable happened and F2P surpassed premium on mobile. And, yeah, some really unexpected things started to happen. Of course, *Angry Birds* was still topping the grossing charts, but now it jumped on the free download train. And man did that train go. Where in 2010 we were looking at downloads in the under 10 million mark, downloads for the top games were reaching the 30–50 million mark. Don't forget, games that primarily started as premium games, even with IAPs, were now available for free. And that didn't hurt revenues one bit. Mobile games were now hitting the US$20 million mark and of all games to beat *Angry Birds*, it was a game and company nobody heard of (unless you were really into that sort of thing).

PopReach with *Smurfs' Village*? You have got to be kidding me!? A Smurf game made this much money? Something must be wrong. Data glitch? Lies all around? The commies? The author was as stupefied as you surely are right now dear reader, as until time of research, this was well, hidden lore. Sure, city builders were the thing. Zynga showed it to us with *Farmville* on the web. PopReach doesn't even have a Wikipedia page! So who is this mysterious player? The company is a little bit of an enigma if you so will, with a barebones website.

Digging a little deeper however reveals that the initial developer was none other than Capcom. One of their divisions, Beeline Interactive made the game, with the IP eventually traveling to PopReach. A silly little research case however, as when looking at historic data charts on AppAnnie, Capcom can't even be seen, and Beeline is only listed as the publisher in Japan. Well, all comes together, and nothing is a surprise anymore. However, that this game outperformed *Angry Birds* did come as a surprise. *Smurfs' Village* is a pure F2P game, and its economy didn't come cheap at US$4.99 being the cheapest IAP.

And here we have another of the dark sides of IAPs. The game was clearly targeted at kids, and it is speculated that children inadvertently were buying more than their parents knew. For one didn't necessarily have to enter the password again for 15 minutes for a repeat in-app purchase. This targeting to kids and excessive spending by minors would soon, rather than later, become quite a headache for the mobile and F2P games industry.

Over the next few years, things didn't really change this trend. F2P was here to stay, for better or worse. Some companies were frantically clinging on to the premium model on mobile, and it cost them dearly. Rovio is one example that didn't manage to embrace F2P fully until *Angry Birds 2* was released and the company was plagued by several lay-offs. However, Rovio was a lucky one, building smartly on the success of *Angry Birds* through smart licensing and the eventual *Angry Birds Movie* in 2016. EA, as well as Gameloft, kept chugging along just fine as well, with some ups and downs, but F2P was the bread and butter of their mobile games.

2012 ended up bringing more players to mobile gaming not just on iOS but also on Android, which was now an established fact. Other platforms have mostly perished and are entering a world of obscurity. Not all was so uneventful. A new rise of games came crashing down, that, while not a phenomenon yet, paved the way for games like *Pokémon Go*—causing landowners a serious headache. The culprit we mean is, of course, *Ingress* from Niantic. Location based games weren't really anything new, but here we have a game that used the smartphone's capabilities really well by using the built-in camera for augmented reality and the GPS functionality for location tracking. The longevity of the game is maybe its biggest surprise and proves there is a market for such games, plus it gets people up and moving around.

The other game that made a stir came from Supercell and is *Clash of Clans*. It took the world by storm, cleverly combining city building with a strategy game where players compete against each other. And Supercell was not resting on its laurels either, ensuring it would stay around.

Increasingly casual and hyper casual games started showing up in 2013 and it ended up being a slightly different year. Of notable mention is *Dots*. A simple puzzle game that shined through its simplicity. And a break-out title, not financially but as a template for future hyper casual game-play was *Flappy Bird*. Games that were released in 2012, such as *Candy Crush*, *Subway Surfers* and *Hill Climb Racing*, were really making a killing in 2013. Business was good and F2P was dominating. But premium was far from dead, and Mojang's *Minecraft Pocket Edition* brought in an esti-mated US$50 million. That, however, is a token gesture compared with *Candy Crush* and *Puzzle & Dragons*—each game was reaching close to US$1 billion in revenue. Those are numbers that boggle the mind, and quite frankly if anyone didn't believe in the power of F2P, you couldn't deny it now. One special thing did happen in this 2012–2013 period. Asian games are slowly coming to the West on mobile. Until now, we mostly only saw Nintendo and PlayStation have traction in Western markets with games produced in Asia, but with *Puzzle & Dragons*, this definitely started changing. Japanese games in particular were and still are massive in their local market, but the way those games are made slowly trickles through, especially to Korea and China. Before, games from those countries come to the United States and Europe in a big way, now, one Western game is going "Big in Japan" first. In 2013, Japanese mobile carrier and exclu-sive reseller of Apple iPhones in Japan, SoftBank, bought a US$1.5 billion share stake in Supercell. Note also that SoftBank owns GungHo Online

Entertainment, the makers of *Puzzle & Dragons*. This catapulted SoftBank to the absolute top by owning two of the three top mobile games on the market. As *Clash of Clans* became the first game to breach the US$1 billion revenue mark in 2014, it came as no surprise that *Clash of Clans* became a top 10 game in revenue in Japan among a crowd of all Japanese games. The author allows for a little anecdote: "I have lived on and off in Japan since 2007, and one thing I noticed when in Japan that year after that deal was that I saw *Clash of Clans* preinstalled on iPhones when shopping for a new iPhone for my relatives." The Japanese are notoriously immune to Western games, but here we have, well, free marketing for a Western game on the local market. Whether the app was really always preloaded is questionable, but if you walked into any SoftBank store at the time, all demo devices had the game on the front screen, while the phone the author bought had the game preloaded.

Welcome to 2015, the year of strategy and RPGs. While largely the same games from 2014 and before kept their popularity, many newcomers had now entered the market. The top games all earned quite a bit of money. The size of new apps in the app stores had not diminished and growth was huge. Many users have trouble finding apps they love, and Apple has a big advantage over Android by having a well curated store. This reflects in the fact that overall, Apple rakes in more revenue from games and apps despite Android platforms getting a lion's share of the downloads.

The newcomers such as *Game of War, Summoners War, Heroes Clash, Boom Beach* and *Warcraft: Hearthstone* among many others showed a clear trend that RPG oriented games were finally on the rise and devices and data networks were getting powerful enough to run such games. While most games were still asynchronous multiplayers in nature, the real-time games were creeping up on the market. The most popular in the genre in 2015 was *World of Tanks: Blitz,* which through its relatively slow gameplay and the popularity it enjoyed on PC had an instant following on mobile. The competition was not sleeping and several games were shown in soft and full launch in 2015, with *War Robots* and *Battle Bay* taking a lead in action packed real-time team vs. team battles.

By 2016, strategy in the form of 4X was slowly on the rise and more RPGs dominated the revenue market. However, the trends of 2014 and 2015 continued, but a major shift happened in the gaming world and it was most felt on mobile with a major new player joining the fray. It wasn't a particular company, nor was it really someone new. We speak of China of course. The gaming market in China was steadily growing over the years, initially mostly trying to bring Western games to the local market, which through the wonderful ever-scrutinizing eye of government wasn't ever easy. It reached epic levels of hassle by this time for Western developers and publishers, and with Chinese developers and publishers not facing this trouble, they started rolling out major games to the West. The biggest players by far were Tencent and NetEase. While the latter wasn't unknown before, Tencent came crashing through the door with what is now known as *Arena of Valor*, the Western version of *Glory of Kings*. And if you haven't heard of them before, you would know them now. Chinese games are generating a big chunk of the global mobile revenue. In 2016, this chunk was still mostly in China and players outside of China didn't really know about those companies, however, this was about change. It was not all about China that year however. Korean Netmarble launched a highly lucrative version of *Lineage II Revolution* on mobile and *Monster Strike* dominated the charts. Supercell finally had a new game with *Clash Royale*, and albeit after a small start, it gained immense traction by the end of 2016, and gave the developer the top three games in global games revenue. That year was also the year Nintendo got some courage and launched its first mobile game under the Nintendo label with *Super Mario Run*. It showed, not surprisingly, that the company is a decade behind the curve of mobile games and entirely missed the point of what F2P is all about. Luckily for the Japanese publisher, people love Mario, and the game was able to turn a decent buck. It isn't close to a lucrative business for Nintendo. Those two years were quite interesting for companies and consumers, with a bigger variety than ever before on mobile, bringing entertainment to more players than ever.

The year of 2017 seems almost uneventful in comparison when we look at the game charts. *Monument Valley 2* followed up its 2014 predecessor with the expected success and Nintendo published another smash hit with *Fire Emblem Heroes*. The top charts throughout the year were still dominated by the same games.

So what exciting things did happen in 2017? Well for one, defying all logic, *Subway Surfers* was the top downloaded game that year, considering it was five years old, correct live ops certainly helped Danish developer Kiloo stay relevant with a single game making that approach more relevant than ever for the mobile games industry. Two games were released: *PUBG Mobile* and *Fortnite*. One might argue that those two games are the two biggest PC to mobile conversions in history. Where the former took a slightly new approach compared with its PC counterpart and jumped on the live ops and F2P bandwagon, the latter brought the same experience with cross-platform play and tailored controls to mobile.

By 2018, *Fortnite* dominated the games charts across all platforms, pulling in a whopping estimated US$2.4 billion in revenue in total of which about US$300 million was from mobile. These sheer numbers caused a bit of a craze in the industry with imitators trying to get a piece of the battle royale pie, albeit with limited success on mobile for most titles. *Knives Out*, as an imitator gained immense traction in Japan, and *Garena: Free Fire* found its niche market in Southeast Asia and South America and is making a killing, but that's about the extent of it.

On the pure mobile side, the picture looks quite a bit different. *Pokémon Go* is still going strong and increased its yearly revenue considerably. *Dragon Ball Z* and *Candy Crush Saga* did likewise. On the side of action games, *Shadowgun Legends* made a splash by having a fabulous competitive shooter experience. One noteworthy game to pick out might be *Meterofall: Journeys*, a rogue-like deck builder.

That brings us to 2019. China is now undeniably a gaming superpower with Tencent and NetEase setting the tone and runner ups Lillith and FunPlus taking their share. Western and Asian games are definitely trying to learn from each other with better and better ways to bring experiences to players and getting players to stay with a game long term. And wouldn't you know, *PUBG Mobile* launched in China, but alas, China being China, it of course couldn't just get past the censors just like that but had to undergo "changes" and launched under the surely no "pun intended" name: *Game for Peace*. It still makes a killing.

Other games in 2019 were the long-anticipated *Mario Kart Tour* and *Dr. Mario World*, which just shows again, that Nintendo still doesn't know how to develop F2P games inhouse. *Call of Duty: Mobile* brings another great franchise to mobile. Thatgamecompany, known for acclaimed games like *Flower* and *Journey*, brought us mobile first *Sky: Children of Light*. And *Archero* and *Auto Chess* redefined what casual action and auto battle games can be. Last but not least, we see AR games getting additions as well with *Minecraft World* and *Angry Birds AR: Isle of Pigs*. The latter was a long time coming, considering *Angry Birds* had been brought into 3D years ago in various forms, even if not in AR. And to top it off, some 2018 latecomers did more than turn a profit, such as *Brawl Stars*. And so, 2019 concluded and we are here, at the beginning of another decade of mobile gaming.

Unfortunately, rising marketing costs and the perpetual flooding of app stores will make it harder and harder for games to be discoverable and profitable. However, the outlook is not all bleak but rather exciting, for technology and creativity on mobile are gaining new heights, augmented and virtual reality are becoming affordable and enjoyable, and accessibility to quality development tools are cheaper than ever. Not all games, learnings, controversies and successes over the years fit in this short chapter and there were and are plenty of fabulous games, some of which are still available on app stores. Many games unfortunately never gained the success they deserved. The reader is encouraged to see Metacritic charts or do a simple "best mobile games of 20xx" search. A little journey down the rabbit hole can reveal exciting things.

BIBLIOGRAPHY

Bruins, M. (2014). Riot on documentary (2002). *YouTube*. Available at: https://www.youtube.com/watch?v=g0lrIi0ce5E.

Business Wire. (2005). JAMDAT Mobile Launches the *Lord of the Rings: Legends* in Europe; Aragorn, Frodo, Legolas and Eowyn come to mobile operators in France, Portugal, Spain and the United Kingdom. *Business Wire*. Available at. https://www.businesswire.com/news/home/20051122005144/en/JAMDAT-Mobile-Launches-Lord-Rings-Legends-Europe.

De Vere, K. (2012). Japan officially declares lucrative kompu gacha practice illegal in social games. *Adweek*. Available at: https://www.adweek.com/digital/japan-officially-declares-lucrative-kompu-gacha-practice-illegal-in-social-games/.

Erickson, T. (2008). The 10 best iPhone games of 2008. *Pocket Gamer*. Available at: https://www.pocketgamer.com/articles/010628/the-10-best-iphone-games-of-2008/.

Evans, B. (2016). The end of a mobile wave; the Dell of mobile. *Benedict Evans*. Available at: https://www.ben-evans.com/benedictevans/2016/4/29/the-end-of-a-mobile-wave.

GamesIndustry. (2004). Electronic Arts and Digital Bridges announce availability of EA Sports™ *FIFA Football 2005 Mobile International Edition*. *GamesIndustry*. Available at: https://www.gamesindustry.biz/articles/electronic-arts-and-digital-bridges-announce-availability-of-ea-sports-fifa-football-2005-mobile-international-edition.

Hearn, R. (2008). The 10 best mobile games of 2008. *Pocket Gamer*. Available at: https://www.pocketgamer.com/articles/010621/the-10-best-mobile-games-of-2008/.

Hoggins, T. (2019). Fortnite earned record $2.4bn in 2018, the "most annual revenue of any game in history." *Telegraph*. Available at: https://www.telegraph.co.uk/gaming/news/fortnite-earned-annual-revenue-game-history-2018/.

James, C. (2006). *Paris Hilton's Diamond Quest* review. *Pocket Gamer.* Available at: https://www.pocketgamer.com/articles/001286/paris-hiltons-diamond-quest/.

Jordan, J. (2017). The rise and rise of EA's "very profitable" $600 million mobile business. *Pocket Gamer.* Available at: https://www.pocketgamer.biz/data-and-research/65008/the-rise-of-ea-mobile/.

Knight, K., Ando, R., Nayak, M. (2013). SoftBank buys $1.5 billion stake in Finnish mobile games maker Supercell. Reuters. Available at: https://www.reuters.com/article/us-softbank-acquisition/softbank-buys-1-5-billion-stake-in-finnish-mobile-games-maker-supercell-idUSBRE99E0ID20131015.

Perez, S. (2018). iOS App Store has seen over 170B downloads, over $130B in revenue since July 2010. *TechCrunch.* Available at: https://techcrunch.com/2018/05/31/ios-app-store-has-seen-over-170b-downloads-over-130b-in-revenue-since-july-2010/.

Russell, J. (2018). Epic Games, the creator of *Fortnite,* banked a $3 billion profit in 2018. *TechCrunch.* Available at: https://techcrunch.com/2018/12/27/epic-fortnite-3-billion-profit/

Sliwinski, A. (2010). Cut the Rope wraps up a million sales. *Engadget.* Available at: https://www.engadget.com/2010/10/15/cut-the-rope-wraps-up-a-million-sales/https://mashable.com/2010/11/17/smurfs-village/?europe=true.

Strickland, D. (2019). Free-to-play made 80% of 2018 digital game revenues. TweakTown. Available at: https://www.tweaktown.com/news/64532/free-play-made-80-2018-digital-game-revenues/index.html.

Sullivan, R. (2005). Gizmondo's spectacular crack-up. *Wired.* Available at: https://www.wired.com/2006/10/gizmondo/.

Wijman, T. (2019). The global games market will generate $152.1 billion in 2019 as the U.S. overtakes China as the biggest market. *Newzoo.* Available at: https://newzoo.com/insights/articles/the-global-games-market-will-generate-152-1-billion-in-2019-as-the-u-s-overtakes-china-as-the-biggest-market/.

Wright, C. (2008). A brief history of mobile games: Introduction. *Pocket Gamer.* Available at: https://www.pocketgamer.biz/feature/10618/a-brief-history-of-mobile-games-introduction/.

CHAPTER 20

Retrogaming as a Form of Digital Preservation

A Cultural and Technological Approach

Marco Accordi Rickards, Micaela Romanini
and Guglielmo De Gregori

CONTENTS

20.1 The Problem With "Retrogaming": Avoiding Ghettoization   360
20.2 The Asteroids' Syndrome: A Taxonomy Framework for
Identifying Games   365
20.3 Interactive Experience: A New Filter to Interpret
Video Games   367
20.4 Video Game as Sports   369
20.5 Video Game as a Product   370
20.6 Video Game as a Utility   372
20.7 Experience and Challenge: The Genetic Code of
Video Games   374
20.8 Conclusion: An Open Source Asset   375
20.9 VIGAMUS—The Video Game Museum: Case History,
Approach, and Methodology   375
Acknowledgements   380
References   380

WHEN THE NOTORIOUS ITALIAN art critic Philippe Daverio wrote about museums in his seminal book *Il museo immaginato* (*The Imaginary Museum*) (2011), he specifically talked about "the *game* of inventing an ideal museum, a place where the Muses can follow the hypothesis of an idea." Video games are an idea, after all, and so are "old games" and "retro games." Tracing back at the creation of the now seven years old core concept of VIGAMUS, Daverio's statements and book come out as a powerhouse ripe with incredibly untapped potential. It must be of no surprise that we are opening our chapter of this book by quoting an anti-conformist, yet very fond of tradition, Italian art historian.

After all, when a cultural institution opens a museum in Rome, the very cradle of modern European culture, it is crucial to understand that everything you're creating will be compared with historical and artistic landmarks the likes of the Colosseum and Fori Imperiali, and of course with actual museums like the Musei Vaticani, a collection of all the classical artifacts that hundreds of ecclesiastic figures commissioned to master painters and sculptors over the course of the years, only to celebrate Beauty and the Divine. Only to add more pressure to this already incredibly difficult task, when tasked with the inception of VIGAMUS, we were also adding the challenge of opening a video game museum that is only one kilometer away from the actual Vatican. Ironically, everything that could have been mistaken as a true obstacle and infinite source of pitfalls, turned around to be our biggest fortune, because we made a virtue out of necessity, understanding that the only way to escape being a niche odditorium made up by old electronic games, was to embrace the true identity of games as a vessel of human ingenuity.

20.1 THE PROBLEM WITH "RETROGAMING": AVOIDING GHETTOIZATION

Although, while we're embracing the concept of "retrogaming" as an incredibly important and fascinating subculture many people among amateurs and creators perceive as relatable to them (eventually identifying with it), we refuse the very notion of "retrogaming" as a crucial cultural tool that is inevitably involved in the task of opening a video game museum. Of course, it's also entirely true that our museum about video games, VIGAMUS—The Video Game Museum of Rome, is also substantially based on the very elemental assumption that games from the past (or the so-called retro games) are interesting and meaningful. Meanwhile, adding the prefix "retro" to an established medium such as "games" and creating an entirely new moniker, tends to be not too respectful of the importance of video games as a form of art; after all, no one would ever call "retromovie" a film directed by Ingmar Bergman, and it's blatantly evident that the point of watching a movie directed by Ėjzenštejn is not about the exclusivity of watching a very old movie that is not available on Netflix, but to observe the magnificence of some of the greatest masterpieces in the history of filmmaking.

The problem with the term "retrogaming" is its tendency to incentivize the notion of games as a novelty, whereas playing the oldest and rarer game available in the collection is the point of the experience, while risking to dismiss the presence of a piece of art told through code as a simple collateral effect. Obviously, VIGAMUS is well connected to the retrogamer and collector ecosystem, but they're just one part of a bigger equation, although a very interesting one. Many collectors, as a matter of fact, will exclusively focus on the rarity of the item, its price on the market, the condition of the packaging; our side of the team, who are less involved in the gaming ecosystem, was baffled to apprehend that there is a minor fringe of video game collectors who do not even bother to pull the real game out of the original packaging, considering the mere act of playing them an insult to their mission of pursuing the perfect collection. Of course, we're not stigmatizing this approach, which greatly serves its purpose in the struggle to achieve a greater common objective: to tell the history of video games. At the same time, the hardcore retrogamer approach was not really of use to us while opening a museum that should have catered to a wide and heterogeneous audience, being located in one of the most visited cities in the world. If we were to tell people the history of games, we had to ditch the most radical expressions of the collectors and the "fetishization" of packagings. We had to focus on the very essence of what was written inside the code, that is directly spawned by the vision in the mind of one or more authors. Becoming aware of this was one of the greatest breakthroughs in the inception of VIGAMUS, and this notion is so strong and well rooted in the Research Center of the museum that even the new expressions of the museum will strictly adhere to the philosophy of putting the content before the container, so that every future physical and digital expression of the vision at the core of VIGAMUS Foundation will be based on that very principle. Incidentally, VIGAMUS seems to have anticipated a trend that is going to be more relevant than ever, with the rise of digital delivery, games as a service, cloud gaming (i.e. Google Stadia), monetized games, etc., items completely eschew the necessity of being based on a physical support, shifting entirely the weight of what's written inside the code or the heart of the game.

While everything we've written so far may seem to dismiss the importance of retrogaming, at the end of the day, the experience of VIGAMUS made us even more aware of the power and importance at the core of the collector's community. While many figures in our Research Center strongly endorse the idea that every game will eventually be put in the cloud, the physical goods ultimately abandoned in favor of digital goods, a museum is still a physical place in "a material world," and we're definitely "material scholars" when it comes to preserving old machines and making them available to our audience. While it's interesting as a thought experiment to imagine a totally virtual museum located in a non-physical world, something that can possibly be experienced through an Oculus Rift (or visionary contraptions like Elon Musk's NeuraLink), we need to be realistic and be aware that the most common visitor of our demography will be interested in substantially three things while entering VIGAMUS: to play games; to remember the games of his or her infancy; and to know something new that can be told to family members and friends. This is a rough estimate based on anecdotal experience collected while working inside VIGAMUS, of course, but those three needs are shared by many different audiences. When creating a place like a video game museum, the sheer complexity of the medium and its history will create confusion in the scholars, ultimately leading to conceptual chaos.

The history of games it is so wide that, just to make some examples, an entire museum could be centered upon the indie scene, the Japanese arcade tradition, the Brazilian bootlegs, the Swedish demoscene, etc. To condense all of this under the same museum is a herculean task, because it would require a vast physical space, a vast collection of items, but most importantly, the coherency and discipline to put the entire history of gaming in a building while not being entirely redundant and be, from an academic point of view, considered a very weird storage with weird items very few people really care about. This is very evident when traveling to Tokyo, Japan, and entering one of the cult retrogaming stores, such as Superpotato. Walking through a three-story building in Akihabara filled with spare Famicoms, forgotten collectibles, it is easy to associate the idea of very old stuff condensed in a place to a "museum" (as many non-technical visitors of the store mostly say), but that would mean to completely ignore the idea of the scientific focus of a museum.

When it comes to making a museum, and talking of museology as a whole, even after thorough studies accumulated during years of experience, it is completely clear that the only dogma to religiously observe when creating a museum, is merely telling a story. Or, to play *the game of inventing an ideal museum*. It's so interesting and peculiar that Daverio uses the word "game" for describing something so rooted in high culture like a museum. At the same time, the sense of the book written by Daverio is not just collecting a series of photos of classical paintings while commenting on them with historical facts, but instead everything is about creating a pattern out of artistic artifacts and telling the history of our world through the visions of the artists who created them. It may sound weird to think that Daverio, a stereotypical art historian donning glasses and a papillon, gave a conceptual spark so strong in the Italian museum landscape that ultimately led to the creation of a museum in the heart of Rome where Shigeru Miyamoto was acclaimed as Giorgio Canova and an old and dusty *E.T.* cartridge coming out of the desert of New Mexico was regarded as precious as an old Egyptian artifact. That is the power of the idea, mind over matter, fact-checked storytelling intended to be enjoyed by a whole array of audiences, made up mainly by unsuspecting visitors, and catering to gamers in a way that will be always subject to the rule of not estranging the true audience of a museum: mankind. If we believe that video games are part of mankind's heritage, we should also act by shaping our museum in a way that will make video games accessible to mankind.

What's so interesting about Daverio's vision, is that the point of museums as an institution is not just preserving and showcasing artifacts, but displaying the spirit behind them. The concept of refusing the intrinsic value of an item can be considered revolutionary when it comes to classical art, where everything is about the item, because the item itself is the witness of an ancient past. When the Louvre is displaying the Mona Lisa, the curators are actually conserving an almost mythical artifact that lived through generations, the very same item that was manipulated by Leonardo da Vinci himself. Obviously, the Mona Lisa is inserted inside the wider cultural framework of the Louvre as a museum, but there is no text panel nor storytelling that can really improve something that is by definition an attraction: the most iconic painting of Leonardo, so powerful that the Renaissance genius created the framework many centuries ago, starting himself the storytelling behind the painting that was reinforced through art critics and even entertainment (think of Dan Brown's bestselling books). At the end of the day, for an item in the same tier as the

Mona Lisa, the organization behind the museum will probably be more concerned with taking care of all the necessary security measures, or disseminating knowledge about the object through publications and even, as of today standards, social media. But if, by absurd, we chose to adhere radically to Daverio's vision, kill our fathers and be completely iconoclastic even towards one of the staples of European culture, i.e. the Louvre, even the conservation of Mona Lisa could be considered a little bit too shallow. On the opposite side, video games are a medium where the oldest artifact (or the old "retrogame") can be traced back to 50 years ago, even being very generous while creating this hypothetical timeline. At this point, it's very obvious that what we're dealing with is not something that carries with it the weight of centuries of history. Even a very rare video game item today, can't be considered nothing more than mere modern antique, a vintage curiosity. So, when conserving a "retrogame" inside a museum, we're dealing with the issue of creating context and meaning around an item without intrinsic value and where the author must be necessarily be king.

When it comes to museology, even if this sentence may sound a little bit too daring, there are no written rules, but only standards to adhere to that can make the difference between achieving the result of assembling a little exhibition and creating a conservation hub that spreads knowledge of something in the entire world. Italy is known all over the world for its monuments and classical artifacts, from which the myth that our sole country possesses more precious items than all the rest of the world put together. This is probably a "propaganda" myth, but at the same time, it's telling the profound truth of Italy as a place dense with culture where even obscure little towns conceal extremely rare and precious artifacts. So, for a little town with no funds for creating a proper museum, and no professional figures with the competences needed for building a framework around objects, even displaying old treasures from the past inside common display cases is an effort that must be truly respected, while at the same time is very far away from today's standards of museology. Collecting old instruments in a little town museum in Sardinia, or spreading knowledge about minerals inside a university exhibition, is definitely a museological effort, but the very idea that under the umbrella term "museum" may reside little showcases and at the same time literally mammoths such as the Louvre, or amazing contraptions like the greatest science museum all over the world, is completely baffling. The point of all of this is that there is no established dogma in museology and a museum is an ideal place that is evolving through time, trying to keep pace with the self-exploration of mankind's own knowledge. The task of creating a taxonomy for a museum is enormous, because of the huge complexity caused by the many nuances involved in the task of preserving culture. Ironically, we can say the same about video games: in the book *Manuale di Critica Videoludica* (2018), Prof. Accordi Rickards theorized what is called the Asteroids' Syndrome, or the inescapable complexity generated by the never ending evolution of games. At the end of the day, creating a video game museum, a place where "retrogaming" (and contemporary gaming as well) can be celebrated, is a task involving a double layer of complexity, or a double diagnosis of Asteroids' Syndrome.

20.2 THE ASTEROIDS' SYNDROME: A TAXONOMY FRAMEWORK FOR IDENTIFYING GAMES

The problem of a fitting denomination for video games is urgent and relevant, because many of the cultural issues regarding so-called electronic games arise from a deep misunderstanding: the notion that games are entertainment objects with no cultural value at all. This was particularly evident to us while facing the effort of creating a museum where "retrogames" were displayed; so, for some interlocutors, we were not just creating a museum out of "stuff that makes teenage kids waste time," but to add injury to insult, for many this stuff was even dusty and totally not "hip" like *FIFA* or *World of Warcraft*.

To think that all video games are equal deprives the medium of its identity and leads to fatal errors, such as thinking that *Ico* (Ueda, 2001) is the same thing as a Las Vegas slot machine; this can sound ridiculous, but it is exactly what happens inside the governments of many countries in the world (Italy included). The difference of value in games is not solely based on their artistic value and the technological effort required to create them, but the scholar needs to transversely take into consideration the time and the context the item was born in and from what it has ultimately been shaped. Where we take out the element of time from "game studies," we would be in a very awkward situation where everyone could just come up and say that *Pong* is a very crude game with no graphics of absolutely no importance, where as a generic triple A game with nice 3D graphics would be perceived as a more important product than *Pong*. This may sound obvious to everyone in an academic context, but at the same time a scholar can't take anything for granted, especially while being tasked with the mission of creating a museum and studying games as a medium. Our mission for VIGAMUS was to speak to a general audience who were legitimately asking us, Why is *Super Mario Bros.* (1985) more important than *Crash Bandicoot*? (1996), and baffled by the idea that an old 2D game is in fact superior to a 3D and more modern game. Our mission was, at the end of the day, to explain not just the game itself, but the historical context and of course the author behind it. In the case of *Super Mario Bros.*, we needed to explain the situation of the "post-*E.T.* crisis" gaming industry and its miraculous rebirth made possible by Nintendo and a genius of game design called Shigeru Miyamoto.

Many students try to avoid the problem of demonstrating the value of video games as a medium on the basis of their penetration in the social tissue. This is of course a valid approach, and certainly the ever-increasing numbers of the games industry can be of help in explaining the evolution and growth of the medium. Reducing to mere numbers the nature of the discussion, and of video games as a whole, however, is only simple palliative care. In fact, it is not possible to receive a true acknowledgement, if we don't understand precisely what a video game is. This is a problem that was faced by already acknowledged media, such as movies; movies, however, were relatively easy to recognize, given their nature of moving images imprinted with a strong narrative subtext. Video games, on the other hand, offer a far more difficult challenge. They are moving images, and they offer a narrative subtext, but they are not movies. They are informed by a code, yet they can be far more than mere software. They convey themes and messages, but at the same time they can be purely ludic spaces, such as chess or *go*. A common misunderstanding is to confound the container with the content: many observers tend to think of video games as an electronic device, since they are, after all, a code-executing program; but this isn't respectful of the fact that a video game can convey the vision of an author and provoke emotions and thoughts in the users. We can bring Microsoft Word as an example: we have a code-executing program, running on a computer machine; *Gone Home* (Gaynor, 2013), similarly, is a code-executing program, running on a computer machine. But no one would ever classify Microsoft Word as a work of art, while *Gone Home* is universally acknowledged as a deep and thought-provoking video game. So, it's pretty obvious that game critics have a naming convention problem.

This situation led me to theorize in our Research Center on the so-called "The *Asteroids*' Syndrome." In *Asteroids*, the classic Atari video game, in order to accumulate a score, the player needed to destroy space debris, which subsequently were fragmented into smaller parts, navigating the whole screen and increasing the difficulty of the game. This easily describes the extremely challenging task of classifying games, which year by year introduce new mechanics, dynamics and variables, and that's the reason why *Pong* and *Mass Effect* may roughly share the same category, but they are not by any means the same object, and not just from a narrative perspective. *Pong* and *Mass Effect* are both games, but the nature of the technology and of the interaction has so profoundly changed during the years between the two games that they can almost be considered two completely different objects. This is a whole different situation, if we take movies as an example; *Arrival of a Train at La Ciotat* (Lumière Brothers, 1896) is of course extremely less convoluted than a Christopher Nolan's movie, but, fundamentally, the vessel is the same: a moving image, projected on a screen. This leads to similar modalities of fruition, since like in 1896, we still regularly sit a in a movie theatre and watch moving images on a screen. While the contents largely evolved, the nature of interaction has changed very little, as we still interact with movies in the same way we did in 1896, even when taking into account the introduction of sound, and presumably this is not going to change for many decades to come. Games, on the other hand, are a completely different story: interacting with *Pong* (Atari, 1972) is not like interacting with *Mass Effect* (Hudson, 2007), since the user experience and the affordances changed accordingly to the technological evolution. We cannot say that they are not both video games, but at the same time, we cannot say that they are the same thing. This led to a crisis in the critical infrastructure corresponding to the concept of "interactive multimedia work" and made me realize that a new definition was needed to correctly frame video games as a phenomenon.

20.3 INTERACTIVE EXPERIENCE: A NEW FILTER TO INTERPRET VIDEO GAMES

This is the reason why I have introduced the concept of "interactive experience." This formulation retains the "interactive" word, needed to express the possibility for the user to alter and modify the virtual world shaped by designers and programmers. "Experience," on the other hands, allows us to not only consider video games with a cultural background, but even the ones that bear no artistic content at all. The term "experience" was used for video games by many journalists, for example, in the case of *Journey* (Chen, 2012), which notably offered an immersive context with a very minimal set of interaction rules, focusing on aesthetics and digital poetry. The term is interesting, since it allows us to describe the nature of video games as a series of processes that unfold in time and space, implying an alteration of the physical and psychical status of the user. Such a definition can be used for many different purposes, and not only when it implies the presence of cultural and artistic contents. Every game produces a modification in the behavior and cognitive structure of the user, as it was observed by many studies in the field of psychiatry and neuroscience. The nature of this modification, however, can take many different shapes. This led me to develop a further classification, which takes into account the mutable nature of video games as a medium. It is notable that this classification is not to be intended as a definitive solution to the video games classification problem, but it can be an open source asset which could and should be freely modified in subsequent studies. This is crucial, since video games, as we have already seen, tend to hugely evolve, and with the introduction of new platforms, such as virtual, augmented and mixed reality, there is a high probability that we will be able to observe a strong shift in the interactive landscape. I will subsequently explain the different categories I have formulated and their peculiarities.

The first category is the so-called Video Game as Culture, or the new incarnation of the "interactive work." This term is used for video games which convey a strong authorial vision, be it through gameplay or through narrative appendices (such as cutscenes). This is a category that is strongly influenced by the technological evolution of electronic games, and it implies many different nuances. Code too can be considered an authorial expression, for example, in games like *Tetris*, where the clarity and ingenuity of game design can become a form of art in itself. But the concept of Video Game as Culture can be more easily understood when it comes to story-driven games that borrow narrative devices from already acknowledged forms of art such as movies. It's very easy to classify a game like *Metal Gear Solid 2: Sons of Liberty* (Kojima, 2001) as Culture, since it is very heavy on cinematographic cutscenes, dialogues and meta-narrative devices (that, conversely, is the very same reason why it attracted so much criticisms from hardcore gamers). *Metal Gear Solid 2: Sons of Liberty* is a particularly good example, because it is a game that was created by author Hideo Kojima at the apex of his success, free from the conditioning of the public and the publishers, that led to the possibility of the designer providing social commentary. This is a very rare situation, in an industry where many games are created according to the trends and the results of focus groups. *Metal Gear Solid 2: Sons of Liberty* also fits in the Video Games as Culture category because there is a strong synthesis between gameplay and narrative, where the latter is empowered by the former. Generally, the strong presence of an author, be it a pure game designer or a narrator, is the main indicator of a Video Game as Culture. A game like *Super Mario Galaxy* (Koizumi, 2007) easily fits in the category given the quality and originality of its gameplay, even though its narrative is just a simple excuse for kickstarting the action. To see the matter from a different perspective, we can identify a Video Games as Culture even in the light of its impact on the public; games like *Pong* or *Space Invaders* (Nishikado, 1978) bear a strong cultural value, even though the experience is limited by techno-logical constraints, and we can observe that in the resonances inside pop culture. Taito's aliens or *Pong's* rackets are an iconography immediately recognized by people, their background and age notwithstanding. Games like *Tomb Raider* have largely contributed to shape the identity of video games in the collective culture, while even advocating important values such as inclusivity and the correct depiction of women as strong leads inside video games. The presence of a message sent by the developers to the players, or the possibility to find a meaning during an experience, is what makes video games an expression of culture.

20.4 VIDEO GAME AS SPORTS

The second category is Video Game as Sports. This is the category that emerged during the "StarCraft crisis" that we mentioned at the beginning of the paper. A sport, by definition, isn't a proper narrative device: while it can certainly produce meanings and stories, these stories are not defined at the beginning by the vision of an author. Of course, sports have been ideated by one or more "game designers," and the rules of play evolved during the decades, but a match of soccer, for example, completely out-lives the intention of the designers. In sports, the athlete takes over com-pletely the intentions of the game designer, and contributes to creating new meanings, while rewriting the borders of the ludic space, introduc-ing strategies and meta-games that were not intended by the original inventors of the game. In Video Games as Culture, conversely, moving outside the original borders is far more difficult, without the risk of com-promising the whole experience, which would result in a deliberate act of hacking. It's also notable that meaning in sports can be found by outside observers and translated into other forms of art; many important authors have written books or movies about sports, with notable examples like the novel *Infinite Jest* (Wallace, 2006); sports competitions are also a com-mon trope in cinema, usually used as a metaphor for life struggles. In

Video Game as Sports the focus shifts from the author to the cyber athlete: playing an eSports game like *League of Legends* (Riot Games, 2009) or *PlayerUnknown's Battlegrounds* (Greene and Tae-seok, 2017) engages a whole different set of competences than a Video Game as Culture.

The athletic preparation that is required by such games is the same that is required by traditional sports, while of course it involves different areas of the body than a dynamic sport like basketball. In a Video Game as Sports, the action is completely deprived of textual meaning, and the rules of play are deeply connected to the competition. The presence of a human opponent is crucial to identify Video Games as Sports; it's also notable that the presence of an opponent guided by an advanced artificial intelligence, with a defined personal agency, can also be considered as a signal of a Video Game as Sports. The human factor is the key to understand the nature of this particular kind of game; of course, there are also cultural games that emphasize the relation with other characters, like *Journey*. The decisive factor, however, is the competition and the total abstraction from the aesthetic and cosmetic context. Games like *Super Smash Bros.* (Sakurai, 2014) are often at the center of a discussion whether they're eSports or not, due to the presence of highly recognizable characters involved in quirky mechanics and "funny moments"; that's the reason why the game also offers the opportunity to be played by eliminating all of the "party game" and to be arcade modified, resulting in a highly technical version of itself. Again, games are like shapeshifters: they can attain different forms and identities, in regard to their use and the modifications from the players. This category also comprises games such as *FIFA 18* (Electronic Arts, 2017) or *NBA 2K18* (Visual Concepts, 2018), which recreate inside a digital structure the mechanisms of the corresponding sport; in rare cases, sports games also tell a story, which would make them fall under the category of Culture.

20.5 VIDEO GAME AS A PRODUCT

The third category is Video Game as a Product, which completely reduces a video game to a commercial object. In this case, it is crucial to identify the relationship between the experience and the use of money and gambling dynamics. The relationship between video game and money has a long history: classic coin-operated games, such as *Ghosts 'n Goblins* (Fujiwara, 1985), required the player to spend money in order to play. That's the reason why the first waves of video games were so difficult, since they needed to accommodate the needs of game companies to make the player spend as much money as possible. In a certain way, we can say that the design of the first video games was shaped by an economic factor (although this would ignore completely the deep structures of games of the yesteryear). This is probably the reason for the confusion between video games and gambling. More recently, money has played a much more radical role in the shapes of electronic games. MMORPGs ("massively multiplayer online role-playing games"), virtual worlds populated by thousands of players simultaneously, have a deep relationship with money, since in-game currency lets the users buy (or sell) items, generating a truly virtual economy. Such economic balance is commonly altered by the presence of malicious players, that use the so-called "bots." Sometimes the "bots" that can be substituted by human players, which harvest resources in precarious conditions, like sweatshop workers. We wouldn't call *World of Warcraft* (Blizzard, 2004) a gambling game, but surely economics play a huge role in the shaping of this persistent world, demonstrating that the presence of money can alter the game design. This leads us to take into account games like *Candy Crush Saga* (King, 2012), where the design is entirely built around the economic factor. In these games, the player can buy items and modifiers through so-called microtransactions. Given that the reason of being for such a game is to engage the player and make him or her spend as much money as possible, it becomes obvious that their gameplay doesn't follow the common rules of good game design. This is the basis of the majority of free-to-play games, games that are available for free on different marketplaces but make their business plan rely on microtransaction. It's easy to see that if a game needs to induce the player to spend money, it should have different methods of communicating fun; fun, in this case, is more of a hook to make the player stay and spend more money. A good example of how a game design can be altered by economics, is the difference between *Plants vs. Zombies* (PopCap Games, 2009), and its sequel, *Plants vs. Zombies 2* (PopCap Games, 2013). A difference so radical that the author of the first game distanced himself from the sequel. *Plant vs. Zombies* was the example of an extremely balanced game, that led the player by the hand with challenges of increasing difficulty, adhering to the famous line by Atari's founder Nolan Bushnell: "Easy to learn, difficult to master." This simple rule was completely overlooked in the sequel, where the gameplay was structured in order to make the player face incredibly hard challenges, making him or her more likely to spend money in power-ups and helpers. Usually this kind of game can also be played by skilled players that are able to master the game without resorting to buying items, but the difficulty is obviously unfair and imbalanced. It is therefore very difficult to classify as a work of art a video game that forces players to spend money; the difference with a cultural video game lies in the intention of the designer. Incidentally, free-to-play games on smartphones tend to not present any kind of narrative, this led some people to compare the so-called F2P games to the first arcade titles. F2P games can also lead a video game to enter the territory of gambling, as a ludic space altered by economics. Actually, many F2P games reflect enormously the difference between a non-paying and paying user, and just like in gambling, the player with the highest amount of money available is also the player more likely to win or at least not lose too much money. This symptom can be observed in many F2P games, especially MMOs, where paying users are advantaged with better equipment and statistics; many imbalanced F2P games for smartphone and tablets are also dramatically unfair, their game design completely enslaved by the whims of paying users. Of course, under this category are actual gambling games, such as digital poker played over the Internet.

20.6 VIDEO GAME AS A UTILITY

The last kind of video game is the Video Game as a Utility. These are games that use the same languages and structures of other types of experiences, but that ultimately lead the user to gain an advantage in real life. The term comprises many different kinds of items, such as simulation, serious games, edutainment titles, digital gamified systems, and utilities. To understand the peculiarity of these objects it is crucial to understand the theory of the Asteroids' Syndrome as a whole. Even in this case, we have software that runs on the same machines as regular games; a very fitting example is *Personal Trainer: Cooking* (indieszero, 2008), for the Nintendo 3DS: its interface resembles the one seen in many other games on the handheld platform, but its objective is to help the user in cooking through simple tutorials, whereas entertainment is a mere byproduct of the experience only in part sparked by the software itself. There are many liminal experiences, though: *Wii Fit* (Matsunaga, 2008) by Nintendo can be certainly classified as a utility, but at the same time it offers ludic experiences meant to be entertaining. It couldn't be otherwise, since the game is meant to make exercising fun; however, at the same time, many features of *Wii Fit*, mainly the diet planning, have nothing in common with games: at the very best they can be defined gamified systems. The crucial difference lies in the intentions of the designers: if the final objective of the game creator is to offer an experience outside of simple escapism, that can be easily classified as a utility. The adherence to reality can be also a feature of other kind of games, such as culture or sports; however, to distinguish the nature of an experience we must also take into account in this case the intentions of the designers. This is the reason why racing games often oscillate between adhering to reality and offering a fun experience, scaling the realism of the simulation, eventually embracing abstract solutions. The percental of simulation and game design-dictated variables, is what makes a game more or less a utility. The spectrum of experiences ranges from arcade racing games to simulators that are actually used by pilots for testing. Simulators can also be used by the military to train the soldiers to use war vehicles or to prepare pilots to venture into space; usually, a simulator makes use of an interface that entirely recreates reality, which is not meant to be fun but that must adhere as much as possible to the real thing in order to educate the user. Another example of utility are serious games, games that starting from their name evoke a didactic purpose. Serious games use the mechanics of commercial games, but for a whole different purpose, mainly in the field of education, therapy, and military; a simulation can be a serious game, but a serious game isn't necessarily a simulation. The landscape of serious games is extremely diverse and fragmented, but what they all have in common is the objective of teaching something through a fun experience; this is the reason why serious games are usually offered in museum and cultural institutions. Under this category also fall immersive installations, usually offered through virtual reality, that let the player navigate through historical environments. Augmented reality games such as *Ingress* (Niantic Labs, 2012) and *Pokémon Go* (Nomura, 2016) may also fall under this category, even though their integration with real-world dynamics could lead to think of them as non-conventional video game experiences, if not non-games at all. Even if games like *Pokémon Go* offer a narrative context, they don't convey any relevancy, and their mechanics are much too simple to be considered culture, incidentally, the effects of these experiences can be assimilated to serious fitness games. It's also interesting to note that such games use real-life locations inside this gameplay, and this led to the preservation of otherwise overlooked cultural artifacts and monuments. We can conclude that *Pokémon Go* is an "involuntary serious game," and at the same time a good example of Video Game as a Utility, while its nature is certainly a good subject of discussion. It's widely been acknowledged today that games have the power to improve the life of an individual, not just by teaching new skills, but also working in conjunction with the findings of neuroscience and improving cognitive-behavioral patterns of the users. A game can be used to make the user adopt particular behaviors that ultimately may lead to an improvement in health and lifestyle of the individual. A game can also be used to mask menial tasks to be performed by many different human users that ultimately lead to important discoveries; this is the case of *Play to Cure: Genes in Space*, which is nothing but a glorified interface that makes the player identify patterns in-game, a knowledge that will be applied to real-life data by scientists.

20.7 EXPERIENCE AND CHALLENGE: THE GENETIC CODE OF VIDEO GAMES

After having identified four potential categories, we can now delve further in the analysis of the identity of video games. As we've surpassed the concept of genre, and enunciated the hybrid nature of video games, it is necessary to understand which are the elements that inform an interactive experience. Our suggestion is that the nature of every game can be fundamentally traced back to two singular elements: *experience* and *challenge*. Experience is the possibility for the user to immerse himself or herself inside a ludic context, interpreting a character and living emotions through its very eyes. Games have the tendency to induce something similar to altered states in the player, something that can also happen while experiencing a movie. Games, however, can be much more powerful, and this is the reason walking simulators, such as *What Remains of Edith Finch* (Dallas, 2017), are so effective. Walking simulator is of course an ironic moniker given by some video game commentators, but it can be useful to explain that the mere act of walking inside a video game can produce meaning; in other words, it's not necessary for an interaction to be complex in order to be meaningful. The principal example of a 100% experiential video game are French author David Cage's titles, such as *Heavy Rain* (Cage, 2010), a template that was subsequently inherited and improved by Telltale Games, in particular with the widely acclaimed series *The Walking Dead* (Telltale Games, 2012), where the action is almost entirely made of Quick Time Events (QTEs). It is notable that in *Heavy Rain*, QTEs are far more difficult than in *The Walking Dead*, but it's the illusion of mastery given to the player in Telltale Games that makes them so universal and likeable, even in the eyes of non-skilled players. Challenge, on the other hand, is the characteristic of a video game that pushes obstacles of various difficulty in front of the players, prompting them to overcome it using their mental or, more rarely, physical skills. The balance between these two aspects is what contributes to shape the identity of a video game. The repartition between experience and challenge is in many cases uneven, and this is the key to understand the DNA of every different video game. There are many cases where these two aspects are very well balanced, like in *The Secret of Monkey Island* (Gilbert, 1990), where we can locate experiential components, such as the brilliant dialogue written by Ron Gilbert and his collaborators, and the challenge components, devised by the puzzle designers. The dualism of experience vs. challenge is less subject to change than the other categories that we have already explored; this dualism, in fact, is meant to comprehend all kinds of video game phenomena, at least for the current state of the art of the medium. Experience vs. challenge can actually explain the very first expression of interactive media, and at the same time even its more recent incarnations, such as virtual and augmented reality.

20.8 CONCLUSION: AN OPEN SOURCE ASSET

It is important to specify that our classification is not a closed box, and it could not be otherwise, since the ever-changing nature of video games dictates the necessity for organic tools of analysis. Our intention is not just to provide a dogmatic scheme, but to create a mindset to better interpret video games. The constant hybridization and changing of electronic games may lead to the finding of new categories, and we will probably see in the next few years a great rise in the number of possibilities given by interactive experiences. We strongly believe in the power of words: to define correctly what a video game is can only lead to a better understanding of the object of our study, resulting eventually, we think, in the widespread acknowledgement of video games as a form of expression of the human ingenuity. This should be the ultimate goal of every video game student: to avoid relativism and to correctly interpret the true nature of electronic games.

20.9 VIGAMUS—THE VIDEO GAME MUSEUM: CASE HISTORY, APPROACH, AND METHODOLOGY

VIGAMUS was opened in 2012, but it was the result of over ten years of networking and development. Marco Accordi Rickards, VIGAMUS's director, started his career as a games journalist and worked on many important outlets, such as *Game Pro*, the Italian edition of *Edge*. From this cultural infrastructure, the basis for the Museum was born. VIGAMUS was inspired by the need of spreading knowledge about the artistic significance of video games, and it was conceived for being accessible to the broadest audience of visitors possibly. This means that we ditched the "manic retrogamer" approach, opting instead for focusing on the "pop culture" aspect of video games. Inside VIGAMUS, we celebrate the stories of the great video game creators, from Nolan Bushnell to Shigeru Miyamoto. The visitors are amazed by the passion and the curious stories of developers of the yesteryear and today, and of course they can play with video game history, with more than 60 interactive stations and hundreds of emulated titles.

Our greatest challenge in our mission was to make the institutions aware of games as a cultural artifact. It may sound silly, but the Italian government thought of video games as slot machines! And this was a problem... So, getting a physical seat was the hardest part, but we somehow managed to get a building inside the center of Rome.

Before opening VIGAMUS, we went to visit our friend Andreas Lange (the director of Computerspielemuseum) who owns the first video game museum ever opened. Even though we opted for a slightly different approach, Computerspielemuseum inspired our vision of a museum as a cultural hub, a place where knowledge is spread and disseminated, which can be visited not just by hardcore gamers, but by families and even people who just don't play or played while in their infancy. To think that someone could display an Atari 2600 like the Mona Lisa probably sounded crazy many years ago, but luckily, Computerspielemuseum paved the way for our Museum and many other which opened later. The strong academic background of Computerspielemuseum inspired us, and made us realize that it was indeed possible to open a Museum about video games in a European capital. I think that was the biggest inspiration: to see a place full of people having fun while learning, such as in Computerspielemuseum, made us understand that we were heading in the right direction.

Of course, there is a strong research component inside our museum, which is incarnated in the Research Center, a place where video game experts and academics discussed about contents even before the inception of the museum. Marco's journalism background played a big role in defining which contents would be fitting for the exhibition. We understood that games can't be boring, we had to communicate the excitement and the wonder of electronic entertainment, an industry, yes, but an industry that is very peculiar in its very nature. I mean, Nolan Bushnell held Atari's meetings inside a Jacuzzi.... At the same time, we knew that we had an important mission, to make people understand that games could be serious and be able to deliver important messages. Think of games like *Metal Gear Solid*. So there is this balance inside the museum between showing the most iconic games and the most significant ones from an industry point of view. This philosophy is well reflected in the entire exhibition: there is the game that is going to make you say: "Oh, I played this game when I was a kid" and then more obscure games that played a pivotal role in the growth of video games as a medium. Again, "pop culture" was really crucial in shaping our exhibition.

Italy hasn't a big history when it comes to video games, our industry is blooming right now, even though we had many glorious developers in the past and sometimes we do organize events about them. So, our museum lives on stories that happened in other countries, such as the United States or Japan. Even so, we pride on telling the most important examples of local history of the video games industry. In 2012, we opened the exhibition *E.T. The Fall*, the first in the world to display the famous *E.T. The Extra-Terrestrial* buried cartridges. We were in contact with the local community of Alamogordo, New Mexico, that provided us with these artifacts, that for a long time were considered the stuff of legends. It was truly an operation of video game archaeology. We also invited in our museum Joe Lewandowski (Vice President of Tularosa Basin Historical Society), which played a crucial role in the excavations that led to the finding of the buried cartridges. So, VIGAMUS played a huge part in making the public aware of the solution to one of the biggest mysteries of video games history.

Thanks to our connection to collectors, we offer many different kinds of items in display. Naturally there are a lot of consoles and home computers, from the most common ones (the ones that people used to have in their living room) to the most ancient and obscure ones. Games are displayed too, in particular the ones players have most fond memories of. Some of the choices reflect personal studies of the members of the Research Center. In all of our studies, we have a strong focus on storytelling and narrative, so one of the areas of the museum is entirely dedicated to the text adventures of Infocom, with all the original goodies (the so-called "feelies"). This can seem counterintuitive, but instead it reflects a very personal view of the Research Center of video games as interactive experiences that can transmit important messages and values. Many Infocom games were thematically and mechanically groundbreaking (think of Steve Meretzky's *A Mind Forever Voyaging*), so every story-driven game of today needs to pay their respects to Infocom. Last, we have unique pieces, with an incredibly high symbolic value; one of our most precious pieces are *Doom*'s Master

Disks, the first disks where the source code of seminal id Software's was copied, and from which all the subsequent copies were printed. For us, it as important as the first copy of the Beatles' *White Album* on vinyl would be for a museum about music. In the future, we hope to make a broader use of technology inside the exhibition itself, integrating augmented and mixed reality with the fruition of the artifacts.

It's extremely important, you simply can't make a museum about games without letting people experience them firsthand. Of course, it's crucial to find a balance, because even if we let people play, we can't act as an arcade and, as a Foundation, we have first and foremost a cultural mission. So, thanks to the constant work of the Research Center, we carefully select interactive experiences with a symbolic significance, paying attention to anniversaries and to the integration with what is written inside the panels. It's like stealth learning: we're letting people play, but they're playing with important games, created by great designers. You come out of the museum with a deeper understanding of the artistic value of games, and with a clear idea of what a video game was, what it is and what it will be. The challenge in maintaining a playable exhibit is the obsolescence of the original hardware, that needs a regular manutention, and in some cases, this can be tricky (like in the case of the dreaded Vectrex…). Thankfully, we have a strong network of collectors able to help us, and many games are offered via legit emulation.

VIGAMUS was conceived as a house for video games and players, not only a museum. A place where people can meet, celebrate, and play together. This philosophy is expressed by the now put to rest VIGAMUS' tagline: "Past, present and future of video games." VIGAMUS was born to accommodate the first generation of gamers, today's gamers, families, and people who want to discover more about this fascinating universe. VIGAMUS puts on display not only the history of video games, but also unique artifacts donated by video game companies and developers from all over the world; among these, the *Doom* Master Disks, donated by the world famous Texan developer id Software, and an original *Space Invaders* cabinet from 1978, donated by Taito Japan and available in free play.

We should mention also our recent exhibition *E.T. The Fall. Atari's Buried Treasures*, which allows visitors to discover one of the most fascinating legends ever known in the history of video games (Atari's cartridges and hardware found in the excavations of the desert of New Mexico, USA). VIGAMUS was the first museum in the world to display the symbols of the collapse of the video game industry in 1983, donated by the

City of Alamogordo and now considered a unique episode of "video game archaeology." Inside Epson Multimedia Conference Center (100 seats), the museum hosts a huge variety of happenings regularly, divided between consumer events designed for the general public and others dedicated to the main video game sensations of the year; seminars about retrogaming and high profile academic roundtables to help families understand more about the medium. Our consumer events are usually organized jointly with Italian and international game companies: for example, through the years we've organized together with Ubisoft Italy many days dedicated to the *Assassin's Creed* saga, inviting as special guest the Italian voice actors of the games, organizing activities such as trivia and art contests, cosplay challenges, and live performances. Consumer events, like AC Day, are the most successful and loved ones. We truly encourage the direct experimentation of video games: through over 55 interactive stations, VIGAMUS allows visitors to experience firsthand the titles that have made the history of video games and the most innovative technologies.

The interactive areas within the structure host not only different types of platforms and software, but also different gaming devices: from pinball, considered the ancestor of the interactive medium, to the coin-ops, symbols of the 1970/1980 arcade mania, to the console stations, up to the Oculus Room, where the audience is able to experience the Oculus Rift virtual reality device, seeing with their own eyes the future of electronic entertainment. The biggest challenges in the preservation of Game Culture are linked to the technology: we can understand clearly that historical cartridges and hardware need to be preserved for future generations, but we can't forget that the console we can see today will get old faster, as we see new console generations released every four to five years.

Additionally, if the digital distribution allows more people to play and more developers to make their games available, it brings additional problems in terms of preserving our game culture. We truly want to encourage the direct experimentation of video games: through over 55 interactive stations, VIGAMUS allows visitors to experience firsthand the titles that have made videogame history and the most innovative technologies. Together with an international network—EFGAMP (European Federation of Video Game Archives, Museums and Preservation projects)—we seek to promote the need of preserving video games in all these incarnations to a broader audience. The federation has as its main purpose the preservation of digital games and other interactive experiences. Games are an important part of the digital media landscape that we live in. The preservation of games presents us with significant challenges in various fields: legal, technological, conceptual, and financial. With the members of EFGAMP we aim to collaborate on these topics. For instance, EFGAMP will focus on ensuring that the overall European legal framework is compatible with the needs of digital preservation and will advance the accessibility of game heritage by establishing and implementing description standards and connecting existing collections. Creating and enabling a strong network among peers throughout Europe—creating a synergy of skills is crucial to obtain a permanent and convincing solution—is of paramount importance. What is at stake is the salvation of an important heritage, which should be kept accessible for the purpose of celebration, education, and innovation.

ACKNOWLEDGEMENTS

We want to thank all the members of VIGAMUS Foundation's Research Center, which provided their insights and perspectives while sharing examples and best practices that were crucial in shaping our study. Their ongoing research on the identity of video games was the biggest contribution to this chapter.

REFERENCES

Accordi Rickards, M. (2014). *Storia del Videogioco. Dagli Anni Cinquanta ad oggi*. Roma: Carocci

Accordi Rickards, M. (2018). *Manuale di Critica Videoludica*. Milano: Unicopli

Accordi Rickards, M, De Gregori, G, Feliciani, R. (2018). *Indagine oltre le Tenebre: H.P. Lovecraft e le opere interattive*. Roma: Eurilink.

Accordi Rickards, M., & Frignani, P. (2010). *Le professioni del videogioco, una guida all'inserimento nel settore videoludico*. Latina: Tunuè.

Accordi Rickards, M., & Padula, A. (2012). *Videogiochi e Propaganda*. Roma: UniversItalia.

Accordi Rickards, M., Romanini, M., & De Gregori, G. (2012). *David Cage. Esperienze Interattive oltre l'avventura*. Milano: Unicopli.

Accordi Rickards, M., & Vannucchi, F. (2013). *Il Videogioco. Mercato, giochi e giocatori*. Milano: Mondadori Università.

Atari. (1972). *Pong*. Atari.

Atkins, B. (2003). *More than a Game. The Computer Game as Fictional Form*. Manchester: Manchester University Press.

Bittanti, M. (1999). *L'innovazione tecnoludica. L'era dei videogiochi simbolici (1958 – 1984)*. Milano: Jackson Libri.

Bittanti, M. (2004). *Per una cultura dei videogames. Teorie e prassi del videogiocare*. Milano: Unicopli.

Bittanti, M. (2005). *Gli strumenti del videogiocare. Logiche, estetiche e (v)ideologie*. Milano: Costa & Nolan.

Bittanti, M. (2008). *Schermi Interattivi. Il cinema nei videogioch*. Roma: Meltemi.

Blizzard Entertainment. (2004). *World of Warcraft*. Online Game. Blizzard Entertainment.

Bogost, I. (2007). *Persuasive Games: The Expressive Power of Videogames*. Cambridge, MA: MIT Press.

Bolter, J. D. (2003). *Remediation. Competizione e integrazione tra media vecchi e nuovi*. Milano: Guerini e Associati.

Cage, D. (2010). *Heavy Rain*. Quantic Dream.

Chen, J. (2012). *Journey*. thatgamecompany.

Crawford, C. (1984). *The Art of Computer Game Design*. Berkeley, CA: McGraw-Hill/Osborne Media.

Dallas, I. (2017). *What Remains of Edith Finch*. Giant Sparrow.

Darley, A. (2006). *Visual Digital Culture: Surface Play and Spectacle in New Media Genres*. London, United Kingdom: Routledge.

Daverio, P. (2011). *Il museo immaginato*. Milan: Rizzoli.

EA Sports. (2018). *FIFA 18*. Electronic Arts.

Flew, T., & Games. (2005). *Technology, Industry, Culture in New Media: An Introduction*. Melbourne: Oxford University Press.

Foster, Wallace D. (2006). *Infinite Jest*. New York: Back Bay Books.

Fujiwara, T. (1985). *Ghosts 'n Goblins*. Capcom.

Gaynor, S. (2012). *Gone Home*. Online Game. Fullbright Company.

Gilbert, R. (1990). *The Secret of Monkey Island*. LucasFilm Games.

Greene, B. and Tae-seok, J. (2017). *PlayerUnknown's Battlegrounds*. Bluehole Studio. PUBG Corporation.

Howard, J. (2008). *Quests: Design, Theory, and History in Games and Narratives*. Wellesley, MA: A. K. Peters.

Hudson, C. (2007). *Mass Effect*. BioWare.

Huizinga, J. (2014). *Homo Ludens: A Study of the Play-Element in Culture*. Eastford, CT: Martino Fine Books.

Indieszero. (2008). *Personal Trainer: Cooking*. Nintendo.

Jenkins, H. (2007). *Convergence Culture: Where Old and New Media Collide*. New York: New York University Press.

Jenkins, H. (2006) *Fans, Bloggers, and Gamers: Exploring Participatory Culture*. New York: New York University Press.

Johnson, S. (2006). *Everything Bad Is Good for You: How Popular Culture Is Making Us Smarter*. London, United Kingdom: Penguin.

Juul, J. (2009). *A Casual Revolution: Reinventing Video Games and Their Players*. Cambridge, MA: The MIT Press.

Kent, S. (2001). *The Ultimate History of Video Games*. New York: Three Rivers Press.

King. (2012). *Candy Crush Saga*. Mobile game. King.

Koizumi, Y. (2007). *Super Mario Galaxy*. Nintendo.

Kojima, H. (2001). *Metal Gear Solid 2: Sons of Liberty*. Konami.

Lumière Brothers. (1896). *Arrival of a Train at La Ciotat*. Société Lumière.

Manovich, L. (2002). *The Language of New Media*. Cambridge, MA: MIT Press.

Matsunaga, H. (2007). *Wii Fit*. Nintendo.

McLuhan, M. (2008). *Understanding Media: The Extensions of Man*. Cambridge, MA: MIT Press.

Metzen, C., & StarCraft, Phinney J. (1997). *Online Game*. Blizzard.

Niantic Labs. (2012). *Ingress*. Niantic Labs.

Nomura, T. (2016). *Pokémon Go*. Niantic Labs.

Nishikado, T. (1978). *Space Invaders*. Taito.

Pajitnov, A. (1984). *Tetris*. AcademySoft.

Poole, S. (2004). *Trigger Happy. Videogames and the Entertainment Revolution*. New York: Arcade Publishing.

PopCap Games. (2009). *Plants vs. Zombies*. PopCap Games.

PopCap Games. (2013). *Plants vs. Zombies 2*. Electronic Arts.

Riot Games. (2009). *League of Legends*. Riot Games.

Sakurai, M. (2014). *Super Smash Bros*. Nintendo.

Telltale Games. (2012). *The Walking Dead*. Telltale Games.

Ueda F. (2001). *Ico*. Team Ico.

Visual Concepts. (2018). *NBA 2K18*. 2K Games.

Wolf, J. P. M. (2001). *The Medium of the Videogame*. Austin, TX: University of Texas Press.

CHAPTER 21

Diversity in Games

How and Why?

Alayna Cole

DISCLAIMER: *I AM A queer woman living with mental illness, which are aspects of my life that have caused me to be oppressed in social spaces. That said, I also have the privilege of being cisgender, Caucasian, and (mostly) able-bodied, of not deviating from the predominant religious and cultural norms of my society, and of living with financial security.*

Games have a problem with diversity.

The IGDA's developer satisfaction survey most recently notes that 61% of game developers self-identify as being solely 'white/Caucasian/ European', 74% as 'male', 81% as 'heterosexual', and 75% as not having a disability. Despite being a global survey, 49% of respondents are working in the USA – but statistics that are specific to other regions reveal similar demographics.

I live in Australia, where 18% of people working in the games industry identify as female (IGEA, 2018). The statistics are not much better in the United Kingdom, where only 19% identify as women and 4% are described as 'Black, Asian, and Minority Ethnic (BAME)' (Creative Skillset, 2016).

The industry is homogenous: predominantly white, cisgender, male, heterosexual, able-bodied, and neurotypical. But it is not just game development companies that lack diversity; it is also the games that are being developed. For example, at the Electronic Entertainment Expo (E3) in 2018, only 8% of games featured exclusively female protagonists (Feminist

Frequency 2018). And that is just the types of diversity that are most commonly being given attention: there are no accessible, up-to-date statistics about the number of people of colour, disabled people, or queer people in games announced at major industry events.

Queerly Represent Me – an organisation of which I am managing director – has some statistics around representations of queer folks in games, but not in comparison to all games being released in any given year. The LGBTQ Video Game Archive is similarly tracking the number of games released with queer characters, narratives, or themes, but not in comparison to games that do not feature these elements. In-depth analysis and holistic study of the representations that exist are being published more, but limited work is being done to increase the quantities of these representations throughout games – and the industry that is making them.

In 2017, a man – James Damore – was fired from his job at Google for writing and circulating a memo entitled 'Google's Ideological Echo Chamber'. The document insists that we stop stereotyping people based on gender, and then proceeds to say that women often 'prefer jobs in social or artistic areas' over coding, 'generally have a harder time negotiating salary, asking for raises, speaking up, and leading', and have a 'lower stress tolerance' and therefore are less likely to work high stress jobs. The memo boils down to saying that women are biologically less likely to be good at or interested in software engineering because of a predisposition to being people-oriented, cooperative, and anxious.

However, 'tech and games are not naturally male-dominated fields' (Golding & van Deventer, 2016: 28). In fact, women's enrolment in computer science and information technology degrees were following a steady, rising trajectory until 1984 – just as marketing companies began to suggest that 'computers and videogames are boys' toys' (Golding & van Deventer, 2016: 28). There is a cyclical relationship between these facets of the games industry: if games are marketed towards boys (and one technique for this is ensuring they feature playable characters that appeal to those boys), then boys are more likely to become interested in games. If more boys are interested in games, they are more likely to be interested in working within the games industry. Once working in the industry, they are more likely to make characters that resemble themselves and their own experiences, and to market those characters – and the games that contain them – to boys like themselves. And the cycle continues.

It is difficult to solve a problem that is cyclical, particularly when the people inside the cycle are unable to see what is occurring. A game audience survey Queerly Represent Me conducted in 2017 asked participants whether they felt representation of diverse identities was important in games and to explain their answer. The main justifications for individuals deeming representation unimportant focused on its 'irrelevance' to a good game and that 'narrative' or 'gameplay' should be prioritised, but a number of participants specifically suggested that games are already 'diverse enough'.

'There's plenty of diversity already', one participant said. Another stated, 'Games are already the most egalitarian form of entertainment. Many games let you make whatever character you want to represent you'. A third respondent suggested that, 'Representation is adequate already, and not of concern to anyone besides those who do not play games, in my experience'.

There are several misconceptions evident in just these three responses. If diversity can be defined as 'including a broad variety of different people with an assortment of backgrounds and experiences, as well as demographics such as gender, sexuality, race, and ability' (Zammit & Cole 2019), then our earlier statistics show that games – and the games industry that are producing them – are not as diverse as they could be. While character creators are impressive, there are limitations to the types of characters that can be built within them (Cole et al., 2017) – and limitations to the positive impact that these 'optional' forms of representation can have on audiences (Cole, 2018: 9). Most harmful, however, is the misconception that the only people who are advocating for increased and improved representation of diversity in games are people who do not play games.

The idea that nobody playing games would like those games to be more diverse is an unconstructive mentality, which is captured well by this respondent: 'sjw [social justice warriors] don't play games and will find eny [sic] reason to make a game look bad … the normal people are already included' (Queerly Represent Me, 2017). Firstly, suggesting that people who aren't currently represented in games are 'abnormal' reinforces the in-group and out-group dynamics that cause us to form bonds with people who appear similar to ourselves and dismiss or exclude people who do not (Henry, 2010). The construction of barriers between dominant and marginalised groups leads to ongoing discrimination. Secondly, this respondent's statement is objectively untrue – the statistics show that many socially progressive people who this respondent might consider 'social justice warriors' do play games (IGEA, 2017; Queerly Represent Me, 2017).

And even without the statistics, all you need to do is look at my game library to know that this 'social justice warrior' is also a game consumer.

But this attitude is indicative of the problem that games have with diversity. Marketing companies actively worked to make games appeal to a subset of the population (Golding & van Deventer, 2016: 28) and now that subset believes they can act as gatekeepers for games and the games industry. As one respondent so eloquently puts it: 'ayy get out of my hobby' (Queerly Represent Me, 2017). Until these gatekeepers acknowledge that women, people of colour, queer folks, people with disabilities, and many other diverse social groups are interested in playing and developing games, marginalised groups are going to feel unwelcome within a medium and industry that they are continuing to play, work in, and engage with regardless of how uncomfortable they are made to feel.

So, how do we solve the problem?

Well, first we need to figure out exactly what the problem *is*. Games are an incredible medium and should be for everyone – and, currently, they are not. Anybody from any social group should be able to access games that interest them and represent them, and that were made by people who are similar to them – in terms of demographics, background, experience, views, personality, and so on. This ideal situation does not describe an overturning or replacing of the dominant group with another dominant group; instead, diversification refers to a broadening of the scope to include those who currently play and develop games while also welcoming new voices.

By broadening the number of people who feel welcome both playing and developing games, we can encourage variety in the games that are being released, steering away from publishers of triple-A titles falling back on the same archetypes because of the financial risk that arises from experimentation, and instead telling new stories from different perspectives.

To achieve this, we need to do more than simply talk about it. Discussions of diversity are often theoretical, and for them to make a difference in the games industry, they need to be accompanied by actionable steps that can be followed by individuals in a range of situations and positions of power.

The ultimate piece of advice that should be followed by all employers, event organisers, and game developers is to hire consultants. And the key word here is hire; do not approach somebody in your network who identifies as being from a marginalised group and expect them to consult on your project for free. Not everybody wants to use their experiences with a particular demographic or social group to give you advice, and particularly not for free. Diversity consultants are able to look at your workplace, event, or game, and provide specific advice to ensure that it is inclusive and accessible.

There are also many guides and resources that will teach you how to alter your hardware and software, your convention space, or your workplace so that it is as diverse, inclusive, and accessible as possible. This is a perfect first step before reaching out for specific advice, particularly if consultancy is outside your budget or cannot be on the agenda yet.

Support is also important and comes in many forms. Individuals and companies can offer financial support to marginalised creators, speakers, and so on to ensure they are valued for their work. Events dedicated to diversity in the games industry suffer from difficulty acquiring sponsors because of the fear that funding an inclusive event is making a political statement; financially supporting these events helps highlight the importance of diversity in games.

Support is not always financial. You can boost the voices of marginalised people by hiring them for your studios, asking them to speak at your events, sharing their work with your networks, nominating them for awards, and publicly celebrating their successes. If you or an ally are offered an opportunity, a job, or a speaking arrangement that you do not need for your career, recommend a marginalised person who does. If a developer represents a diverse cast of people in their game, give them positive feedback and encourage them to continue supporting marginalised people through representation.

Games have a problem with diversity. But they do not have to. We have the power to boost marginalised people, support their work, and irrevocably change the games industry.

REFERENCES

Cole, A. (2018). Categories of representation: Improving the discussion and depiction of diversity. *TEXT Journal*. Special issue: "*Writing and Gaming.*" Accessed 5 February 2019, from http://www.textjournal.com.au/speciss/issue53/Cole.pdf.

Cole, A., Barker, D., & Zammit, J. (2017). Impossible identities: The limitations of character creation systems. *Presented to the DiGRA International Conference*, Melbourne, Australia.

Creative Skillset. (2016). *2015 Employment Survey: Creative Media Industries*. Accessed 5 January 2019, from https://www.screenskills.com/media/1562/2015_creative_skillset_employment_survey_-_march_2016_summary.pdf.

Damore, J. (2017). *Google's Ideological Echo Chamber.* Accessed 5 February 2019, from https://web.archive.org/web/20170809220001/https://diversitymemo-static.s3-us-west-2.amazonaws.com/Googles-Ideological-Echo-Chamber.pdf.

Feminist Frequency. (2018). *Gender Breakdown of Games Featured at E3 2018.* Accessed 5 January 2019, from https://feministfrequency.com/2018/06/14/gender-breakdown-of-games-featured-at-e3-2018/.

Golding, D., & van Deventer, L. (2016). *Game Changers: From Minecraft to Misogyny, The Fight for the Future of Videogames.* South Melbourne, VIC: Affirm Press.

Henry, E. A., Bartholow, B. D., & Arndt, J. (2010). Death on the brain: Effects of mortality salience on the neural correlates of ingroup and outgroup categorization. *Social Cognitive and Affective Neuroscience,* 5, 77–87.

IGDA. (2018). *Developer Satisfaction Survey 2017: Summary Report.* Accessed 5 January 2019, from https://cdn.ymaws.com/www.igda.org/resource/resmgr/2017_DSS_/!IGDA_DSS_2017_SummaryReport.pdf.

IGEA. (2017). *Digital Australia 2018.* Accessed 5 February 2019, from https://igea.net/2017/07/digital-australia-2018-da18/.

IGEA. (2018). *Australian Video Game Development: An Industry Snapshot FY 2016–17.* Accessed 5 January 2019, from https://igea.net/2018/01/australian-game-developers-march-generating-118-5m-spite-limited-recognition-support/.

Queerly Represent Me. (2017). *Game Audience Surveys: 2017.* Accessed 5 February 2019, from https://queerlyrepresent.me/resources/survey-results.

Zammit, J., & Cole, A. (2019). Establishing a language of diversity: Preliminary findings. *Presented to the DiGRA Australia Conference,* Sydney, Australia.

Index

2D art sprites, 283
2D art style, 247
2D cartoons, 247
2D digital puppetry, 246
2D drawings, 258, 259, 264
2D information, 257–258
2D vector line art, 247
2D visual clues, 258
3D animation, 247, 257, 258
3D games, 231, 308, 310
3D information, 258
3D mesh geometry, 212, 215
3D modeling and animation tools, 247
3D models, 201, 202, 208, 210, 250,
    257, 258
3D positioning, 297
3D tree models, 211
6-11 framework, 4–7, 17
8-bit games, 128, 129
"8 Kinds of Fun" taxonomy, 5

AAA games, 39, 128
AAA methodologies, 185–186, 191,
    194–197, 275, 296
Able Gamers, 41
Abstract art, 152
AC Day, 379
Achievement motive, 77
Action blurs, 282–283
Actions, 4, 8, 9, 11, 16, 106–107
Activision, 190, 191
Adams, Ernest, 126, 142
Adobe AE, 258
Adobe Illustrator, 261
Adobe Photoshop, 197, 276
ADSR, *see* Attack, decay, sustain, release
Adventure games, 7, 12, 15, 134, 165, 167

Advertising, 57, 120
Aesthetics, 56, 145, 147, 152, 153,
    236–240, 367
AGE framework, 4, 8, 14, 17, 147
Agile development, 191
AI, *see* Artificial Intelligence
Akron Art Museum, 147
Aladdin (film), 146
Alexander, Christopher, 158
Alpha Bear (2015), 133
Alvarez, Julian, 144
Android, 352, 353
Android OS, 346
Angry Birds, 350, 351
    2009, 347–349
    2016, 351
Angry Birds AR: Isle of Pigs, 355
Anrgy Birds 2 (2015), 118, 349, 351
Anthem, 189, 191
Anthropy, Anna, 143, 146
Apex Legends, 190
AppAnnie, 351
Apple, 42, 120, 346, 347, 353
Apps, 57–58, 70, 75, 85, 89
App Store, 197, 346, 347, 349
    Android, 343
    Apple, 120, 343, 349
AR, *see* Augmented reality
Arcade games, 39, 129
Arcade style minigames, 15
Arc-based teleportation, 318, 325
Archero, 355
An Architectural Approach to Level Design
    (Totten), 143, 158
Arc System Works, 247
Arena of Valor, 354
Arrival of a Train at La Ciotat (1896), 367

Artgames, 145
Artifacts, 360, 363, 364, 373, 376–378
Artificial Intelligence (AI), 14, 234
Artificial movement, 307, 309
Artillery Simulator, 350
Artists' Games, 145
Art styles, 118, 151, 153, 210, 247, 276,
      278, 284
Artworks, 144–146, 147, 148, 157, 277
Asian games, 352, 355
Asphalt 4: Elite Racing, 347
Assassin's Creed, 39, 379
Asteroids (1979), 134, 366
Asteroids' Syndrome, 365–367, 372
Asymmetric game, 22
Asymmetry, degrees of, 23–24
Atari, 40, 371, 378
Atari 2600, 376
Atari Flashback Consoles, 128
Atari VCS, 128, 134
Attack, decay, sustain, release
      (ADSR), 290
Attention economy, 64, 87
Audio-driven gameplay, 300
Audio file compression, 298
Audiogames, 39
Audio middleware, 288–289, 296–298
Audio pre-production, 289
Audio sources, 297
Audio tools, 288–289
Audyssey, 41
Augmented reality (AR), 108, 229, 305,
      352, 373
Auto-Chess, 190, 355
Automatic color updating, 262
Automatic gap-closing method, 263
Automatic inbetweening, 250, 251
Automatic stroke layering method, 259
Autonomy, 20, 26–29, 82
Auto Race (1976), 341

Bach, Johan Sebastian, 148
Balloon Shooter, 100
Bandersnatch (2018), 166, 168–170, 175
Banner Saga (2014), 137
Barone, Eric, 195
Barriers in games, 37–39, 43–44
Basecamp, 337

Basic life support (BLS), 100
Battle Bay (2015), 353
Battlefield, 350
"Battle royale" approach, 134
BBC, 41
BBC Micro, 39
BCD, *see* Building City Dashboards
BCD WebGL, 203, 205
Beatles, 378
Beat Saber, 307
Beat the Whites with the Red Wedge,
      148, 152
Beaux arts-style architecture, 153
Beaver Snap Game, 83
Beeline Interactive, 351
Behavioral economics, 58, 348
Behavioral engagement, 22, 24
Behavioral learning process, 81
Behaviourist learning perspective, 70,
      74, 82
Bejeweled, 344, 345
Belonging and power motives, 77–78
Bergman, Ingmar, 361
Best Friends list, 75, 85
Beyond Boredom and Anxiety (1975), 129
Billboard, 218–220
BIM, *see* Building Information Modeling
Binaural microphone, 300
Bioware, 295
Blind-accessible games, 39
Blind computer operators, 38
Blind gamers, 39
Blog posts, 48
Blood and Laurels (2014), 176–178
Blood & Truth, 306
BLS, *see* Basic life support
Blue Lava Wireless, 345
Boom Beach, 353
Boon, Ed, 39
Boundary shape interpolation, 251–252
Boundary stroke, 267–268
Branching, 14, 167, 298
Brawl Stars, 123, 355
Brilliant Computing, 40
Building City Dashboards (BCD), 201–206
Building Information Modeling
      (BIM), 158
Buried Treasures, 378

Burnout, 345
Bushnell, Nolan, 371, 376
Butler, Alan, 147

C64 Mini, 128
CAD, *see* Computer Aided Drafting
Cage, David, 167, 374
Caillois, Roger, 144
Calinescu, M., 165, 166
Call of Duty: Mobile, 355
Campaign Clicker (2016), 133
Candy Crush, 295
Candy Crush Saga (2012), 355, 371
Capcom, 351
CASA, 201
Casual games, 352
CCMs, *see* Cooperative communication
    mechanics
CCPIG, *see* Competitive and Cooperative
    Presence in Gaming
    questionnaire
CD-ROMs, 39
Cedar products, 295
Character Controller, 203
Chat notifications, 80
Chat systems, 337
"Cheating," 41
Chillingo, 350
Chinese games, 354
Chip and Dale Rescue Rangers 2
    (1993), 134
Choose-your-own-adventure (CYOA), 166
Cibele, 146
City Engine, 201
City of Alamogordo, 379
Civilization (1991), 132
Clark, Naomi, 143
Clash of Clans, 352, 353
Clash Royale, 354
Cloud-based communication, 338
Cochlear implants, 103
Cognitive-behavioral patterns, 374
Cognitive biases, 58
Cognitive perspective, 70, 80, 83
Cognitive psychology, 56
COGS, *see* Cost of goods
Colin McRae Rally 2005, 345
Collaborative games, 25, 29

Color management, 260–265
    automatic color updating, 262
    coloring, 251, 260–261
    gap closing, 262–264
    region types, 261–262
    vector flood fill-based gap closing,
        264–265, 268–269
Colosseum, 360
Columbian Exposition (1893), 153
Combat (1977), 134
Comfort rewards, 106
*Command & Conquer 3: Tiberium
    Wars,* 345
Commodore 64, 128
Competence, 20, 28, 29, 53, 76, 77, 80, 84,
    85, 88
Competition, 7, 21, 66, 74, 76, 82, 85, 87,
    88, 107, 128, 134, 341, 343, 344,
    353, 369, 370
Competitive and Cooperative Presence
    in Gaming questionnaire
    (CCPIG), 21
Competitive games, 24, 26, 295
Computer Aided Drafting (CAD),
    158, 201
Computer games, 95–97
Computer graphics techniques, 228
Computerspielemuseum, 376
Concurrency pattern, 25
Conflict theory, 315
Constructivist artwork, 149
contemporary art, 145, 147
Context-aware inbetweening method, 254
Context mesh interpolation, 255
Contraceptives, 105
Conventional 2D flat experiences, 311
Cooperation-oriented obstacles, 25
Cooperative communication mechanics
    (CCMs), 31
Cooperative games, 22, 24
Core mechanic, 151
Corporate game development, 185
Cost of goods (COGS), 187
Cost Per Install (CPI), 121
Coupling, concept of, 22–25
CPI, *see* Cost Per Install
Crash Bandicoot, 197, 366
Crash Bandicoot: Mutant Island, 345

Crossfading, 298, 299
Croucher, Mel, 14
Crusader's Quest, 284
Csikszentmihalyi, M., 21
Cubic interpolation, 253
Cultist Simulator (2018), 175, 176, 178
Cultural games, 370
Culyba, Sabrina Haskel, 151
Cuphead, 146, 148
Curiosity, 7, 12, 15, 16, 127, 134, 313, 364
Curve reconstruction method, 255
Custom controllers, 41
Cut the Rope, 350
Cybersickness, 314–316, 323
CYOA, *see* Choose-your-own-adventure

Dakar 2007, 345
Damore, James, 384
Dark pattern design, 54, 55, 57–60
Dataset Diptych 01, 147
Dataset Diptych 06, 147
Daverio, Philippe, 360, 363, 364
da Vinci, Leonardo, 363
DAW, *see* Digital audio workstation
DBSC, *see* Disk B-Spline Curve
DDLC, see Doki Doki Literature Club
    (2017)
Dead Nation (2010), 131
Dead Space, 311
de Cervantes, Miguel, 154
Defender (1980), 39
Degrees-of-freedom (DoF), 305–306
DEM, *see* Digital Elevation Model
Denoiser hardware/software, 295
Department of Geocomputation, 201
Depth perception, 304, 305, 310, 311
"Designer's Notebook: The Role
    of Architecture in
    Videogames"(Adams), 142
Design ethics, 59
Design principles, 127–139
    overview, 127–128
    retro and modern, 128–138
        mixing genres, 136–137
        relying on emotional hook, 133–135
        short game sessions and tight
            controls, 129–132
        straightforward goals, 133

teaching, challenging and
    rewarding players, 135–136
technical and experiential
    limitations, 137–138
using familiar theme, 132–133
Design thinking, 150–159
    architectural, 152–156
        for analysis criteria, 152–153
        applied to non-architectural works,
            154, 156
        for planning game design and art
            goals, 153
    empathy and pre-design, 150–152
    level design as architectural process,
        157–159
Desolus, 153
Destiny, 189, 191
Deus Ex Machina (1985), 14
Dialogue levelling, 295
Digetic interface, 311
Digital assets, 234
Digital audio workstation (DAW), 290,
    292, 295
Digital Bridges, 345
Digital Chocolate, 344
Digital Elevation Model (DEM), 207
Digital hologram, 311
Digital poetry, 367
Dillon, Roberto, 147
DiRT, 345
Disabled gamers, 38
Discord, 196
Disk B-Spline Curve (DBSC), 252
Disney, 146
Dithering, 215, 278–279
DitherTemporalAA, 215
Diversity in games, 383–387
The Division 2, 39
DIY arcade cabinets, 128
Djaouti, Damien, 144
DoCheckSegment, 225, 226
Document management systems, 337
DoF, *see* Degrees-of-freedom
Doki Doki Literature Club (DDLC,
    2017), 174
Donkey Kong (1981), 129, 133
Don Quixote (de Cervantes), 154
Doom, 377, 378

Doom VFR (2018), 127
DOTA, 295
Dots, 352
Dr. Mario World (2019), 355
Dragon Ball Z, 355
Dragon Quest, 148
Dragon Quest Builders, 190
Dropbox, 338
Dublin 3D city model, 201–202
Dungeon Boss vs. Star Wars: Galaxy of
    Heroes, 118
Dys4ia, 146
Dystopias, 65, 87

E3, *see* Electronic Entertainment Expo
EA, *see* Electronic Arts
EA Mobile, 345
East Coast Games Conference (ECGC), 144
Edge, 347, 375
Edge deformation-gradient features, 254
Edging, 281
EFGAMP, *see* European Federation
    of Video Game Archives,
    Museums and Preservation
Electronic Arts (EA), 187, 189, 344, 345,
    347, 349–351
Electronic Entertainment Expo (E3), 383
Electronic games, 365, 368, 371, 375
Elevation models, 207, 209
"Eliza effect," 169
Emoji, 75, 77, 78, 81
Emotion, 4–6, 8, 10
    anger, 5
    contagion, 20
    excitement, 6
    experience, 4, 8, 10–16, 48, 78, 79,
        84, 147
    fear, 5, 10
    joy/happiness, 6, 10
    pride, 6, 10
    sadness, 6
    visuals, 228
Emotion perspective, 73
Empowering players, 135
Enjoyment, 20, 21, 23, 29, 31, 66, 100, 347
Entertainment Software Association
    (ESA), 19
Epson Multimedia Conference Center, 379

Ericcson, Stefan, 345
ESA, *see* Entertainment Software
    Association
"E-score," 54
eSports game, 370
ESRI, 201
E.T. The Extra-Terrestrial buried
    cartridges, 377
E.T. The Fall (exhibition), 377, 378
Eternal Darkness: Sanity's Requiem
    (2002), 173
European Federation of Video Game
    Archives, Museums and
    Preservation (EFGAMP), 379, 380
Evil Controllers, 41
Experience *vs.* challenge, 374–375
Experimental art, 153
Exploitationware, 65, 87
Extended reality (XR), 236, 305
External speech synthesisers, 39

F2P, *see* Free to Play games
Fabric, 296
Facebook, 67, 68, 70, 348; *see also*
    Gamification elements
Fallout, 190
Fantasy game, 188
Farmville, 351
The Fast and the Furious, 345
Feature points-assisted inbetweening,
    265–267
Feedback, 30, 48, 54, 70, 74, 80–84, 86, 89,
    90, 106, 123, 152, 159, 241, 295
Ferrari, Mark, 284
Field of view (FOV), 315, 317
Field recording, 292
FIFA, 189, 365
FIFA 18 (2017), 370
Fighting games, 7
Final Fantasy, 147
Final Fantasy XV, 300
Financial support, 343, 387
FindStartPoint, 225
Fire Emblem Heroes, 354
First-person games, 14
First-person perspective (FPP), 13,
    203, 228
First-person shooters (FPS), 6, 7, 13, 287

Flappy Bird, 130, 352
Flashback Classics (2016), 127
Flick Kick Football, 350
Flipper books, 246
Flood fill algorithm, 264
Flood fill method, 251, 261
Flood Resilience (FR) controller, 204
*Flow: The Psychology of Optimal
         Experience* (1990), 129
Flower, 355
FMOD, 296
Foley recording, 292
Foliage Component, 222
Folmer, Eelke, 41
Football Manager, 39, 137
Forbidden Forest (1983), 134
Fori Imperiali, 360
Fortnite, 190, 354, 355
FOV, *see* Field of view
Fox, Toby, 195
FPS, *see* First-person shooters
FR, *see* Flood Resilience controller
Freeman, Nina, 146
Free to Play (F2P) games, 118, 119, 125,
         348–352, 354, 355, 372
French gothic church, 149
Friends' birthdays, 79, 82
Friends list emojis, 75, 77, 78, 81
Friends Screen, 80
Friendversaries, 76, 79, 81
Frogger (1981), 8–11
Fruit Ninja, 350
Fullerton, Tracy, 151, 158
Full motion video, 39
Fun, 6, 8, 10, 13, 28, 29, 65, 90, 126, 197,
         228, 345, 350, 371–373
Functional creep, 89
Fundraising, 79, 81, 85
Funka, 41
Funnel conversion, 120
FunPlus, 355

Gacha boxes, 349
GAG, *see* Game Accessibility Guidelines
Gamasutra, 126, 142
Gambling game, 371, 372
Game accessibility, 37–49
    barriers, 43–44

    GAG, 42–43, 44–48
    history, 38–42
    overview, 37–38
Game Accessibility Guidelines (GAG),
         42–43, 44–49
Game Accessibility Special Interest Group
         (GA-SIG), 41, 49
Game analysis theories, 143–150
    collected work, 146–149
    levels as unique works, 149–150
    single work, 144–146
Game Art, 145
Game audio, 287–301
    definition, 287–288
    elements, 290–301
        examples, 298–301
        implementation, 295–298
        music, 290–291
        sound design, 291–293
        voice, 293–295
    in production pipeline, 288–289
Game balancing, 24, 29, 31
Game Boy (1989), 341–344
Gameboy Advance (GBA), 186, 187
Game culture, 379
Game designers, 3, 14, 21, 29, 30, 31, 38,
         130, 138, 143, 147, 150, 151, 186,
         187, 369
Game design patterns, 23, 27, 31, 56
Game Design Vocabulary (Anthropy and
         Clark), 143
Game Developers Conference (GDC), 126,
         132, 143, 144
Game documentation, 233
Game Gear, 341
Game imaging technology, 231
Game level design, 228–242
    aesthetics, 236–240
        HUD, 237–238
        hue and saturation, 239
        humans and their faces, 240
        leading lines, 238
        location and size, 236
        rhythm, 239
        shape, 237
    components, 232–235
        description, 233–235
        geometry, 232–233

elements, 240–242
  critical paths, 242
  limited backtracking, 242
  milestones and landmarks,
    241–242
  multiple choices, 242
  player and NPCs, 240–241
  sub-and side-tasks, 241
  time, 242
genres and levels, 230
"Presence" approach, 228–230
and concepts of space, 229–230
Gameloft, 343, 345, 346, 347, 350, 351
Game mechanics, 153, 175, 179
Game music, 147
Game of War, 119, 353
Gameplay, 4–5, 9, 11, 12, 15–16, 43–46,
    133–137, 142–144, 154, 230–231,
    368–369, 371
Game Pro, 375
Games analysis, 3–17
  6-11 framework, 4–7
  AGE framework, 4
  Frogger (1981), 8–11
  Loading Human (2016), 11–16
    color appreciation, 13
    curiosity, 15
    movement and object
      manipulation, 16
    self-identification, 13–15
    storytelling and puzzle solving,
      15–16
  overview, 3–4
"Game Spaces," 152
Games preservation, 379–380
Gamevil, 345
Game & Watch (series), 341
Gamification, 53–60, 64–66
  dependency, 57–58
  exploitation, 58–59
  open questions on, 59
  overview, 53–55
  privacy, 56–57
  related work, 56
Gamification elements, 84–85
  selected, 69–70
  in Snapchat, Instagram and Facebook,
    70–83, 86

badges and achievements, 70,
    76–77, 85, 88
  challenge, 70, 83, 85
  clear goals, 70, 79–80, 84–86
  feedback, 70, 80–81, 84, 86
  leaderboards, 69, 75, 85, 88
  levels, 70, 77–78, 85
  points, 69, 73–74, 84, 86, 88
  progress, 70, 82–83, 85, 88
  rewards, 70, 81–82, 84–86, 88
  stories and theme, 70, 78–79, 84, 86
  SNS and UX principles, 86–87
Gap-aware coloring tool, 264
Gap closing, 262–264
Garena: Free Fire, 355
GA-SIG, *see* Game Accessibility Special
    Interest Group
Gates, concept of, 26
Gaze-based locomotion, 319, 325
GBA, *see* Gameboy Advance
GDC, *see* Game Developers Conference
GDC Level Design Workshop, 149
Gee, James Paul, 144
Geiss, Matthew, 150, 151
Genetic algorithms, 210
Genre-mixing approach, 135–136
Geographic Information Systems (GIS),
    201, 207
Ghosts 'n Goblins (1985), 370
Gilbert, Ron, 375
GIS, *see* Geographic Information Systems
Gizmondo, 345
Glory of Kings, 354
Glu, 345, 350
Gmail, 338
Golden Boot 2019, 350
Gone Home (2013), 366
Google, 346
Google Cardboard, 318, 324
Google Docs, 337, 338
"Google's Ideological Echo Chamber," 384
Google Slide, 337
GPS, 352
G/P/S model, 144
Grand Theft Auto V, 147
Graph-based vector region searching
    method, 265
Graphical user interface (GUI), 146

Grayboxing, 158
Greater London Authority, 201
Gridrunner (1982), 131
Group flow, concept of, 21
GUI, *see* Graphical user interface
Guillemot, Michel, 343
GulliVR, 322, 323
GungHo Online Entertainment, 352–353
Gym mode/fitness related app, 58

Half Life 2, 40
Hall, Edward T., 229
Handheld games, 341, 343
HandyGames, 344
Hanging with Friends, 39
Hansoft, 193
Hanson, C., 163–166, 173
Hardware platform and input device, 106
Harry Potter, 345
Hashtag statistics, 75
Hawkins, Trip, 344
Head-mounted displays (HMDs), 314,
　　　316–319
Head movements tracking, 316, 323–324
Head Up Displays (HUD), 228, 236–239, 311
　　2D, 300
Health games, 95–111
　　animal health, 108
　　designing, 105–108
　　　automation, 107–108
　　　principles, 105–107
　　health personnel training, 96, 98–100
　　overview, 95–98
　　patient training, 97, 100, 102–103
　　policies, 97, 104–105
　　therapy, 97, 103–104
　　uses, 108–110
Health Points (HP) value, 222
Heavy Rain (2010), 374
Height-field, 207
Hellblade: Senua's Sacrifice, 300
Helsinki City Simulator, 200
Heroes Clash, 353
Hero of Sparta, 347
Heterotopias, 87
Hidden persuasion techniques, 90
Hideo Kojima, 138, 368

Hildebrand, Grant, 158
Hill Climb Racing (2013), 352
HMDs, *see* Head-mounted displays
Hololens, 305
Home micros, 39
Horror game, 5, 6, 8
Hourglass nudge, 81, 86
HP value, *see* Health *Points* value
HTC VIVE, 305, 317
HUD, *see* Head Up Displays
Huizinga, Johan, 144
Hybrid models, 207
Hyltander, Anders, 96
Hyper casual games, 352

IAPs, *see* In-app purchases
IBM, 42, 342
IBM Simon, 342
Ico (2001), 365
IDEO Design Consulting Company, 150
id Software, 378
IGDA, 41, 383
Igroup Presence Questionnaire (IPQ), 314
Il museo immaginato (*The Imaginated
　　Museum*, Daverio), 360
Immersion, 13–15, 24, 27, 147, 228, 230,
　　236, 295, 309, 310, 314, 316
Immersive Tendencies Questionnaire
　　(ITQ), 315
Impossible Mission (1984), 136
In-app purchases (IAPs), 343, 348–356
Inbetween drawings, 246
Inbetweening, 247, 248, 250–257, 269
　　feature points-and motion path-
　　　assisted, 265–267
　　linear interpolation, 253
　　non-linear interpolation, 253–254
　　stroke connectivity, 254–256
　　user interactions, 256–257
　　　feature point, 256
　　　motion path, 256–257
Inclusive design, 38
Indie and indie games, 185–197
　　AAA methodologies, 185–186, 191,
　　　194–197, 275
　　audio, 293
　　developers, 196, 197

failure, 187–189
and large videogame company,
    190–191
mistakes, 195
predictability, 192
task micromanagement, 193–194
Infinite Jest (Wallace), 369
Infocom, 377
Information sharing, 25, 27, 41
Infoterra, 201
In-game mechanics, 31
Ingress (2012), 352, 373
INSIDE, 300
Instagram, 68–70, 89; *see also*
    Gamification elements
Instant games, 83
Instinctive behaviors, 4–6, 8
aggressiveness, 7
collecting, 6
color appreciation, 7, 13
communication, 7
competition, 7
exploration/curiosity, 7
greed, 7
protection/care/nurture, 7, 10–12
revenge, 7
self-identification, 6, 10, 12–14
survival, 3, 8, 10
Interactive experience, 367–369
Interactive film, 168
Interactive multimedia work, 367
Interactive music, 291, 296
Interactive Tree Creator, 211, 219, 220
Interactive urban design tool, 201
Interactive work, 368
Interest perspective, 73, 74, 79–81, 83
Interface elements, 43
International Society for Presence
    Research (ISPR), 229
Interpersonal communication, 229
Interpolation method, 250
Intrinsic interpolation method, 253
Intuitive controls, 20
Invisible unsubscribe option, 57
iOS, 39, 352
iPad, 348
iPhone, 346–348, 352, 353

iPhone OS 2.0, 346
IPQ, *see* Igroup Presence Questionnaire
ISPR, *see* International Society for
    Presence Research
Italian museum, 363
ITC tool, 217
ITQ, *see* Immersive Tendencies
    Questionnaire
Izotope RX series, 295

J2ME, *see* Java 2 Micro Edition
Jacobs, Jane, 158
JAMDAT, 343–345
Java 2 Micro Edition (J2ME), 342
Jessel, Jean-Pierre, 144
Jira, 193
Jobs, Steve, 348
Johnson, Ollie, 148
Journey (2012), 355, 367, 370
Juul, J., 164

Key performance indicators (KPIs),
    121–122, 125
Killer Instinct, 39
Kiloo, 354
Kineographs, *see* Flipper books
Kleiman, Jonathan, 150
Kleinman, E., 173
Klotz, 342
K-neighborhood method, 254
Knives Out, 355
Koichi Sugiyama, 148
Konami, 8
Korean Netmarble, 354
KPIs, *see* Key performance indicators
Kremers, Rudolf, 142, 158
KungFucious, 307
Kyma, 292

Lahman, Scott, 343
La Mancha, 154
Lange, Andreas, 376
Laparoscopic surgery, 98
LapSim, 96
Layer-dependent color management, 262
Layer-independent coloring scheme, 262
Layering, 299

LazyBrush, 264
League of Legends (2009), 370
"Learn More" option, 57
Legend of Zelda (series), 147
Lego Worlds, 190
Lemmings, 345
Level Design: Concept, Theory, and Practice (Kremers), 142
Level Design Lobby Podcast, 149
Level Design Workshop, 143
Lewandowski, Joe, 377
LGBTQ Video Game Archive, 384
Licensed games, 346
Lifetime value (LTV), 121, 122
Likes, 67, 68, 70, 74, 88
Lillith, 355
Lineage II Revolution, 354
Linear audio, 287
Linear games, 232
Linear interpolation, 253, 266
LineTrace functions, 226
Lissitzky, El, 148
Lissitzky's Revenge, 148, 151, 153, 158
Little Nemo and the Nightmare Fiends, 153, 158
Little Nemo in Slumberland, 153
Live Paint, 262
Live recordings, 290–292
Loading Human (2016), 11–16
   color appreciation, 13
   curiosity, 15
   movement and object manipulation, 16
   self-identification, 13–15
   storytelling and puzzle solving, 15–16
Locus of manipulation, 28, 29
London Connects, 201
Loot boxes, 6, 349
Lord of the Rings, 344
Los Angeles basin, 200
Louvre, 363, 364
Love Rocks (2015), 346
Low-pass filter, 298
LTV, *see* Lifetime value
LucasArts, 197
Lunar Lander, 38
Lyndon, Donlyn, 158

Machine learning techniques, 210

Machine zone, 64–65
Madden, 39
MAGFest, *see* Music and Gaming Festival
Magic Leap, 305
Mandelbrot, B. B, 207
Maniac Mansion, 12
"Manic retrogamer" approach, 376
Manipulative timing, 55
Manuale di Critica Videoludica, 365
Manual gap closing, 251, 263
Maplestory, 348
Marginalised people, 385–387
Mario Kart Tour (2019), 355
Marketing creatives, 120
Marketing department, 189, 191, 386
Marvel catalog, 344
Mass Effect (2007), 165, 367
Massively multiplayer online role-playing games (MMORPGs), 371
Master Disks, 377–378
Match-three puzzle games, 296, 346
Mattel, 341
MaxMSP, 292
Mayer, Mark, 153/4
Maynooth University, 201
McCay, Winsor, 153, 246
MDA Framework, 145, 147
Mechanics, Dynamics, Aesthetics (MDA) model, 4, 5
Medical model of disability, 37
Meier, Sid, 118, 132
Mellen, Brice, 39
Memories, 78, 79, 84
Meretzky, Steve, 377
Merge Actors tool, 220, 227
Mesh Collider, 201
Messenger app, 68
Meta-data, 68
Meta game, 117, 118
Metagame mechanics, 170, 173
Metal Gear, 138
Metal Gear Solid, 377
Metal Gear Solid 2: Sons of Liberty (2001), 368
Metal Gear Solid (series), 293
Meterofall: Journeys, 355
Microsoft, 41, 42
Microsoft Kinect, 318

Microsoft Word, 366
Microsuasion, 67–68
Microtransactions, 371
MIDI, 290
Milton Bradley MicroVision, 341
A Mind Forever Voyaging, 377
Minecraft, 39, 189, 190
Minecraft Pocket Edition, 352
Minecraft World, 355
Mini-consoles, 128
Minigames, 97, 103, 107–108, 118, 137
Minigore (2009), 131
Missile Command, 40
Mitchell, A., 165–167, 169, 173, 175, 178
Mixed Reality (MR), 305
    games, 236
MMORPGs, *see* Massively multiplayer
        online role-playing games
Mobile devices, 97, 345
Mobile games
    design, 117–126
        audience, 118
        casual, midcore *vs.* hardcore game,
            118–119
        genre and art style, 118–119
        KPIs, 121–122
        live operation, 124–126
        monetization, 119–120
        onboarding, quality assurance and
            player support, 123–124
        user acquisition and marketing,
            120–121
    history, 341–356
        advent of iPhone, 346–348
        first phone games, 342–346
        in-app purchases, 348–356
        original handheld games, 341
Mojang, 352
Mona Lisa, 363–364, 376
Monetization, 119–120, 348
Monopoly, 345
Monster Strike, 354
Monument Valley 2, 354
Moore, Charles, 158
Mortal Kombat, 39
Motion path-assisted inbetweening,
        265–267
Motion sickness, 16, 138

Motivation, 54, 64–66, 82, 100
    gamification, 69
    mechanisms, 70, 84, 88, 90
    psychology, 68
    theory, 20
Mouse Orbit script, 203
MR, *see* Mixed Reality
MSVEs, *see* Multiscale virtual
        environments
MSX computers, 138
Multiplayer games, 19–22, 25, 188
Multiple 3D-based cel-shading rendering
        methods, 247
Multiscale virtual environments
        (MSVEs), 322
Musei Vaticani, 360
Museology, 363, 364
Museum exhibitions, 147
Music and Gaming Festival (MAGFest), 143
MySpace, 348
Myst (1993), 134

Namco, 41, 345
Narrative, 228, 368, 369, 377
    elements, 165
    experiential, 164
    linear, 14, 164, 179
    structures, 167
Naughty Dog, 197
NBA 2K18 (2018), 370
Need for Speed, 345, 350
Need for Speed: Undercover, 347
NES, 128
NetEase, 354, 355
Netflix, 169, 361
Networked Minds Questionnaire
        (NMQ), 22
N-Gage, 344
Niantic, 352
Nier Automata (2017), 174, 175
Ninja Theory, 300
Ni No Kuni 2 (2018), 137
Nintendo, 41, 304, 341, 343, 352, 354, 355,
        366, 372
Nintendo 64, 39
Nintendo DS, 343
Nintendo 3DS, 372
Nintendo Switch, 42

Nitsche, Michael, 142
NMQ, *see* Networked Minds
        Questionnaire
Node-based teleportation, 318, 324–325
Noise, 210, 290, 292, 295
Nokia & Co., 342, 344, 346
Nolan, Christopher, 367
Nom, 345
Nom 2, 345
No Man's Sky, 190
Non-action-oriented games, 133
Non-interactive media art works, 145
Non-linear audio, 300
Non-linear games, 232
Non-linear interpolation, 253–254
Non-narrative games, 179
Non-playable characters (NPCs), 7, 14,
        177, 228, 233, 236, 241
Non-visual aesthetics, 287
Norman, Zack, 343
NPCs, *see* Non-playable characters
NTT DoCoMo's I-Mode platform, 342

Occluded stroke, 267
Occlusion, 257–260
    handling based on boundary strokes,
        267–268
    high-level information, 258–259
    region and region analysis, 259–260
Oculus Kickstarter, 304
Oculus Rift, 305, 308, 362, 379
Oculus Room, 379
Odyssey Magnavox, 40
Omni-directional ball-bearing disc
        platform, 321
Omni-directional treadmills, 321
OneSwitch, 41
OneSwitch.org.uk, 41
Online community building, 66, 68
Online marketing strategies, 68
Online social interaction, 66, 67, 86, 90
Open World: Video Games &
        Contemporary Art
        (exhibition), 147
Optacon, 38
Ordnance Survey, 201
Organic sounds, 292
Organic users, 121

Original Sound Track (OST), 291
Overwatch, 295
Oxenfree (2016), 174

Pac-Man, 129, 186
Paid users, 121
PaintVerticesLerpAlongAxis function, 227
Pandora's Box, 349
Panning, 297
Paper prototyping, 158
Paris Hilton's *Diamond Quest* (2006), 346
Partial rereading, 165, 166
Passage, 146
Penny Arcade Expo (PAX), 143
Perceived behavioral interdependence, 22
Perceived relatedness, 20
Peripheral vision, 309
Personal Trainer: Cooking (2008), 372
Persuasive games, 68
Phantom limb pain (PLP), 103
Photogrammetric methods, 201
Photorealistic imaging techniques, 201
Physically disabled gamers, 41, 44
Picofun, 344
PikPok, 350
Ping system, 31
Pitfall (1982), 132, 133
Pixel art, 275–285
    action blurs, 282–283
    colour shading, 277–278, 280
    dithering, 278–280
    edging, 281
    games, 275, 284
    Pointillism, 278
    practices, 276–277
    traditional, 284
Plants vs. Zombies, 349, 371
Plants vs. Zombies 2 (2013), 371
Playdead, 300
Player communication, 30–31
Player feedback and ability, 106
Player interdependence, 19–31
    approaches, 22–29
        complementarity and coupled
            interactions, 22–25, 31
        interface design, 27–29, 31
        level design, 25–26, 31
    challenges, 29–31

definition, 21–22
social player experience, 19–21
Players' engagement, 4, 105–106
PlayerUnknown's Battlegrounds
(2017), 370
PlayStation, 352
PlayStation 4, 42
PlayStation Classic, 128
PlayStation VR, 305
PlaytestCloud, 123
Play to Cure: Genes in Space (2014), 374
PLP, *see* Phantom limb pain
PocketGamer, 126, 347
Pointillism, 278
Pointing device, 317
Poison theory, 315
Pokémon Go, 352, 355, 373
Pokémon Ride, 100
Pong, 38, 365, 367, 369
PopCap, 350
Pop culture, 369, 376, 377
PopReach, 351
Populous (1989), 135
Pop-ups, 58
Portal, 40
Portal 2 (2011), 31
Positional audio, 297
Postural instability theory, 315
PQ, *see* Presence Questionnaire
Premium games, 119, 196, 349
"Presence" approach, 228–230
and concepts of space, 229–230
Presence Questionnaire (PQ), 314
Procedural assets creation in Unreal
Engine 4 (UE4), 210–227
Interactive Tree Creator, 211–224
automatic billboard generation,
218–219
branch intersection blending,
214–215
force reaction and dynamic wind,
220–222
fruit placement, 217
leaf placement, 215–217
main concepts, 212
preparing trees for use, 220
root, branch and sub-branch
placement, 212–214

tree chopping, falling fruits, leaves
and debris, 222–224
wind weighting, 218
smart spline generator, 224–228
main concepts, 224
merging to static mesh, 227
recursive surface align algorithm,
225–226
vert count optimization with spline
thicken function, 226, 227
Project Gotham Racing: Mobile, 345
Prostate biopsy, 109
Proxemics, 229
"Pseudo-restarts," 174
PSVR games, 13, 306, 308
PSVR platform, 11
Psychological models, 65, 88–90
"Psychological shenanigans," 58
PUBG, 190
PUBG: Mobile, 119, 354, 355
Pure Data, 292
Puzzle & Dragons, 352
Puzzle games, 133, 138, 296, 345,
350, 352
Puzzles, 13
cooperative switch, 25
environmental, 12, 15
shared, 25
solving, 15–16, 28
Puzzles & Empires, 123

QA, *see* Quality assurance
QTEs, *see* Quick Time Events
Quake, 295
Quality assurance (QA), 123–124
Queerly Represent Me, 384, 385
Quick Time Events (QTEs), 374

Racing games, 42–44, 231, 345, 373
Raiders of the Lost Ark (1981), 132
Rapture Seekers, 344, 347
Raster-based 2D animation, 248, 268
Raster-based drawing systems, 260
Realism, 210, 305, 310, 315, 320
Red Dead Redemption 2 (2018), 128
Redirection methods, 322
Reed, A., 164
Reflective rereading, 165, 166, 175

Relude, *see* Rapture Seekers
Render Target texture, 219
Reorientation techniques, 322
Replaying, 163–179
    for completion/closure, 170–174
    definition, 163–166
    for understanding, 174–178
    for variation, 166–170
Research Center, 361, 362, 366, 376–378
Retrofitting, 38
Retrogaming, 127, 359–380
    Asteroids' Syndrome, 365–367
    genetic code, 374–375
    interactive experience, 367–369
    museum and, 360–365
    open source asset, 375
    Video Game as Product, 370–372
    Video Game as Sports, 369–370
    Video Game as Utility, 372–374
    VIGAMUS, 375–380
Return on investment (ROI), 195
Reverb implementation, 297
Rewind mechanics, 166, 169, 170
Rhythm games, 137, 287
"Rhythm of interdependence," 30
"Rhythm violence," 291
Rickards, Marco Accordi, 365, 375, 376
Ridge Racer 3D, 345
Riot-E, 344
Roach motel business model, 58
Robotron (1982), 131
Rohrer, Jason, 146
ROI, *see* Return on investment
Role-playing games (RPGs), 118, 134, 137,
        157, 165, 230, 349, 353, 371
Rollings, Andrew, 142
Room-scale tracking, 316, 323–324
Rovio Entertainment, 344, 346, 347,
        349–351
RPGs, *see* Role-playing games
RuneScape, 348

SAAM, *see* Smithsonian American Art
        Museum Arcade
SAAM Arcade at the Smithsonian
        American Art Museum
        (2018), 152

Sample libraries, 293
Samplers, 290–291
Save the Date (2013), 171–174
SBM, *see* Sketch-based modeling
Scene Capture 2D component, 219
Schell Games, 151
Schreiber, Ian, 126
Schu¨ll, Natascha, 65
Schweizer, Bobby, 142
Sci-fi games, 188, 292
Scott Pilgrim vs the World, 283
Scrabble, 350
Scramble, 342
Screenshot notification, 81
Scrum methodology, 151
Season One, 168
Second screen gaming, 27
The Secret of Monkey Island (1990), 375
Sega, 341
Sega Genesis, 146
SEGA Genesis Classics (2018), 127
Self-determination perspective, 73, 75, 77
Self-determination theory, 20, 30, 31
Self-esteem, 74, 84
Sensors, 97, 103, 321
Serious games, 65, 98, 108, 145, 152, 372, 373
SetMainDirectionVector, 225
Sexually transmitted illnesses (STIs), 105
Shadowgun Legends, 355
Shape distortion, 256
Shared control, 28–29, 31
Sharp, John, 145
Shigeru Miyamoto, 363, 366, 376
Shinji Mikami, 146
Shout-for-shout campaigns, 76
Siemens, 342
SimCity, 135, 345
SimCity 2000, 186, 187
Simple rereading, 165
The Simpsons, 345
Sims, 58
The Sims 2, 345
Simulated cavity navigation
        environment, 100
Simulator sickness, 315
Single-player story games, 188
Singular work theory, 145, 146

The Sinking of the Lusitania, 246
Skallagrigg (Horwood), 38
Skeletal animation, 246
Sketch-based modeling (SBM), 258
Skipping Stone, 345
Sky: Children of Light, 355
Skyrim (2011), 165
Skyrim VR, 317
Slack, 338
Slender: The Eight Pages (2012), 134
Smart spline generator, 224–228
  main concepts, 224
  merging to static mesh, 227
  recursive surface align algorithm,
    225–226
  vert count optimization with spline
    thicken function, 226, 227
Smithsonian American Art Museum
  (SAAM) Arcade, 145
Smooth movement, 284, 307, 308
Smurfs' Village, 351
Snake, 342
Snapchat, 68–70; *see also* Gamification
  elements
Snap Games, 73, 83, 86
Snap Score, 73, 76, 77, 83, 85, 86
Snap Streaks, 83, 84
Snap Streaks and *Stories,* 69, 73–74, 77, 78,
    81, 86, 87
Snap turns, 308
SNS, *see* Social networking sites
Social appreciation, 74, 87, 88
Social benefit, 66
Social capital, 87
Social comparison, 66, 67, 73, 74, 82, 84,
    88, 90
Social justice warriors, 385–386
Social media, 48, 65–68, 86–88, 90
Social media game, 63–90
  double-edged game, 64–65
  ethics, 87–90
    design and fun, 90
    psychological models, 88–89
    social comparison, 88
    surveillance, 89–90
  gamification elements, 84–85
    selected, 69–70

  in Snapchat, Instagram and
    Facebook, 70–83, 86
  SNS and UX principles, 86–87
gamifying social media, 65–70
  interrelation between gamification
    and social media, 66–67
  persuasive design application,
    67–68
  selected platforms, 68–69
Social model of disability, 37
Social networking sites (SNS), 66–68, 70,
    80, 82, 85–90
Social practice, 178
Social presence, 20–22, 24, 26–31
Social Presence in Gaming Questionnaire
    (SPGQ), 21, 22
Social relatedness, 84, 88
Social relations, 67, 75
Socio-psychological effects, 20
SoftBank, 352, 353
Software instruments, 290
Software Product Line Engineering
    (SPLE), 107, 110–111
Software Product Line (SPL), 107–108
Sony, 197, 346
Sony PlayStation, 128
Sound effects, 40, 137, 143, 144, 292, 293,
    296, 298
Sound volume, 43, 45, 46, 122, 124, 227,
    295, 297
Space, Time, Play (2007), 142
SpaceChem (2011), 165
Space Invaders, 369, 378
Space Invaders for Blind (2003), 39
Spatial interface, 311
SpecialEffect, 41
"Special Feature" option, 40
Speech mechanisation in children, 103
SPGQ, *see* Social Presence in Gaming
    Questionnaire
Spider and Web (1998), 173
SPL, *see* Software Product Line
SPLE, *see* Software Product Line
    Engineering
Spline Components, 212
Spline interpolation methods, 253
Spline Mesh Component, 212, 226

Split-screen settings, 27
sponsored *Lenses,* 78, 79
Spore Origins, 347
Sprint, 344
Spy vs. Spy (1984), 134
Square Enix, 190, 300
Stanford Design School, 150
The Stanley Parable (2013), 174
Stardew Valley, 195
Star Wars, 186
Statik (2017), 138
Stereotyping, 189, 384
Stickers, 78, 79
Stifled, 134, 307, 310
STIs, *see* Sexually transmitted illnesses
Storygames, 163–167, 170–171, 173, 175,
        178, 179
Storytelling, 6, 12, 15–16, 78, 79, 86, 142,
        240, 363, 377
Story Views, 73
Stroke-based interpolation, 252, 253
Stroke correspondence, 250
Stroke occlusion, 250–251
Studio MDHR, 146
Subway Surfers, 119, 352, 354
Summoners War, 118, 353
Super Boom Boom, 345
Supercell, 352, 354
Supercollider, 292
Superhot, 307
Super Mario Bros. (1985), 135, 165, 366
Super Mario Galaxy (2007), 369
Super Mario Run, 343, 354
Super Nintendo, 146
Superpotato, 362
Super Smash Bros. (2014), 370
Survival horror games, 5, 6
Sweep line algorithm, 259
Symmetric game, 22
Synergies creation, 23
Synthesizers, 290, 292

Taito, 39, 378
Tales from the Borderlands (2014), 168
Tapping and pushing, 319
Tap Tap Dance, 347
Team involvement and attention, 22
Teleportation, 307, 320, 324–325

Teleport locomotion approach, 317
Telepresence, 229
Telltale Games, 168, 374
Tempest (1981), 131
Temple Run (2011), 133
Tencent, 354, 355
Terrain asset and 3D game map, 207–210
    array to vector conversion, 209–210
        elevation model, 209
        volumetric model, 209
    geometry, 209–210
    representation, 207
        height-field, 207
        voxel-map, 208
Tetris, 164, 171, 172, 342, 344, 345, 350, 368
Thatgamecompany, 355
This is the Police (2016), 137
Thomas, Frank, 148
Threes (2014), 165
Throughput *vs.* permanence, 336–337
Timing, 28, 44, 55, 74, 148, 257
Tomb Raider, 345, 369
Toms, Kevin, 137
Top-down approach, 8, 12
Top Fan badge, 76
Topology structures, 254
Toys 'R' Us, 187
Tracked controllers, 318
Traditional I/O approaches, 316–317
Trait perspective, 70, 75, 77, 82
The Transformational Framework
        (Culyba), 151
Transparency, 57, 65, 89, 90, 215
Tree chopping system, 222
Trello, 337, 338
Trophies and *Charms* features, 76, 77, 81,
        83, 86
Trustworthiness, 53–54
TuckerSoft, 168, 169

UA, *see* User Acquisition
UA-Games, 41
Ubisoft, 343, 344, 379
Ubisoft games, 39
UE4, *see* Unreal Engine 4
UE4 Blueprint system, 211
UE4 Marketplace, 211, 224
UI, *see* User Interface

Ukraine Space Agency, 345
Uncharted, 197
UnderControl, 105
Undertale, 137, 174, 195
Unity, 39, 149, 201–206
Unity 5, 296
Unreal Engine, 39, 296
Unreal Engine 4 (UE4), 224, 227; *see also*
    Procedural assets creation in
    Unreal Engine 4 (UE4)
Untold Games, 11
USB condenser microphone, 294
User Acquisition (UA), 121, 122, 195
User engagement, 54, 64
User eXperience (UX) design, 55,
    56–59, 86
User Interface (UI), 201, 206, 311, 316
usertesting.com, 123
UV-Aligned method, 247
UX design, *see* User eXperience (UX) design

VAC, *see* Vector Animation Complex
Valve, 40, 191
V&A Museum, *see* Victoria and Albert
    (V&A) Museum
VC, se Visualization Controller
VCS console games, 40
Vection, 315
Vector Animation Complex (VAC), 247,
    254, 256
Vector-based 2D animation system,
    245–269
    color management, 260–265
        automatic color updating, 262
        coloring, 251, 260–261, 269
        gap closing, 262–264,-268
        region types, 261–262
        vector flood fill, 264–265, 268–269
    inbetweening, 250–257, 268
        feature points-and motion path-
            assisted, 265–267
        linear interpolation, 253
        non-linear interpolation, 253–254
        stroke connectivity, 254–256
        user interactions, 256–257
    occlusion, 257–260, 269
        handling based on boundary
            strokes, 267–268

high-level information, 258–259
region and region analysis,
    259–260
overview, 246–248
vs. raster-based techniques, 248, 268
system architecture, 249–250
Vector flood fill-based gap closing,
    264–265, 268–269
Vector Graphics Complex (VGC), 254
Verbal commands and symbols, 79
Verner, Jordan, 39
Vertex Color node, 218
Vertex Laplacian coordinates, 254
Vestibular system, 315, 317
VFX, *see* Visual special effects
VGC, *see* Vector Graphics Complex
Victoria and Albert (V&A) Museum, 147
Video calls, 336
Video game archaeology, 379
Video Game as Culture, 368, 369
Video Game as Product, 370–372
Video Game as Sports, 369–370
Video Game as Utility, 372–374
Video game museum, 360, 365
Video Game Museum (VIGAMUS),
    360–362, 375–380
Videogames: Design/Play/Disrupt
    (exhibit), 147
Video Game Spaces: Image, Play, and
    Structure in 3D Worlds
    (Nitsche), 142
Views, 80
VIGAMUS, *see* Video Game Museum
Virtual Boy, 304
Virtual cities creation, 200–206
    developing UI, city layers and
        simulations, 201–206
Virtual currency, 120
Virtual London, 201
Virtual model, 200
Virtual museum, 362
Virtual office, 331–338
    communication, 335–337
        throughput *vs.* permanence,
            336–337
    cost and, 331–333
    infrastructure, 337–338
    time zones, 333–35

daily reports and tracking output, 333–334

dedicated space to work, 334–335

"standup" meetings and mental health, 335

Virtual OSX machine, 338

Virtual reality toolkit (VTK), 108

Virtual reality (VR), 12, 13, 16, 97, 98, 108, 138, 229, 230, 236, 304–312

blurring, 308–309

arm swing movement, 308

head-oriented movement, 308–309

environmental hazards, 306–307

designing for safety, 306–307

digital boundaries, 306

going all in, 306

experiences, 14

general aids, 309

adding stabilising factor, 309

simplifying visuals, 309

variable peripheral vision, 309

headsets, 27

key traits, 305–306

degrees-of-freedom, 305–306

depth perception, 305

nausea, 307

avoidance, 307

overview, 304

tricking eyes, ears and brain, 307–308

snap turn, 308

teleport, 307

types, 304–305

augmented reality/mixed reality (AR/MR), 305

extended reality (XR), 305

uncanny valley, 310–311

scale, 310

stylization, 310

view change, 310–311

user interfaces, 311

Virtual Studio, 335–337, 338

VirtuSphere, 321

Visual art, 144, 146, 148, 154

Visual cues, 31, 57, 133

Visual design, 60

Visual design and communication, 57

Visual fidelity, 309

Visualization Controller (VC), 204

Visual novel approach, 137

Visual programming software, 292

Visual special effects (VFX), 240, 283

Voice snippets, 300

VOID, 306

Volumetric model, 207–208, 209

Voxel models, 207

VPaint, 247

VR, *see* Virtual reality

VR-based PC and PS4 game, 11

VR Beirut 3D project, 201

VR locomotion, 313–325

design implications, 323–325

overview, 313–314

presence and cybersickness, 314–316

stationary approaches, 316–319

gestures, 318–319

teleportation, 317–318

traditional I/O approaches, 316–317

walking-inspired techniques, 319–323

multiscale navigation, 322–323

natural walking, 319–320

physical treadmills, 321

redirected walking, 321–322

walking in place, 320–321

VR navigation system, 109–110

VTK, *see* Virtual reality toolkit

Waiting times, 30

The Walking Dead (2012), 165, 166–169, 374

Walking-inspired techniques, 319–323

multiscale navigation, 322–323

natural walking, 319–320

physical treadmills, 321

redirected walking, 321–322

walking in place, 320–321

Walking simulator, 374

WAP, 342

Warcraft: Hearthstone, 353

War Robots (2015), 353

Web games, 348

Western games, 352–354, 355

What Remains of Edith Finch (2017), 374

What Video Games Have to Teach Us About Learning and Literacy (Gee), 144

White Album, 378
Wii balance board, 319
Wii Fit (2008), 372
Wiki, 337
Williams, 39
Wireframe sequences, 15, 16, 47
Without Wheels, 41
The Wolf Among Us (2013), 168
Wolfenstein, 345
Works of Game (Sharp), 145
World of Goo, 347
World of Level Design, 149
World of Tanks: Blitz (2015), 353
World of Warcraft, 333, 365, 371
Worms, 350
Wwise, 296

Xbox Adaptive Controller, 41
Xbox One, 42
XR, *see* Extended reality

Yang, Robert, 143
Yankelevitz, Ken, 40
Yatt, Barry, 152
YouTube, 143, 169, 195

Zelda Ocarina of Time, 39
Zenonia, 347
Zimmerman, Eric, 126
Zork, 134, 165
Zork: The Grand Inquisitor, 39
Zynga, 351
Zynga Poker, 347

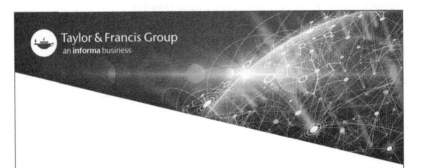

Printed and bound by CPI Group (UK) Ltd, Croydon, CR0 4YY

23/10/2024

01778265-0002